Richards

Gorgias
Sophist and Artist

Studies in Rhetoric/Communication
Thomas W. Benson, Series Editor

GORGIAS
SOPHIST AND ARTIST

Scott Consigny

University of South Carolina Press

UNIVERSITY OF SOUTH CAROLINA BICENTENNIAL

© 2001 University of South Carolina

Published in Columbia, South Carolina, by the
University of South Carolina Press

Manufactured in the United States of America

05 04 03 02 01   5 4 3 2 1

Library of Congress Cataloging-in-Publication Data

Consigny, Scott Porter
  Gorgias, sophist and artist / Scott Consigny.
    p. cm.
  Includes bibliographical references and index.
  ISBN 1-57003-424-9 (cloth : alk. paper)
  1. Gorgias, of Leontini. I. Title.
B305.G32 C66 2001
183'.1—dc21   2001001824

For Mille

Contents

Editor's Preface   ix
Acknowledgments   xi
Translations, Abbreviations, and Stylistic Conventions   xiii

Seeking the Sophist   1

Part One   Rhetoricity
   1   Beyond Subjectivism and Empiricism   35
   2   The Rhetoricity of *Logos*   60

Part Two   Community
   3   Beyond Spontaneity and Duty   95
   4   The Agonistic Community   119

Part Three   Performance
   5   Beyond Epiphany and Transparency   149
   6   The Epideictic Performance   167

The Place of Gorgias   203

Notes   213
Bibliography   225
Index   235

Editor's Preface

Gorgias of Leontini (c. 483–375 B.C.E.) was a teacher of rhetoric, sometimes called a sophist, who traveled as an ambassador from Sicily to Athens in 427 B.C.E., where he created a sensation with his eloquence. His rhetorical teachings and his orations attracted a wide following but also attracted the scorn of Plato, who represented Gorgias in the dialogue as teaching a false rhetoric. In *Gorgias, Sophist and Artist*, Scott Consigny argues that earlier accounts of Gorgias are incomplete and unsatisfactory. Understanding Gorgias today is complicated by the fragmentary and in some cases dubious records that remain of his works. Even in the texts that remain, Gorgias is typically ambiguous, even playful. Consigny argues that two schools of interpretation have attempted to deal with the problems of interpreting Gorgias, and that both are unsatisfactory. An "objectivist" account attempts to reveal Gorgias' original intent. A "rhapsodic" account accepts that it is impossible to discover original intent and instead uses Gorgias as a stimulus for contemporary, subjective theorizing. Consigny proposes a middle way that accepts the impossibility of a truly objective account but that nevertheless appeals to the scholarly community with a reading of Gorgias that renders him comprehensible as well as internally and contextually consistent. Using this approach as the basis for a close study of the texts, Consigny discovers a Gorgias who differs from the two prevailing narratives of his work as either an evolutionary step on the road to the triumph of rationalism or as an echo of an earlier, irrational, tribal Greece. Consigny proposes a third way, reading Gorgias as an anti-foundationalist who rejects the foundationalist claims of both logical and mythic thought. Consigny shows that his view resolves many of the difficulties that had previously appeared to be contradictions in Gorgias' work, and prompts us to see Gorgias as an important contributor to the development of Greek culture. This is a complex, closely argued, and sometimes dazzling book, and a welcome addition to the University of South Carolina Press series in rhetoric and communication.

Acknowledgments

I would like to thank Stanley Cavell, David Smigelskis, Wayne Booth, Lloyd Bitzer, and Stanley Fish, extraordinary teachers who introduced me to many of the topics I explore in this book. I would also like to thank Bob Hollinger, David Roochnik, Joseph Kupfer, Tom Kent, Michael Mendelson, and David Russell, colleagues and friends with whom I have enjoyed many lively discussions about those topics. Third, I would like to express my gratitude to Richard Leo Enos, Edward Schiappa, John Poulakos, and Victor Vitanza, whose writings on Gorgias have inspired my work, and whose specific comments on my interpretations have been invaluable. I would also like to thank Barry Blose, my editor at the University of South Carolina Press, whose encouragement and comments have been most helpful. Finally, I would like to thank Eva Lanczos for her assistance throughout the process of writing this book.

Translations, Abbreviations, and Stylistic Conventions

Gorgias' extant works, translated by George Kennedy, may be found in Rosamund Kent Sprague's *The Older Sophists*. I use these as default translations with two exceptions. For Helen, I use Kennedy's revised translation, which he appends to his translation of Aristotle's Rhetoric; and for the Epitaphios, I use the translation by Thomas Cole, which he includes in his The Origins of Rhetoric in Ancient Greece. For the transcription of Gorgias' On Not-Being by the anonymous author of Melissus, Xenophanes, Gorgias, or MXG, I use the translation by T. Lovejoy and E. S. Forster in Barnes' Collected Works of Aristotle. In citing specific remarks by Gorgias, I use the lettering and numbering protocol in Sprague, which follows that of the 1908 Diels and Kranz compendium of the writings of the Older Sophists, in which the letter A designates commentary and the letter B designates works attributed to Gorgias himself. The exceptions are Gorgias' four major extant texts, On Not-Being (B3), the Epitaphios (B6), Helen (B11), and Palamedes (B11a), which I cite parenthetically as N, E, H, and P respectively, followed by the line number. Translations of Plato and Aristotle are taken from the Loeb editions. With respect to the difficult issue of gender references in personal and possessive pronouns, I attempt to use gender-neutral terms as much as possible, but otherwise I opt for his and he for the sake of clarity.

Gorgias
Sophist and Artist

Seeking the Sophist

The sophist is not the easiest thing in the world to catch and define.

Plato, Sophist

It is only if we give them our soul that [the works of ancient times] can go on living: it is *our* blood that makes them speak to *us*. A really "historical" presentation would speak as a ghost to ghosts.

Nietzsche, Human All Too Human

Recovering Gorgias

During the past several years, scholars have become increasingly interested in the ancient Greek Sophist Gorgias of Leontini. This scholarly turn marks a striking reversal in the status of Gorgias, a figure who has been marginalized in Western thought and culture ever since he was depicted by Aristophanes as a barbaric sycophant, by Plato as a shallow opportunist, and by Aristotle as an inept stylist.[1] In part, the current appreciation of Gorgias is an outgrowth of the project, initiated in the nineteenth century by G. W. F. Hegel and George Grote, of "rehabilitating" the Sophists; for most recent studies of Gorgias reaffirm the collapse of what Henry Sidgwick in 1872 was already calling the "old view" of the Sophists, one that portrayed them as an unscrupulous band of charlatans who "taught the art of fallacious discourse" and who propagated "immoral practical doctrines [through] plausible pernicious sophistries" (289). But recent studies have elevated Gorgias' standing even further than that accorded him by scholars engaged in sophistic rehabilitation, most of whom portray Gorgias as less significant than his eminent "colleague" Protagoras, and some of whom exclude Gorgias from the company of Sophists altogether.[2] Certainly not all scholars would concur with Victor Vitanza's claim that Gorgias is the principal precursor of our own "Third Sophistic"; and indeed, many academic philosophers continue to ridicule any attempt to depict Gorgias as a serious thinker or able writer.[3] But the attention currently accorded Gorgias by scholars in numerous fields has transported this once marginal figure closer to the centers of what Richard Rorty calls the Conversation of the West (1980, 494).

In their diverse inquiries, scholars have explored the substance and style of Gorgias' four principal extant texts, his pedagogy, and his political activities. Concerning *On Not-Being*, many philosophers and historians of philosophy now read Gorgias' baffling text as a significant contribution to pre-Socratic philosophy in general and to Eleatic ontology and epistemology in particular; and several scholars argue that Gorgias' remarks on language, knowledge, and truth anticipate the views of such twentieth-century thinkers as Heidegger, Derrida, Wittgenstein, Ayer, Rorty, and Fish.[4] Regarding the *Encomium of Helen,* scholars of Greek mythology increasingly cite Gorgias' account of Helen of Troy as rivaling the accounts by Homer, Sappho, Stesichorus and Euripides in importance;[5] historians of Greek science and medicine consider Gorgias' remarks about the magical and pharmaceutical nature of *logos* significant in the development of "psychotherapy" in fifth-century Greece;[6] students of Greek theater emphasize the influence Gorgias had on Euripides;[7] and feminist scholars read Gorgias' account as illuminating the status of women in Greek society.[8] In their readings of the *Defense of Palamedes,* legal historians have found Gorgias' reasoning to be a significant contribution to the development of dicanic argumentation, and Platonic scholars have found the defense to be a model for the composition of Plato's own *Apology.*[9] Concerning the *Epitaphios* or *Athenian Funeral Oration,* cultural historians have read Gorgias' text as a significant contribution to the genre of *epitaphios,* a source for Plato's parodic *Menexenus,* and a subtle critique of the propagandist rhetoric of fifth-century imperial Athens.[10] In respect to Gorgias' notorious style, many historians find his antithetical and figurative manner of writing seminal in the development of Greek rhetorical theory and practice; and literary scholars have argued that his distinctive manner of writing and speaking adumbrates such genres and styles as Menippean satire, mannerism, the sublime, the grotesque, and the carnivalesque.[11] Concerning his educational theories and practices, several theorists credit Gorgias for originating a pragmatic pedagogy that not only anticipates Isocrates and Quintilian, but remains vitally relevant today.[12] And in regard to his political activities, some historians now contend that by urging Athens to undertake its ultimately disastrous Sicilian campaign, Gorgias played a more important role in the subsequent defeat of imperial Athens than previously believed; while others suggest that Gorgias' advocacy of cultural Panhellenism anticipates some twentieth-century "post-colonial" thought.[13]

But although he may no longer be relegated to the margins of scholarship, Gorgias nevertheless remains elusive and enigmatic. Indeed, one may argue that in his emergence in discussions of the nuances of pre-Socratic philosophy, the intricacies of Greek mythology, the complexities of Greek politics and diplomacy, the formalities of Athenian legal argumentation, and the subtleties of Greek rhetorical theory and style, the figure we call Gorgias has become even more elusive and puzzling than he was to fifth and fourth century Athenians. For just as Gorgias appears to have "astonished" his first Athenian audience in 427 B.C.E., to have puzzled Socrates, who importunes Gorgias to "draw aside the veil" from his elusive rhetoric (*Gorgias* 460a), and to have perplexed Isocrates with his "subtleties" in *On Not-Being* and his transgressions of genre in *Helen,* Gorgias continues to confound contemporary scholars.[14] Of course, some dispute among scholars about a Sophist like Gorgias is to be expected, for the entire company of Sophists has always had a reputation for subtlety, ambiguity, and controversy. But even in comparison with discussions of his sophistic colleagues, disagreements about Gorgias are striking in their nature and scope. For while scholars may differ over the meaning of Protagoras' notions of "measure" and "man," the nature of Hippias' "cosmopolitanism," the rationale behind Prodicus' attention to synonyms, the significance of Thrasymachus' remarks on justice, or the implications of Antiphon's concept of truth, their disagreements tend to occur within a framework of general consensus about the views of the particular Sophist in question. But in discussions of Gorgias, such consensus is seldom found, and critics dispute vehemently what issue if any he is discussing, what he means by his various claims, and whether he even holds the position for which he is arguing. To use an analogy from the fine arts, if interpretations of Protagoras, Prodicus, or Antiphon are akin to portraits by a school of Renaissance painters that illuminate various nuances of character or temperament, then renderings of Gorgias are more like renderings by Picasso or Francis Bacon, in which the nature and very existence of the model is called into question. In his myriad guises and diverse voices, identified with seemingly inconsistent positions on a variety of issues, Gorgias has thus acquired the dubious distinction of being perhaps the most elusive of the polytropic quarry hunted in Plato's *Sophist*.

In the face of this intense scholarly disagreement about Gorgias, I intend in this book to articulate a coherent account of this enigmatic thinker and writer. Given this objective, I will use the remainder of this Introduction for several preliminary tasks. First, I will delineate the principal obstacles to articulating a coherent and comprehensive reading of Gorgias, impediments deriving from the condition of his extant texts, the elusive nature of his own thinking and writing, and our lack of definitive information about the contexts in which he composed and performed his works. I refer to our interpretive situation as a "hermeneutic aporia," an impasse in which the obstacles we encounter seem to prevent us from articulating an account of Gorgias that is in any sense definitive or even more persuasive than radically antithetical readings. Second, I argue that the two principal strategies that scholars have urged as a means of escaping this aporia, the "objectivist" and the "rhapsodic" strategies, fail to provide us with a means of articulating a compelling and defensible reading of Gorgias. I then delineate the hermeneutic model I will use in my reading of Gorgias, one that draws on Stanley Fish's notion that interpretation is a game played by members of an "interpretive community." Attending to readings that attempt to render Gorgias' work cogent, consistent, and coherent, I delineate three rival accounts of Gorgias currently advanced by scholars in the interpretive community, readings I identify as "subjectivist," "empiricist" and "antifoundationalist." Finally, I sketch the three sections of this book in which I will articulate and defend an "antifoundationalist" reading of Gorgias, attending first to his agonistic model of language, his rhetoricist conception of inquiry, and his endorsement model of truth; next to his communitarian ethics and Panhellenic politics; and third to his parodic, figurative, and theatrical performances.

The Hermeneutic Aporia

I turn first to the principal obstacles to understanding Gorgias, those deriving from the condition of his extant texts, the elusive nature of his writing, and our lack of definitive information about the contexts in which he composed and presented his works. The first class of impediments includes the lacunae in Gorgias' oeuvre and in individual texts, and the questionable authenticity and accuracy of some works.[15] Perhaps the primary obstacle among these is that most of what the Suda refers to as a "great deal" of Gorgias' writing, over a lifetime of a hundred and nine years, appears to be lost altogether, while those few texts that do remain are in the form of paraphrases and copies (A2).[16] The lacunae in Gorgias' oeuvre are of course a severe impediment, in that any interpretation based on a limited amount of an author's writing must be acknowledged as potentially wildly inaccurate and at best partial. Furthermore, of the extant works that are included in the Diels-Kranz collection, which scholars today tend to accept as authoritative, most are themselves fragmentary and often corrupt. Of Gorgias' four principal works, *On Not-Being* (B3), the *Epitaphios* or Athenian funeral oration (B6), the *Encomium of Helen* (B11), and the *Apology for Palamedes* (B11a), only *Helen* and *Palamedes* appear to exist in their entirety, and each is questionable in several places. The *Epitaphios* may be a small fragment of a considerably longer funeral oration; and *On Not-Being* exists only in summary form, indeed in two paraphrases that differ in significant ways. Among other extant fragments are one remark from the *Olympic Speech* (B7–8a), and the opening line from the *Encomium for the People of Elis* (B10). Diels and Kranz also include a dozen "unidentified" remarks and aphorisms attributed to Gorgias by various ancient authors as well as four remarks they consider to be of "doubtful authenticity."

A second difficulty posed by the condition of Gorgias' texts derives from the questionable accuracy and authenticity of the texts attributed to him. Concerning *On Not-Being*, Gorgias' original work is lost, and we possess only two quite disparate paraphrases, that of Sextus Empiricus in *Against the Professors*, and that of the anonymous author of *Melissus, Xenophanes, Gorgias*, or *MXG*, a text included in the Aristotelian corpus. It is possible that both versions are summaries of an earlier work by Gorgias or that each draws on intermediary sources, for each work omits material that is presented in the other. Concerning *Helen* and *Palamedes*, a quite different sort of scholarly hurdle arises. Both works, as they exist in the Cripps and

Palatine manuscripts, appear to be transcriptions of Gorgias' original texts rather than mere paraphrases. And although the two extant transcriptions of *Helen* differ slightly, they are by no means as diverse as the two extant paraphrases of *On Not-Being*.[17] But although most scholars now consider the transcriptions to be accurate, it is instructive to observe that before the canonization by Diels and Kranz many scholars did not appear to attribute either work to Gorgias. Of the three most influential nineteenth-century "rehabilitators" of the Sophists—Hegel, Grote, and Nietzsche—none refers to either work in his discussions of Gorgias; and two of the most respected nineteenth-century British classicists adamantly repudiate each as spurious. R. C. Jebb thus asserts that both works are "generally admitted to be later imitations" (1876, cxxvi), and that *Helen* in particular does not "bear any distinctive marks of the style of Gorgias"; and E. M. Cope contends that both *Palamedes* and *Helen* "are now regarded as imitations of his manner by some later Sophist" (1856, 67). It is somewhat disconcerting to note concerning the *Epitaphios* preserved by a scholiast on Hermogenes from one of the lost texts of Dionysius the Elder, that the scholiast describes the extant text as "an example of the style" of Gorgias' speeches (B6a), suggesting that the text may merely be an imitation of Gorgias' style, and not a work composed by Gorgias himself. And most of Gorgias' extant "aphorisms" are paraphrases by authors who lived centuries after Gorgias uttered them, and none is cited in historical context.

If Gorgias' texts are obscured by the vagaries of historical transmission, they are also rendered elusive because of the nature of his writing itself. Many of Gorgias' assertions are ambiguous because he does not define the terms he uses to advance his principal theses and arguments. In *On Not-Being,* for instance, he does not specify whether his term *exist* is be construed in its "existential" sense, in its "veridical" sense, that of "being true," or in its predicative or copulative sense. In the *Epitaphios,* he uses such terms as *dike* (justice) and *pistis* (faithfulness) to praise the slain warriors, but does not tell us what he means by these accolades. In *Helen,* he does not define the principal terms he uses in defending Helen's departure with Paris, leaving open to interpretation what he means by such terms as *tyche,* a term denoting chance and contingency, and *logos,* a polysemous term that denotes discourse, argument, and rational order.[18] In *Palamedes,* he does not define such pivotal terms as *aletheia* (truth), *dike* (justice), *time* (honor), or *kairos* (the opportune or the timely); and in his diverse aphorisms, he leaves tantalizingly ambiguous such key terms as *dike* (justice) (B21), *apate* (deception) (B23), and *doxa* (opinion) (B26). Further complicating his failure to define these and other terms, Gorgias frequently presents his central ideas in elusive and ambiguous metaphors, similes, and puns. He states, for example, that *logos* is a great dynast (H8) and a drug (H14); that love is a disease (H19); that Nature is a judge who casts a vote of death against everyone (P1); that the citizens of Larisa are akin to pots manufactured by the famous Larisan potters (A23); that philosophers are like the suitors of Penelope (B29); and that orators are like frogs croaking in water (B30). Each of these tropes is ambiguous, and what Gorgias actually means by any of his assertions is often open to an array of interpretations.

Further complicating an interpretation of Gorgias is his pervasive playfulness; for as several commentators have noted, it is unclear when he is being "serious" in his assertions. Aristotle, for example, notes that Gorgias himself recommends responding to seriousness with jests, and to jests with seriousness (*Rhetoric* 1419b3); and he characterizes Gorgias' own writing as pervasively "ironic" (*Rhetoric* 1408b18–21). As readers, we must decide whether to read Gorgias' texts as "serious" theses, as playful *paignions*, or perhaps as both. To cite only one instance of the hermeneutic challenge posed by this playfulness, Gorgias in *Helen* addresses a variety of epistemological and ethical issues, including the nature and power of language; the epistemological status of poetry and science; the limits of free choice in the face of chance, fate, and compulsion; the conflict between obligations to one's family and the pursuit of personal happiness; and the struggle between Greeks and barbarians. But he characterizes his own work as a *paignion* or "amusement" (H21), suggesting that the text may not in some sense be "serious." If we read his remark as disavowing the text's seriousness, it is unclear whether we should discount the content of the entire text and thereby refrain from attributing any of the views expressed to Gorgias; whether we should discount only some of the arguments and conclude that Gorgias means what he says about, say, the nature and power of language; or whether we should read Gorgias as meaning everything he asserts. Our interpretive task lies not only in determining if and when Gorgias is being playful in his various assertions, but in deciding whether and to what extent such playfulness may obviate interpretation itself.[19]

While our attempt to understand Gorgias is obstructed by the condition of his texts and the nature of his writing, it is also made difficult because of the ambiguity and diversity of the contexts in which he composed and performed his works. It would be enormously helpful to be able to place Gorgias' texts in a detailed historical narrative, and to situate them vis-à-vis the political, social, legal, cultural, and intellectual institutions and events in Leontini, Larisa, and other cities in which he composed and performed; but we are limited in any such undertaking and must frequently resort to speculation.[20] We are told that Gorgias was born between 480 and 490 B.C.E. in the small city of Leontini, a colony in eastern Sicily established by the Chalcideans and allied with Athens, and that he died over a hundred years later, perhaps in Thessaly. We know little about Gorgias' family life, save that his father was Charmantides and that he had a brother, Herodicus, a physician whom he apparently accompanied at times, and a sister whose grandson dedicated a golden statue to him at Delphi. He may or may not have married.[21] Gorgias appears to have studied under Empedocles of Acragus in southern Sicily, but we do not know when, how long, or in what capacity.[22] He may have also have studied with the rhetoricians Corax and Tisias in the eastern Sicilian city of Syracuse, but we know very little about these two figures and nothing of Gorgias' relationship with either man.[23] Concerning his political activities, we know that Gorgias led an embassy from Leontini to Athens in 427 B.C.E., requesting military assistance against Syracuse, but we know nothing about his political activities in Leontini before 427 or even what the political institutions in Leontini were. After 427 Gorgias appears to have moved to mainland Greece, where he traveled to Athens, Larisa, and other cities. He spoke frequently at Panhellenic festivals, becoming "conspicuous" at Olympia, Delphi, and elsewhere, but we do not know whether he was involved in the organization of the festivals themselves.[24]

Gorgias' principal profession was teaching, and his students are said to have included Polus, Meno, Aspasia of Miletus, Pericles, Critias, and Isocrates. He is also said to have influenced Thucydides, Agathon, Alcidamas, and many other writers.[25] But though Gorgias may have influenced his students' thought and manner of writing, their own views offer little guidance for understanding Gorgias' thought. One of Gorgias' students in Sicily was Polus of Acragus, who subsequently taught and apparently wrote a text on rhetoric. Plato inserts the "coltish" Polus into the *Gorgias;* but we should not necessarily attribute to Gorgias the views expressed by Polus. Nor should we attribute to Gorgias the radical egoism expressed by the purely fictional Callicles, even though Plato depicts Callicles as sympathetic to Gorgias. Isocrates, also a student of Gorgias, appears to have been influenced by several of his mentor's ideas; but we cannot presume that Isocrates fully understood Gorgias' thought, given that he condemns Gorgias for his "arid" remarks in *On Not-Being* (*Antidosis* 268) and his "violations" of genre in *Helen* (*Helen* 14–15).[26] Two other Athenian students of Gorgias include the opportunistic Alcibiades, who promoted Athens' disastrous Sicilian campaign, and the notorious Critias, who became a member of the tyrannical Athenian "Thirty"; but we have no reason to assume that Gorgias condoned the political activities of either man. One of Gorgias' students in Thessaly was Meno, who in Plato's *Meno* extols Gorgias' characterization of virtue and his putative "theory of pores"; but the Platonic Meno's account of these topics may not accurately represent Gorgias' own views. In respect to style, Gorgias appears to have influenced the writing of Alcidamas and Lycophron as well as the style of authors as diverse as Hippocrates, Thucydides, Isocrates, and Agathon, whose "euphuistic" style Plato parodies in the *Symposium*.[27] But although these men may have imitated some features of Gorgias' manner of writing, we should not assume that Gorgias used tropes, *topoi,* arguments, or genres for the same reasons as any of his putative imitators.

If we should not assume that Gorgias concurs with his teachers or students, neither should we assume that he shares all the views of the thinkers and teachers he is most frequently associated with, the Sophists. Most scholars include Gorgias among the "Older Sophists," the diverse array of individuals who taught and lectured throughout fifth- and early fourth-century Greece. But while we may classify Gorgias as a Sophist, we ought not conclude that he would always concur with Protagoras, Hippias, Antiphon, and Prodicus. Rather, we should recognize that the Sophists were a rather heterogeneous family of thinkers, writers, speakers, and teachers who discussed a variety of ontological, epistemological, ethical, political, and stylistic topics, and who presented their views in different genres and venues. In respect to Protagoras, arguably his most important "colleague," we may find that Gorgias shares some of Protagoras' principal views, and that attending to Protagoras' views may illuminate those of Gorgias. We may be able to illuminate Gorgias' thought if we attend to Protagoras' contention that "man is the measure of all things" (DK80.B1), that every *logos* can be opposed with a rival *logos* (DK80.B6a), and that it is possible to make an apparently weaker *logos* stronger (DK80.B6b). But we must also recognize that Gorgias appears to depart from Protagoras in crucial ways. To cite only three examples, Gorgias does not advocate agnosticism but discusses the gods in several texts, he promotes Panhellenism rather than democracy, and he appears to place enormous emphasis on the heuristic function of style and delivery. We may also attend to the ideas of other Sophists to illuminate Gorgias; but we ought not conclude that by defining "sophistry" or "sophistic rhetoric" we will thereby be able to understand Gorgias' distinctive ideas, his art of inquiry and argument, his multifarious style, or his theatrical delivery.

If we cannot rely on the remarks of his mentors, students, and colleagues in our interpretation of Gorgias, neither can we rely uncritically on the portrayals of Gorgias given by his two most influential critics, Plato and Aristotle. Plato provides indispensable insights into Gorgias' views, notably that Gorgias participates in an "ancient quarrel" between rhetoric and philosophy; that he considers probabilities more significant than any putative context-invariant "truths" (*Phaedrus* 267a); that he articulates an anti-essentialist, family-resemblance conception of virtue (B19, *Meno* 71e-72a); that his primary ethical concerns are honor and shame (*Gorgias* 461b); that his multifarious style is both festive and combative (*Gorgias* 447a); and that his objective as educator is to liberate and empower his students (*Gorgias* 452d).[28] But while these insights are invaluable, we must recognize that Plato depicts Gorgias with his own philosophically weighted vocabulary and assesses him from within his own conceptual framework. Indeed, it is instructive to emphasize that Gorgias himself describes the *Gorgias* as a playful satire rather than an accurate account of his own views (A15a). We must also be cautious of Aristotle's account of Gorgias. We may learn a great deal from Aristotle's observations about Gorgias' conception of the art of rhetoric, notably that Gorgias' "epideictic" performances are overtly theatrical and frequently playful (*Rhetoric* 1366a29–32); that he is concerned with praise and blame (*Rhetoric* 1414b29); that he uses associative or "paralogical" reasoning (*Rhetoric* 1418a32); that he deploys localisms, neologisms, epithets, and metaphors in his "frigid" and quasi-poetic style (1405b34–1406b4); that he frequently writes ironically (*Rhetoric* 1408b18–21); that he considers "seriousness" to be a rhetorical strategy rather than an inherently desirable moral trait (*Rhetoric* 1419b3); and that in teaching the art of rhetoric he has students memorize model speeches rather than learn the rules of the art (*Sophistical Refutations* 183b36). But although his remarks illuminate Gorgias' conception of rhetoric, we must recognize that Aristotle, like Plato, is by no means neutral or impartial in his characterization, and that he describes and evaluates Gorgias from within a conceptual framework that is diametrically opposed to that of Gorgias.

Given the fragmentariness and questionable authenticity of much of his oeuvre; the ambiguous, figurative, and ludic nature of his own writing; the dearth of specific information about the contexts in which he composed his works; the ambiguous relationship between his views and those of his mentors and students; and the openly partisan characterizations of his work by his Athenian adversaries, we find ourselves in what may be termed a *hermeneutic aporia,* or impasse, in that we appear to have no obvious means of articulating and defending a particular account of Gorgias' thought. On the one hand, it is not clear how we may attribute to Gorgias any "position" on any issue or any overall philosophy, given that we do not know if or to what extent the fragmentary collection of his texts is representative of his overall philosophy, whether or not he really means what he is reported to have said in any of his works, or what he means by his undefined terms and elusive metaphors. Describing Gorgias as holding a particular position on any issue thus seems highly suspect if not completely arbitrary. Conversely, given the nature of Gorgias' works, it seems possible to attribute *any* position to Gorgias we wish, since any construal may be rendered consistent with the fragmentary, ambiguous remnants of his writing, and no interpretation can be judged more or less viable. For if a critic encounters a remark by Gorgias that appear to be inconsistent with his or her interpretation, he or she may always resort to claiming that the particular remark in question was not really made by Gorgias, that it is not representative of his overall thought, that the terms themselves have a different meaning, or that remark is merely ironic or playful. The hermeneutic challenge, in this respect, is not only one of articulating a coherent and comprehensive account, but of being able to argue in a meaningful way that a given interpretation is preferable to other plausible readings of Gorgias. For if any reading is consistent with one or another construal of some of the extant fragments, and all apparent contradictions in a given interpretation can be resolved by diverse recourses, then every attempt to attribute a particular position to him is suspect, and every attempt to decide which reading is preferable is futile.

The Objectivist and Rhapsodic Escapes

In the face of this hermeneutic aporia, scholars have proposed two sorts of "escapes," ways of reading Gorgias that appear to circumvent the ostensibly insurmountable obstacles to articulating a compelling interpretation. Each of these proposed escapes, I suggest, fails to provide a way out of the hermeneutic aporia. We may label the first approach "objectivist," in that its goal is to articulate an objectively valid or "correct" account of Gorgias by identifying his *original intentions* in the text without imposing our own biased assumptions or conceptual schemes on them.[29] This objectivist approach is first proposed by Plato, who depicts understanding as a process of "drawing aside the veil" of speech in order to discern Gorgias' real meaning (*Gorgias* 460a). Plato expands on what "drawing aside the veil" involves in the *Ion,* where he indicates that interpretation involves understanding an author's original intentions. He thus insists that a rhapsode engaged in interpretation must "understand the meaning of the poet," and that this requires him to "interpret the *mind of the poet* to his hearers" (*Ion* 530c). Plato further indicates that understanding an author's original meaning involves examining his precise words and the meaning they had in his own historical context, namely "his own region and dialect" (*Protagoras* 341a-d). Plato's objectivist approach to interpretation has been extremely influential, and it informs the views of contemporary theorists such as Emilio Betti and E. D. Hirsch. Betti maintains that "it is our duty as guardians and practitioners of the study of history to protect this kind of *objectivity* and to provide evidence of the epistemological conditions of its possibility" (177–78, emphasis added); and Hirsch contends that an interpreter must discern a "determinate" meaning, namely the author's intended meaning, for "the meaning of a text is the author's meaning" (25). Following Plato's lead, he asserts that "the interpreter's primary task is to reproduce in himself the author's "logic," his attitudes, his cultural givens—in short, his world. Even though the process of verification is highly complex and difficult, the ultimate verificative principle is very simple—the imaginative reconstruction of the speaking subject" (242). Hirsch argues that the "activity of interpretation can lay claim to intellectual respectability only if its results can lay claim to validity" (164). An objectively "valid" reading trumps every other interpretation, for it recovers an author's original meaning without imposing anachronistic conceptual schemes upon an author.

This objectivist approach has been advocated by numerous Gorgian scholars, including Jacqueline Romilly, George Kerferd, Thomas Cole, and Edward Schiappa. Among these scholars, Schiappa has articulated this objectivist approach most eloquently, and I will address his account in order to show why it fails to provide a way out of the hermeneutic aporia. Schiappa states that in order to understand any of the Sophists, we must base our reading on "historical fact" (1991, 65), and reconstruct the Sophists' ideas "in their own words and intellectual context," rather than relying on our own anachronistic terminology. He thus asserts that his goal is to attain "a thorough and comprehensive recovery of each Sophist's thinking as far as the available evidence permits," and to "understand sophistic thinking in its own context as far as possible" (1991, 81). He acknowledges that every such reconstruction must necessarily be incomplete, since given the limits of our knowledge "there is no such thing as a final, *objective, impersonal historical account,*" one that exactly replicates the Sophists' own ideas. But Schiappa insists that "it does not follow that all [readings] are equally valuable or 'valid,'" for some are clearly more accurate than others in their fidelity to *objective facts,* while others "stretch the original context and anachronistically inject later developed abstractions" (1990b, 308–10; emphasis added). Schiappa thus echoes Jacqueline Romilly, who chastises those scholars who turn their back on "history as it was lived, within the framework of fifth-century Athens" in order to detect in the Sophists "their own particular problems and prejudices." (1992, xi). He iterates Kerferd's claim that we should read the Sophists "without presuppositions" (1989, 13); and he embraces Alan Bloom's contention that "if we were to study history according to our tastes, we would see nothing but ourselves everywhere," given that "thought is the prisoner of whatever place it is to be found [if] it cannot *break the bonds of the present*" (cited in Schiappa 1991, 67–68).

In order to "break the bonds of the present" and arrive at a more objective and accurate account of Gorgias and the other Sophists, Schiappa advocates two complementary hermeneutic strategies. First, he argues that we should ground our reading on the Sophists' original words or *ipsissima verba,* rather than relying on interpretations and commentary by subsequent scholars. We should identify and privilege "data" rather than "theories," attending solely to those fragments that are authentic, accurate, and free of subsequent interpretation. In so doing, we should "bracket" our own anachronistic philosophical terminology and concepts as much as possible, so as to discern the Sophists' own thought in their own words, and to avoid "improper and premature schematization" (1991, 21). Rather than transplanting their fragments from their original context into subsequent conceptual frameworks, we should avoid any philosophical terminology that the Sophists themselves did not actually use.

Second, Schiappa argues that we must ground our interpretation of what the Sophists themselves meant in their own *historical context,* namely that of fifth-century Greece; for it is only within this context that their original words have meaning. Drawing on the work of Havelock, Ong, and others, Schiappa characterizes the Sophists' "fifth-century historical framework" in respect to the traditional topic of *mythos* and *logos.* He identifies the "mythic-poetic" culture of early Greece as "a constellation of certain social practices, including specific forms of discourse (primarily oral poetry), patterns of explanation (typically theistic), and political orientations (elitist)"; and he describes the subsequent "rationalistic" culture exemplified by Aristotle as a culture in which "oral and written prose challenged poetry, anthropocentric or 'scientific' explanations challenged theistic traditions, and radical democracy challenged more elitist forms of government" (1991, 30). Using this distinction, Schiappa characterizes fifth-century Greece as a period of *transition* from the more primitive culture based largely on mythical thinking to the fourth-century culture relying on rational inquiry. Positing this putative historical transition or progression as "objective fact," Schiappa concludes that most of Gorgias' thought and style may be understood as "advancing the art of written prose in general, and argumentative composition in particular" (1995, 317).

While Schiappa's objectivist strategy may appear on its face to escape the hermeneutic aporia by situating Gorgias' original words in his own historical context, it fails for two reasons. First, Schiappa's attempt to attend solely to Gorgias' "actual words," or *ipsissima verba,* is futile, for as noted above, all of Gorgias' "actual words" are lost. Since all of his extant texts and remarks exist in the form of transcriptions and paraphrases of questionable authenticity and accuracy, it is impossible to stipulate any of Gorgias' "original words" without relying on an array of interpretive assumptions and speculations about Gorgias and the authors who have transcribed and paraphrased him. Although most Gorgian scholars today tend to accept as authoritative the collection of Diels and Kranz, this does not mean that we have finally arrived at an "accurate" collection of Gorgias' works, one that corrects the "errors" of such nineteenth-century scholars as Jebb or Cope, who considered *Helen* and *Palamedes* inauthentic. On the contrary, the acceptance of Diels and Kranz's collection indicates that our discussions of Gorgias depend on our own historically contingent assumptions, judgments, and speculations about such matters as whether or not a particular text is sufficiently representative of Gorgias' thinking or manner of writing to be assigned to him; and whether and to what extent the transcribers of Gorgias' works may have misunderstood his original terms or arguments and thereby altered his original texts. But even if we stipulate that some of Gorgias' extant texts are comprised of his "original words," this does not enable us to avoid using our own anachronistic terminology in reading

Gorgias. For we must still translate his words into contemporary English, and hence into our own conceptual schemes, in order to understand their meaning; and to do this, we must use our own terms and conceptual schemes. For as every experienced translator recognizes, translation requires interpretation; and every interpretation involves making assumptions and adopting specific procedures. In Rorty's terms, "translation is necessary if 'understanding' an author is to mean something more than engaging in rituals of which we do not see the point, and translating an utterance means fitting it into *our* practices" (1984, 52n. 1). While Schiappa insists that in order to decipher Gorgias' original intentions we should "bracket" our own anachronistic terms and concepts, he fails to recognize that this practice is simply not possible.

Schiappa's second error is that he sees "historical placement" as an objective project that does not rely on our own culturally biased assumptions and judgments. He fails to see that every historical placement of Gorgias' texts, both in respect to the specific contexts in which he wrote and the more general contours of fifth-century Greek history and culture, is speculative and contestable. As noted above, we possess very little specific information about the specific political, economic, social, and cultural milieus of Leontini, Syracuse, Phaerae, and elsewhere in which Gorgias composed and presented his texts; thus, in order to characterize those contexts, we must rely on an array of contestable assumptions, procedures, and judgments. And regarding what Schiappa calls the general "framework" of Greek culture in which Gorgias lived and wrote, we must see that any characterization of its dominant features and how they may have influenced Gorgias' writing is perhaps even more speculative and disputable. Although Schiappa situates Gorgias' work in terms of a traditional historical narrative that depicts Greece as evolving from an irrational culture informed by *mythos* into a rationalistic culture informed by *logos,* we must recognize that this narrative is not an objective fact but a highly questionable tale that many scholars in the twentieth century have repudiated as positivistic and simplistic. The disputable nature of the evolutionary narrative may be exposed by contrasting it with a rival narrative, one that may be termed an "agonal" narrative of Greek culture. [30] In the agonal narrative advocated by an array of comparative mythologists, cultural anthropologists, and historians of philosophy and rhetoric, Greek culture is depicted, not as an evolution from the putative irrationality of myth to the rationality of *logos,* but as a sequence of disputes between people holding rival conceptions of rationality, truth, and value—disputes that Plato first characterized as manifestations of an "ancient quarrel" between philosophy and rhetoric. In the agonal narrative, foundationalist thinkers such as Orpheus, Parmenides, and Plato are depicted as seeking objective truths and moral laws; while "pragmatic" thinkers such as Gorgias and Protagoras are seen as insisting that truths and moral codes are constructed by members of contingent communities.[31] Whether we find the evolutionary or agonal narrative more convincing, we ought not conclude that either is "objectively true." Rather, we should see that every account of Greek culture and history is ultimately a narrative or story that we tell and that the project of placing Gorgias in Greek culture and history does not depend on "historical accuracy" but on which story we find more believable. Rather than assuming, with Schiappa, that we are able to situate Gorgias' texts in an "objective historical setting," we must recognize that any characterization of what constitutes an "objective setting" is no more than a "likely story."

Although we should repudiate as misguided the objectivist attempt to understand Gorgias by attending only to his original words and placing them in an "objective" historical framework, we need not follow the advice of those scholars who encourage us to read Gorgias in any way we choose, without any concern for whether our reading may be more or less plausible than rival readings. This is the advice of scholars who contend that, rather than attempting to discern what Gorgias or any of the other Older Sophists may have actually meant in their various texts, we should use their extant remarks as inspiration for creating our own personal philosophies. Like objectivism, this strategy finds one of its earliest and clearest articulations in the work of Plato. If objectivist scholars adopt Plato's objectivist model of interpretation in the *Ion*, these scholars may be said to adopt the approach of Ion himself, a rhapsodist who uses the words of characters in the *Iliad* or *Odyssey* to create a novel dramatic performance without concerning himself with Homer's own views.[32] Also like objectivism, this rhapsodic approach to reading has a long history, one that has affinities in the ancient world with the radical skepticism of Pyrrho, who contends that knowledge about any object or text is impossible and that we must rely solely on our own individual perceptions and judgments. It also has affinities in the modern world to radical solipsists like Dostoyevsky's underground man, who maintains that knowledge is illusory and that listening to other people is of value only insofar as it serves to promote his own unbridled personal freedom.[33] Among its recent advocates are Gilles Deleuze and Felix Guattari, who argue that "reading a text is never a scholarly exercise in search of what is signified, still less a highly textual exercise in search of a signifier. Rather, it is a productive . . . exercise that extracts from the text its revolutionary force" (106). Rather than attempting to understand an author's intention in a text, they urge readers to create their own personal "readings," none of which can be deemed more persuasive than another. For a book "is not an image of the world, still less a signifier. It is not a noble organic totality, neither is it a unity of sense. . . . In a book, there is nothing to understand, but much to make use of. Nothing to interpret or signify, but much to experiment with. . . . Find scraps of book, those *which are of use to you or suit you*" (50; 67–68, emphasis added). Each act of reading, in this model, is an artistic performance in which a reader draws freely upon a text to create his or her own radically novel work of art.

This rhapsodic approach to Gorgias is advocated most prominently by John Poulakos, who contends that since apprehending the Sophists' own views is impossible, we are better served by constructing our own "neosophistic" conceptions of knowledge, power, and art. Repudiating as misguided any attempt to discern the original intentions expressed in any of the Sophists' texts, Poulakos asserts that such efforts erroneously "assume that the discourses attributed to the Sophists are stable objects of investigation, objects, that is, that can be explored disinterestedly, examined closely, and possessed epistemologically"; and they incorrectly "assume that we, the present interpreters, can indeed recover and have access to the past-as-it-was and can disregard, untroubled, the distance separating our times, our society and our culture from that of the ancients" (1995, 5). Moreover, Poulakos contends that attempting to recover the meaning of any of the assertions or arguments made by Gorgias or any of the other Sophists is wrong-headed, since the Sophists did not "really mean" what they wrote in their extant texts. Rather, according to Poulakos, "what they have left behind is not what they really believed. Their works represent only sketchy illustrations of what can be done with language" (1995, 25). Poulakos argues that our purpose in reading the Sophists should not be to "correct prior views on the sophists and offer truer interpretations," nor to "resolve conflicts between competing interpretations," but "to treat the rhetoric of the sophists so as to *stimulate some new thinking on our own rhetorics*" (1995, 4–5, emphasis added). In order to stimulate new thinking, Poulakos adopts a deliberately idiosyncratic strategy of reading, whereby he selects three terms from some of the Older Sophists' "rhetorical compositions and reported practices," and constructs what he labels "sophistic rhetoric," in respect to these three terms. He acknowledges that his strategy of reading is selective, but he argues that this is not a weakness, for "no set of terms, no set of illustrative texts, and no reconstructed cultural horizon can exhaust the sophists' rhetoric" (1995, 56). Selecting the terms *kairos* (timeliness), *paignion* (play), and *dunaton* (the possible), Poulakos defines sophistic rhetoric as "the art which seeks to capture in opportune moments that which is appropriate and attempts to suggest that which is possible" (1983, 36). Poulakos implies that insofar as Gorgias, Protagoras, Critias, Prodicus, Hippias, and others engaged in what he calls "sophistic rhetoric," they merit the title of Sophist.

Although Poulakos may appear to offer an escape from the hermeneutic aporia, I suggest that his rhapsodic approach is irrelevant to our project of understanding Gorgias and that his substantive account of sophistic rhetoric is too reductive to be of much use. On the one hand, Poulakos' approach is irrelevant, since he repudiates as misguided the entire project of making sense of Gorgias and presents his own account as his own personal creation. If the sole criterion for assessing the viability of any reading is the extent to which it generates a reading of value in a reader's own life, then any attempt to argue that one reading is preferable to another is misguided and self-contradictory. We should thus not expect Poulakos' account to illuminate any of Gorgias' own ideas about such matters as the nature of truth, knowledge, or language; the role of honor and shame in ethics; the nature of Panhellenism; or any of the other topics he discusses. Of course, if we agree with Poulakos that Gorgias does not really mean anything he says in his texts, then we are relieved of such an effort and should attend only to his conception of "rhetoric."

But even if we limit our investigation in this way, we find that Poulakos' account fails to illuminate Gorgias' practice in his four extant works. For attempting to understand Gorgias' art of rhetoric in respect to the three terms *kairos, paignion,* and *dunaton* is highly reductive and says nothing about Gorgias' strategies of invention; his deployment of paradigmatic and associative modes of reasoning; his use of parody, puns, metaphors, epithets, and other tropes; or his deliberately histrionic mode of delivery. This is not to deny that Gorgias considers *kairos* to be important, that he is indifferent to what is possible, or that he composes playful *paignions;* but it is to deny that Gorgias' entire art of rhetoric is reducible to these three terms. Moreover, Poulakos' definition of sophistic rhetoric is extremely vague and does not distinguish Gorgias' ideas or practices from those of his most ardent adversaries. Poulakos has no grounds for excluding from his category of "sophistic rhetors" individuals such as Socrates, whose views differ radically from those of Gorgias. For one could argue that Socrates, Plato, and even Aristotle attempt to "capture in opportune moments that which is appropriate" and to "suggest that which is possible." Indeed, many of the views articulated by Plato in his dialogues are far more original or novel than those of, say, Prodicus, the Sophist whom Gorgias himself ridicules "for speaking what was old-fashioned and had often been said before" (A24).

A rhapsodic strategy of reading is also employed by Victor Vitanza, who engages in what he calls a "wild/savage" practice that affirms his own *"sovereign subjectivity"* (1997, 319, 253). Repudiating as misguided any attempt to understand any of Gorgias' own thoughts, Vitanza asserts, "I place very little value in the authorial fantasy" (1997, 237). Indeed, Vitanza never pretends to speak of Gorgias at all, and instead concerns himself solely with the interpretation of Gorgias advanced by Mario Untersteiner, referring in one passage to "Gorgias' (Untersteiner's) view" (1997, 131). Instead of pretending to "understand" Gorgias, Vitanza professes his goal to be the creation of a "Third Sophistic," one generated from his own subjective perspective. He thus asserts that "discussing the possibilities of a Third Sophistic in rereadings of Gorgias' text will allow me to initiate a reinvestigation of a sublime-sovereign *subjectivity*" (1997, 237; emphasis added). He remarks, "I am thoroughly persuaded that if we are to reclaim the Sophists, it must be done by searching for third ('some more,' sovereign, sublime) subject positions" (1997, 237). The strategy of "reading" that Vitanza uses in his creative project is one that he labels "topical deformation." In one such instance of topical deformation, Vitanza explains that he arrived at his understanding of "Gorgias" via Jacques Lacan by characterizing "*subjectivity* in terms of the *topos* 'out of the possible comes the possible,' or 'out of negation comes affirmation.'" He explains, "I achieved this reading by way of Lacan's discussion of the real (the impossible) and its trilemma (imaginary, symbolic, real), which I eventually paralleled with Gorgias' trilemma (in "On the Nonexistent or on Nature") . . . it was a reading of Gorgias across these Lacanian *topoi* that allowed me to reach for a non-Humanist subjectivity" (1997, 252). Using his anti-method of topical deformation, Vitanza appropriates the figure he refers to as "Untersteiner's Gorgias" into his own Third Sophistic. Since he makes no claim that his reading in any way represents any of Gorgias' own thoughts, Vitanza eludes the charge that his account is arbitrary or reductive. But rather than providing a viable way of escaping the hermeneutic aporia, Vitanza altogether abandons the project of making sense of Gorgias' thought and writing. His rhapsodic exhibitions may illuminate his own neosophistic ideas and inspired strategies of reading, but they offer little guidance for understanding Gorgias' own views.

The Interpretive Community

In order to avoid the Scylla of objectivism and the Charybdis of rhapsodism in our attempt to escape the hermeneutic aporia that we face in seeking Gorgias, I suggest that we adopt a model of interpretation that may be characterized as pragmatic, conventionalist, or "communitarian"—a model adumbrated by Protagoras and developed more recently by such scholars as Hans-Georg Gadamer, Kenneth Burke, Richard Rorty, and Stanley Fish.[34] This model locates the criteria for assessing any reading in the shared practices or conventions of reading that constitute and regulate what Fish calls an "interpretive community" of readers, rather than a putatively determinate historical text or the arbitrary whim of an autonomous reader. In this model, a "reading" is made possible only within the practices of an established community of readers who consent to the assumptions, practices, and procedures of the specific interpretive project. Many of these assumptions and practices are not explicitly spelled out but are relied upon by scholars in the field to the extent that being a scholar involves an unchallenged use of them. These practices include, among others, using the terminology of the appropriate scholarly discourse; deploying modes of argumentation, authentication, and citation deemed acceptable by other scholars; and conforming to the conventions of genres such as the essay or scholarly text published by recognized journals and presses in the field. The practices also involve a general consensus about which interpretive projects are worth undertaking at any given time, a recognition of what scholars have said about the subject, and an acceptance of some authors and texts as authoritative. These shared practices enable members of the interpretive community to identify and agree upon the accuracy and authenticity of particular texts, to delineate what counts as a persuasive interpretation of a text, and to rule out some readings as inappropriate. The precise nature of these scholarly strategies, assumptions, and judgments, and hence what counts as scholarship in the field, may well change over time; but this does not mean that the changing conventions enable scholars to arrive at a closer approximation to the "real meaning" of a text; nor does the change in scholarly practices indicate that these procedures themselves are optional or arbitrary. Rather, the change indicates that what it means to be a scholar changes over time and that if individuals egregiously transgress those conventions, they will simply not be considered to be members of the scholarly community.

In this model of interpretation, there is no original and determinate text to be discovered, for texts themselves are fabrications made available through the use of hermeneutic conventions. That is, there are no "uninterpreted texts" that exist apart from, and prior to, interpretations. Since the texts themselves are available only through the conventions and procedures of the interpretive community, it is only within these interpretations that an author's thought becomes available, and there is no external entity or meaning that the interpretations represent. In Fish's terms, assertions about the "truth, correctness, validity, and clarity" of any given text are not made "in reference to some extracontextual, ahistorical, noninstitutional reality, or rule, or law, or value," but are instead "intelligible and debatable only within the precincts of the context or situations or paradigms or communities that give them their local and changeable shape" (1980, 342–43). Conversely, while there are no independent "texts" for scholars to be faithful to, there are also no unbridled, autonomous readers who are able to interpret the texts in any way they choose and still remain viable members of the interpretive community. Every member of the interpretive community is constituted by shared practices and procedures of communicating and reading, and individual readers are thus regulated and indeed constituted by the practices of the communities to which they belong. Thus, "meanings are the properties neither of fixed and stable texts nor of free and independent readers, but of interpretative communities that are responsible both for the shape of a reader's activities and for the texts those readers produce" (Fish 1972, 322). Whereas an objectivist like Schiappa may depict himself as an autonomous agent who is able to leap beyond our contemporary "anachronistic" critical vocabulary in order to understand an author such as Gorgias in his own words and in his own time, and a rhapsodist like Poulakos may consider himself to be an original artist who creates his own personal understanding of Gorgias, the communitarian reader repudiates the notion of an original text and an individual autonomous reader altogether and maintains, with Fish, that "an individual's assumptions and opinions are not 'his own' in any sense that would give body to the fear of solipsism. That is, he is not their origin (in fact, it might be more accurate to say that they are his); rather, it is their prior availability which delimits in advance the paths that his consciousness can possibly take"; for "interpreters act as an extension of an institutional community" (1972, 320–21).

Insofar as scholars consent to the array of practices and conventions of the interpretive community, their work is *cooperative;* for they rely on the work of others in the community, and without the agreed-upon procedures and conventions, they would be unable to understand any text. But if every scholarly project is cooperative, it is also *competitive,* in that its objective is to articulate a persuasive or compelling reading of a text or author. Stated another way, interpretation is a "game" played by members of the interpretive community, in which each scholar's objective is to articulate an account that is more persuasive than rival interpretations. Indeed, the only criterion for the viability of a reading is its persuasiveness, its power to convince other members of the community. Every reading is thus inescapably "partial," both in the sense that it is partisan and represents the position advanced by a culturally situated reader and in the sense that it articulates only one perspective among other possible readings. Using Protagoras' terms, we may say that every reading may be opposed by a rival or "opposed" reading (DK80. B6a) and that a scholar's task is to make his account "stronger" than those of his rivals (DK80.B6b). Furthermore, while a scholar may challenge existing readings, he may not honestly do so on the grounds that other readings fail to replicate what an author "really meant"; for the only way to determine what an author "really meant" is with another interpretation. Again using Protagoras' terms, we may say that it is "impossible to contradict" any interpretation by reference to unmediated facts (DK80.A1) and that it is only possible to refute a reading with another, more persuasive reading. Since the texts themselves are available only through the conventions and procedures of the interpretive community, it is only within these interpretations that an author's thought becomes available; there is no "external" entity or meaning that the interpretations "represent." In order to judge whether a reading is viable, scholars must assess it in respect to *rival interpretations* advanced by other members of the interpretive community. In those instances in which scholars agree upon a reading, this does not mean that they have finally unearthed the real meaning of a text and have finally "gotten it right." It simply means that no scholar in the community has been able to effectively challenge the prevailing reading.

Adopting this "communitarian" model of interpretation, my purpose and procedure will differ significantly from that of objectivists like Schiappa and rhapsodists like Poulakos. Unlike Schiappa, my goal is not to articulate a "valid" interpretation that replicates Gorgias' original intentions as impartially and objectively as possible, for I maintain that such a goal is illusory. Rather, my goal is to articulate an account of Gorgias that is more compelling than other accounts currently articulated in the scholarly community. In respect to procedure, I will not privilege Gorgias' "original words" as the only means of grasping his views and in so doing eschew our own terminology as anachronistic and distorting. Rather than avoiding such terms as *rhetoric, hermeneutics, subjectivism, empiricism, antifoundationalism,* and others that do not appear in Gorgias' oeuvre, I will rely extensively on these terms, considering them to be essential for articulating competing accounts of Gorgias' thought and for judging which account is most viable. This does not mean that I will attend only to "interpretations" and ignore Gorgias' own views; for I hold that to articulate Gorgias' own views is not to flee our own terminologies but to articulate an interpretation in terms that we deem more persuasive than rival accounts. Nor will I presume that I can situate Gorgias in an "objective" historical and cultural context, such as that informed by a putative evolution from *mythos* to *logos* that Schiappa embraces. For I maintain that we, as members of the interpretive community, must determine the nature of Gorgias' "historical context" by engaging in interpretation and deciding which narrative we find most compelling. To understand Gorgias, we must situate him in various intellectual, political, and artistic contexts; but in so doing we must decide which contexts we consider most pertinent, and what the nature of those contexts is in each case. For we do not possess an independent means of accessing Gorgias' historical situation that enables us to circumvent our own partisan interpretive strategies—a kind of privileged, direct route that reveals the way things really were. My hermeneutic approach does not suggest that I will ignore "history" and attend only to contemporary, anachronistic concerns; for every interpretation situates Gorgias "historically," albeit in a different way; and which "historical" account we consider viable is itself a function of the interpretation we accept as most persuasive. Rather than ignoring history, I reject only the positivist notion that "history" is composed of a progression of unmediated facts that may be apprehended by an unbiased observer and transmitted in an objective and neutral vocabulary. As such, my approach is thoroughly "historicist," for I see every historical account as itself an historically conditioned narrative or "genealogy," and every historian as inescapably situated in his or her own contingent historical perspective.

While I reject the purpose and method of objectivist readers, I do not embrace the goal and procedure of rhapsodic readers like Poulakos. Unlike Poulakos, I do not take as my goal the creation of my own personal views of rhetoric or philosophy, ideas that may enable me to cope with exigencies in my own life. I agree with Poulakos that scholars should strive for novel or original readings and that a valuable consequence of interpreting Gorgias is that it may inspire readers to generate their own ideas about language, rhetoric, interpretation, or other matters. But I suggest that in order to determine whether a reading is truly novel or original, we must compare and contrast it with existing readings. A reading may seem quite new to a reader who is unaware of the work of other scholars, while to other scholars in the field the reading may be derivative and commonplace. Moreover, I suggest that while interpreting Gorgias may provide us with guidance for developing our own views about the issues and topics that Gorgias himself discusses, this does not obviate the need to first understand him. For only if we understand Gorgias' views, and are able to differentiate his views from those of other thinkers, will we be able to draw meaningfully upon his views in developing our own. For if we understand Gorgias' position on a given topic, we will be able to enter meaningfully into the conversation, position ourselves vis-à-vis Gorgias, and articulate our own perspective. While I reject the objectivist goal as illusory, I do not thereby conclude with Poulakos that this prevents us from articulating a compelling and defensible account of Gorgias' thought, one that we consider more persuasive than rival accounts. Indeed, I suggest that to dismiss every attempt to "understand" Gorgias as theoretically impossible is to accept the objectivist thesis that "understanding" means possessing a direct or unmediated access to Gorgias' own thought, independently of our own assumptions and judgments. And this, I contend, fails to recognize that understanding any text means accepting an account of it that we find more persuasive than every rival account. In respect to the strategy of reading I use, I reject Poulakos' idiosyncratic strategy of selecting three terms from the works of the Sophists, constructing a schematic model of "sophistic rhetoric," and characterizing Gorgias as a Sophist insofar as he fits this model. Instead, I attend to the rival terminologies that scholars have used in their interpretations of Gorgias; flesh out their competing portrayals of Gorgias' views about a variety of issues; assess the rival readings in respect to their consistency, coherence, and cogency; and develop and defend the reading that I find most compelling.[35]

Five Stipulations

In articulating and defending my interpretation of Gorgias, then, I will rely on the shared conventions of the scholarly community, for it is these conventions that enable us to generate viable readings. But as noted above, these conventions are not sufficient for developing a coherent and defensible reading of Gorgias, given the condition of his texts, the elusive nature of his writing, and the obscurity of the contexts in which he composed. If we reject as illusory the objectivist search for a valid interpretation and dismiss as irrelevant the rhapsodic proliferation of free-floating fabrications, we must turn to our conventions themselves as a way out of our impasse. But how can our conventions guide us? The answer, I suggest, is that we must further *stipulate* or agree about some of the features of Gorgias' work; and if we can come to some consensus, we will be able to arrive at a more limited number of plausible readings of Gorgias. These stipulations are neither universal nor absolute, but are grounded in our own existing interpretive practices and customs, and are open to examination and challenge. As such, we may choose to modify them in the ongoing "circular" project of articulating an account of Gorgias, the result of which is what John Rawls calls a "reflective equilibrium," wherein our understanding of Gorgias is congruent with our own interpretive conventions, stipulations, and judgments. Not all scholars will agree to these stipulations, and in those cases their readings will lie outside the boundaries of what I consider the mainstream construals of Gorgias. But I suggest that, given our customary practices, the stipulations are reasonable, and that in fact most Gorgian scholars do accept them. Prior to articulating and defending my reading of Gorgias, then, I will delineate five stipulations that most Gorgian scholars have made and will attempt to justify each stipulation. These involve the stipulations about the authority of the Diels-Kranz collection, the cogency of thought we attribute to Gorgias, the logical consistency of his assertions, the thematic coherence of his work, and the stylistic design of his writing.

    The first stipulation is that we accept the authority of the Diels-Kranz collection of Gorgias' works, so that when we speak of Gorgias, we are speaking of the Diels-Kranz Gorgias. As noted above, prior to the publication and acceptance of this 1908 collection, scholars such as Hegel and Grote did not appear to attribute *Helen* or *Palamedes* to Gorgias; and Cope and Jebb specifically argued against such an attribution. It is conceivable that the current scholarly consensus may change and that compelling arguments may lead us to agree with these earlier scholars. I am not assuming that Diels and Kranz provide us with the "true" texts of Gorgias, such that a scholar with the proper credentials and authority could never challenge one or another of them. Rather, I am only claiming that, given the assumptions, criteria, procedures, and judgments of Gorgian scholars, the collection is authoritative to the extent that the figure we call "Gorgias" is the figure we identify as the author of these texts. I will not ignore critics who wrote prior to Diels-Kranz; on the contrary, I will argue that the three principle readings of Gorgias originate in nineteenth century authors Hegel, Grote, and Nietzsche. But their readings remain powerful because they are consistent with Diels-Kranz; and, it may be argued, one of the reasons scholars today accept the Diels-Kranz collection as authoritative is because most scholars tend to read Gorgias in one of these three ways. The Diels-Kranz collection will not be altered because a scholar discovers Gorgias' true thought; it will be changed if a scholar advances a rival reading that is more compelling than current readings. By stipulating the authority of Diels-Kranz, we place the burden of proof on a critic who wishes to reject or ignore one or more texts; and we agree to marginalize those readings that reject the authority of Diels-Kranz without justifying their rejections.

The second stipulation is one of *cogency,* wherein we agree to attribute cogency or power to Gorgias' thought and writing. In this stipulation, we consent to a principle of hermeneutic "charity," wherein we attempt to "do the best for the text," or make what we consider to be the strongest case for Gorgias. This stipulation is not unreasonable, given that during much of his life Gorgias was highly respected as a philosopher, moralist, and artist. His metaphysical treatise *On Not-Being* was widely known throughout Greece, drawing attention from an array of philosophers.[36] Furthermore, Gorgias was respected as a moralist and political figure, serving as ambassador for his native city of Leontini and becoming "famous" at the festivals where he promoted Panhellenism (B9).[37] And Gorgias was admired as an artist rivaling Aeschylus in importance; extolled by Philostratus as the "father" of the Sophists' art; and credited with inventing improvisational oratory, myriad figures of speech, and entire genres of discourse. A colleague of some of the most eminent poets and playwrights of his time, Gorgias was featured in the comedies of Epicharmus and appears to have influenced many of the tragedies of Euripides.[38] I do not maintain that we should rely on ancient testimony in assuming that Gorgias is a cogent thinker and artist; but I am suggesting that we place the burden of proof on those critics who contend that Gorgias has no ideas worth taking seriously, that he doesn't understand the issues he is discussing, and that he is inept in his use of style.[39] The stipulation of cogency does not mean that we must preclude the possibility that his critics are correct in dismissing him as an amoral confidence man and inept stylist; and it certainly does not mean that we must agree with anything that he says. Rather than ignoring criticisms of Gorgias, I only submit that it is reasonable to consider interpretations that are able to characterize Gorgias as a compelling thinker and skilled artist to be prima facie more persuasive than those readings that simply dismiss his thought as shallow and his writing as inept.

The stipulation of cogency is linked to the next three stipulations: logical consistency, thematic coherence, and stylistic design. The first of these, logical consistency, means that we stipulate that Gorgias considers consistency to be a high priority and that if a reading is able to render Gorgias' remarks consistent, we ought to consider that reading *prima facie* more plausible than a reading that fails to resolve apparent inconsistencies. Stated another way, I will consider an interpretation that fails to resolve any ostensible contradictions in Gorgias' assertions about such matters as the nature of truth, knowledge, justice, or freedom to be weaker than an interpretation that is able to resolve ostensible contradictions. The stipulation of logical consistency may be defended on two grounds. First, Gorgias himself emphasizes the importance of consistency in several of his works. In *On Not-Being* he rebuts his adversaries for their inconsistent statements about existence, knowledge, and language; in *Helen* he shows that the poets are inconsistent in their condemnation of Helen; and in *Palamedes* he argues that treasonable behavior is inconsistent with his desires or abilities and that we ought not trust Odysseus, who is "most inconsistent" (*enantiotata*) in implying that Palamedes is both wise and mad. And, he asks, "How can one trust a man of the sort who in a single speech says to the same man the most inconsistent things about the same subjects?" (P25). Second, most scholars have considered consistency to be extremely important and have either condemned Gorgias for his inconsistency or made a strenuous effort to resolve inconsistencies in Gorgias' assertions. Plato concludes that Gorgias is inconsistent in professing to teach his students about justice, since some of them are unjust; Adkins argues that a "universal determinism of action could easily be generated from what is said in the *Helen,* and that such a determinism is not consistent with the *Palamedes*" (1983, 122); Robinson argues that Gorgias is inconsistent in his assertions about the nature of Being in *On Not-Being;* and Roochnik concludes that the "relativism" of Gorgias is untenable because it is self-contradictory. I do not mean to suggest that we must conclude that Gorgias *is* consistent in his assertions; we may well concur with Plato, Adkins, Robinson, or Roochnik that Gorgias' thinking is inconsistent and that no attempt to resolve his inconsistencies is persuasive. But if we draw this conclusion, we must consider it a serious flaw in Gorgias' thought; and if we are engaged in making the best case for Gorgias, we must consider readings that fail to resolve apparent inconsistencies to be weaker than those that do.

A stipulation closely related to that of consistency concerns the overall coherence of what may be called Gorgias' "world view." Specifically, I suggest that we should attempt to render Gorgias' work thematically coherent, such that his remarks on various topics form an integrated whole. This stipulation differs from the stipulation of logical consistency in that it emphasizes the holistic or integral nature of his views on diverse subjects, rather than the consistency of his assertions on the same subject. Specifically, it involves delineating a coherence among Gorgias' views on an array of topics such as truth, language, communication, knowledge, and rhetoric; the nature of the individual and the community; the nature of virtue or excellence; the social values of justice, equality, freedom, and friendship; and the purpose and nature of education and art. It may be argued that stipulating that Gorgias' thought on these various topics is coherent is presumptuous; but I suggest that for Gorgias this stipulation is indeed warranted. Gorgias himself suggests that he sees a connection between epistemological and ethical matters, praising the Athenian warriors for their intellectual and moral virtue. Many of Gorgias' most astute readers have seen his views as coherent and have drawn upon that coherence to praise or chastise him. Plato, for example, draws a connection between Gorgias' repudiation of truth and acceptance of probability, his art of rhetoric as a form of pandering to stereotypes and the status quo, and the amoral consequences of his teaching. In the modern era, a number of scholars have delineated connections between Gorgias' epistemological and ethical views. E. R. Dodds suggests that Gorgias' affirmation of empiricism is integrally related to his Utilitarian ethics; and Untersteiner argues that Gorgias' subjectivist epistemology is integrally connected to his irrationalist ethics. Although we may not agree with these construals, I suggest that insofar as they are able to discern a unity in Gorgias' thought, these readings merit consideration as viable on the grounds that they render Gorgias' overall worldview to be coherent.

While scholars have attempted to render Gorgias' work thematically coherent, many have also sought to find an integral or purposive relationship between the "substance" of his work and his notorious "Gorgianic" style. In consenting to this stipulation, we presume that Gorgias is a skilled stylist whose manner of writing and performing is deliberate and functional, and we place the burden of proof on those critics who assume that there is no meaningful relationship between Gorgias' putative thought and his outlandish figuration, or who dismiss Gorgias as an inept stylist who simply is unable to communicate clearly. This stipulation will pit us against an array of Gorgias' ancient critics such as Plato, who characterizes Gorgias' style as a "delightful feast" of words designed solely to entertain his audiences; and Aristotle, who argues that Gorgias' style is too artificial and frigid to be effective. And it will lead us to challenge an array of modern critics, including W. H. Thompson, who contends that in Gorgias' writing "the sacrifice of sense to sound, perspicuity to point, [is] manifest throughout" (1871, 176); Bromley Smith, who sees Gorgias' metaphors as far-fetched and tasteless (1921, 357); George Kennedy, who states that Gorgias "flagrantly indulged" in his Gorgianic figures (1989, 184); Neil O'Sullivan, who argues that Gorgias' bombastic "Aeschylean" style was considered "striking" in 427 B.C.E. only because of its obsolescence (21); J. D. Denniston, who maintains that two words suffice for characterizing Gorgias' style, "wholly bad" (1952, 10); and John Robinson, who dismisses Gorgias' style with the single epithet "repellent" (1973, 52). In stipulating that Gorgias is a skilled and deliberate stylist, I will consider those readings which fail to show how his thought and writing are interrelated to be less convincing than those interpretations which are able to explain the nature and purpose of his distinctively "tropical" style.

Subjectivist, Empiricist, and Antifoundationalist Readings

Given these stipulations, I undertake three interrelated tasks in developing my reading of Gorgias. First, I identify the most persuasive readings of Gorgias that scholars have articulated. Second, I integrate and develop the reading of each school, combining the work of individual scholars who share the same view of Gorgias but who examine different aspects of his work. Third, I assess the readings of the rival schools, judging which of them presents the most compelling account of Gorgias. In identifying, developing and assessing these three rival accounts, I must make two disclaimers. First, although I do not intend my classification of these rival readings to be controversial, in that I draw from the descriptions scholars have given of their own accounts and those of their rivals, I recognize that alternative characterizations of the most persuasive positions in current discussions of Gorgias may be offered. Second, I recognize that not every scholar who has recently written on Gorgias, and whom I classify as adhering to one or another of the rival schools, will necessarily accept every aspect of the "composite" reading that I develop. In developing the rival "constructions" of Gorgias' thought and art, I attempt to show how each reading offers a coherent account of what may be called his metaphysics and epistemology; his ethics and politics; and his "rhetoric"; or, stated another way, his conception of truth, inquiry, and language; his conception of the individual and the community, and the sort of community he advocates; and the manner in which he presents his ideas. I recognize that each school allows for varieties of emphasis and focus; and that the way I situate various scholars is open to challenge.

If we attend to those scholars who attempt to render Gorgias as a consistent and coherent thinker and artist, we will be able to identify three distinct schools of interpretation. I identify these three readings as the "subjectivist," "empiricist," and "antifoundationalist" accounts, using labels that several of the scholars themselves have deployed to describe their own accounts and those of their adversaries. The first two schools of Gorgian criticism originate in the writings of the two nineteenth-century authors who have been credited with initiating the project of "rehabilitating" the Sophists, Hegel and Grote. Hegel's 1832–33 *Lectures on the History of Philosophy* and Grote's 1869 *History of Greece* have been so influential that until recently most subsequent scholars engaged in discussions of Gorgias and the other Sophists have tended to adopt one or another of the readings. The identification and characterization of the two prevailing schools is itself widely accepted among sophistic scholars. Kerferd thus observes that "it has become common to classify the defenders of the sophists into two groups, the one . . . stemming from Grote, and the other the

Hegelian" (1989, 10); Susan Jarratt remarks that the Hegelian and Grotian readings "created two different sets of sophists" (5); Schiappa, who embraces the empiricist reading, notes that "Despite the lingering of the Platonic and Hegelian traditions, most contemporary students of the Sophists accept Grote's general position" (1991, 10); and A. A. Long, also a partisan of Grote's position, writes that "on the sophists nothing has ever surpassed Grote"; while "for philosophical stimulus (but not for scholarly accuracy)," Hegel is recommended (Long 1999, 366).[40]

In the reading originating with Hegel and developed by Untersteiner, Rosenmeyer, Verdenius, Versenyi, White, and Miller, Gorgias emerges as advocating what Hegel calls *subjectivism* (355). In this reading, Gorgias is construed as maintaining that each individual fabricates his or her own subjective reality or truth, that objective knowledge is impossible, and that every claim to describe objective reality is deceptive. Among scholars who attribute this view to Gorgias, Mario Untersteiner contends that Gorgias posits a "tragic antithesis" between our perception and the world from which we are isolated (1954, 150); and Eric White argues that Gorgias sees reality as a Heraclitean flux in which every unprecedented, kairotic moment is apprehensible only through subjective intuition (1987, 16, 34). Some adherents of this school portray Gorgias' ethical and political views as integrally related to his subjectivism, construing him as attempting to liberate himself and his audiences from the "prison-house of language." Untersteiner argues that for Gorgias every moral decision is "irrational," and William Race argues that Gorgias embraces a romanticist ethic which urges individuals to pursue their romantic desires. Politically, Gorgias sees every government as repressive, whether power is wielded by a tyrant, by the few, or by the many, and he promotes a politics of rapture modeled on the Dionysian festival. Concerning Gorgias' rhetorical style, Untersteiner argues that Gorgias deploys the trope of antithesis to show or display the antithetical opposition between individuals and the chaotic reality that lies beyond language, an antithesis that cannot be expressed logically without self-contradiction (194); and White suggests that Gorgias "restlessly experiments with the style of utterance in the hope of producing genuine novelty," a poet of *kairos* who recreates himself and his world anew in each epideictic performance.

Although many scholars read Gorgias as a subjectivist, they are countered by a school of critics who read Gorgias as advancing a diametrically opposed epistemology, that of *empiricism*. In Guthrie's summarizing phrase, Gorgias and his sophistic colleagues "shared the general philosophical outlook described . . . under the name *empiricism*" (1971, 8–10). The empiricist school, which includes Grote, Loenen, MacDowell, Dodds, Enos, and Schiappa, construes Gorgias as a scientific empiricist whose emphasis on observation and rational argument anticipates the science and logic of subsequent thinkers such as Aristotle. These scholars tend to read Gorgias in *On Not-Being* as rejecting the "transcendent" and nonempirical realm of Being affirmed by Parmenides and affirming the existence of a material world accessible through the senses. Concerning language, they contend that Gorgias overtly repudiates the deceptive use of language by magicians, poets, practitioners of witchcraft, and men like Odysseus, and uses rational argumentation to arrive at the truth. Furthermore, the empiricist camp tends to read Gorgias as a liberal in his ethics, promoting the greatest happiness of the community as a whole or advocating an ethics of duty in which morality demands adherence to universally valid moral laws accessible to the uniquely human faculty of reason. They read Gorgias as a vigorous partisan of democracy who maintains that individuals should be free and equal because of their possession of a rational moral faculty. In respect to his own rhetorical style, Gorgias uses antitheses to accentuate and clarify his conceptual distinctions, and he illustrates his ideas with lucid metaphors and other appropriate figures of speech.

Although these two readings tend to dominate current discourse about Gorgias, several scholars have recently begun to articulate a third account, one that has been labeled *antifoundationalist*. In this construal, Gorgias repudiates as misguided the project of seeking a criterion for knowledge and language. This reading originates in the writings of Nietzsche, who argues that the Sophists articulate a "tropical" model of language in which every assertion is inescapably figurative; they embrace an "agonistic" model of inquiry in which knowledge as constructed through rival rhetors; and they construe "truth" as a label of endorsement rather than an objective state of affairs. More recently, the antifoundationalist reading has been suggested by Rorty, who construes the Sophists as resisting the attempt by such philosophers as Parmenides and Plato to discover an "unshakable foundation" for knowledge and discourse (1980, 157). It is also promoted by Richard Lanham, who construes Western intellectual history as an ongoing quarrel between serious foundationalist thinkers intent on discovering ultimate truths about the world and absolute rules for governing behavior, and pragmatic, playful thinkers like the Sophists who see language as a repertoire of rhetorical maneuvers that enable communities to fashion their own truths and values (1976, 1–4). The antifoundationalist reading is explicitly urged by Fish, who asserts that "antifoundationalism *is* rhetoric, and one could say without too much exaggeration that modern antifoundationalism is old sophism writ analytic" (1989, 347). The reading is also advocated by Jarratt, who characterizes "the sophists' emphasis on *dissoi logoi*—contradictory propositions—as the *anti-foundation* of any knowledge" (1991, 70, emphasis added). Among scholars who have begun to develop this reading in detailed studies of Gorgias' individual texts, Alexander Mourelatos (1987) explores Gorgias' antirepresentationalist model of language in *On Not-Being*; Nicole Loraux examines the way Gorgias simultaneously deploys and exposes his own use of established commonplaces or *topoi* in praising the Athenian warriors in the *Epitaphios* (1986, 221–262); and James Porter (1993) examines Gorgias' parodic repudiation of the poets' claim to foundational "truths" in *Helen*.

Rhetoricity, Community, Performance

In this book I will draw upon, elaborate, and synthesize the studies of the antifoundational school of critics, arguing that their reading resolves many of the inconsistencies in the subjectivist and empiricist readings, and provides a more viable explanation of Gorgias' style or manner of writing. I develop this argument in three parts. In part one, "Rhetoricity," I examine Gorgias' conceptions of language, knowledge, and truth. I discuss the subjectivist and empiricist construals of Gorgias and argue that each is contradicted by many of Gorgias' assertions. I then develop an antifoundationalist reading of Gorgias, arguing that in *On Not-Being* Gorgias repudiates the notion that there is a foundational "truth" in the world, that knowledge consists in the apprehension of this truth, and that words acquire meaning by representing an independent "reality." In his three-part argument he shows that attempts to characterize this putative truth are inevitably self-contradictory; that even if such a truth existed, we could not apprehend it; and that even if we could apprehend it, we could not communicate it to others. Stated another way, Gorgias shows that a foundationalist model is unable to account for everyday claims to knowledge or the practice of everyday communication. In place of this model, Gorgias articulates and uses an agonistic model of language in which discourse is a repertoire of maneuvers in various agons or games, inquiry involves a competitive and cooperative struggle between rival rhetors, and "truth" is a term of endorsement given by a community to accounts it finds persuasive. In Gorgias' construal, claims to truth are not evaluated in reference to independent criteria, but are always judged in reference to the practices, conventions, and criteria agreed upon by individuals in a community. Truths are neither subjective expressions of intuitive insights nor accurate replications of a context-independent domain but are persuasive narratives fabricated in rhetorical contexts that persuade and win the endorsement of a situated community.

In part two, "Community," I discuss the ethical and political dimensions of Gorgias' antifoundationalism. In opposition to the subjectivist and rationalist readings, I suggest that Gorgias is a *conventionalist* who sees habitual practice, or *nomos*, as informing individuals and communities and who characterizes morality as adherence to the social conventions of particular communities. Gorgias' principal ethical terms are thus *honor* and *shame*, wherein the ultimate authority lies neither in universal moral laws nor in the subjective desires of autonomous individuals, but in the members of a communities themselves, mutually trusting people who concur in their moral judgments about one another. In Gorgias' ethics, individuals strive to obtain their own goals within the parameters of socially sanctioned agons or contests guided by considerations of honor and shame, terms of moral approbation or condemnation rendered by other members of their community. Rather than urging people to free themselves of rational restraint or to adhere to universal moral laws, Gorgias invites people to become engaged in the agons of their community. In respect to his political views, I characterize Gorgias as a Panhellenist who endorses the conventions of the Greek community. Gorgias is not a relativist who sees every political arrangement as equally desirable, for he vigorously supports Hellenic culture, and opposes "barbarians" who aggressively assault it as well as imperial cities who seek to enslave other cities. Gorgias' advocacy of the agon as a venue for fashioning truths and values leads him to oppose repressive tyranny; but his embrace of the agon does not entail a commitment to democracy as the only possible form of government. Instead, Gorgias advocates a pluralistic Panhellenism in which diverse political arrangements are possible but in which people in various cities live harmoniously with one another.

In part three, "Performance," I examine the stylistic and performative aspects of Gorgias' epideictic performances, focusing on his notorious figuration and histrionic manner of presentation. I examine the subjectivist thesis that Gorgias uses "poetic" devices to express truths that cannot be articulated in rational prose and the empiricist reading that Gorgias uses figurative language to communicate clearly in oral settings, and I argue that each of these readings is contradicted by Gorgias' stylistic practice. As an alternative to these accounts, I argue that Gorgias' style may best be characterized as "parodic," in that he adapts to the conventions of diverse discourses while playfully drawing attention to the conventions of those discourses and the rhetoricity of every text. In his performances, Gorgias adapts his manner of writing to the conventions of distinct genres in order to compose novel texts, but he foregrounds the conventions of the discourse in order to expose the strategies his foundationalist rivals use to deceive audiences into believing that their arguments or texts are objectively valid. In his four extant works, he deconstructs the assertions by self-effacing Eleatic philosophers who present themselves as speaking the voice of reason, the utterances of poets who present themselves as divinely inspired, the assertions by biased litigants who present their accusations as true, and the orations of prominent Athenian citizens who depict their city as the fount of justice. Gorgias' parodic performances are an integral part of his pedagogy, for by displaying the rhetoricity of every text, he shows his audience that all arguments, including his own, are contingent, situated fabrications that are "true" only insofar as they are endorsed by specific audiences. Gorgias' objective is not to transmit objective truth or to inculcate universal moral principles, but to encourage people to become engaged in the agons of their culture. For it is by engaging in these agons that people are able to liberate and empower themselves, while fostering solidarity in the Panhellenic community.

Throughout the three main sections of this book, I argue that the antifoundationalist reading makes a stronger case for Gorgias than the subjectivist and empiricist readings, rendering Gorgias' work logically consistent, thematically and artistically coherent, and consequently more compelling or cogent. But which reading we ultimately accept will not depend solely on the cogency it lends to Gorgias, but also on whether it is congruent with our conception of Greek and Western culture. For every interpretation involves placing an author in a cultural context; and the way we construe that context will influence the way we place and thus read Gorgias. In the concluding chapter of the book, I address the ways in which our conception of Greek and Western culture may determine how we situate Gorgias. Attending to the two principle narratives of Greek culture, I suggest that our interpretation of Gorgias is correlatively related to which of these narratives we find most persuasive. If we adopt the *evolutionary* narrative, we will be inclined to situate Gorgias in respect to this evolution and hence will tend to embrace either the subjectivist or empiricist reading. Subjectivists from Hegel to Vitanza thus read Gorgias as a proponent of irrationality who depicts *logos* or reason as inherently deceptive and repressive, an advocate of liberation who seeks to overthrow the repressive regime of *logos,* and a creative artist who uses poetic devices to expose the deceptions of *logos* and to suggest new ways to recreate oneself and one's world. Empiricist scholars from Grote to Schiappa, in contrast, read Gorgias as an advocate of reason who promotes rational inquiry as a way to dispel the deceptions of myth-bound poets, a supporter of democratic governments who affirms the equality of rational individuals and rejects the repressive social orders legitimized by traditional myths, and a proponent of lucid prose who deploys antitheses, analogies and logical reasoning to convey his ideas clearly and effectively. I suggest that if we adopt the *agonal* model of Greek culture, we will see Gorgias as neither a proponent of mythic or logical thought, but as an antifoundationalist thinker who sees both *mythos* and *logos* as contingent upon the conventions of a community and who challenges both claims by philosophers that they possess a privileged route to the truth and assertions by poets that their words are divinely inspired. If we adopt this reading, we will be inclined to grant him a seminal and pivotal role in Greek culture, seeing him as a clever Sophist and skilled artist who displays his antifoundationalist views in a variety of parodic, epideictic performances. And if, with Fish and other scholars we see this struggle as informing much of Western history, such that the ancient quarrel between rhetoric and philosophy continues to this very day in terms that are "exactly those one finds in the dialogues of Plato and the orations of the sophists" (1989, 483–85), then we may be inclined to grant Gorgias an even more important role as a thinker and artist, one who stands as our own precursor in an ongoing struggle against the deceptions of foundationalist thought.

Part One
RHETORICITY

1

BEYOND SUBJECTIVISM AND EMPIRICISM

> To the Sophists the content is mine, and subjective.
> Hegel, *Lectures on the History of Philosophy*

> Gorgias' positive, sensualistic theory of knowledge is very prominent indeed
> J. Loenen, *Parmenides, Melissus, Gorgias*

In this chapter I examine the two prevailing readings of Gorgias' notions of truth, knowledge, and language. I first examine the subjectivist reading initially proposed by Hegel and developed subsequently by Untersteiner, Rosenmeyer, Gronbeck, Miller, and White. In this reading, Gorgias posits an unbridgeable gulf between reality and human awareness and construes every use of language to be deceptive insofar as it purports to represent the real nature of things. He maintains that it is only by escaping the "prison-house of language" and experiencing the world subjectively in a nonrational "kairotic moment" that we are able to experience the truth. I next examine the empiricist reading first advanced by Grote and subsequently articulated by Loenen, MacDowell, Romilly, Enos, and Schiappa. In this construal, Gorgias rejects as unreal the transcendental domain of Being posited by the Eleatics and affirms instead the reality of the physical world, one that we may perceive empirically through our sensory "pores" and describe accurately with a scientific discourse. I argue that while each of these interpretations is internally coherent, each is contradicted by a variety of Gorgias' own statements.

REJECTING FRIVOLITY AND NIHILISM

Before examining these two readings of Gorgias, we may note that both vehemently reject the view that Gorgias is not a significant philosopher and that, rather than engaging in serious inquiry in any of his texts, he instead composes what Arthur Pease calls "paradoxical encomia," playful *paignions* in which he defends positions that are unpopular, paradoxical, or patently absurd (Pease 1926, 27).[1] This reading of Gorgias is first suggested by his Athenian critics, notably Isocrates, Plato, and Aristotle. Isocrates argues that like many Sophists, Gorgias is not a serious philosopher who attends to important issues facing the city, that instead he is a frivolous writer who composes trivial works akin to those praising bumblebees or salt (*Helen* 10.11–12). Gorgias displays his frivolity in *On Not-Being*, in which his primary objective is to exhibit his own ability to make an obviously preposterous position appear stronger.

Isocrates thus remarks that "there are some who are much pleased with themselves if, after setting up an absurd and self-contradictory subject, they succeed in discussing it in tolerable fashion; and men have grown old, some asserting that it is impossible to say, or to gainsay, what is false, or to speak on both sides of the same questions . . . and still others waste their time in captious disputations that are not only entirely useless, but are sure to make trouble for their disciples. . . . For who could surpass Gorgias, who dared to assert that nothing exists of the things that are" (*Helen* 10). In a similar vein, Plato characterizes Gorgias as a playful orator who delights his audiences with an elegant "feast" of words (*Gorgias* 447a) and who maintains that "there is no need to know the truth of the actual matters," for "one merely needs to have discovered some device of persuasion which will make one appear to those who do not know to know better than those who know (*Gorgias* 459bc). Plato also refers to Gorgias as a Sophist as well as a festive orator, and in so doing he includes him among the class of verbal athletes who are mere jugglers of words rather than true philosophers intent on finding the truth (*Sophist* 235a).² In this respect, Gorgias is akin to the antilogistic Dionysodorus, who argues that if you own a dog, and your dog is the father of puppies, then the dog is your father and your siblings are puppies (*Euthydemus* 298e). Aristotle also appears to consider Gorgias a frivolous orator, excluding him entirely from his inventory of pre-Socratic philosophers in the *Metaphysics* and discussing him primarily as an orator who composes playful epideictic texts. In some passages, Aristotle suggests that he also considers Gorgias to be a Sophist, a person whom Aristotle denigrates as one whose goal is to make money by appearing wise or clever and whose means of doing so typically involves the deployment of fallacious or "sophistic" arguments.³

This construal of Gorgias has been remarkably resilient, and many academic philosophers today still dismiss Gorgias as a clever wordsmith rather than a bona fide philosopher. John Robinson thus argues that we should not really take Gorgias seriously as a philosopher, and that his "bizarre" stab at metaphysics in *On Not-Being* reveals little more than his own ignorance and ineptitude. For rather than seriously challenging Parmenides, Gorgias' silly, embarrassing, and specious text betrays more than anything else the fact that he has "not the slightest understanding even of what the issues are" (Robinson 1973, 59). Unconcerned with engaging in a meaningful discussion about the nature of truth, knowledge, or language, Gorgias is only a "clever mimic" whose text is a slapdash pastiche of dubious arguments. Echoing his Athenian precursors, Robinson concludes that Gorgias trivializes philosophy so as to render it "an extension of the art of controversy, raised perhaps to a higher level of abstraction, but otherwise unchanged" (60). In a similar vein, Martha Nussbaum dismisses Gorgias as a shallow opportunist who scorns "traditional philosophical ways of attending to validity and clarity" and who deploys fallacious arguments to deceive and manipulate his audiences. Condemning Gorgias' motives as well as his intelligence, she argues that "if one secretly, or openly, despises rational argument and wishes, like Gorgias, to win fame and fortune by some other means, what more convenient doctrine to espouse in the process than the Gorgianic view that there is no truth anyway, and it's all a matter of manipulation, more or less like drugging? Then one's failure to exhibit the traditional rational virtues will look like daring rather than sloppiness" (1990, 21).

Clearly, we are justified in repudiating the notion that Gorgias is a frivolous orator rather than a philosopher worth taking seriously. A student of Empedocles, a colleague of Protagoras, and a teacher of Lycophron and Alcidamas, Gorgias appears to have been quite readily accepted by many of his philosophical contemporaries. Furthermore, both Sextus Empiricus and the author of the *MXG* consider Gorgias' *On Not-Being* a viable work of philosophy, and Philostratus insists that Gorgias and the other Older Sophists treat philosophical issues.[4]

If Isocrates and Plato argue that Gorgias is not really a philosopher, we must recall that they each have their own restrictive definitions of philosophy and that neither appears to consider the other a true philosopher. Moreover, if Plato protests that Gorgias is not a true philosopher, perhaps he protests too much, since he addresses Gorgias' ideas explicitly or implicitly in a dozen dialogues.[5] And if Aristotle himself omits Gorgias from his exclusive list of pre-Socratics, it is significant that most scholars until quite recently have attributed the *MXG,* a text that treats Gorgias as a serious philosophical rival, to Aristotle; for attribution of the text to a philosopher of Aristotle's stature suggests that many scholars have considered Gorgias a philosopher worth taking seriously.

If we examine Gorgias' own remarks about the nature of "philosophy," we may well conclude from *On Not-Being* that he is critical of the Eleatics and perhaps of most other philosophers of his own time; but this does not mean that he repudiates philosophy altogether. His only explicit comment about philosophy is in the form of a metaphor, namely that "those neglecting philosophy and devoting themselves to general studies were like the suitors who, though wanting Penelope, slept with her maids" (B29). Gorgias' praise of philosophy may be faint, for he suggests that it is a form of seduction, that it may fail to capture its elusive prey, and that it may involve risking one's own well-being; but he does suggest that he considers philosophers to be more respectable than those who engage in "general studies."

More literally, the argument that Gorgias fails to qualify as a philosopher because he does not address serious issues and because he violates what Nussbaum calls "traditional philosophical ways of attending to validity and clarity" (1990, 220) is without merit. Among the "philosophical" topics that Gorgias discusses with sophistication are existence, truth, knowledge, and communication (in *On*

Not-Being); free will and love (in *Helen*); morality and political commitment (in *Palamedes*); heroism and the role of the state in human affairs (in the *Epitaphios*); and, in his extant aphorisms, topics such as existence and appearance, justice and friendship, honor and beauty.

Rather than agreeing with Robinson (1973), who asserts without explanation or argument that in *On Not-Being* Gorgias has "not the slightest understanding even of what the issues are" (59), I submit that it is more accurate to say that Robinson fails to understand Gorgias. Concerning his use of argument, Gorgias deploys such conventional modes of reasoning as argument by example, induction, the if-then counterfactual, and the disjunctive "tree" method extolled by Plato in the *Sophist*. Gorgias' three-part argument in *On Not-Being* is cogent and memorable; his defense of Helen is original and at times compelling; and his seminal deployment of the notions of "motive and opportunity" in *Palamedes* has become paradigmatic of many subsequent legal defenses. If some of Gorgias' arguments are not "formally valid," this certainly does not warrant the conclusion that he scorns "traditional philosophical ways of attending to validity and clarity" or that he "despises rational argument." Certainly not every argument advanced by Plato, Augustine, or Nietzsche is formally "valid." And if Robinson finds Gorgias' style "repellent," he betrays the parochiality of his own tastes. Is Kant or Hegel any less a philosopher because we find their style repellent? And if some scholars conclude that Gorgias' texts cannot be seriously philosophy because they are too playful or witty, they fail to recognize that seriousness and playfulness are by no means mutually exclusive and that philosophers from Plato to Derrida have presented serious ideas in a playful manner.

While the subjectivist and empiricist schools reject the contention that Gorgias is not a significant philosopher at all, they also reject the thesis even if he *is* a bona fide philosopher, Gorgias' putative "philosophy," that of radical *nihilism,* is so preposterous that it is unworthy of consideration. Among Gorgias' ancient and modern readers, this interpretation is also not without some support. In one passage Isocrates suggests that he considers Gorgias' arguments in *On Not-Being* to be serious rather than frivolous, and that Gorgias is a bona fide nihilist who argues that "nothing at all" exists (*Antidosis* 268). The anonymous author of the *MXG* also appears to read Gorgias as defending nihilism, for in his refutation of Gorgias' arguments in part one, he argues that "it does not follow from what he [Gorgias] has said that nothing is. . . . For the exact opposite seems then to become the consequent," namely that "all things are" (*MXG* 978b4–10). Among modern scholars, the nihilist reading also has some supporters: Bromley Smith describes Gorgias as a "nihilist" (1921, 334); John Dewey argues that Gorgias is "the first pure nihilist in philosophic theory [and] also the last" (1902, 177); and Richard Bett contends that Gorgias advances a "nihilistic and extraordinary view" in which truth becomes nonexistent and in which "every impression and opinion is false" (1989, 150–152).

The primary objection to the nihilist reading is that it renders *On Not-Being* patently self-contradictory. For Gorgias' own arguments in the work assume that everyday objects do in fact exist and that we are able to know about them and communicate information about them. Thus, in part one he flatly asserts that "it is not, in fact, true that the existent does not exist" (N67). In part two Gorgias further indicates that he is not defending nihilism; for when he argues that we are unable to grasp "the existent" in our minds, he distinguishes between our ability to think of things that *do* exist, such as men and chariots, and to think of things that obviously do not exist, such as flying men, chariots racing on the sea, Scylla and Chimaera. He points out that "Scylla and Chimaera and many other nonexistent things are considered in the mind" (N80), and he maintains that "if one considers a man flying or chariots racing in the sea, a man does not straightaway fly nor a chariot race in the sea" (N79). Clearly, Gorgias cannot be arguing that nothing *whatsoever* exists; for if he were, his arguments in part two would make no sense. For each argument depends on the assumption that we are quite able to distinguish between things that exist and things that do not exist. In part three, Gorgias further repudiates nihilism. He asserts that, for example, "that by which we reveal is *logos*, but *logos* is not substances and existing things. Therefore we do not reveal existing things to our neighbors, but *logos*, which is something other than substances. Thus, just as the visible cannot become audible, and vice versa, similarly, when external reality is involved, it would not become our *logos*" (N84). Gorgias distinguishes between existing things and *logos*, or discourse, but he never asserts that things and words "do not exist." Finally, Gorgias thoroughly repudiates nihilism in each of his subsequent works, in which he speaks of a variety of "existing" things, ranging from tangible objects to nonvisible gods. If we assume that Gorgias is consistent in his argumentation in *On Not-Being* and in his oeuvre as a whole, then we cannot read *On Not-Being* as a defense of nihilism.

THE SUBJECTIVIST READING

The first school of criticism portrays Gorgias as a subjectivist who posits an ontological and epistemological gulf between the individual subject and external reality, such that individuals are unable to apprehend or gain access to the truth and are consequently condemned to dwell within their own deceptive, subjectively generated conceptual and linguistic domains. The subjectivist account of Gorgias may said to originate in the modern era with Hegel, who interprets Gorgias and the other Sophists in the context of his model of the "dialectical" progress of human thought, wherein the views of the Sophists occupy a position that is antithetical to the "objective"

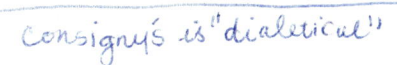

thought of the Ionian natural philosophers. For Hegel, the history of Western thought follows a universal pattern, one proceeding through the positing of a thesis, the emergence of its negation in an antithesis, and a subsequent synthesis. By applying this model to Greek philosophy, Hegel discerns three grand periods, the first extending from Thales to Aristotle, the second encompassing the Hellenistic period, and the third a Neo-Platonic synthesis. Within the first period Hegel also identifies a dialectical triad, wherein the positivist "thesis" is advanced by the Ionians, Thales to Anaxagoras. In this model, thought emerges from objective, sensuous determinations; and reality is seen as comprised of objective, sensible natural elements such as water, air, and fire. The antithesis of objectivism, in Hegel's account, emerges in the writings of the Sophists, who present finite, individual *subjects* as determining their own perceptions and thoughts and who initiate "an age of subjective reflection" (1995, 350). Rather than seeking objective theoretical and moral truths, the Sophists contend that each individual is his or her own ultimate source of truth and value; and they leave it to "particular subjectivity to make itself first and fixed, to relate everything to itself" (355). In the Sophists' account, articulated in Protagoras' contention that "man is the measure of all things," the source and criterion of what is real is subjective individual experience. In effect, the Sophist bases all judgments solely on his own subjective experience; and every judgment depends "on the pleasure of the subject alone which shall prevail" (337).

If he contrasts the Sophists with their objectivist predecessors, Hegel also contrasts them with their Athenian critics, Socrates, Plato, and Aristotle, who in Hegel's account synthesize Ionian objectivity and Sophistic subjectivity. Hegel thus observes that the standpoint of the Sophists differs from that of Socrates and Plato in that "the mission of Socrates was to express the beautiful, good, true and right, as the end and aim of the individual, while with the Sophists . . . all this was left to the individual will" (366). Stated another way, the difference between the Sophists and Plato is that the former posit the subjective individual as the "ultimate basis" or *foundation* of knowledge and action, while Socrates and Plato posit truth and the good as objective criteria. In Hegel's terms, "something fixed there must be. This is either the good, the universal, or the individuality, the arbitrary will of the subject. . . . To the Sophists the satisfaction of the *individual himself* was now made ultimate, and since they made everything uncertain, the fixed point was in the assertion, 'It is my desire, my pride, glory, and honour, particular subjectivity, which I make my end'" (370; emphasis added). Hegel also contrasts the subjectivism of the Sophists with the "spiritual" culture informed by Christianity. He thus asserts that "in Greek culture the time had not yet come when, out of thinking consciousness itself, the ultimate principles had become manifested, and thus there was something firm to rest upon, as is the case with us in modern times . . . where culture is, so to speak, introduced under the protection and in pre-supposition of a spiritual religion . . . of the eternal nature of Spirit and of the absolute end, of the end of man, to be in a spiritual way actual and to posit himself in unity with the absolute spirit" (365). Thus the Sophists not only encapsulate subjectivism in Greek culture, but they also exemplify the subjectivist position in Western culture as a whole, one iterated by the "subjective idealists" of Hegel's own time. So if Hegel "rehabilitates" the Sophists by incorporating them into the Western philosophical tradition rather than dismissing them as opportunistic charlatans who deploy fallacious arguments to appear intelligent, he in effect identifies them with what he sees as advancing a misguided position, one that has been corrected by the progress or development of reason itself.

Although he depicts all the Sophists as subjectivists, Hegel singles out Gorgias as particularly pivotal, given his systematic critique of the possibility of attaining and communicating knowledge of objective reality in *On Not-Being*. Concerning *On Not-Being*, Hegel writes that "in the first [stage] he proves that (objectively) nothing exists, in the second (subjectively) that assuming that Being is, it cannot be known; and in the third place (both subjectively and objectively) that were it to exist and be knowable, no communication of what is known would be possible" (379). In Hegel's reading, Gorgias' argument is that human beings, being finite and limited, are unable to say anything about objective Being that is not contradictory. For "if Being is, it is contradictory to predicate a quality to it, and if we do this, we express something merely negative about it" (380). Specifically, "In speaking of Being and non-being, we always say the opposite to what we wish. Being and non-being are the same, just as they are not the same; if they are the same, I speak of the two as different: if different, I express the same predicate of them, diversity" (382). Concerning part two of *On Not-Being*, Hegel reads Gorgias as contending that even if an objective reality existed, it could never be known; and he argues that Gorgias offers as an alternative a subjective "idealism" in which each individual fabricates his or her own world. Attending to Gorgias' argument that if what is presented to the mind is accepted as real, then "everything that is presented also exists, but no one says that if a flying man, or wagon riding on the sea were presented to us, it would exist" (383), Hegel infers that "Gorgias on the one hand pronounces a just polemic against absolute realism, which, because it represents, thinks to possess the very thing itself, when it only has a relative [awareness], but he falls, on the other hand, into the *false idealism* of modern times, according to which thought is always subjective only, and thus not the existent, since through thought an existent is transformed into what is thought" (383; emphasis added). Hegel reads part three of Gorgias' treatise as complementing his subjective idealism. For, he asserts, Gorgias' argument that language is categorically different from the objects it purports to name results in the complete impossibility of conveying information about "objective reality." And since Gorgias denies that any attempt to communicate about objective reality is possible, he suggests that only "subjective" and hence "relative" notions can be conveyed to others. Gorgias, in short, is a subjective idealist, for whom objective reality is neither knowable nor articulable in words.

Hegel's depiction of the Sophists as subjectivists has been enormously influential, as is evidenced in the writing of historians such as Eduard Zeller and Wilhelm Nestle, who iterate Hegel's fundamental view of the Sophists as "subjective" theorists who deny the possibility of objective knowledge.[6] But Hegel's characterization of the Sophists is perhaps given its most succinct iteration in the writings of Søren Kierkegaard, who points out that as subjectivists, the Sophists were able to provide a secure foundation for ordinary perception and speech. Adopting Hegel's overall reading, Kierkegaard observes that "since reflection had shaken the *foundations* of everything, Sophistry assumed the role of remedying the momentary need. Thus reflection in Sophistry was checked in its precarious outflowing and was controlled at every moment, but the security that bound it was *the particular subject*. . . . But when the foundations of everything have been shaken, what can then become the firm ground that is to save the situation? Either it is the universal (the good, etc.) or it is the *finite subject*, his propensities, desires, etc. The Sophists seized the latter expedient" (1989, 205; emphasis added). What is crucial in Kierkegaard's account is his insistence that while the Sophists shake the foundations of knowledge by denying access to objective reality, they nevertheless provide a new foundation for knowledge and communication. Hence, although Gorgias denies the existence of "objective reality," he does not so much undermine or annihilate everyday notions of what is real, but instead preserves such notions on a new *foundation*, that of individual subjectivity. In this respect, Gorgias and his sophistic colleagues "thought themselves able to satisfy the demands of the times, not by shaking the *foundations* of everything, but, after having shaken the *foundations,* by making it all secure again" (297; emphasis added).

From Logos to Kairos

Few scholars today ascribe to Hegel's dialectical model of intellectual history, but many continue to be influenced by his subjectivist account of the Sophists in general and of Gorgias in particular. But unlike Hegel, who repudiates Gorgias' subjectivism as misguided, they argue that Gorgias' "subjectivism" is coherent and cogent. But what precisely is the "subjective truth" that Gorgias embraces? For several subjectivist scholars, the answer is the ephemeral and unique experience that Gorgias discusses in part three of *On Not-Being*. In his argument against the possibility of communicating what is real, Gorgias asserts that "the objects which even one and the same man perceives at the same moment are not all similar, but he perceives different things by hearing and by sight, and differently now and on some former occasion" (*MXG* 980b). In Guthrie's summarizing phrase, all truth for Gorgias is "individual and temporary," rather than objective and permanent (51).

Using Plato's distinction, we may say that Gorgias embraces the view that "nothing ever is, but is always becoming" (*Theaetetus* 152d). For Gorgias holds that what is ultimately real is not a stable, unchanging realm of Being, but a mutable, ever-changing flux that may only be experienced subjectively and that resists every attempt to grasp it with the mind or categorize it with words. Gorgias denies what is typically seen as "objective" reality because the sole reality is that which each of us must experience subjectively. In Eric White's terms, Gorgias sees reality as immediately present, "an unending flux . . . not unlike the one put forward by Heraclitus" (1987, 16). Reality is not to be found in the artificial, rationally constructed domain that Parmenides says exists outside of time and place; rather it is a concrete instant in an ongoing life, one that is temporal as well as spatial and as such is "constantly changing, in a condition of ceaseless flux" (28). Reality is a "primordial flux that thought must overlook if it would construct an enduring edifice of knowledge"; it is the "swarming continuum," a "primal anarchy and formlessness" (34).

The term that several scholars see as the key to Gorgias' subjectivist epistemology is *kairos*. The Greek term *kairos,* as Richard Onians (1973) points out, denotes an opening that is limited in respect to space as well as time, and derives from the arts of archery and weaving. In archery, the term *kairos* denotes the aperture created by aligning axes set at intervals in a straight line through which a skilled archer such as Odysseus is able to shoot an arrow (*Odyssey* 21); and in weaving, the term denotes the opening in which a weaver inserts a woof-thread through the warp in using a loom. As a temporally and spatially limited opening, the term *kairos* denotes an "occasion," "opportunity," or "critical moment" (Onians 1973, 345–46).

Gorgias is credited by Dionysius of Halicarnassus as being the first thinker who attempted to write about the elusive notion of *kairos,* even though he did not "write anything worth mentioning" (B13). But if he does not define *kairos,* Gorgias appears to consider the notion extremely important, and he explores it in several of his extant texts. In Untersteiner's assessment, "The ethic, aesthetic and rhetoric of Gorgias are all based on *kairos*" (1954, 160). In the *Epitaphios,* Gorgias suggests that the ability to discern and act upon a *kairos* is a "divine" achievement, indeed the defining virtue of the gods. He states that "the most godlike and most common code" is to do what is fitting "at the fitting time" (E11, Smith 1921). In *Helen,* he suggests that failure to function effectively in a critical, kairotic moment may result in disaster, as when, upon seeing terrible sights, people may abandon thought "of the present moment" and hence experience "useless labor and dread diseases and hardly curable madness" (H17). And he characterizes Palamedes' situation during his trial as a kairotic moment in which he must speak effectively, an unprecedented moment for which he is completely unprepared and one in which he cannot rely on any earlier strategies. Palamedes thus exclaims, "Where shall I start to speak about these matters? What shall I say first? To what part of the defense shall I turn my attention? For an unsupported allegation creates evident perplexity; and because of the perplexity, it follows that I am at a loss in my speech, unless I discover something out of the truth itself and out of the *present necessity*" (P4; emphasis added). Finding himself in an unprecedented moment, Palamedes relies on *kairos* to invent a defense. He thus remarks that "the present occasion (*kairos*) requires me to make my defense in every possible way" (P32).

In the subjectivist reading, Gorgias' notion of *kairos* is integrally related to his conception of subjective truth. First, the kairotic experience is ephemeral or fleeting, one that is always radically unprecedented and unique. In this subjectivist model the only reality is the present moment, and both the past and the future are always fabrications of memory or projections of the imagination. The kairotic experience is radically subjective and can never be measured or assessed with any "objective" instrument such as a clock, which merely reinforces the deceptive and illusory reality constructed with the faculty of reason. In one of his aphorisms, Gorgias appears to endorse this view, for he ridicules popular orators who live by the *clepsydra*, or "water clock," the apparatus used to limit the time permitted each orator in a legal and political setting. Specifically, he asserts that orators are "like frogs; for the latter [make] their cry in water and the former before the water clock" (B30). That is, to the extent that we measure our lives by external instruments rather than experiencing reality immediately in kairotic experiences, we will be unable to rise above the consciousness of amphibians. Only if we overcome the illusory temporal order imposed by water clocks and experience a radically subjective new moment, will we be able to escape the illusory medium of reason.

Rather than being measurable by clocks, kairotic experiences frequently rupture the measured routines of everyday experience. In Bernard Miller's terms, the *kairos* is "the way we measure our lives on the basis of critical events that disrupt the normal sequence of chronos" (1987, 169). If we are able to experience life kairotically and to overcome temporal objectification, we may become open to the temporal dimension of our own human *Becoming*, and as such we may cease thinking of ourselves and our world in the reified terms of *Being*. Our kairotic reality will be a process of change in which our own personal consciousness lies at the very heart. Our kairotic moments will, in this respect, provide us with an "opening" or aperture to the domain of Becoming in which we undergo transformation ourselves.

If the kairotic experience is unique and unprecedented, it is also "irrational," and it eludes any attempt on our part to comprehend it rationally or logically. In Eric White's terms, the kairotic experience is an irrational attunement to the "living present," such that the Gorgian "*kairos* stands for precisely the *irrational novelty* of the moment that escapes formalization" (1987, 20; emphasis added). The kairotic awareness is irrational in the sense that it lies beyond the reach of "reason" as a faculty with which we delineate connections between concepts, objects, or events. We are able to have a truly kairotic experience only if we overcome the limits of rational thought and become open to an encounter with "unforeseen spontaneity" (White 1987, 14). Since the ongoing flux of Becoming is "a succession of discontinuous occasions" rather than a measurable duration or comprehensible historical continuity, experiencing each new moment requires us to resist any attempt to impose our own artificial, logical order. In this respect, the *kairos* demands that we forget the past and not think of the future; for we cannot rely on any prior rational account of the nature of things, given that each new moment demands a radically novel perception. The Gorgian *kairos* thus designates a spontaneity, a fusion with the world of becoming that may take the form of "poetic frenzy" or "divine madness" but never takes the form of clear-headed observation or rational reflection (Miller 1984, 169). And because it is completely nonrational, the kairotic experience tends to be "incomprehensible to ordinary mortals" who are confined to the domain of reason (Segal 1972, 120). In order to achieve kairotic awareness, we must "leap" beyond the limits of *logos* into the unpredictable, chaotic flux of an irrational Becoming.

Since every kairotic moment is unprecedented and irrational, any attempt to describe it in language is misguided, for every description "reifies" the experience and conceals its fleeting, unnamable nature. Attempting to categorize or name the flux of Becoming is as futile as trying to grasp a river with a sieve, for as soon as a word is uttered, the flux itself has changed. If what is truly real is a fleeting and nonrepeatable momentary experience, then every verbal description is deceptive insofar as it imputes order and meaning; for language is itself an abstraction, an artificial construction that bears no meaningful relationship to the irrational kairotic moment. In this respect, *logos,* as a faculty and verbal apparatus that enables us to articulate "rational accounts," is ultimately *autonomous,* creating a deceptive virtual world that belies the nonrational flux, one that Bruce Gronbeck describes as "one more remove from reality" (1972, 30). In Thomas Rosenmeyer's terms, language for Gorgias is "altogether unrelated to reality," for it is "not a reflection of things, not a mere tool or slave of description, but is its own master. *Logos* is a great *dynastes* . . . a creator of its own reality" (1955, 231–32). Every rational account is inescapably deceptive, for "if speech and reality are not commensurable, then those statements which convey to the audience the impression that they are being confronted with a new knowledge, i.e., those statements which seem to impart information, are by nature *apeteloi*. All *peitho*, therefore, is *apatelos*. . . . *Apate* signals the supersession of the world of the *logos* in place of the epic world of things" (1055, 232).

Given that he affirms the kairotic moment as that which is ultimately real, we may understand why Gorgias repudiates the project of apprehending the truth in *On Not-Being* through the artificial categories of the Eleatics. Insofar as we accept these categories as real, we will remain separated from true experience, for every rational account of objective truth is false or deceptive. If we think that our intellectual categories or terms mirror how things "really are" or believe that even our own assertions are true, we are self-deceived. In this respect, White argues that the *Not-Being* that Gorgias refers to is akin to the *Tao* in Lao-tse's *Tao Te Ching*, in which "the *Tao* that can be told is not the eternal *Tao*. The name that can be named is not the eternal name" (1987, 34).

In Untersteiner's terms, Gorgias sees the kairotic experience as the only way in which we may overcome the "tragic antithesis" between our limited human minds and the chaotic reality that lies beyond our comprehension and language. Indeed, the very essence of reality is contradiction itself, and there is a "contradictory antitheses hidden in the essence of things" (1954, 150). For Untersteiner's Gorgias, human existence is "tragic" because when we attempt to comprehend the world with our rational minds and in so doing rely on rational discourse or *logos*, we are never able to grasp the real nature of things. In Untersteiner's terms, "Man cannot escape the antitheses. His thoughts discover only the opposite poles in all propositions which try to explain reality philosophically. The reality reached by dialectic expresses only *aporiai*. . . . All human experience . . . [is] brought to a standstill in the face of reason, which can no longer decide anything and therefore ends by denying on a rational basis every relationship between man and man, and finally all coherence within the individual himself" (1954, 159–60). Since reality is inescapably contradictory and antithetical when approached rationally, and human thought and language are inescapably rational, or confined to *logos*, it is impossible for us to comprehend or describe the nature of reality. Thus "Gorgias attacks . . . *all* the metaphysicians who had in any way sought to define the nature of reality" (149). Gorgias' target in *On Not-Being* is not only the Eleatics but all philosophers who attempt to understand reality logically; and his assault is "directed against all philosophical theories, rationalist or empirical" (151).

While he argues in *On Not-Being* that language is inherently deceptive, the subjectivist Gorgias appears to iterate the thesis in *Palamedes* and *Helen*. In *Palamedes*, Gorgias appears to repudiate the notion that words enable us to represent things and events in the world, asserting that "if then, by means of words, it were possible for the truth of actions to become free of doubt [and] clear to hearers, judgment would now be easy from what has been said. But . . . this is not the case" (P35). That is, neither events nor things in the world can ever be represented in the deceptive *logos* in which we communicate. We are only able to experience kairotic truth when we repudiate and overcome the artificial rational structures and procedures that reason and language or *logos* "stamps" in our psyches (H13) and experience our lives as moments of transformation and change. When we retreat to the artificial, virtual world fabricated by reason and rational discourse, we retreat from the truth of becoming.

Gorgias also appears to depict language as inherently deceptive in *Helen*. As Guthrie points out, Gorgias explicitly states that *logos* is always deceptive, for when he writes that "all who have and do persuade people of things do so by molding a false argument" (H11, K1), what he means is that "knowledge is in general impossible and fallible opinion the only guide" (1971, 272, n.1). Guthrie also cites another passage, in *Helen* 13, in which Gorgias repudiates the possibility of attaining knowledge of "objective" truth. In this passage Gorgias argues that meteorologists, philosophers, and popular orators do not speak the "truth" but instead deceive their audiences. Guthrie concludes that for Gorgias "what appears to me *is* for me, and what appears to you *is* for you" (51). Concerning its deceptiveness, Gorgias asserts that *logos* operates as a mode of magic or witchcraft, casting a "spell" upon us (H10). And in a striking metaphor, he asserts that *logos* is a drug, a *pharmakon* that governs the psyche as much as medical drugs may direct the forces in the body (H14). Under the influence of the drug of reason, we are only able to experience a world that is censored by the dictates of reason. In Anthony Cascardi's terms, we are confined in a "virtual prison-house," wherein "our thoughts and our existence, our mind as much as our being" is trapped within an "obstinate, intransigent cellophane margin: we are caught in the ambiguity of not knowing being from non-being because of the opaque gossamer of words" (1983, 220). The more lucid our accounts of things, the more they only reveal how distant we are from the truth. In Shakespeare's provocative metaphor, our mind is a flower preserved in the distilled essence of a perfume, a "liquid prisoner pent in walls of glass."[7]

Gorgias is not alone in maintaining that human beings are unable to comprehend the ultimate nature of things. Indeed, as Plato points out, this is the traditional view of many poets whom he opposes in what he calls the "ancient quarrel" between poetry and philosophy (*Republic* 607b5) and whom he specifically associates with Gorgias when he characterizes Gorgian rhetoric as poetic (*Gorgias* 501c-502d). Associating Gorgias with his poetic precursors, several scholars characterize Gorgias' view of truth and knowledge as a "mythic" worldview, one that in Greece preceded the birth of *logos* or reason. According to Ernst Cassirer, the "mythical" mind is one in which man is fused with the cosmos, a condition that was lost with the "permanent separation" of man and the gods. In this construal, Gorgias affirms *mythos,* a nonrational apprehension of life that rationalists since Aristotle have dismissed as "primitive" and simplistic. His consciousness is shaped by a collective tradition rather than autonomous, disengaged reflection. For Eric Havelock, the "mythical" state of mind is one of "a state of total personal involvement and therefore of emotional identification with the substance of the poeticized statement" which results in "total loss of objectivity"; the poet's *mimesis* is the ability to "make his audience identify almost pathologically" with the content of what he is saying" (1963, 44–45). The mythic and oral state of mind is "passive, communally oriented, non-critical oral consciousness that ruled the society," according to Connors (40). In Walter Ong's formulation, mythic and oral thought is "redundant and copious," repeating and amplifying its materials; it remains close to the "human lifeworld" and does not much venture into abstract thought; and it is "empathetic and participatory" rather than objectively distanced (1982, 36–56). And Havelock remarks that "works of genius, composed within the semi-oral tradition . . . constituted or represented a total state of mind which is not our mind and which was not Plato's mind; and that just as poetry itself, as long as it reigned supreme, constituted the chief obstacle to the achievement of effective prose, so there was a state of mind which we shall conveniently label the 'poetic' or 'Homeric' or 'oral' state of mind, which constituted the chief obstacle to scientific rationalism, to the use of analysis, to the classification of experience, to its rearrangement in sequence of cause and effect" (1963, 46–47).

Repudiating Subjectivism

How convincing is this reading of Gorgias? I submit that it is ultimately unpersuasive, for it is contradicted by a number of Gorgias' assertions about existence, knowledge, and language. For Gorgias explicitly and repeatedly *repudiates* the notion that we are severed from the real world by an ontological and epistemic abyss and that the only reality we experience is subjective, fleeting, and incommunicable. While he clearly repudiates what he calls the "existent" in *On Not-Being,* contending that various accounts of it contradict one another, that we are unable to apprehend such an entity either through our senses or intellects, and that even if we could we would be unable to communicate anything meaningful about it to others, he repeatedly affirms that we are quite warranted in our belief that ordinary things truly exist, that we are quite able to distinguish between what exists and what is merely imaginary, and that we are able to communicate our knowledge to other people. In part two of *On Not-Being,* for instance, Gorgias clearly holds that such ordinary things as men and chariots truly exist and that they differ from things that do not exist such as flying men, chariots racing in the sea, and imaginary creatures such as Scylla and Chimaera (N79–81). Indeed, his entire argument in part two, that we are not warranted in relying on our rational intellect alone in determining what truly exists, is based on the assumption that we already know and are quite easily able to distinguish between what truly exists and what does not. And while he argues in part three that we are unable to communicate anything about the "existent" to others, he assumes throughout his entire treatise that we are quite able to understand one another on most matters, even the abstruse topics he addresses in the text itself. Gorgias also affirms the existence of the everyday world in his subsequent texts. In the *Epitaphios,* he never expresses any doubt whatsoever about the real achievements and virtues of the warriors; in *Helen* he affirms an array of facts about Helen, her parents, and her suitors; and in *Palamedes,* he depicts Palamedes as being deeply enmeshed in the very real world of the Greeks.

Although he consistently depicts people as being engaged in a natural and social world, Gorgias also suggests that they are able to understand and speak meaningfully about the *gods* and the domain that they reputedly inhabit. Rather than being separated by an unfathomable gulf from an incomprehensible and chaotic domain known only to the gods, Gorgias suggests that human beings and gods all live in more or less the same domain, think about the same things, and even experience the same emotions. He frequently presents the gods as intervening in human affairs, displaying many human traits, and at times leading people astray. In the *Epitaphios,* he affirms that humans and deities dwell in the same world and have the same emotions, observing that he must avoid provoking the "wrath of the gods" (E3–5) in his assertion that the warriors possess a virtue that is "instilled by gods" (E7). In *Helen,* Gorgias depicts the gods as capable of playing an even more active role in human life, insisting that Helen's father is Zeus himself (H3). He argues that it is quite possible that the gods determined Helen's behavior, that "it is impossible to prevent a god's predetermination by human premeditation" (H6), and that she may have been coerced by the god Eros who "prevails over the divine power of the gods" as well as over mere mortals (H19). In *Palamedes,* Gorgias affirms the presence of the gods in everyday life, having Palamedes exclaim that a traitor is an enemy of the gods in part because he "dishonors what is holy" (P17) and that Odysseus' charge against him is "godless" (P36). Concerning his own character, finally, the inscription by Eumolpus on Gorgias' statue at Olympus reads: "His statue stands as well in the vale of Apollo / Not as a show of wealth, but of the piety of his character" (A8), indicating that his family and acquaintances perceived Gorgias as a person who displayed respect and piety for the gods, not as a person who considered them absent from everyday life.

Second, Gorgias repudiates the subjectivist notion that we are unable to acquire knowledge about the world. Instead, he identifies various sorts of human knowledge and distinguishes quite sharply between knowledge and opinion. He uses a variety of terms to denote knowledge, including *episteme* (P3), *mathesis* (H13), *gignosko* (E15, 24), *sophia* (H1, 4; P25), *eidos* (H5, P24,15), and *sineste* (P15). In the *Epitaphios*, he praises the warriors for their knowledge and judgment (E15), and he remarks that every rhetorical contest requires knowledge (B8). In *Helen*, he observes that "what is becoming to a soul is wisdom (*sophia*) (H1) and that "to tell the knowing what they know is believable but not enjoyable" (H5). Gorgias has Palamedes remark that he possesses intelligence, or *sophia* (P25), a trait for which he is honored. Distinguishing knowledge from mere "opinion" (*doxa*), Gorgias remarks in *Helen* that "if everyone had a memory of all that is past, a conception for what is happening at present and a foreknowledge of the future, communication would not be as it is. But as it is, there is no easy way of either recollecting the past or investigating the present or divining the future, so that on most subjects most men have only opinion to offer the mind as counselor; and opinion is slippery and insecure" (H11).

Although Guthrie reads Gorgias as holding that "knowledge is in general impossible and fallible opinion the only guide" (1971, 272n. 1), Gorgias makes no such claim. On the contrary, he asserts that in some cases it *is* possible to acquire knowledge, even though *most* but not all men, in *most* but not necessarily all cases, tend to fall back on opinion. By implication, Gorgias suggests that some men, in some cases, possess knowledge that is neither "slippery" nor "insecure." He does not delineate in this passage what this "certainty" consists of, but he indicates that certainty in some instances is indeed possible. Gorgias further distinguishes between knowledge and opinion in *Palamedes*, asserting, "Therefore, it is quite clear that you do not have knowledge of the things about which you make accusation. It follows that since you do [not] have knowledge, you have an opinion. Do you then, O most daring of all men trusting in opinion, a most untrustworthy thing, not knowing the truth, dare to bring a capital charge against a man? Why do you share knowledge that he has done such a deed? But surely it is open to all men to have opinions on all subjects, and in this you are no wiser than others. But it is not right to trust those with an opinion instead of those who know, nor to think opinion more trustworthy than truth, but rather truth than opinion" (P24). Gorgias thus clearly distinguishes between knowledge and opinion and suggests that such a distinction may be made in diverse situations.

Gorgias not only depicts people as quite knowledgeable about the real world, but he also explicitly repudiates as "absurd" the notion that true knowledge is inward or "subjective." In part two of *On Not-Being*, he argues that if things considered in the mind are existent, then we must conclude that everything we can think of must exist. We are able to conceive of flying men and chariots racing in the sea, but if our sole criterion is a "subjective" one, we must thereby conclude that these exist. But this, he argues, is absurd, since flying men and chariots in the sea *do not exist*. Consequently, merely thinking something exists does not make it exist, and things considered subjectively are not existent. In *Helen,* Gorgias again explicitly rejects the subjectivist notion that we are confined to a world that we personally concoct. In one of his most succinct repudiations of epistemic subjectivism, he asserts that "the objects of sight do not have the nature we would like them to have but *that which they happen to have*" (H15; emphasis added). He remarks that "to tell the knowing what they know is believable but not enjoyable" (H5). Distinguishing knowledge from mere opinion, Gorgias remarks that "on most subjects most men have only opinion to offer the mind as counselor; and opinion is slippery and insecure" (H11). Guthrie asserts that Gorgias repudiates the possibility of knowledge, holding that "knowledge is in general impossible and fallible opinion the only guide" (1971, 272, n.1), but Gorgias never makes this claim. As Robinson accurately points out, Gorgias asserts that in some cases it *is* possible to acquire knowledge, even though *most* but not all men, in *most* but not necessarily all cases, tend to fall back on opinion. Gorgias' implication is clearly that some men, in some cases, do possess knowledge that is neither "slippery" nor "insecure" (Robinson 1973, 51–52).

Third, Gorgias repudiates the subjectivist view that language is isolated from reality and that every assertion is inescapably deceptive. Instead, he affirms that some assertions may be judged to be true and others false. In the *Epitaphios,* he states that his objective is to speak truthfully about the slain warriors, avoiding divine nemesis and human envy (E5). In *Helen,* Gorgias' opening assertion that *truth* is the "fairest ornament" of *logos* clearly implies that he believes some assertions are true. He states his objective to be "to prove that those who censure her are liars; to demonstrate the *truth;* and to put an end to ignorance concerning Helen" (H2; emphasis added). He delineates an array of truths about Helen, corrects the erroneous notions that her father was a mortal, and relates information about her suitors. He asserts that some people, such as the seductive Paris, may use language to deceive their victims; he compares language to a drug that influences the mind the way a drug influences the body, suggesting that language may be used to manipulate others; he asserts explicitly that some uses of language "bewitch the soul with a kind of evil persuasion"; and he rhetorically asks, "How many speakers on how many subjects have persuaded others and continue to persuade by modeling false speech?" (H11).

But Gorgias does not imply thereby that *every* use of language is inevitably deceptive and that it is impossible to speak the truth. And he never advances the subjectivist thesis that language is deceptive because it is unable to correspond to "things as they really are" and hence that it confines us to an autonomous domain of our own creation. In *Palamedes,* Gorgias also addresses deception, in particular the false accusation by Odysseus that Palamedes has committed treason. Palamedes must refute this false claim, showing that his own account is true solely through the use of language and argument, without supporting evidence or witnesses. Palamedes admits that his task is not easy, given that it is not possible "through words to make the truth about reality pure and clear to the hearers" (P35). But rather than suggesting that it is impossible to speak truthfully and that every assertion is deceptive, Gorgias instead shows that even in instances in which there is no physical evidence, individuals like Palamedes may nevertheless articulate the truth.

THE EMPIRICIST READING

In part because of these contradictions in the subjectivist account, a number of scholars have articulated a radically different reading of Gorgias' ontological and epistemological views. In contrast to the subjectivist reading, these scholars read Gorgias as affirming the existence of an objective reality that we are able to apprehend empirically and discuss meaningfully. This empiricist reading originates in Grote's interpretation of *On Not-Being,* which he reads as affirming the existence of a physical world and an assault on the putative "transcendental" or "ultra-phaenomenal existence" affirmed by Parmenides and other Eleatics (1869, 173). Concerning Gorgias' argument that "nothing exists," Grote remarks,

> In our sense of the words, it is a monstrous paradox: but construing them in their legitimate filiation from the Eleatic philosophers immediately before him, it is a plausible, not to say conclusive, deduction from principles which they would have acknowledged. The word Existence, as they understood it, did not mean phaenomenal, but ultra-phaenomenal existence. They looked upon the phaenomena of sense as always coming and going—as something transitory, fluctuating, incapable of being surely known, and furnishing at best grounds only for conjecture. They searched by cogitation for what they presumed to be the really existent Something or Substance—the Noumenon, to use a Kantian phrase—lying behind or under phaenomena, which Noumenon they recognized as the only appropriate object of knowledge. . . . Now the thesis of Gorgias related to this ultra-phaenomenal existence, and bore closely upon the arguments of Zeno and Melissus, the Eleatic reasoners of his elder contemporaries. He denied that any such ultra-phaenomenal Something, or Noumenon, existed, or could be known, or could be described" (173).

In short, Gorgias maintains that reality is physical or material rather than "transcendental," and that we are able to apprehend reality through our senses. Gorgias is not a subjectivist who denies the possibility of objective knowledge but an empiricist who affirms that sensory experience is the sole source of knowledge about an independently existing physical reality. In J. Loenen's terms, Gorgias repudiates the Eleatic notion of "an absolute reality not perceptible by the senses," a domain of eternal Being that transcends the everyday world of physical things (1959, 106).

While he repudiates the notion of a transcendental Being, the empiricist Gorgias affirms the existence of everyday material objects, and indeed he may be characterized as a *materialist*. In Loenen's terms, "Gorgias' positive view of the world [is] a materialist's view of the world" whereby reality is comprised solely of physical objects and forces (1959, 190). Gorgias thus follows Anaxagoras, asserting that the sun is a "red-hot stone" (B31) and not, say, a deity such as Apollo, who races his chariot across the sky (or over the sea, as Gorgias remarks in *On Not-Being*); and he argues that the material world is populated with objects such as chariots and material men who live in a material world but not with immaterial mythical beings like Scylla and imaginary flying men (N79). Gorgias' materialism extends to human beings as well, for he appears to construe the psyche as a kind of material entity rather than as a mystical entity that is able to transcend the material world. Gorgias does not develop this theory in detail, and in Charles Segal's terms, "Gorgias probably does not think in terms of such a consistent materialism as Democritus. His psyche, nevertheless, is in contact with the physical phenomena and operates in ways analogous to theirs. In thus treating the emotions as real, almost physiological entities, Gorgias indicates a kinship with the scientific rationalism of Greek medicine" (1972, 104–6). Moreover, as Dodds insists, Gorgias also expresses a kinship with the scientific orientation of most of the other Sophists. Unlike Hegel and most subjectivist scholars, who read Gorgias and his sophistic colleagues as subjectivists whose views are diametrically opposed to Ionian objectivism, Dodds insists that there is no "sharp line of distinction between *sophistai* and *phusikoi* (natural scientists)" (1973, 94), and that Gorgias warmly embraces Ionian physicalism. Among the Sophists he is no exception, for his scientific empiricism is quite in accord with Hippias' study of geography, Prodicus' examination of physiology, and Antiphon's study of mathematics.[8]

A materialist, Gorgias bases his epistemology on the notion that we are able to apprehend the true nature of things through our own physical sensory apparatus. He thus argues that in order to acquire knowledge we must rely on our senses and not on our intellects alone. In Loenen's terms, Gorgias' "empirico-sensualistic theory of knowledge" is the "fundamental presupposition of the entire second part [of *On Not-Being*] (and of the third part as well)" (1959, 193). Specifically, Gorgias argues that merely conceiving of something in our minds, using our intellect or faculty of reason, can never guarantee that the object really exists; for we are able to conceive of imaginary objects like flying men and seaborne chariots. That is, "conception of an object is in itself no proof of its existence. Thus the statement that 'things that are thought do not actually exist' means the fact of their being thought is no warrant for their actual existence" (194). Instead of relying on intuition or rational reflection, processes which would presumably enable us to discern the ultimate nature of things, we must always rely on the testimony of our senses if we wish to understand the world. For our senses provide the "exclusive criterion of the actual existence of the objects which are perceived by a particular organ." Consequently, Loenen points out, Gorgias holds that "thought too would have to be the exclusive criterion of the actual existence of that which is merely thought; this, however, appears not to be the case (the example of the chariots on the sea here recurs); hence, it is not the reality that is thought. Here again Gorgias' *positive, sensualistic theory of knowledge* is very prominent indeed: thought differs from sense-perception in that in itself it does not guarantee the reality of its object; the actual existence of a thing can only be established by the senses" (195; emphasis added). In short, "the things we see do not have the nature which we want them to have, but the nature which each actually as" (H15).

Gorgias thus not only affirms empiricism as a general philosophical theory; he also identifies the specific physiological apparatus with which we are able to apprehend the empirical world, namely the *pores* or apertures of our senses. As Richard Enos (1976) points out, Gorgias appears to derive this theory from his mentor, Empedocles, whose theory of pores accounts for the way in which we are able to perceive the world. For Empedocles "placed trust not with the gods, but with human senses—a concept which Gorgias readily accepted. Man's ability to acquire knowledge, and for that matter to perceive existence itself, was dependent upon the degree of his sense-perception. Empedocles' view of knowledge led him to dismiss the possibility of perceiving the gods and of communicating with them, for they were beyond the *positivistic reality of the senses*. As a student of Empedocles, Gorgias accepted his teacher's concept of sense-reality" (1976, 41). Specifically, Gorgias holds that "for a thing to be comprehended it must be understood through the human media of the understanding; i.e., *sense-perception*. . . . Man's finite sense limitations, however, restrict him to perceptions based upon the optimum capacity of his senses, and in this respect thoughts beyond *positivistic experience* have no referential existence beyond the imaginative extrapolations of the thinker" (47; emphasis added).

In Gorgias' theory, our pores enable us to perceive the material "effluences" emitted by objects; and each sense differs in the type of effluence it is able to receive. In Plato's terms, Gorgias holds that "existing things have some effluences"; that we have "pores into which and through which the effluences are carried"; and that "some of the effluences fit some of the pores, but some are smaller or larger."

Hence "color is an effluence of things commensurate and perceptible to sight," and one could "define what voice is, as well, in this way and smell and many other similar things" (*Meno* 76aff.). Since each sense differs in respect to its pores and the effluences it is able to receive, each sense is effluence-specific, and the sight, for instance, cannot perceive sounds.

Gorgias holds that we must rely on our senses for information, but he also suggests that we require the assistance of the faculty of reason to attain knowledge. First, this is because our sensory pores provide us with sensory-specific information; for it is through reason that we synthesize the diverse sensory information we receive and are able to understand the structure of the world. Our knowledge will be only probable rather than certain, for we must often rely on hypotheses and guesses. But through careful observation and rational reflection, we may approximate the truth. So when Gorgias states that he is concerned with probabilities rather than with "truths" (*Phaedrus* 267a), he is speaking as an objective scientist and rejecting the metaphysical or mystical notion that we are able to apprehend absolutes through pure reason or, presumably, through the procedure or introspective reminiscence advocated by Plato himself, whereby our eternal souls recall past lives in heaven.

Second, we require reason to insure that we are not mistaken in our perceptions; for if we permit our passions or desires to interfere with our perception, we will not see things as they are. Our emotions and desires bias our perception, leading us to mistake what really exists. Gorgias thus remarks that we may be carried away by fear or erotic desire and thereby lose our presence of mind. Helen, for instance, may have been carried away by her desire for Paris. Other people are led to err because of fear, for "whenever men at war, enemy against enemy, buckle up in the armament of bronze and iron, whether in defense or offense, when their sight beholds the scene, it is alarmed and causes alarm in the soul, so that often they flee in terror from future danger as though it were present . . . thus does sight engrave upon the mind images of the seen" (H16–17). Only if we remain dispassionate, presumably, will we be able to discern the true nature of things, and reason enables us to control our passions and desires. In a similar manner, Palamedes tells his judges that he will not appeal to their emotions, for "it is not right to persuade you with the help of friends or entreaties or appeals to pity, but it is right for me to escape this charge by means of the clearest justice, *explaining the truth, not deceiving*" (P33; emphasis added).

In Gorgias' materialistic and empiricist philosophy, language acquires an important epistemic and communicative role. For language is the means by which we name things in the world and are thereby able to communicate what we perceive to others. Gorgias thus articulates what Loenen (1959) calls a "correspondence" theory of language, wherein the meaning of a word is the object it names in the world. In this correspondence theory of language, words are signs of material things, for "words are based on perception by the senses of things actually existing outside us (instances mentioned are taste and color), and this is why words do not make manifest the outside world, but the outside world makes known words.' . . . Words are mere signs of the reality perceived by the senses and they are significant only in relation to this reality" (1959, 197–98). Words derive their meaning from "personal sense-perception," and hence "words as such cannot make anything known" (203). When Gorgias asserts that we are unable to communicate our perceptions through words, he does not mean that communication is impossible. On the contrary, he means that communication is possible only if we all perceive the same material things. We are unable to convey our sensory experiences to others if they have never experienced it themselves; but if they have had the experience, then communication will be successful. In Loenen's construal, "the words of A as such cannot make known to B what A perceives, for the very reason that B does not perceive it himself; in other words, what is to A a significant word, to B is a mere meaningless and unintelligible sound" (197). In this respect, communication is impossible in the sense that it is not possible to transmit an awareness of an object to another person through words. Insofar as words are names of things, however, communication is quite possible if a person is already familiar with the object in question.

In respect to the traditional *topos* of *mythos* and *logos,* the empiricists strongly oppose those subjectivist readers who identify Gorgias as an advocate of *mythos* and an adversary of *logos*. For the subjectivist camp, Gorgias opposes *logos*, construed as reason and rational discourse, because it abstracts us from immediate experience and confines us in a deceptively lucid prison-house of language. It is only if we are able to break free of that prison that we are able to experience life in nonrational kairotic moments. To the empiricists, who read Gorgias as advancing a materialistic ontology, an empiricist epistemology, and a representational theory of language, Gorgias is clearly aligned with other members of the fifth-century Greek Enlightenment who advance the cause of reason and who struggle against the irrationalism of all sorts of "mythical" thinkers. A clear-headed scientist who sees the world as an empirically accessible material domain, Gorgias repudiates as mere figments of the imagination the myths created by poets about such nonexistent creatures as Scylla and Chimera (N79). Indeed, as Dodds suggests, Gorgias would presumably deny the existence of the gods altogether and would concur with his student Critias that "religion is an artificial moral sanction, deliberately invented to bolster up the laws" (DK88 B25) (Dodds 1973, 97). For Gorgias repudiates the pseudo-sciences of witches and magicians as promoting errors and deceptions, and he rejects the discourses of the poets who believe that they are able to apprehend the truth through "divine" inspiration.

Disavowing Empiricism

How persuasive is the empiricist reading of Gorgias? Although it appears to resolve some of the contradictions generated in the subjectivist account, I suggest that it too is contradicted by a variety of Gorgias' assertions. Concerning his argument about the nature of reality in *On Not-Being*, the empiricist camp contends that Gorgias denies Parmenides' domain of Being, which Grote identifies as the "noumenal" realm, but that he affirms the phenomenal, changing world of Not-Being. But Gorgias does not argue this; instead, he argues that *neither* realm exists, emphatically repudiating the ultimate reality of *both* domains. Gorgias vehemently argues that the realm of Not-Being, that of appearances, is no more ultimately real than the domain of Being affirmed by Parmenides. He does not argue that the domain of Not-Being exists but that neither the "existent" nor the "non-existent" exists (N66). Gorgias also explicitly repudiates empiricism in part two of *On Not-Being*, rejecting the empiricist claim that knowledge is ultimately grounded on sense perception. Instead, he insists that sense perception does *not* provide access to the nature of things, writing that "just as objects of sight are said to be visible for the reason that they are seen, and objects of hearing are said to be audible for the reason that they are heard, and we do not reject visible things on the grounds that they are not heard, nor dismiss audible things because they are not seen (since each object ought be judged by its own sense, but not by another), so, too, things considered in the mind will exist even if they should not be seen by the sight nor heard by the hearing, because they are perceived by their own criterion" (N81). Rather than affirming an empiricist theory of knowledge, Gorgias explicitly repudiates it, arguing that the senses do not provide information that allows us to affirm the existence or nonexistence of anything in the world.

One of the reasons that we cannot rely on sense perceptions, according to Gorgias, is that they do not provide us with neutral, objective information. Instead, our senses are themselves influenced by our emotions and other factors. When Gorgias states in *Helen* that "the things we see do not have the nature which we want them to have, but the nature which each actually has," he seems to be advancing an empiricist epistemology. But this reading is not warranted; for the context of Gorgias' remark is that the faculty of "sight" (*opsis*) is influenced by emotions such as fear. For "we see not what we wish but what each of us has experienced; through sight the soul is stamped in diverse ways" (H15). That is, what we see is always a matter of contingency; we always see what "happens" to be the case in a given circumstance (H15); and this contingency involves an arrangement of the situation in which our own emotional engagement plays a vital part. Moreover, Gorgias suggests that "sight" is not a neutral faculty that provides objective information about the world; instead, it functions as a kind of independent agent that is influenced by a variety of heterogeneous forces, is frequently misleading, and is

visual rhetoric

not to be trusted. Gorgias thus suggests that although we may wish to see things as they "really are" in their own "inner nature," this is not possible; and we can never rely on our sight to see what "really exists" any more than we can rely on *logos*, which stamps the psyche as a drug influences the body (H14). And concerning Gorgias' putative "theory of pores," it is incorrect to conclude that his endorsement of such a theory commits him to an empiricist conception of knowledge. Indeed, the very contrary is the case; for the theory allows for the possibility that our perceptions, and presumably our "pores," change depending on our emotional state. This appears to be the view advocated by Empedocles, who suggests that the emotional states of love or hate enable us to perceive these emotions. Hence, "By love do we see Love, and Hate by grievous hate" (DK109).[9]

While he denies that we are able to apprehend the nature of things empirically through our senses, Gorgias also maintains, conversely, that we may affirm the reality of some things that are *not* empirically observable. In particular, he repeatedly affirms the existence of various *gods*, beings who may be real but who are not empirically observable. As noted above, Gorgias refers to the gods in the *Epitaphios*, *Helen*, and *Palamedes* as playing an active role in human affairs. In the *Epitaphios*, he observes that praising the warriors too excessively would encroach on the proper territory of the gods and elevate the warriors too highly among other people. Furthermore, Gorgias includes in his evidence that the warriors do what is "fitting" the fact that they erect tributes to Zeus and that they behave reverently toward the gods (E30, 35). In *Palamedes*, Gorgias again stresses the important role the gods have in human behavior, arguing that committing treason shows disrespect to the gods (P17). But Gorgias' references to the gods are not limited to these instances in which humans respect gods they believe in. He also refers to the gods as a possible explanation for human behavior. In *Helen*, he delineates two scenarios for Helen's behavior in which the gods play active roles: in one case, several gods determine that Helen will elope with Paris; in another case, the god Eros acts on his own to impel her to fall in love with Paris. Gorgias never says that the gods are empirically observable; indeed, he suggests that in some cases it is disputable whether the gods are actually present. In *Helen*, for instance, he notes that people disagree over whether Helen's father is Zeus or the mortal Tyndareus; and while he argues that Zeus is her father, Gorgias does not suggest that the issue is resolvable by "empirical observation."

Gorgias also repudiates the empiricist thesis that scientific assertions, which are presumably grounded on empirical observation, are "privileged" in the sense that they differ in kind from the proclamations of opinionated orators and the utterances of "inspired" poets. Instead, he suggests that there is no epistemological difference between poetry, science, and oratory and that scientific discourse is indistinguishable from the discourse of orators, philosophers, or even poets, whose speech differs from those of other people only because it is "metered" (H9). For the meteorologist, or astronomer, like the poet, philosopher, and popular orator, presents an opinion, or *doxa;* and as such his assertions are no more privileged in their status than those of any other speaker or writer. Specifically, Gorgias asserts that "to understand that persuasion, joining with speech, is wont to stamp the soul as it wishes, one must study, first, the words of astronomers who, substituting opinion for opinion, removing one and instilling another, make incredible and unclear things appear true to the eyes of opinion; second, forceful speeches in public debate, where one side of the argument pleases a large crowd and persuades by being written with art even though not spoken with truth; third, the verbal wranglings of philosophers in which, too, a swiftness of thought is exhibited, making confidence in opinion easily changed" (H13). Rather than privileging the remarks of astronomers because they are grounded on empirical evidence, Gorgias contends that their remarks are merely opinions designed to *displace* a currently held opinion. Gorgias does not construe science as an empirical study, grounded on the testimony of the senses, wherein one attains an increasing approximation of the "real nature of things"; and he does not construe scientific discourse as the articulation or communication of such truths. Instead, he suggests that scientific discourse, like the discourse of poets, philosophers, and popular orators, is thoroughly *rhetorical,* concerned with demolishing opinions and displacing them with others.

Gorgias thus clearly repudiates the dogmas of empiricism as forcefully as he rejects those of subjectivism. He vehemently rejects the subjectivist theses that what we ordinarily accept as real does not exist and that the only real world is an unnamable flux of "becoming"; that what we ordinarily accept as knowledge is erroneous and that the only real "knowledge" is a nonrational, kairotic experience of the unprecedented present; that every rational account we attempt to give of what is real is invariably deceptive, for it abstracts from the immediate moment and reifies experience in deceptive, artificial categories; and that consequently the only "honest" speech consists of poetic allusions to the unnamable made in antithesis, metaphor, and other figures of speech. But if he rejects subjectivism, Gorgias also repudiates the empiricist theses that the real world is ultimately material, that our knowledge of this world depends on the data we receive through our sensory "pores," and that descriptions and explanations of the world are valid only if they accurately represent the elements and structure of the material world. But if Gorgias repudiates both of these epistemologies, how does he see the world? Specifically, how does he construe truth, knowledge, and discourse? I now turn to a reading that provides answers to these questions.

2

THE RHETORICITY OF LOGOS

> Gorgias of Leontini began from the same position as those who have abolished the criterion, but did not follow the same line of attack as the school of Protagoras.
>
> Sextus Empiricus, *Against the Schoolmasters*

> Another word for antifoundationalism *is* rhetoric, and one could say without too much exaggeration that modern antifoundationalism is old sophism writ analytic.
>
> Stanley Fish, *Doing What Comes Naturally*

I have argued that the subjectivist and empiricist readings are each contradicted by a number of Gorgias' assertions. In this chapter I develop a third account, one in which I depict Gorgias as an antifoundationalist who rejects as misguided the project of discovering an objective or subjective truth and who instead sees truth as a label of endorsement awarded by a community to an account that it finds most persuasive. To this end, I first discuss the notions of foundationalism and antifoundationalism. I then argue that Gorgias repudiates the foundationalist position in *On Not-Being*, in which he argues that it leads to the absurd consequences that we cannot have knowledge and that we cannot communicate meaningfully. In his three-part argument, Gorgias repudiates the notion that there is a criterion that exists "in the world itself" that underwrites our claims to knowledge; he rejects the notion that we possess a mental faculty that enables us to discern such an order; and he rejects the notion that language is able to communicate anything about any such independent order or meaning. I then examine the model of language, inquiry, and truth that Gorgias develops in his subsequent texts. I argue that Gorgias construes language as an array of maneuvers or tropes that people use in various socially sanctioned agons or games; that he characterizes inquiry as a debate between rival rhetors in sanctioned agons of the culture; and that he depicts *truth* as a label of endorsement, a prize awarded by the audience or community to the accounts they find most persuasive.

FOUNDATIONALISM AND ANTIFOUNDATIONALISM

Characterizing Gorgias' thought as "antifoundationalist" may on its face seem egregiously anachronistic, given that the term is of recent vintage and is commonly used to characterize the rhetorical philosophy of the later Wittgenstein, the neopragmatism of Rorty and Fish, and the deconstructive projects of Derrida and Lyotard.[1] But although the term is relatively new, this does not prevent it from being extremely useful for illuminating fifth-century Greek thought in general and that of Gorgias in particular. For as many philosophers, classicists, and literary theorists have argued, returning to the Greek origins of today's discussions may clarify the terminology and basic positions of today's debate. David Roochnik argues that the contemporary debate between foundationalist and antifoundationalist thinkers about "the nature, the limits, the fate, of reason and rational inquiry" is the *very same debate* that is examined in extraordinary detail in Plato's dialogues, wherein Socrates argues against Gorgias, Protagoras, Hippias, Thrasymachus, and other Sophists; and that "returning to the Greek origins of today's debate can illuminate the basic terms and structure of that debate" (1991, 226). Other scholars iterate this point, emphasizing that while Western thought is diverse in its concerns, there is a remarkable continuity in the way in which many thinkers have formulated their views of language, knowledge, and truth: Joseph Margolis locates the origins of today's debate in pre-Socratic philosophy, observing that foundationalism is the "presumption of the classical (the Parmenidean) canon: the canon that holds that reality possesses invariant structures and that human science is capable of—indeed, is formed specifically for—discerning just those structures" (1992, 20–21); Tom Rockmore and Beth Singer write that Plato's theory of ideas and Aristotle's doctrine of *ousia* are concerned with versions of this problem and are in part responses to the earlier views proposed by Heraclitus, Anaximander, and Parmenides (1992, 3); Alexander Nehamas suggests that Plato relies on a distinction between foundationalism and antifoundationalism in his account of philosophy and sophistry, whereby the true philosopher is a person who accepts the Forms as "foundations" for knowledge, while the Sophist is trapped in the "groundless" world of appearance (1999, 118). And Stanley Fish asserts that the current debate between "foundational and antifoundational thought" not only originates with the Greeks but that "the history of Western thought could be written as the history of this quarrel." Rather than being a radically new development in Western thought, the contemporary quarrel between foundational and antifoundational thought is a replay of the ancient Greek debate in which "its terms are exactly those one finds in the dialogues of Plato and the orations of the sophists" (1989, 483–85).

In order to understand the notion of antifoundationalism and to see how it may be used to illuminate the writings of Gorgias, it is useful first to sketch the "foundationalist" view of truth, knowledge, and language that it opposes. Typically, foundationalists see truth or reality as an independent "ground," a starting point or origin that is ontologically, logically, and temporally prior to human inquiry and knowledge; that is independent of the contingencies of human life, culture, and language; and that serves as a criterion for claims to knowledge and meaningful speech. In Roochnik's terms, foundationalist thinkers maintain that "there are rational standards immune to the vagaries of history, that men and women of knowledge have access to these standards, these Forms, which can function as stable anchors of our lives and various modes of discourse" (1991, 226). The ground thus functions as what Fish calls a "reference point or checkpoint against which claims to knowledge and success can be measured and adjudicated" (1989, 342).

Foundationalist thinkers disagree about the precise nature of the objective foundation and characterize it in various ways. Hesiod depicts the "foundation" as the earth itself, the "secure foundation" that emerges from a void or rupture between sky and earth (*Theogony* 116ff.).[2] The notion that the *earth* is the original foundation is important for Athenians like Isocrates, who see themselves as *autochthonous,* or having a birth directly from the earth itself.[3] Several sixth-century Ionian philosophers identify the ground as an aspect of nature, specifically water (Thales), air (Anaxagoras), or fire (Heraclitus). The early Italian and Sicilian philosophers identify the foundation with god (Xenophanes), with number or harmony (Pythagoras), with Being (Parmenides), with four "roots" (Empedocles), or with atoms in a void (Leucippus). Plato identifies the ground as the Forms or Ideas, and Aristotle identifies the ground as the essential entities that populate the world.

Second, foundationalists tend to characterize human knowledge as the apprehension or observation of the truth that exists in the world. They differ, however, about whether and how we are able to apprehend this objective truth, and they privilege different human faculties and modes of inquiry for obtaining knowledge of it. Some poets state that we are unable to discern truth without divine inspiration. A common poetic convention, that of Homer and Hesiod, is that the only route to the truth is to hear it as reported by the muses (Homer *Iliad* 2.485; Hesiod *Theogony;* Pindar *Paean* 6.51ff.). Hesiod thus writes, "This word first the goddesses said to me—the muses of Olympus, daughters of Zeus who holds the aegis: 'Shepherds of the wilderness, wretched things of shame, mere bellies, we know how to speak many false things as though they were true; but we know, when we will, to utter true things.' So said the ready-voiced daughters of great Zeus, and they . . . breathed into me a divine voice to celebrate things that shall be and things that were aforetime" (*Theogony* 27–32). Some poets, such as Shelley, contend that the faculty of the "imagination" enables a genius to apprehend the true nature of things; others suggest that erotic passion, alcohol, or other stimulants may trigger the requisite escape from the mundane sobriety in which most of us dwell.[4] Only by escaping our rational prisons, presumably, are we able to experience the ongoing flux of Becoming.

Conversely, some philosophers contend that we are able to apprehend the truth through rational reflection or empirical observation. Thus, Heraclitus admonishes his readers to attend to the *logos* that is inherent in the nature of things; Parmenides, who identifies the ground of knowledge with the domain of Being, argues that we are able to apprehend Being if we think correctly, relying primarily on our innate faculty of reason. He remarks that "the same thing is for knowing as is for being" (Fragment 3); that "what is for saying and for thinking of must be" (Fragment 6); and that "the same thing is for thinking as is for-the-sake-of (or cause-of-that-for) which there is thought" (Fragment 8.34). For Parmenides, the correct route to understanding of Being involves a retreat from attention to the physical world to an inward reflection and intuition that Tom Rockmore calls a "direct, intuitive grasp of an underlying sphere of reality" (6). Other thinkers, such as Empedocles, contend that perception or sensation provides a reliable means of apprehending the true nature of things and that our perceptual openings or "pores" enable us to perceive the effluences emitted by material objects. This reliance on sensory experience is also affirmed by various medical authors in the Hippocratic tradition. The thinkers whom Dodds calls "Greek rationalists" suggest that we may apprehend (or at least approach) the *logos* inherent in the world by using the faculty of reason and following a rational method of inquiry.[5] Plato thus argues that we may approach the true nature of things through dialectical reasoning whereby we become able to assemble diverse aspects of things and divide the world into its proper classifications (*Phaedrus* 265d-266c). Using Derrida's term, we may describe these thinkers as *logocentric,* in that they affirm that rational inquiry will lead them to understand the true order of things.[6] Derrida writes that in logocentrism there is an "absolute proximity" between discourse and the meaning of Being, a natural relationship between "being and mind, things and feelings" (1976, 11–12).

Third, foundationalist thinkers usually maintain that we are able to convey our knowledge of the truth in some type or mode of discourse. Many poets suggest that mythic narratives about the gods are the best means of characterizing the ultimate nature of things and that figurative language is the only way to speak about a truth that lies beyond the realm of ordinary human apprehension. To many poets, mundane prose is inadequate for articulating the hidden nature of things. They concur with Aeschylus that human speech is deceptive insofar as it purports to speak the truth about reality itself.[7] Parmenides, on the other hand, who sees Being as comprehensible and logical, maintains that correct human speech is able to articulate Being and is, in effect, coterminous with Being. And Aristotle contends that unequivocal, literal prose is the best way to articulate the true nature of things without distortion. He thus remarks that "spoken sounds are symbols of affections of in the soul, and written marks symbols of spoken sounds. And just as written marks are not the same for all men, neither are spoken sounds. But what these are in the first place signs of—affections of the soul—are the same for all; and what these affections are likenesses of—actual things—are also the same" (*De interpretatione* 16a3–8). Despite differences in the way they picture the world, each foundationalist thinker maintains that there is an order or truth in the world that we may approach or apprehend if we use the appropriate faculty or are properly inspired and that we may communicate this truth if we speak in the proper manner. In this respect, both the myths of Hesiod and the rational accounts of Aristotle are attempts to communicate the essential nature of things that the poet or philosopher has himself understood. To rationalists like Aristotle and Thucydides, the mythical accounts should be displaced with logical explanations, but both the poets and the philosophers are engaged in more or less the same foundationalist project.

Rather than attempting to find a reliable route to the true or essential nature of things and to articulate an adequate means of speaking about it, antifoundationalists tend to repudiate the entire project as misguided, reductive, and unnecessary for knowledge and meaningful discourse. In Rorty's terms, the antifoundationalist is an "ironist," a person who "faces up to the contingency of his or her own most central beliefs and desires" and who has "abandoned the idea that those central beliefs and desires refer back to something beyond the reach of time and chance" (1990, xv). Rather than seeking to discern an objective criterion that antedates human inquiry and discourse by following a privileged procedure, antifoundationalists tend to present a very different account of language, inquiry, and truth. First, many antifoundationalists characterize discourse as a form of social behavior in which words acquire meaning, not by referring to independent entities in the world, but by playing a role in what Wittgenstein calls language games, human forms of life involving, and in various respects informed by, speech. They thus reject the notion that any use of language is able to provide an impartial, unbiased account of the true nature of things or a transparent window upon an independent "reality." Second, antifoundationalists maintain that inquiry is itself always partisan, wherein every claim to understanding is always a biased interpretation advanced by a culturally situated human being. Rather than being impartial or objective, every assertion is always generated within a web of assumptions, procedures, and judgments; and the notion that any viewpoint is impartial is misguided and often self-deceptive. Third, antifoundationalists reject the idea that some assertions accurately represent an objective reality and that such a context-invariant ground or referent is needed to serve as a criterion to distinguish true and false speech. For every such "ground" or criterion, they maintain, is *itself* a human construct, articulated in a language that is inevitably situated in a particular time, place, and culture; subject to the biases and perspectives of those who articulate it; and consequently never able to serve as an unbiased criterion. While antifoundationalists are quite willing to use terms such as *truth* and *reality*, they contend that the meanings of these terms vary from situation to situation and that they are determined through persuasive argumentation in specific debates rather than by simply observing how things really are. Thus, antifoundationalists are quite able to distinguish between true and false assertions, between knowledge and opinion, and between what is real and what is merely apparent; but they contend that all of these distinctions are *topoi*, or commonplaces, verbal distinctions that acquire meaning only in the specific language games in which they are deployed, and that they are always "inextricable from the social and historical circumstance in which they do their work" (Fish 1989, 344–45).

When we construe foundationalism and antifoundationalism in this way, we can see that the two prevailing schools of Gorgian interpretation both depict Gorgias as a *foundationalist* thinker engaged in a project of finding a privileged source or ground for knowledge and truthful discourse. Rather than being antithetical, the subjectivist and empiricist readings are in this respect essentially the same, for each construes Gorgias as seeking a criterion that lies outside or beyond the contingent domain of human discourse. In the subjectivist reading, Gorgias posits an ontological and epistemological gulf or chasm between the human subject and external reality, a gulf imposed by reason or *logos* itself, such that we are unable to apprehend the true nature of things. The ultimate source of truth lies in the individual subject, and the only way to apprehend the real is to escape the prison-house of reason and experience an unmediated kairotic moment. In the empiricist reading, Gorgias identifies the foundation as a material world that is accessible through empirical observation and articulable in a discourse that is grounded on those observations. The subjectivist's discourse is true only if it represents his immediate, kairotic experience, and the empiricist's discourse is truthful only if it represents an objective material domain; but while the referent of discourse differs, both accounts are foundational in that they rely on a criterion that antedates and validates discourse. The characterization of Gorgias as a foundationalist thinker is made explicit by Frank Walters (1994), who writes that Gorgias and his Sophistic colleagues are foundationalists whose principle concern is finding a secure ground for discourse and knowledge. Walters writes, "Epistemology, the problem of knowing and of representing knowledge, is inherent to the Sophists' thinking and writing about Being; they make Being the primary object of intellectual and moral inquiry. In this sense they are *foundationalists,* agreeing with their rivals that Being—what it is, how it is known, and how it should be represented—is the great project of a rational and moral person's life" (144; emphasis added).

Abolishing the Criterion

If we construe Gorgias as an antifoundationalist, we may read *On Not-Being* as a three-part argument that challenges the project of grounding knowledge and discourse on any sort of nonlinguistic criterion by showing that it results in undesirable absurdities. In this construal, Gorgias does not attempt to demonstrate, as the subjectivists maintain, that truth is beyond conventional apprehension, that we are confined to a deceptive domain fabricated by *logos,* and that we are unable to communicate meaningfully and truthfully with each other. Nor does he attempt to prove, as his empiricist readers contend, that reality is ultimately material rather than immaterial or supernatural, that we can obtain knowledge about the physical world through empirical observation, and that we can only communicate in a discourse that is accurately grounded on empirical perception. Rather, he argues that the foundationalist project is fatally flawed because it cannot characterize the nature of things without self-contradiction, it cannot explain how we are able to acquire knowledge, and it cannot explain how communication is possible. Gorgias argues that every attempt to discern and articulate the nature of a foundational referent that exists independently of discussion of it and that serves as an independent ground or criterion for our claims to knowledge and meaningful communication leads to self-contradiction or absurdity. In Sextus's phrase, "Gorgias of Leontini began from the same position as those who have abolished the criterion, but did not follow the same line of attack as the school of Protagoras" (N65).

Before discussing his three-part argument, it is useful to attend to Gorgias' ambiguous term *exist.* Following several contemporary scholars, I read Gorgias as using the term in more or less the same way as other ancient philosophers such as Parmenides, Plato, and Aristotle appear to use it. Specifically, in Charles Kahn's terms, the ancient Greek term *einai,* or 'exist,' is best understood in a "veridical" rather than an "existential" sense, in that "the most fundamental value of *einai* when used alone (without predicates) is not 'to exist' but 'to be so,' 'to be the case,' or 'to be true'" (1976, 250). In a similar formulation, Alexander Nehamas argues that when most ancient philosophers use the term, they deploy it in a "definitional" sense. In this construal, to say that something "is" the case is to assert that it is "what it is to be" the case (1999, 133–34). We may thus characterize "is" as "what it is to be F." This is the "definitional" or "veridical" sense of the term that Plato's Socrates uses when, in seeking the essential nature of something, he asks the *ti esti* question: What is virtue, justice, or friendship? The definitional sense of *is* is closely related to the notion of Being for Parmenides and Plato, who contend that to say of something that it is "what it is to be F" is to identify and define its *essential nature.* As Nehamas suggests, this may be why Parmenides denies that the mutable everyday realm of becoming and passing away, which he denotes with the term *Not-Being,* is "real" in the sense that the unchanging realm denoted by *Being* is real. Using Nehamas's example, if we say a particular piece of wood *is* wood in the definitional or essentialist sense, we must mean that the particular piece of wood is *what it is to be* wood. But we would certainly not want to say this about a particular piece of wood, primarily because the wood will eventually decay and no longer exist. As such, it cannot be the same as a *definitional* or essential quality, for that is not something that can decay or cease to exist. Consequently, for Parmenides and

Plato, we must identify another ontological domain, one in which "essential" qualities and entities reside; and this is the realm of Being. In order to gain access to this domain or understand the defining properties of things, we cannot simply rely on our senses, for they only provide us with sights, sounds, tastes, and smells, all of which are mutable and none of which tells us what it is to be a piece of wood or, say, good or just or beautiful. Instead, we must use another faculty, that of rational thinking. When Parmenides states that "the same is for thinking and Being," he thus appears to mean that if we think correctly, we can accurately define such things as justice and love and wood. He further suggests that we can articulate these true accounts if we speak accurately and correctly, such that our spoken words represent or manifest the true nature of things.

Plato appears to use the term *exist* in more or less the same way, distinguishing two distinct ontological domains that are denoted by the terms *Being* and *Not-Being*. In the *Sophist*, for instance, Plato identifies the realm of Being as that which is unchangeable and real, and says that the everyday domain of Not-Being is that of appearance and change. Definitions of things do not change, whereas things in the world, subject to becoming and passing away, do change. Plato remarks that most people (including the Sophists) concern themselves only with Not-Being, the realm of appearance, while the true philosopher dwells in the domain of Being. Aristotle adopts a similar distinction between Being and Not-Being, characterizing the difference in terms of the essential and the accidental. What is essential to any given thing is part of what defines it; whereas what is accidental is that which merely happens to be associated with something in a given situation. Thus Aristotle states, "The accidental, then, is what occurs, but not always nor of necessity, nor for the most part. Now we have said what the accidental is, and it is obvious why there is no science of such a thing; for all science is of that which is always or for the most part, but the accidental is in neither of these classes" (*Metaphysics* 11.8). Aristotle also agrees with Plato that the Sophist is unconcerned with what is essentially real. For while philosophers like himself are able to grasp what is essential in their accounts of things and thus speak the truth, nefarious Sophists draw on what is merely contingent or accidental in order to fabricate fallacious arguments. Consequently, "Plato was in a sense not wrong in ranking sophistic as dealing with that which is not. For the arguments of the sophists deal, we may say, above all with the accidental . . . the accidental is obviously akin to non-being" (*Metaphysics* 6.2). "None of the traditional sciences busies itself about the accidental . . . but only sophistic; for this alone busies itself about the accidental, so that Plato is not far wrong when he says that the sophist spends his time on non-being" (*Metaphysics* 11.8). For Aristotle, a Sophist like Gorgias thus concerns himself with contingency, or the accidental associations of things, and is thereby able to deceive people with fallacious arguments.[8]

If we construe the "existent" in this way, we may read Gorgias as arguing that there is no true or essential reality; that if there were, we could not know it; and that even if we could know it, we could not explain or communicate it to another person. This means that Gorgias is opposed both to the notion that the ultimate reality is an unchanging domain of Being or an always-changing domain of Not-Being or flux. He not only rejects Parmenides' eternal Being, but he also rejects the "Protagorean" notion that the immediate experience of each person is real.[9] For Gorgias repudiates the notion that *either* realm is "real" in a definitional sense; consequently, he denies that there is an "independent" domain that justifies our claims to be speaking the truth, be it a transcendent Being or an unmediated Becoming of which we are a part. So while he repudiates the notion of an essential nature of things, Gorgias does not thereby affirm that the domain of appearance or Not-Being is the "real world." We should not conclude, however, that because he repudiates the idea that there is an essential feature of things, or a definitional realm of Being, that he thereby sees everything as contingent or accidental and that he somehow affirms the realm of Becoming as "real." Gorgias does not accept the distinction itself as one that designates distinct ontological realms or that designates a difference between things that holds in every situation. He is quite willing to distinguish, in specific situations, between what he considers true and what he considers merely apparent; but in each case his distinction will acquire meaning only within the context in which he employs it; and what counts as true or apparent, or real or unreal, will vary depending on the context in which he makes the distinction.

In part one of *On Not-Being,* Gorgias argues against the existence of both Not-Being and Being. In his "special proof" in the *MXG,* he contends that we cannot say of Not-Being that it "exists" in the sense of being what it is to be Not-Being, for to do so would be analogous to saying that a given piece of wood is what it is to be wood; but since a piece of wood changes and decays, it cannot be a defining essence. Gorgias then argues that Being cannot exist, maintaining that every attempt to characterize any such putative referent as either Being or Not-Being (N66), as "eternal or generated" (N68–72), as "one or many" (N73–74), or as "mobile or stationary" (*MXG*) is self-contradictory. And since every attempt to characterize "the way the world really is" is self-contradictory, we may conclude that it is pointless to attempt to talk about "the way the world really is." In effect, Gorgias rejects the project of searching for "what truly exists," a project undertaken by Parmenides and subsequently by Plato.

What is absolutely crucial in Gorgias' argument in part one is that he argues that *both* Being and Not-Being, do not exist in a foundational or essentialist sense; there is nothing that is "what it is to be X," whether it is the realm of Being or the realm of Becoming. Gorgias is not a subjectivist who maintains that we are separated from the true world of Being by an ontological and epistemological "gap." This is because the putative domain of Being does not exist in an essentialist way. But Gorgias is also not an empiricist, for he does *not* affirm that the realm of Not-Being or appearance is real, while the noumenal realm of Being is unreal; that is, he does not maintain that the everyday world of "empirical" experience is the fundamentally real world, while the transcendental or metaphysically unchanging domain of Being is a fabrication or is unreal. Stated another way, Gorgias argues against essences; but in so doing, he does not embrace the putative realm of appearance, or Not-Being, that Parmenides and Plato posit as the ontological alternative to Being. Instead, Gorgias argues that this domain also does not exist, that it is not essentially or ultimately the true world.

In part two of *On Not-Being*, Gorgias continues his assault on the notion that there is something that exists in an essentialist sense, such that we can say that something is "what it is to be" that thing. Gorgias' focus is epistemological rather than ontological, and he considers the two routes that have been proposed for apprehending reality. These two routes are the mind or thinking (*nous*), as proposed by Parmenides, and sensation (*aisthesis*), as proposed by Plato's Protagoras. In a manner similar to his mode of argument in part one, Gorgias repudiates both routes, each of which seeks a foundation or independent referent for our knowledge. As several scholars point out, both the *MXG* and Sextus are fragmentary, and it is impossible to say how Gorgias relates his discussion of knowledge and that of sensation. But it is consistent with both texts to read Gorgias as repudiating both the mentalist and the sensory conceptions of knowledge.

In a foundationalist model of knowledge, we attain knowledge of what exists by grasping it in one of two ways, either through sensation or by grasping it in our minds directly, whereby we must rely on our mind as the sole criterion for what exists or does not exist. Gorgias argues that sensation does not lead to knowledge; for each sense enables us to apprehend only that which is specific to it: vision enables us to perceive sights, hearing enables us to perceive sounds, but none of these alone leads to knowledge. Hence, Protagoras is incorrect insofar as he holds that knowledge is perception. But Gorgias also argues that knowledge is not possible through direct apprehension by the mind either. For this alternative leads to absurd consequences, such as the impossibility of imagining nonexistent things or maintaining that conceivable things like men flying and chariots racing in the sea do exist. If we say with Parmenides that "the same is for thinking and Being," then we must conclude that false statements and thoughts are not possible. But since we are clearly able to see that some ideas are not valid, we should conclude that Parmenides' thesis is absurd.

The fatal flaw in the foundationalist theory of knowledge is that if we posit the existence of an independent referent or criterion designed to ground or justify our knowledge, we are unable to know anything about such a putative referent. For if we require this referent or ground to serve as a criterion for our knowledge, such that our claims to knowledge are only valid insofar as they accurately represent the referent, then we can never know whether or not we know anything at all. The requirement that the referent serve as a criterion engenders an unbridgeable gulf or chasm between the way the world really is from what may be called the point of view of the world, and the way the world is from our own human point of view. Moreover, we have no way to know if our own view of things ever matches or corresponds to the way the world really is. For to judge the accuracy or inaccuracy of the match requires us to have *another* point of view, one that is independent of both the "subjective" human point of view and the "objective" world's point of view. Gorgias thus argues that if we posit a putative referent or criterion for our knowledge, "it is unknowable and incomprehensible to man" (N77). If "things considered in the mind" do not match the external criterion, then "the existent is not considered" (N77). But, he argues, "things considered (for this must be our starting point) are not existent," and "the existent is not therefore considered" (N78). For if things considered in the mind are existent," and the criterion for existence is that we consider them, then "the conclusion is that all things considered exist, and in whatever way anyone considers them. Which is absurd. For if one considers a man flying or chariots racing in the sea, a man does not straightaway fly nor a chariot race in the sea. So that things considered are not existent" (N79). Gorgias thus attacks Parmenides' theory of knowledge (the same is for thinking and Being) by arguing that it leads to agnosticism: we have no way of knowing what is or is not real if we are confined to our minds. Since we are able to conceive of chariots racing in the sea and flying men, both of which contradict common sense, reliance on the mind alone can never guarantee that we are thinking about the way things really are, that "the same is for thinking and Being." Since the mind leads us to consider absurdities like flying men and seaborne chariots, there is no reason to think that the mind is a trustworthy source of knowledge.

But if Parmenides' mentalist theory cannot lead us to things as they really are, Gorgias continues, neither can the perceptualist theory; for perceptions do not provide a way to get any closer to the way things really are in the world. This is because each sense only affords access to its own domain: sight to what is visible, hearing to what is audible. And no sense provides access to what is apprehensible in the mind. Attending to the theory that we can assess knowledge on the basis of perception, Gorgias argues that perception can never provide us with knowledge of what exists or does not exist, of what is true or false. He thus argues that "just as objects of sight are said to be visible for the reason that they are seen, and objects of hearing are said to be audible for the reason that they are heard, and we do not reject visible things on the grounds that they are not heard, nor dismiss audible things because they are not seen (since each object ought be judged by its own sense, but not by another), so, too, things considered in the mind will exist even if they should not be seen by the sight nor heard by the hearing, because they are perceived by *their own criterion*" (N81; emphasis added). We attribute visibility or audibility to things because we see or hear them. But even though we cannot hear visible things or see sounds, we do not conclude that they do not exist. By analogy, we have no way of knowing whether things we consider in the mind exist or not, if we assume that they are knowable only "by their own criterion." Therefore, he concludes, "the existent is not an object of consideration and is not apprehended" (N82).

In part three of *On Not-Being*, Gorgias continues his assault on the foundational model, arguing that even if we assume that we are able to have knowledge of the true or essential nature of things, we could not put our knowledge or apprehension into words. Consequently, we could never communicate anything about the criterion. Gorgias offers three arguments to support this thesis. First, in what Mourelatos (1987, 41) labels the "categorial" argument, Gorgias argues that a speaker cannot communicate information about an object that is visually perceivable, since *logos* is of a different *category* than things. In this argument, Gorgias attacks the empiricist notion that words represent phenomena, asking: "But even if they are knowable by us, how, he asks, could any one indicate them to another? For how, he says, could any one communicate by word of mouth that which he has seen? And how could that which has been seen be indicated to a listener if he has not seen it? For just as sight does not recognize sounds, so the hearing does not hear colors but sounds; and he who speaks, speaks, but does not speak a color or a thing" (*MXG* 98019–21). Gorgias argues that just as one cannot convey colors through sounds, so one cannot convey colors or sounds or any other "perceptible" through *logos,* which is ontologically different from the objects it purports to communicate. The speaker, in uttering words, can no more speak the "thing itself" than sight can apprehend sounds. In Sextus's rendition, for something to be communicated, it must be in the form of *logos* (N84–85). But then *logos,* and not things, is all we communicate, since "*logos* is not the same as the underlying realities or the actual things" (N85). By analogy, "just as the visible cannot become audible and vice versa, so too, since reality obtains outside of us, it could not become our own *logos*" (N84). Gorgias concludes his argument by asserting, "When, therefore, one has not a thing in the mind, how will he get it there from another person by word or any other token of the thing except by seeing it, if it is a color, or hearing it, if it is a noise? For he who speaks does not speak a noise at all, or a color, but a word; and so it is not possible to think a color, but only to see it, nor a noise, but only to hear it" (*MXG* 980b4–8). That is, if a speaker is to communicate to a listener some entity that belongs to the external world, the listener must form some idea about that entity; but the idea would be something *other* than the object referred to.

Next, Gorgias argues that words cannot communicate subjective mental images or perceptions. In what Mourelatos (1987) labels the argument from "perceptual sameness," Gorgias argues that no one grasps the same mental image as anyone else (*MXG* 980b18–19). The assumption in this argument is that in order for communication to occur, two people must mentally grasp the *same thing*. This is the case if language is depicted as representing things "outside" it, as in the foundationalist model of *logos*. Gorgias argues, "But even if it is possible to know things, and to express whatever one knows in words, yet how can the hearer have in his mind the same thing as the speaker? For the same thing cannot be present simultaneously in several separate people; for in that case the one would be two" (980b8–11). Gorgias' argument is that if communication requires that two people grasp the same thing, something that is external to *logos* and in some way signified by *logos*, it is impossible for the speaker and listener to mentally grasp the *same thing;* for since the speaker and listener are two distinct persons in different places, it is impossible for them to have the *same* entity or referent in their minds. If each person's perceptions are his own, it is inconceivable that they can be the same. Gorgias continues with another counterfactual conditional, namely, that if "the same thing *could* be present in several persons, there is no reason why it should not appear dissimilar to them if they are not themselves entirely similar and are not in the same place; for if they were in the same place they would be one and not two" (*MXG* 980b11–14). In this argument, Gorgias asserts that even if the very same entity somehow *were* in two people, that same entity would not necessarily appear the same to each of them, given that they are situated differently. Gorgias' argument appears to be drawn from the analogy of perspective, in that things seen from two different perspectives appear differently. Gorgias' argument assaults the "subjectivist" notion that words refer to subjective mental entities, for he argues that individuals are unable to "transfer" their subjective mental ideas to others.

If we read Gorgias as an antifoundationalist and see *On Not-Being* as a three-part assault on the foundationalist project, then we see that both the subjectivist and empiricist readings of his work are misguided. Gorgias repudiates the notion that there is any essential nature to anything that exists "from the point of view of the world itself" and is independent of the situated human discourse used to describe it. In short, there is no "true account of the world." Gorgias does not advance a "subjectivist" view that posits an epistemological gulf between the mind and an independent truth, for this thesis presumes that such a domain *does* exist, whether it is physical or metaphysical. By rejecting the notion of a foundational criterion, Gorgias thereby erases the possibility of an epistemological gulf that it engenders. Conversely, Gorgias does not advance an empiricist account in which knowledge is grounded on material objects and is perceptible through the senses, for such an account merely describes the putative foundational criterion in another way and as such is subject to the same difficulties as any foundational model of truth and knowledge. The empiricist model also posits an "external" domain that serves as a standard or criterion, depicts knowledge as the accurate attendance or observation of such criterial entities, and characterizes truth as correspondence to them. Gorgias repudiates this version of the foundationalist project as being as misguided as the subjectivist version. This does not mean that he denies the possibility of articulating truths, knowledge, or meaningful communication. On the contrary, he insists throughout *On Not-Being* that truths are not only possible but are commonplace, that we know what exists and does not exist, and that we routinely communicate the truth. What he denies is that the "truth" is a property of the "world itself" and that this true nature of things is a foundation, or reference point, or criterion, for what we say.

THE GAMES OF DISCOURSE

If Gorgias repudiates the foundationalist notion that there is a truth in the world that is independent of our contingent discourses, it would seem that he rejects the possibility of truth, knowledge, and meaningful discourse altogether. As such, he would seem to abandon us to a radical solipsism, in which we are not only prevented from apprehending anything about the world itself, but in which we are prevented from experiencing kairotic moments that are replete with meaning. Unable to apprehend or experience the truth, we would appear to condemned, like Samuel Beckett's nomadic vagabonds, waiting endlessly for an audience with Godot, dwelling in a shadowy realm of *doxa*. And even if we could ever apprehend the truth, we would, like the mad slave Lucky, be unable to articulate what we have apprehended to others, reduced to nonsensical references to other texts, our "qua qua qua" a pointless string of unintelligible sounds. But this is not the condition into which Gorgias places us, for he offers an alternative to the foundationalist worldview that preserves truth, knowledge, and meaningful discourse. He does not articulate this alternative in *On Not-Being*, and indeed, as Robert Wardy points out, "far from constituting a theory of *logos*, [Gorgias' text] confronts us with a picture of what language cannot be, with what it cannot be assumed to aspire to be" (1996, 24). But if he does not develop his alternative account of language and truth in *On Not-Being*, Gorgias does do so in his subsequent works. In the *Epitaphios, Helen,* and *Palamedes,* and in several of his aphorisms, Gorgias articulates an account of language, knowledge, and truth that does not depend upon a context-invariant or independent criterion but instead locates the source of truth in the institution of the agon, or "contest," a contingent practice engaged in by members of the Hellenic community.

Gorgias is not the only ancient Greek thinker to see the agon as an institution in which people generate knowledge and truth. As historians since Burckhardt and Nietzsche have repeatedly observed, the agon is perhaps the most pervasive and definitive institution of ancient Greek culture. Burckhardt thus argues that the agon is "the paramount feature of life" in ancient Greece, to the extent that "life on all levels was influenced by the agon" (1998, 166); that the agon is a distinguishing feature of the Greeks, one he calls "a motive power known to no other people" (162); and that the agonism of the Greeks pervades every aspect of Greek life. Burckhardt explains: "Daily life from childhood on, the agora, conversation, war and so forth played their part in educating each boy for the agon. The existence that resulted from all this was of a kind never known before or since anywhere on earth—all of it *saturated and dominated by the agon*" (183).

As a defining feature of Greek culture, the agon informed the Olympian, Pythian, Nemian, and Isthmian games; the various city and Panhellenic festivals; the government of the polis; and the production of much theater and art. As Nietzsche notes, the "Greek artists, the tragedians, for example, wrote in order to triumph; their whole art cannot be imagined without competition" (1986, 116). For "every great Hellene hands on the torch of the contest; every great virtue kindles a new greatness" (1976, 36). Consequently, "with festivals and the arts, they also aimed at nothing other than to feel *on top,* to *show* themselves on top" (1990, 3). For the Greeks, according to Nietzsche, "every talent must unfold itself in fighting: that is the command of Hellenic popular pedagogy. . . . And just as the youths were engaged through contests, their educators were also engaged in contests with each other. . . . In the spirit of the contest, the sophist, the advanced teacher of antiquity, meets another sophist . . . the Greek knows the artist only as engaged in a personal fight" (1976, 37).[10]

Another way of speaking about the Greek emphasis on the agon or game is in terms of *play.* For as Nietzsche points out, a distinctive characteristic of Greek life is the importance of play, their tendency and ability to encompass all of life within the horizon of playful competition. Nietzsche remarks that "what is unique to Hellenistic life is thus characterized: to perceive all matters of the intellect, of life's seriousness, of necessities, even of danger, as play" (1989, 3). In this respect, Nietzsche depicts the Greeks as using the agon to transform the potential destructiveness of physical combat into a creatively playful activity that encourages contestants to overcome not only their adversaries but their own prior achievements and limits.[11]

Drawing on this insight into the importance of the agon, I submit that Gorgias sees language itself as inescapably "agonistic" in the sense that he sees every use of language as occurring in an agon or game. He does not specifically argue for or defend this conception of language, but he repeatedly speaks of language in this way and frequently draws attention to the fact that he is participating in a contest in his own texts. He thus depicts every utterance as being performed in accordance to recognizable conventions and suggests that it is only within conventional, recognizable games that words and actions acquire meaning. In this respect, Gorgias depicts language as ludic or "agonistic," and he frequently portrays speech as a competitive confrontation of speakers. In his *Olympic Speech,* for example, he compares speaking to the Olympic games themselves, noting that "speech, like the summons at the Olympic games, calls him who will, but crowns him who can" (B8). And he observes that his own speech is contestive, for "a contest such as we have requires two kinds of excellence, daring and skill; daring is needed to withstand danger, and skill to understand how to trip the opponent" (B8). Gorgias thus suggests that in many instances speech involves "demolishing an opponent" (B12), destroying a rival claim as one would destroy an enemy in battle. Not surprisingly, the praise given Gorgias by his grandnephew on the golden statue erected at Olympia mentions Gorgias' teaching as one of training for contests: "No one of mortals before discovered a finer art / Than Gorgias to arm the soul for contests of excellence" (A8).

Gorgias often underscores the competitive nature of language by using a "warfare" metaphor in his account of speaking and writing. The warriors he praises in the *Epitaphios* use words as part of their military encounters; Paris's seduction of Helen is a form of battle; and Palamedes' confrontation with Odysseus is a battle for his life. Gorgias would presumably agree with the words Plato has him speak in the *Gorgias,* when he states that "our use of rhetoric should be like our use of any other sort of [agonistic] exercise" (*Gorgias* 456e). To use speech is to engage in athletic or military contests. In each of these instances, Gorgias characterizes speech as a form of behavior, a "maneuver" in a game. In this respect, it is significant that Gorgias presents himself as Palamedes, an inventor of games (P30). And when Gorgias describes his own discourse about Helen of Troy, he characterizes his writing as a *paignion,* a playful "game" (H21).

Insofar as he characterizes language as consisting of a family of games, Gorgias implies that language is a form of human action. In *Helen,* he argues that when poets, magicians, and witches use language, they act upon people's emotions and that if Paris seduced Helen with words, his speech acts are analogous to rape, a kind of verbal violence meriting serious punishment. Specifically, Gorgias asserts that language may become an apparatus of *force* and that "persuasion has the same power as necessity . . . for speech, by persuading the soul that it persuaded, constrained her both to obey what was said and to approve what was done" (H12). Gorgias underscores his notion that speaking is an action in a compelling metaphor, asserting that language itself is a "powerful lord" (*dunastes megas*) that acts as it wishes upon people (H8). Like a dynast who forces others to accept his decrees, speakers often attempt to impose their ideas on others.

In *Palamedes,* Gorgias further develops his conception of language as a form of behavior, an activity designed to effect results. In a case of treason, words themselves become deeds, for betrayal may take the form of providing information to an enemy. And the same importance of words emerges in the trial; for if Palamedes is able to speak effectively and to convince the judges of his innocence, then his words will be more important than any action. Palamedes argues that the decision of the judges is more important than life itself, for to speak inappropriately and to bring shame upon oneself is worse than disease and death. He admonishes the judges to utter the correct verdict, asserting that "if you give an unjust verdict, you will make a mistake, not only in regard to me and my parents, but by your action you will make yourselves responsible for a dreadful, godless, unjust, unlawful deed" (P36).

If he construes language as action, Gorgias suggests that the converse is also true, namely, that all human action is informed by language and is itself a form of discourse. In *Palamedes,* he asserts that discourse must precede every action, that "before any future deeds it is necessary first for there to be discussions" (P6). In this particular instance, Gorgias is speaking of the need to have a discussion before any treasonous deeds may be undertaken, but this is an instance of his general view that *logos* in effect precedes and informs actions. Before any gesture or movement becomes a meaningful action, there must be a discursive context in which it acquires meaning; and an action becomes meaningful only within the context of a human frame of reference whose horizon is discursive. In a striking metaphor that Aristotle denounces as "far-fetched," Gorgias remarks that that "you shamefully sowed these and wretchedly reaped" (*Rhetoric* 1406b4), suggesting that agriculture is within the purview of human culture and that, like any other *techne,* it is subject to the moral judgment of honor and shame. And in his simile about Penelope, Gorgias suggests that sexual intercourse is akin to philosophical inquiry, remarking that "those neglecting philosophy and devoting themselves to general studies were like the suitors who, though wanting Penelope, slept with her maids" (B29). In each of these instances, Gorgias suggests that language and action are not only correlative but coterminous: every utterance is an action, and every meaningful action lies within the horizon of language. Gorgias would thus presumably *not* agree to the distinction Plato has him make between rhetoric and the other arts, that "in rhetoric there is no such manual working, but its whole activity and efficacy is by means of speech" (*Gorgias* 450bc).

While in one sense Gorgias confines *logos* by restricting it to human language and thereby removing the denotations of the structure of the world and the universal human faculty, he expands the denotation in the sense that it denotes all of human action. The domain of *logos* as language consists not only of marks and vocal sounds but also of facial expressions, gestures, and every purposive bodily movement. Gorgias' world is a thoroughly linguistic world in which every gesture and action is meaningful. In Gorgias' view even silence becomes a part of language, rather than a condition in which we may escape the horizon of discourse. He thus states that the warriors consider the most divine and common code to do what is fitting, "whether in things done or not done, said or left unsaid" (E12–13). To "keep silence," for the warrior, is as much a form of action, and hence as important a strategy in his various agons, as is speaking.

In Gorgias' agonal model of language, the most fundamental element of discourse is the maneuver, or *trope;* and discourse as a whole is composed of maneuvers that may be used in various games. These linguistic tropes or maneuvers, made by participants in verbal contests or struggles, are analogous to the maneuvers a wrestler uses to strike or trip an opponent (B8). Gorgias thus differs sharply from foundationalist theorists such as Aristotle, who maintain that individual terms are the fundamental units of language and that terms are labels of things and events in the world. In Aristotle's representationalist model of language, nouns are literally "names" of things in the world, and figurative language, or tropes, are alterations of literal use. For Gorgias, the tropes of discourse are not variations on a previously existing "literal" speech, in the sense that "literal" speech consists of a set of labels that name actual things in the world. For as Gorgias argues in *On Not-Being,* there *are* no such independently existing things that antedate their articulation in a particular language and serve as a criterion for correct speech. So unlike Aristotle, who sees tropes such as metaphors and puns as "deviations" from the proper function of language, that of naming essential features of the world itself, Gorgias sees *all* language as inherently tropical, consisting of tropes or "maneuvers" in specific games. For Gorgias, literal speech is not the foundation or ground for figurative speech; rather, literal discourse designates the family of tropes that a community is so accustomed to using that they no longer realize that they are tropes. As Nietzsche observes about the Sophists' conception of language, tropes or figures of speech are not "occasionally added to words but constitute their most proper nature. . . . What is usually called language is actually all figuration" (1989, 25).

This does not mean that Gorgias is unable to distinguish, in specific instances and in specific discourses, between a "literal" and "figurative" use of words. But for Gorgias, what counts as "literal" arises from using a particular set of tropes in a familiar way. When, as users of a language, we take some tropes or modes of speaking for granted and no longer attend to their use, our tropes become *topoi,* or "commonplaces," ways of using words that we accept as literal. The "everyday" is thus generated and reinforced through conventional uses of words, and the way we are persuaded to speak shapes the way we see and describe the world in which we live. Literal language, in this respect, is the language we accept and use as members of a linguistic community, our commonplaces so familiar to us that we accept them as representations of the "real world."

In Gorgias' model of language, words acquire meaning in a very different manner than they do in the foundationalist model of language. In a foundationalist or representational model, the meaning of a word derives from its relationship to an entity or referent in the "world," or to an idea in the "mind"; and both the world and the mind are posited as existing outside and prior to the use of the word. For Gorgias, in contrast, the meaning of a given word is the use we give it in a particular verbal game or agon. When we participate in verbal discussions and make various verbal moves in our interactions with others, we thereby make meaningful assertions. The maneuvers we make in a particular agon, like the maneuvers of a wrestler in a match, do not acquire meaning by referring to an external reality that validates or explains what the maneuver means. Instead, the verbal maneuvers acquire meaning from their role in a particular agonistic discussion. In short, the meaning of words arises from their being used in a family of games or agons, not from the putative entities in the world that they purport to represent. As Plato has Gorgias' student Meno point out, Gorgias regards *virtue* as a term that has a family of meanings:

> First of all, if you take the virtue of a man, it is easily stated that a man's virtue is this—that he be competent to manage the affairs of his city, and to manage them so as to benefit his friends and harm his enemies, and to take care to avoid suffering harm himself. Or take a woman's virtue: there is no difficulty in describing it as the duty of ordering the house well, looking after the property indoors, and obeying her husband. And the child has another virtue—one for the female, and one for the male; and there is another for elderly men—one, if you like, for freemen, and yet another for slaves. And there are very many other virtues besides, so that one cannot be at a loss to explain what virtue is; for it is according to each activity and age that every one of us, in whatever we do, has his virtue; and the same, I take it, Socrates, will hold also of vice. (*Meno* 71e-72a).

For Gorgias, the term *virtue* has a variety of meanings, depending on when and where it is used and in which linguistic contexts. A word does not have meaning because it represents a thing in the world or an idea in the mind; rather, a word has meaning because we *use* it in our lives, and thereby assign it a meaning.

We may describe Gorgias' model of language as "nonrepresentational" in that he repudiates the notion that language represents or imitates an independent, external reality. Instead, he suggests that the way we see the world is shaped by the games we play and the discourses we use. Attending to things in the world, in this respect, reveals our own linguistic conventions rather than the way the world "really is." He makes this point in *On Not-Being,* contending that "it is not the case that discourse is something that represents external reality; rather, it is the external reality that comes to be communicative [explanatory] of the discourse" (N85). What Gorgias suggests is that what we take as "external reality" reveals to us the meaning of our words or the various ways we use language. That which we accept as real and those truths we take as "commonplace" reveal who *we* are and how we use language in our interactions with others. Rather than seeing language as representing things in the world, Gorgias inverts the relationship between things and words, and suggests that examining what we take as real and what we posit as "external" shows us how we use words. Stated another way, there is no independent criterion for the use of language, and there are no independently existing "things" that are named or mirrored in literal speech. As maneuvers or turns that we make in various games, our tropes give "meaning" to terms; and the meaning of a term is always its use in the particular game at hand. In effect, Gorgias inverts the foundationalist's account of meaning, in that he holds that a word does not have meaning because it represents an object; instead, a word represents an object because it is accepted and used in particular ways. Gorgias thus posits use, practice, or custom as explanatory of meaning; and meaning emerges only in the domain of rhetorical, situated communication, a domain that is not dependent upon a prior, more fundamental domain of external things in the world. We do indeed speak of things in the world, but these "things" are made possible and thereby fabricated through our routine practices in various rhetorical situations; and the meaning of our words lies in the use to which we put them in everyday life.

This does not mean Gorgias holds that we are unable to discuss things or events, or that every discussion is inevitably severed from the truth. Within any given language game, stipulations about what is real and unreal are typically quite clear, and in playing the game, we are quite able to distinguish between truth and opinion, or reality and appearance. But what Gorgias does deny is the notion that language as a whole must somehow "represent the world" in order to be true. For if language consists of maneuvers in games, it simply makes no sense to say that the maneuvers somehow "represent the way things really are." In *Helen,* for example, Gorgias delineates four quite distinct "discourses" that various authors have used in their discussions of Helen, which we may identify roughly as theological, political, legal, and medical. The *theological discourse* includes a diverse family of written accounts of the gods and demigods in epic, lyric, dramatic, and other genres; performances by rhapsodes; and pronouncements by private individuals as well as by official oracles at sites such as Delphi. The *political discourse,* that found in Herodotus' history, for example, concerns the relationship between the Greeks and non-Greeks. The *legal discourse* consists of arguments in specific trials and legal discussions in various dramatic and philosophical works. The *medical discourse* is found in the texts of the Hippocratic school as well as in various magical and philosophical treatises. This discourse includes discussions of the nature of *logos* as a quasi-pharmaceutical and its power to influence human perceptions, beliefs, and behavior. Gorgias further develops this discourse in his account of *eros,* which he depicts as a psychological disorder or "disease," arguing that as a disease, *eros* distorts Helen's perceptions and desires, leading her to behave irrationally and to abandon her ethical commitments (H19). Each of these discourses enables us to characterize and discuss Helen and the forces acting upon her in meaningful ways, but none enables us to see her as she "really is"; and to say that one of the discourses offers a "closer approximation to reality" is quite meaningless.

Insofar as he construes terms as acquiring meaning through their use in different language games, Gorgias avoids the charge that he is inconsistent in his characterizations of what is real and what is merely apparent. For when he uses these terms in various contexts, the terms acquire meaning by the specific context and discourse in which he uses them. In the theological, political, and medical discourses he identifies in *Helen,* for example, what counts as ultimately "real" varies. In the theological discourse, for example, the decrees of the gods are real, and the notion that Helen has free choice is an illusion. In the medical discourse, however, the gods themselves become a fiction, and *logos* is akin to a drug that controls the mind. But though he suggests that "reality" is a function of discourse and that in different contexts, using different discourses, what counts as real and what counts as imaginary changes, this does not mean that Gorgias is committed to the view that reality is out of reach or is beyond the scope of language. What is "real" is precisely what is designated as real in a given language that people accept and use. Nor is Gorgias committed to the view that reality is ultimately a flux of Becoming that lies beyond every use of language. For he says nothing whatsoever about any such "ultimate reality," and in *On Not-Being,* he argues that the foundationalist notion that such an external reality exists is part of a misguided view of language and the world. Rather than antedating language, the very idea of what is "real" emerges only within the specific discourses in which we use it.

Since he sees words as acquiring meaning from their role in various agons or games, Gorgias is quite able to distinguish, in particular instances, between such concepts as truth and falsehood, reality and appearance, and knowledge and opinion. For the meanings of these terms do not derive from their representation of the world as it really is and do not characterize distinct ontological realms. Instead, the meanings of the terms are determined by their use in specific agons, each of which is informed by stipulated criteria applicable to the game at hand. In *Palamedes,* for example, Gorgias has Palamedes assert that he *knows* that he is innocent and that

Odysseus only has an opinion: "It is quite clear that you do not have knowledge of the things about which you make accusation. It follows that since you do [not] have knowledge, you have an opinion. . . . But it is not right to trust those with an opinion instead of those who know, nor to think opinion more trustworthy than truth, but rather truth than opinion" (P24). But in this assertion, Gorgias does not commit himself the notion that there is a domain of "truth" that we may grasp through reason or the intellect and a less-real domain of "appearance" or *doxa* that we grasp through mere observation or opinion. For the meaning of what is true or what is apparent differs in each situation, and the manner in which something is established as "true" and the arguments in support of such an assertion may well vary from agon to agon. Each word is anchored in a specific verbal and social practice, and its use or meaning is always governed by the conventions and rules of the agon at hand. Gorgias also states in *Helen* that his audience "knows" about the way in which Paris and Helen sailed to Troy (H5), but he does not suggest that there are shared procedures that Palamedes and the audience of *Helen* follow to arrive at such knowledge or that the status of their knowledge is comparable. What counts as opinion and what counts as knowledge vary from case to case. In this sense, Gorgias would not object to Plato's portrayal of him as distinguishing between knowledge and opinion (*Gorgias* 454ce). But he would adamantly dispute Plato's foundationalist conclusions that he is concerned only with opinion and not with knowledge, that he thinks we are only able to have opinions about things and never attain knowledge of what is true, that our ability to distinguish between knowledge and opinion is the same in every situation, and that our distinction between knowledge and opinion in a given context in any way suggests that there are two distinct ontological domains of, say, Being and Not-Being, to which our terms ultimately refer.

Insofar as he espouses an agonistic model of language, Gorgias differs sharply from foundationalists in respect to the nature of communication. In a typical foundationalist model of language, a speaker who attempts to communicate must use words that represent or name objects in the world or his ideas about those objects and then use words to convey his thoughts to another person. Gorgias repudiates this conception of communication in the third part of *On Not-Being* when he argues that if communication functions in this way, then we can never truly communicate, for the same thought cannot be in two people at the same time, and the same person "perceives different things by hearing and by sight, and differently now and on some former occasion" (N980b15). Gorgias' game model of language avoids the puzzles generated by the foundationalist model. For in Gorgias' model, the criterion for successful communication is not the successful transference of an "idea" between two "minds," but rather the fact that the people are playing the game in question. What happens to occur in one player's "mind" is quite irrelevant to the playing of the game, and communication is not explained by any such inner exploration. In Gorgias' model, a person cannot have a mental intention to move a piece in, say, a game of draughts, unless he is already playing the game. In this respect, Gorgias inverts the explanatory roles of the "mind" and "behavior." For the foundationalist, our words and external behavior are meaningful because they convey our inward thoughts; for Gorgias, however, our thoughts have meaning only because we are already engaged in playing various games. That is, the practice of playing the game is logically prior to the possibility of forming an intention or idea, and our activity of playing games with other people antedates not only what we accept as real but even what we are able to think about. Inward thoughts and impressions do not antedate effective communication; on the contrary, the practice of communication, in a variety of verbal games, makes inward reflection possible.

The Rhetoric of Inquiry

In conjunction with his agonistic model of language, Gorgias develops an agonistic "debate" model of inquiry in which a community generates knowledge and truth. For Gorgias, formal inquiry is an agon in which rival rhetors engage in a public debate in order to persuade an audience of the viability of their respective positions. The starting point of every inquiry is a conflict or rivalry between two or more people, each of whom are typically members of the community. Gorgias displays this initial conflict in each of his extant texts. In *On Not-Being*, he begins by addressing the statements or positions of several principal players, whom he identifies as his rivals. As the author of the *MXG* remarks, "To prove that nothing exists he collects the statements of others, who in speaking about what is seem to assert contrary opinions (some trying to prove that what is is one and not many, others that it is many and not one; and some that existents are ungenerated, others that they have come to be, and he argues against both sides" (*MXG* 979a). In the *Epitaphios*, Gorgias positions himself vis-à-vis an array of other Athenian orators who have delivered funeral addresses in Athens and who typically use the occasion to praise Athens and promote its hegemony. In *Helen*, Gorgias presents himself as taking a position in the ongoing debate about Helen, situating himself vis-à-vis an array of epic, lyric, and dramatic poets who have written about Helen and whom Gorgias characterizes as "univocal and unanimous" in their condemnation of her (H2). In *Palamedes*, Gorgias takes on the role of Palamedes and positions himself in a legal dispute in which he is falsely accused of treason. In each of these four instances, Gorgias situates himself in respect to specific participants in a recognizable and familiar agon, addressing their stated positions and identifying his own overtly partisan position in opposition to theirs.

In Gorgias' agonistic model, "inquiry" is initiated in a conflict, disagreement, or rivalry between two (or more) people. In this respect, Gorgias differs from Plato and Aristotle, who suggest that inquiry begins with an individual's personal experience of "wonder."[12] The agon is not a quest for a transcendent goal that lies beyond the horizon of a person's life. If a puzzle or aporia arises, as it does for Palamedes, who remarks that he is at a loss as to where to begin his speech, the puzzle emerges in the context of an accusation or categorization by a rival (P5). Rather than originating from a solitary inward experience or a journey beyond the everyday, Gorgias indicates that the origin of his speech lies entirely within an established and recognized agon. In the foundationalist model of inquiry that Gorgias delineates in *On Not-Being,* an epistemological chasm stands between the individual and the truth that he seeks. For Gorgias, however, the only chasm is one that is created by an accusation or charge made by an enemy or rival whose accusation or categorization separates the accused from others in the community: Helen is thus scorned, and Palamedes is placed in custody, forced to stand trial as an accused traitor. Unlike Parmenides, for example, Gorgias does not present himself as withdrawing from the muddled discourses of the undiscerning horde in order to journey to a rarified perch from which he is able to observe the truth and correct the misguided views of everyone else. His inquiry is not a solitary quest for a preexistent truth but a struggle in which he attempts to make his own position stronger than that of his rival.

In some instances, rival rhetors engage in face-to-face debate in which both are present in the same location, as in *Palamedes;* while in other situations, a rhetor's rival may be absent, as in an *Epitaphios,* in which rival orators are those who have spoken at previous and future funerals. But in every instance, the agon involves an audience or community of people who determine which rhetor emerges victorious in the agon. Thus, the agon is always a community undertaking, involving rival rhetors and a judge or audience of the contest. Indeed, the Greek term *agon* denotes an "assembly" of people, typically people who gather for a competition such as the Olympic Games, as well as the competition itself. The community may consist of a determinate group of warriors, as in *Palamedes;* it may be comprised of members of a distinct profession, such as meteorologists who present their views to each other (H8) or the Eleatic philosophers who argue among themselves, as in *On Not-Being;* or a community may be a general audience, such as those who attend a festival. But in each instance the audience is an active participant in the inquiry from its inception to its outcome. Gorgias is thus very clear in each of his works about who his audience is, whether it be rival metaphysicians, critics of Helen, attendees of an Athenian festival, or the judges of Palamedes; and his remarks are always specifically addressed to them. In none of these instances does Gorgias simply expresses his personal feelings or speak "from his heart"; nor does he present his words as intended for a "universal" audience, perhaps one made up of all rational beings. In this respect, Gorgias differs from foundationalist thinkers such as the poet Orpheus, who refuses to engage in agons; and he differs from Parmenides, who belittles the community of ordinary mortals as pathetic fools who are "tossed about, as much deaf as blind, an undiscerning horde by whom to be and not to be are considered the same and not the same" (Fragment 6).[13]

The community or audience is engaged in the process of inquiry from the very inception of the agon, for it is their beliefs that demarcate the conceptual site of the inquiry. It is within the domain of the audience's beliefs that the rhetors operate, and if they "stray" from this domain of beliefs, they risk losing the contest. Stated another way, the rhetors always dwell within the *commonplaces,* the shared persuasions of the audience; and the persuasiveness of any discourse depends on how well he is able to position himself in respect to these beliefs. The commonplace, or *topos,* denotes the "place," or conceptual location, within which the rhetor functions and in which he finds his arguments. The commonplace, as a belief or viewpoint held by a particular audience, is often one that they typically take for granted and accept as something that "goes without saying." These range from superficial stereotypes to highly technical notions about the nature of truth, inquiry, and communication held by a professional community of Eleatic philosophers. The *topoi* also embody the values of the community, in the sense that they comprise what the community considers important. As Perelman and Olbrechts-Tyteca note, "The particular places that are accorded special importance in various societies enable us to characterize those societies" (1969, 113). Insofar as the rhetor begins his speech within the arena of the commonplaces, he does not draw from a privileged domain accessible only to himself, an independent "truth" of which he has prior knowledge; nor does he simply express what he is experiencing subjectively, in an arbitrary and creative manner. Instead, he invents by situating himself in a specific cultural context, attending to the beliefs or commonplaces of his audience, and generating a position vis-à-vis his rival. The commonplace shared beliefs of the audience, in this respect, demarcate the horizon within which are the possible points of departure for a rhetor's speech, the domain from within which he generates his discourse.

The commonplaces do not merely demarcate the conceptual arena or site within which the rhetors locate arguments; they comprise the subject matter about which they speak. The commonplace or *topos* is thus the "topic" of the discourse, demarcating the issue under dispute. When Gorgias addresses such topics as the nature of existence, the virtue of the Athenian warriors, the infamy of Helen, or the innocence of Palamedes, he thus addresses specific issues or topics that are being disputed. The *topos* or conceptual place, in this respect, is a verbal articulation of the shared or "common" beliefs of the community; and the *topoi* designate the common places or sites in which people are able to communicate. In his four texts,

Gorgias does not invent a radically new topic, one that has never been considered or discussed; nor does he generate an issue from within his own private or subjective experiences. The topics of his texts are those that are currently debated and are of concern to specific audiences. In *On Not-Being,* Gorgias draws on the beliefs that what exists may be characterized as Being or Not-Being; that Being is either ungenerated or generated, limited or unlimited, one or many, in motion or at rest. In the *Epitaphios,* the commonplaces include the notion that words are inadequate for praising the warrior's heroic deeds, that the warriors possessed and displayed great virtues, and that their death glorifies the city of Athens. These commonplaces or *topoi* provide the vocabulary that may be used in discussion of the subject. But the subject itself, in this context, is inseparable from the commonplaces and is indeed "created" by the commonplaces. In this sense the commonplaces inform the subject matter about which a rhetor speaks.

As a point of departure, the rhetor does not attend to an independent "reality" but to the *topoi* themselves: his discourse is composed entirely of *topoi*. Thus Loraux remarks that Gorgias' *Epitaphios* is a striking instance of his writing, a work made up entirely of commonplaces "in which all new thought may be reduced to a received or already formulated idea, in which all formal invention follows an already established model" (1986, 229). But this is the case for each of Gorgias' works; there is never a "departure" from the realm of the commonplaces, even though he frequently manipulates those *topoi* in such a way as to generate an "outrageous" position in the debate. Gorgias' text is not bereft of substance, as his critics frequently contend; for to Gorgias the "substance" or "topic" of a text is the beliefs, tropes, or forms of life engaged in by the community. In this sense, altering the *topos* in a particular context enables the rhetor to literally change the subject. Stated another way, the subject matter of the discussion does not lie "outside" the discussion but is instead fabricated in the course of the agon itself.

Insofar as he characterizes the commonplaces as the source and subject matter of the agon, Gorgias differs sharply from authors like Parmenides who present themselves as departing from commonplace beliefs and seeking a truth that lies beyond the realm of everyday discourse in a distinct ontological realm. For Gorgias, a rhetor always functions within the domain of the audience's beliefs; and though he may challenge them, he does so through rearrangement or emphasis or inversion. To say that he "departs" from the realm of beliefs merely means that he is no longer convincing and that he is losing the debate. In effect, the rhetor supports his position by referring to other commonplaces, arguing that a particular belief is incongruent with other beliefs that his audience does not wish to give up. In effect, the *topoi* demarcate "reality"; there is no other noncontextual reality to which they refer or which they represent. There is no place or location beyond the *topoi* about which the rhetor speaks. Invention always involves remaining in the *topoi,* altering the *topoi,* or moving to other *topoi* of the audience. In this respect, Gorgias never attempts to create the illusion that his view is true in itself; but he emphasizes from the outset that he is inventing his position from within the commonplace beliefs themselves, that his own view is made possible because of beliefs and procedures that are already in place, and that he is demarcating his position according to the conventions of the agon at hand. He thus differs from "objectivist" philosophers and scientists, who present themselves as apprehending a truth independently of the agon, and from "subjectivist" poets, who present their text as a dim imitation of a fleeting experience that is ultimately inexpressible in words.

In order to compete effectively in a debate, a rhetor requires an art or *techne,* a skill or learned ability that enables him to debate effectively in verbal agons. For without such an art, every encounter would be completely novel, and he would find himself always at the mercy of contingency. We may term this art *rhetoric,* literally 'the art of the rhetor,' even though Gorgias does not use the word in his extant texts. The Greek term *techne,* which derives from the *tekton,* or 'wood worker,' denotes a wide variety of arts, among which are agriculture (B16), pottery making (A23), pharmacology and medicine (H14), athletics (B8), poetry (H9), meteorology (H13), magic and witchcraft (H10), communication, trade, and military strategy (P30), to cite only the arts mentioned by Gorgias himself. In its most general sense, a *techne* involves the capacity to function effectively in a given situation, what Nussbaum calls a "deliberate application of human intelligence to some part of the world, yielding some control over chance; it is concerned with the management of need and with prediction and control concerning future contingencies" (1986, 95). Gorgias' art of rhetoric is not a "method," a *meta-hodos,* a procedure that involves following a set of rules that enables a rhetor to grasp a previously existing truth. For in agonistic confrontations, no such procedure is possible, and a rhetor must be able to respond to the unpredictable maneuvers of his rival.

Gorgias' art of rhetoric is universal in its application, one that enables a rhetor to become a master of language or *logos* as a whole (*Gorgias* 449d). Because language is made up of the discursive maneuvers people use in various agons or games, a skilled rhetor will be able to excel in many of these games and in so doing will be able to speak authoritatively on an array of subjects. The scope of Gorgias' art of rhetoric in this sense is universal, in the sense that there is no subject or topic that lies outside the purview of the art. A skilled rhetor should be able to address any issue that may arise, to engage in any agon whatsoever. As Gorgias himself boldly proclaims, he is able to respond to any question that is thrown at him (A1a). Moreover, rhetoric is a universal art in the sense that there is no other art, no "competing" skill that a rhetor may use, no privileged "method" that lies outside his own art of rhetoric that provides "access to the truth." Since there is no domain that exists independently of the commonplaces of the community other than the commonplaces of another community, perhaps another profession, the only *techne* for generating truths is the art of rhetoric, the mastery of *logos*. Stated another way, Gorgias' art of rhetoric also involves the antecedent stage of "inventing" a position, of generating and establishing a position in an agon. This is because for Gorgias there is no other art that antedates the rhetorical art, no other means of arriving at the truth.

Insofar as he construes rhetoric as a universal art, Gorgias suggests that a skilled rhetor may presumably compete with diverse professionals, for there is no essential difference between the diverse arts, each of which involves mastery of *logos*. When Gorgias describes poets, scientists, and philosophers, he characterizes them all as rhetors who use language to persuade audiences. Thus, the poet's speech is distinctive only because of its use of meter; the astronomer engages in rhetoric, "substituting opinion for opinion, removing one and instilling another, makes incredible and unclear things appear true to the eyes of opinion"; and philosophers, rather than engaging in a dispassionate search for the truth, instead engage in "verbal wrangling in which, too, a swiftness of thought [quick-wittedness] is exhibited, making confidence in opinion easily changed" (H9, H13). For Gorgias the art of rhetoric is universal, and disciplines such as poetry, meteorology, or philosophy are specializations within the art of rhetoric itself. There is no inherent reason why a rhetor could not function as a poet, scientist, or philosopher, given that each is a rhetorician; but a rhetor will respect the specialist for mastering a distinct vocabulary. As Plato has him remark, "The orator is able, indeed, to speak against every one and on every question in such a way as to win over the votes of the multitude, practically in any matter he may choose to take up: but he is no whit the more entitled to deprive the doctors of their credit, just because he could do so, or other professionals of theirs" (*Gorgias* 457ab).

During the process of rhetorical debate, each rhetor strives to find opportunities or "openings" in which he can "strike" his rival (B8). The outcome of the contest often depends on which rhetor is able to bring about, discern, and act effectively in such critical moments. The term Gorgias uses to characterize these momentary opportunities is *kairos,* a term that denotes an opportunity or occasion, a critical moment that arises within the context of a competitive, agonistic situation. As such, the *kairos* is an opportunity the rhetor discerns and helps to bring about during the course of the agon, given his perspective and abilities or skills. The opening or *kairos* does not exist "on its own," apart from the perceptions and actions of an individual, any more than an opening in a particular moment of play in a game exists independently of the positions and skills of the players. Rather, the *kairos* emerges only when a player is engaged in the contingencies of a particular situation and occurs within that situation. What is an opportunity for a highly skilled and powerful archer at a given moment in a battle will not be an opportunity for a weaker, less-skilled, and less-alert archer who is unable to discern an opportunity or act effectively in the situation. Conversely, the archer does not bring about the opening independently of the situation, through an act of will or on a whim. It is only insofar as he is engaged in a struggle with a rival in a specific context, terrain, and time that he is able to help bring about such an opening; the *kairos* is the opportunity to strike a vulnerable point in his opponent. In effect, a rhetor must be able to discern an opening, and to penetrate it is to articulate a way out of an impasse, a way of escaping the constraints or "binds" that one's adversary effects. In order to succeed, the rhetor must always improvise and innovate in order to adapt to the contingencies of the moment; and when he discerns an opportunity, he must act swiftly and effectively, seizing the occasion and turning it to his advantage.

Insofar as he depicts a *kairos* or opening as arising only during the course of play in which a player seeks an opportunity to strike his rival, Gorgias does not suggest that it is some sort of metaphysical capacity for perceiving the true nature of things, one that involves a "leap outside of language," as his subjectivist readers suggest. The notion of leaping outside of language has no meaning in Gorgias' model any more than the notion that a wrestler would attempt to leap outside of his own maneuvers in a wrestling match in order to "really" win the bout. For the *kairos* or opportunity only arises in the contest itself and only has meaning within the parameters of the contest at hand. The *kairos* is an opportunity for action that arises in the course of an agon, not an opening through which a rhetor is somehow able to transcend language and observe a metaphysical flux or discern a tragic antithesis between the subjective mind and objective Being. A *kairos* or opportunity arises through an interaction of rhetor and situation; it is an opportunity or opening that a given rhetor may discern in part because of his skills and abilities, but also in part because of the manner in which he is situated vis-à-vis his adversaries and the way things are taken to be. It is difficult to define because what constitutes a *kairos* differs from situation to situation, and what is a *kairos* to one rhetor may well not be to another. The *kairos* as opportunity is neither a subjective experience nor an objective opening; it is not an unprecedented "instant" that lies beyond *logos,* an opening into an unnamable metaphysical domain that the creative individual seeks to access. This opening is not "objectively" apprehensible in the sense of being independent of his own presuppositions and procedures, for it is itself created by one's own position and skills as well as those of one's adversary in a particular moment in the agon.

Truth as Endorsement

Gorgian inquiry is informed by the agon in its outcome as well as in its inception and procedure, for the objective of each rhetor is to win the game at hand. Gorgias frequently emphasizes this objective in his account of diverse activities. He thus speaks of Helen's suitors as *philonikou,* or "lovers of victory" (H4). In the *Epitaphios,* he praises the warriors who defeat enemies and establish trophies to advertise their accomplishment (E28–29); and in *Palamedes,* his entire endeavor is to defeat his rival, Odysseus. The rhetor does not depict things as they really are; instead, he presents an account that the audience finds compelling. Long writes, "For Gorgias speech-making is like a ball game where he has done all he can with the ball but must now pass it on to others instead of trying to score himself" (1984, 237). But if he depicts the rhetor's objective as victory, this does not mean that Gorgias is indifferent to truth and that he is merely an opportunist intent upon appearing wise to an audience. For Gorgias sees truth as an award, a term of praise, or a decoration that the audience awards to the account they find most persuasive. In Gorgias' succinct phrase, the fairest "ornament" of *logos* is truth (H1). Just as a community decorates or ornaments its heroes, so it decorates the account of the victorious rhetor with the ornament of "truth." In opposition to the foundationalist, who views truth as existing outside all human contexts and serving as criterion for assessing various claims, Gorgias holds that truth is an accolade or ornament (*kosmos*) awarded by a community to an assertion or argument it considers persuasive.[14] In short, truth is a matter of *endorsement,* not an inherent feature of an independent domain that some assertions accurately represent. As such, *truth* is a laudatory term, wherein to say that an assertion is "true" is to praise or compliment it but not to assert the empty claim that it somehow corresponds to reality.

As an antifoundationalist, Gorgias distinguishes between appearance and truth, between what is probable and what is certain. But he does not distinguish between them on the basis of two distinct ontological realms, two different classes of things which opinion and knowledge refer to. Rather, he suggests that the distinction between opinion and truth is situational and must be made anew in each case, based on the arguments at hand. Gorgias rejects the notion that individuals create their own truths and maintains that the community has the authority to decide what is true, an authority that is itself contingent and situated. He asserts that opinion, being "slippery and insecure, casts those relying on it into slippery and insecure fortune" (H11). But this does not mean that every opinion is false; nor does it mean that there is an alternative class of privileged assertions that are true because they correspond to the way things really are. Rather, because opinion is slippery, it means that assertions will presumably attain the status of truth only after they are submitted to the scrupulous examination of a respected community.

Gorgias is not a subjectivist who holds that every assertion is invariably deceptive because it can never bridge the tragic abyss between words and the world. In this subjectivist construal, every use of language that purports to "speak the truth" is a deception since it presents itself as attaining what it can never attain, namely, an accurate depiction of things as they really are. But this is *not* what Gorgias asserts, either in *On Not-Being, Helen,* or *Palamedes;* and it is impossible to reconcile his remarks in *Helen* and *Palamedes* with such an account of truth. In *Helen* he does not assert that *every* statement is a deception; rather, he simply suggests that many people have been deceptive. In *Palamedes,* he maintains that he would like to argue from the "truth" but that he cannot, not because it is *never* possible to speak the truth, but because in this case, in which there is no evidence and are no witnesses, he cannot draw upon what the jury would consider to be the truth. The "two teachers," the truth and the present necessity, are more perilous than resourceful (P4). For Palamedes to rely on what he himself deems the truth is perilous, for until his beliefs are endorsed by the judges, they do not have the status of truth.

If truth is construed as endorsement, and assertions attain the status of truth by persuading a community rather than reflecting a preexistent domain or state of affairs, then different communities as well as "professions" within the communities are able to generate truths in their various discourses. Consequently, people in disciplines as diverse as meteorology and poetry are able to articulate "truths," in that they are able to persuade their respective audiences. Thus Gorgias asserts that truths are established by meteorologists who "substituting opinion for opinion, removing one and instilling another, make incredible and unclear things appear true to the eyes of opinion" (H13). Truths are also established by rhetors engaged in forceful speeches in public debate, where one side of the argument pleases a large crowd and persuades; by philosophers engaged in "verbal wrangling . . . in which, too, a swiftness of thought is exhibited, making confidence in opinion easily changed" (H13); and by poets who are able to persuade people into a condition of unanimous and univocal agreement (H2). In each of these instances, the "truth" of an assertion or argument is determined by its *persuasiveness,* what Gorgias calls its ability "to stamp the soul as it wishes" (H13). In each of these cases, Gorgias implies that true statements are not based on an independent domain and that persuasion is not grounded on anything more secure or foundational than the contingent practices of justification accepted by a community.

Gorgias' repudiation of a referential truth that lies beyond the arguments and choices made in an agon does not mean that he affirms the ultimate reality of mere "appearance," or "Becoming"—one in which the world itself is seen as change, mutability, and multiplicity rather than as possessing a permanent structure. For Gorgias, every such assertion about the world itself is merely a position advanced in a situated agon and is hence open to rebuttal. We may well be persuaded by a meteorologist who says that the universe obeys a strict set of laws, but this merely means that we are momentarily persuaded by his account; it does not mean that the universe has those laws independently of our judgments and that rival accounts of the universe may not challenge his claim. Gorgias in effect says absolutely nothing about any putative "truth about the world in itself"; and this may be why some of his foundationalist rivals maintain that he is indifferent to, or severed from, the truth. But for Gorgias, the notion of a "truth in itself" is a meaningless phrase, analogous to saying that a trophy or award exists "in itself," independently of the people who awarded it and the person who received it. To say that an account is "really" true, or that it is "certain," merely means that a particular rhetor has presented a highly convincing case, one that we cannot, at the moment, counter with a persuasive retort. Since every claim is contestable, an absence of disagreement on an issue does not mean that people have discovered an objective truth; rather, it means that they are so convinced by one account that they simply do not question it. Gorgias is even able to speak of the "eternal," with the implicit proviso that its meaning is determined in a specific agon and that the criteria for "eternality" are those that we stipulate in each agon. Thus, in *On Not-Being*, he uses the *topos* of "the eternal and the generated" to argue against the notion of a criterial "existent"; in the *Epitaphios*, he suggests that yearning for the warriors is permanent or deathless and that the bodies of the warriors and the mourners are transient and subject to death; in *Helen*, he says that the desire for victory and honor among Helen's suitors is unconquerable; and in *Palamedes*, he says what is eternal is honor, in contrast to individuals whose bodies may be destroyed. In each case, Gorgias depicts the "eternal" as a notion that is socially constructed, a term in a commonplace, and a value of a given community.

Gorgias' antifoundationalist notion of truth as endorsement illuminates his enigmatic remarks about the "deceptiveness" of discourse. In *Helen*, he exclaims, "How many men have persuaded and do persuade how many, on how many subjects, by fabricating false speech! For if everyone, on every subject, possessed memory of the past and [understanding] of the present and foreknowledge of the future, speech would not be equally [powerful]; but as it is, neither remembering a past event nor investigating a present one nor prophesying a future one is easy, so that on most subjects most men make belief their mind's advisor" (H11). In this assertion Gorgias does not suggest, as the subjectivist camp contends, that all language is inherently deceptive because it is severed from objective truth by an unfathomable gulf and operates in its own autonomous domain. Nor does he imply that some discourse is deceptive because it does not accurately represent the determinate facts of the physical world. Instead, Gorgias argues that the deceptiveness of discourse arises when we forget that we are always engaged in rhetorical games.

In Gorgias' construal, there is no objective, nonsituated, or nonrhetorical way of seeing "things as they really are," because every viewpoint is made possible only within the conventions of a particular agon. Every account is always a partial and partisan assertion by a rhetor engaged in a specific agon. In some cases, clever rhetors are able to conceal their own situatedness and, consequently, the rhetoricity of their texts. In so doing, they effectively efface themselves before what appears to be an objective truth, presenting their partisan rendering as if it were a neutral account of "the way things really are," and in this respect they deceive their unwitting audiences. But as members of the audience, this does not mean that we must necessarily be deceived by clever rhetors; it only means that we may be deceived if we forget that there will always be alternative ways of construing the situation and that we, as situated members of the community, ultimately decide what is true.

Part Two
Community

3

Beyond Spontaneity and Duty

> The ethic, aesthetic and rhetoric of Gorgias are all based on *kairos*.
>
> Mario Untersteiner, *The Sophists*
>
> [The sophistic movement] shows the same typical traits as the liberal thought of the eighteenth and nineteenth centuries: the same individualism, the same humanitarianism, the same secularism, the same confident arraignment of tradition at the bar of reason.
>
> E. R. Dodds,
> *The Ancient Concept of Progress and Other Essays on Greek Literature and Belief*

I have argued that Gorgias is an antifoundationalist who construes discourse as a repertoire of maneuvers or tropes, who depicts inquiry as debates between rhetors in an array of socially sanctioned agons, and who characterizes "truth" as an accolade awarded by a community to those accounts they find persuasive. I now turn to Gorgias' ethical and political views. In this chapter I examine the subjectivist characterization of Gorgias advanced by Race and Untersteiner that Gorgias is a romantic and an irrationalist who urges people to escape the tyranny of reason or *logos*, pursue a life of passionate intensity, and unite with others in euphoric Dionysian festivals. I then discuss the empiricist reading of Gorgian ethics advanced by Grote, Dodds, and Enos, which depicts Gorgias as a liberal "universalist" who grounds moral behavior on universal moral laws accessible to reason and who advocates egalitarian democracy as the political embodiment of morality. I argue that both of these accounts of Gorgias' ethical and political views are contradicted by many of his remarks. In chapter 4 I argue that Gorgias articulates a conventionalist and agonistic model of ethics and politics that is consistent with his antifoundationalist hermeneutics.

Rejecting Hedonism

Before examining the subjectivist and empiricist accounts, we may note that both camps reject the notion that Gorgias is a hedonist who maintains that a person is justified in performing any action that enables him to gratify his own desire for pleasure. This reading is suggested by some of Gorgias' early critics, such as Aristophanes, who depicts Gorgias as a "rascal," a "sycophant," and a "barbarian." Specifically, Aristophanes writes that

> There is in Phanae by the
> Waterclock a rascally race
> Of those who live by their tongues,

> Who reap and sow
> And gather in and play the sycophant
> With tongues. They are
> Barbarians by birth,
> Gorgiases and Philips
>
> (A5a, *Birds* 1694ff.).

Aristophanes' depiction is quite harsh, for "rascal" (*panourgos*) denotes a person who is willing to use any means to achieve his ends; a sycophant, in fifth-century Athens, is a person who criminally abuses the courts by bringing suits for his own personal gain rather than for a just cause;[1] and a "barbarian," in Aristophanes' depiction, typically embodies the antithesis of the "Greek" intellectual and moral virtues of wisdom, moderation, justice, and courage.

Isocrates is somewhat less critical of Gorgias, though he also chastises him for his selfishness, suggesting that that he is more concerned with earning money than with serving a particular polis or Greece as a whole. Isocrates thus remarks that among the Sophists, "Gorgias of Leontini acquired the most money . . . since he did not inhabit any one city steadily, not spending money for public benefits nor being required to pay a tax, moreover neither marrying a wife nor begetting children but being free of this continual and most expensive demand" (*Antidosis* 15, 155–6). Indifferent to the social good, reluctant to live in any one city for an extended period of time lest he be required to pay taxes, Gorgias lives the life of a selfish wanderer, one of the "teachers who do not scruple to vaunt their powers with utter disregard of the truth," for he believes that "those who choose a life of careless indolence (*alazoneuesthai*) are better advised than those who devote themselves to serious study" (*Sophists* 13.2).

Echoing these criticisms, Plato also suggests that Gorgias' principal concern is mercenary, quipping that by "giving exhibitions and associating with the young, [Gorgias] earned and received a great deal of money from this city" (*Greater Hippias* 282bc). Plato also observes that Gorgias is not concerned with imparting virtue to his students (Meno 95c); he suggests that Gorgias, like his hedonistic student Philebus, believes that pleasure is the highest good; and he implies that Gorgias is willing to manipulate others in order to gratify his own hedonistic desires, given that he professes an art of rhetoric by which "all things are willingly but not forcibly made slaves" (*Philebus* 58a).

Several modern scholars also characterize Gorgias as a hedonistic opportunist. Arthur Adkins remarks that Gorgias' defense of Helen is morally suspect, for such augments "are intended to excuse, and which could be applied, so far as I can see, *to any misdeed whatsoever*" (1983, 122). And Martha Nussbaum suggests that Gorgias is a selfish opportunist who is concerned only with his "fame and fortune"

(1990, 220). But perhaps the most extensive characterization of Gorgias as a hedonist is mounted by E. M. Cope, who suggests that Gorgias nourishes and endorses the views expressed by Callicles in Plato's *Gorgias*. For Cope, Gorgias is a hedonist who holds that the highest good is the satisfaction of subjective appetites or desires and that conventional rules of "morality" are undesirable constraints on instinctive drives. Cope argues that Calliclean egoistic hedonism is the logical consequence of Gorgias' arguments in *On Not-Being* that nothing exists, for his repudiation of external reality has as its consequence the repudiation of all objective ethical rules. Cope denounces all the Sophists as egoists who are culpable of subverting objective moral principles, for they disseminate "principles of reasoning the tendency, though not the objects, of which was to undermine the foundation of man's religious, moral, social and philosophical creed" (1854, 149). But he condemns Gorgias as particularly reprehensible, for Gorgias' nihilism undermines the objective criteria needed for ethical judgment and thereby encourages "falsehood and fraud" (154). For "as in the one case all absolute and general truth is denied, so in the other the obligation of existing laws and customs is attacked: and on the same ground, viz. that they are *subjective* and therefore change with the caprice of the *subject*" (180; emphasis added). Insofar as he rejects a foundational moral law, Gorgias subverts morality; for by "allowing *each individual* to set up for himself his own standard of right and wrong, [the Sophist] virtually abrogates all universal principles to which mankind appeal" (156; emphasis added). With his sophistic colleagues, Gorgias is guilty of "quackery and ostentation, fallacious reasoning for the purpose of deception, vast pretensions and slender performance in their profession of teaching, to which Plato adds philosophical and practical principles subversive of public and private morality" (169).

While he acknowledges that Gorgias does not defend hedonism in the *Gorgias*, Cope suggests that Gorgias condones Callicles' version of it. In defending hedonism, Callicles distinguishes between nature (*phusis*) and convention (*nomos*). The natural motivation of each person is to satisfy his nonrational appetites such as thirst, hunger, and sex. The satisfaction of these drives, which is experienced as pleasure, becomes the ultimate "good." The natural good is thus "satisfying each appetite in turn with what it desires" (1854, 492a), and the happy or flourishing life is one of "luxury and licentiousness and liberty" (492c). To achieve these ends, a person requires power or force; hence the desires, "if they have the support of force, are virtue and happiness." Virtue for Callicles is the power to overcome all restraints, for they prevent one from attaining one's truest ends. In nature, there are no rules that restrict one's attempts to achieve this end; the only limitation is power. Any means are justified by these ends, and rather than placing constraints on one's drive for power, the "right" is seen as any act that serves to increase one's pleasure.

Hence, each person strives to be as powerful as possible so as to be able to satisfy his own drives. In seeking to satisfy his drives, the egoist may need the assistance of others who are skilled in attaining goods, and he will have to resist those people who attempt to obstruct him. Presumably, he may often encounter resistance from others, especially if he deprives them from attaining scarce resources; in nature, life is an ongoing struggle. He must thus be able to manipulate other people, both to increase his own power to satisfy his selfish ends and to prevent others from restricting his own strivings. Life is always a struggle between people and a striving to satisfy one's desires. Callicles justifies this control of others as "natural," for he considers it natural for the strong to rule over the weak. Thus he asserts that nature "proclaims the fact that it is right for the better to have advantage of the worse, and the abler of the feebler." This is the case not only in the "animal world, but in the states and races, collectively, of men—that right has been decided to consist in the sway and advantage of the stronger over the weaker. For by what manner of right did Xerxes march against Greece, or his father against Scythia? . . . Why, surely these men follow nature—the nature of right—in acting thus" (483de).

While in nature Callicles' strong beast may rely primarily on physical force to overpower others, in society he requires another sort of power. For in society the weak band together to constrain the strong and thereby establish morality and laws, unnatural "conventions" designed to prevent the strong from dominating them. The weak agree to restrict their own natural drives rather than experience the inevitable defeat they would face were they to compete with the strong. In order to enforce their conventions, the weak instill the emotion of shame in people so that they heed conventional restraints; and in so doing, they "disguise their own impotence, and are so good as to tell us that licentiousness is disgraceful, thus enslaving—as I remarked before—the better type of mankind; and being unable themselves to procure achievement of their pleasures they praise temperance and justice by reason of their own unmanliness" (*Gorgias* 492ab). Those who enact laws are weak, and "it is with a view to themselves and their own interest that they make their laws and distribute their praises and censures; and to terrorize the stronger sort of folk who are able to get an advantage, and to prevent them from getting one over them, they tell them that such aggrandizement is foul and unjust, and that wrongdoing is just this endeavor to get the advantage of one's neighbors" (*Gorgias* 483bc). While in nature it is "right for the better to have advantage of the worse, and the abler of the feebler," in society the conventions dictate that such actions are unjust. And this, according to Callicles, is why by convention "it is termed unjust and foul to aim at an advantage over the majority, and why they call it wrongdoing" (*Gorgias* 483cd).

If the superior individual is to remain strong in a society in which conventional morality and law prevail, he requires the power of deception, whereby he overpowers others by pretending to accept their "conventional" beliefs and laws. Only then will he be able to manipulate them and become their master. Since people are moved by verbal persuasion, the strong man requires a mastery of rhetoric, the art of verbal deception or "flattery," whereby he persuades others by pleasing them. A hedonist himself, the strong man sees all people as ultimately motivated by the drive for pleasure; and to control them, he attempts to convince them that in giving him power over them, he will render their own lives more pleasurable. He will not try to improve or "correct" their hedonistic drives; instead, he will condone and foster those drives, using them for his own gain. In effect, he will use rhetoric to transform others into "willing slaves." Through his mastery of rhetoric, the Calliclean egoist thus becomes a "natural" man in a social setting, manipulating others to become his slaves.

How convincing is Cope's notion that Gorgias endorses Calliclean hedonism? I suggest that it is not persuasive at all, for unlike Callicles, Gorgias sharply repudiates hedonism in several of his works. He personally repudiates hedonism in his own life, attributing his health and longevity to "never doing anything for the sake of pleasure" (A11); and he presents several arguments against hedonism in *Helen, Palamedes,* and the *Epitaphios*. In each of these works, Gorgias depicts human objectives or goals as nonselfish and nonhedonistic; indeed, the goals he praises are those of helping others and revering one's parents, family, country, and gods. In the *Epitaphios,* Gorgias praises the warriors for their social conscience and sense of justice. Rather than acting out of personal gain or selfish gratification, they give their lives for the sake of the city; and in so doing, they exhibit such other-directed virtues as reverence, respect, justice, and loyalty. Not only do they give "help to those unjustly afflicted and punishment to those unjustly flourishing," but they are

> reverent to the gods by means of justice,
> respectful to parents by means of care,
> just to fellow citizens by equality,
> loyal to friends by faithfulness
> (E21–24)

Rather than being motivated by selfish desires, the warriors' principal goals are to help others and to protect their city against enemies to the extent of sacrificing their lives for others. Gorgias also depicts the warrior Palamedes as possessing virtues that are other-directed rather than egoistic. He has Palamedes condemn the traitor as "the enemy of all: the laws, justice, the gods, the bulk of mankind. For he contravenes the law, negates justice, destroys the masses, and dishonors what is holy" (P17). And he defends himself on the grounds that "in every respect from beginning to end my past life has been blameless, free from all blame" (P29). Palamedes further asserts, "I am not only blameless but also a great benefactor of you and the Greeks and all mankind, not only of those now alive but [also] of those to come. . . . I am inoffensive to the older, not unhelpful of the younger, not envious of the fortunate, but merciful to the unfortunate; not heedless of poverty nor valuing wealth ahead of virtue, but virtue ahead of wealth; neither useless in council nor lazy in war, doing what is assigned to me, obeying those in command" (P30–32). Palamedes does assert that people are motivated by a desire for gain; but he contends that the "gain" he seeks is not the satisfaction of his own egoistic desires but rather that of assisting his countrymen, honoring his parents, and serving his country in war.

Gorgias also repudiates the view that a person may use any means to gratify his desires, repeatedly emphasizing the importance of constraining violence. In the *Epitaphios,* he asserts that the most divine and common law is that of doing one's *duty,* claiming that the warriors

> attained an excellence which is divine and a mortality which is human . . . believing that the most godlike and universal law was this:
> in time of duty dutifully to speak and to leave unspoken, to act [and to leave undone].
>
> (E5–9)

Gorgias praises the warriors for behaving justly, defending their city, helping those who are "unfairly unfortunate," and punishing those who are "unjustly flourishing." In *Helen,* he characterizes his own objective as the attainment of justice, defending a person whom he claims has been unjustly impugned. He argues that if Paris physically raped Helen, he deserves to be condemned: "If she was seized by force and illegally assaulted and unjustly insulted, it is clear that the assailant as insulter did the wrong and the assailed as insulted suffered wrongly. It is right for the Barbarian who laid barbarous hands on her by word and law and decree to meet with blame in word, disenfranchisement in law, and punishment in deed, while she who was seized and deprived of her country and bereft of her friends, how should she not be pitied rather than pilloried? He did dread deeds, she suffered them. Her it is just to pity, him to hate" (H7).

Gorgias goes even further in his critique of using unjust means to attain one's ends, broadening the notion of violence to include deceptive speech. He thus contends that if Paris used speech to manipulate Helen, he ought to be condemned as engaging in violence. Rather than condoning violence or suggesting that no action is subject to ethical praise or condemnation, Gorgias argues that some actions deserve blame, dishonor, and punishment, while others merit praise or reward. And in *Palamedes,* Gorgias repeatedly emphasizes the importance of justice. He observes that he invented written laws, the guardians of justice (P30); he condemns treason as an act that "contravenes the law and negates justice" (P17); he reminds the judges that "by seeming unjust" they will acquire a reputation that is worse than death (P35); and he concludes that "if you give an unjust verdict, you will make a mistake, not only in regard to me and my parents, but by your action you will make yourselves responsible for a dreadful, godless, unjust, unlawful deed, having killed a man who is your fellow soldier, useful to you, a benefactor of Greece, Greeks killing Greek, though convicting him of no clear injustice nor credible fault" (P37).

THE ETHICS OF LIBERATION

As an alternative to the hedonistic reading, several members of the subjectivist school characterize Gorgias as a "romanticist" or "irrationalist" who urges us to liberate ourselves from the tyranny of reason or *logos*. This account is grounded in the view that Gorgias sees discourse or *logos* as inherently deceptive and confining insofar as it purports to describe things as they really are. The romantic Gorgias thus characterizes *logos* as a "powerful lord" or dynast (*dunastes megas*) (H8) which, in Derrida's terms, is profoundly "violent" in its infiltration into the human psyche (1981, 115). An imperious despot, *logos* dictates what we are able to do as well as what we are able to say and think. In Cascardi's terms, Gorgias maintains that *logos* confines us within a "virtual prison-house," wherein "our thoughts and our existence, our mind as much as our being" is trapped within an "obstinate, intransigent cellophane margin: we are caught in the ambiguity of not knowing being from non-being because of the opaque gossamer of words" (1983, 220). The prison-house of *logos* is one in which every word is a lie and every attempt to articulate a truth is self-deception. In many instances, the coercive power of *logos* is overt and explicit. As Gorgias delineates in *Helen,* many people are "enchanted" by the intonations of magicians, moved to tears by poets, bound by the words of sorcerers because they believe in the power of their binding spells. And Helen herself is manipulated by Paris's explicit words. Palamedes also is legally confined because of explicit words, namely the persuasive accusations of treason made against him by Odysseus. In each of these instances, persuasive speech has the same effect as coercion or force; and, as Gorgias observes, "persuasion, though not having an appearance of compulsion, has the same power (H12).

But Gorgias also suggests that *logos* may operate covertly as well as overtly; we are not aware that we are puppets manipulated by its invisible and insidious strings. Gorgias thus asserts that *logos* is a power "which by means of the finest and most invisible body effects the divinest works" (H8). It is an irresistible power that insinuates itself into our psyche and stamps or impresses itself as it wishes. When it functions covertly, *logos* deceives us by leading us to erroneously believe that it liberates us and that insofar as we heed it, we are thereby free. Under the influence of the crafty and well-crafted *logos,* "*all things are willingly but not forcibly made slaves*" (A26; emphasis added). *Logos* makes us "willing slaves" in the sense that we are led, with self-deceived philosophers like Plato, to believe that if we heed the dictates of reason we will thereby become in touch with our truest selves and will be able to liberate ourselves from our "irrational" drives and other modes of contingency that prevent us from being truly moral and who we "really are." We are deceived into believing that we must heed the dictates of reason in order to become free; while in reality, those dictates are the strings that constrain us. Although *logos* appears to enable us to make "free" choices, it in fact restricts and controls our choices. Since *logos* imposes its deceptions upon its users, it follows that one is never able to "escape" its illusions and the choices of action it permits. Insofar as we accept the dictates of reason, we allow *logos* to predetermine what we are able to perceive and articulate as free choices. For *logos* imposes itself upon the psyche through its established forms, and it thereby prescribes what we are able to see and what we accept as rational or irrational. In this respect, we do not accept an argument because it is "rational"; rather, we accept certain positions as rational because we are already imprisoned by the protocols of the dominant *logos*.

An apparatus of confinement as well as deception, the "voice of reason" silences its opposition, enslaving us by presenting itself as the very criterion by which we make any decision. As "logic," it presents itself as the highest court, the impartial judge whom we gladly obey. We fail to see that we accept this *logos* because we are already enslaved by it and by its covert repression of alternative *logoi* and the possible modes of perception they may permit. For if we accept certain patterns of speaking, we deceive ourselves into accepting these patterns as representing reality. Because we accept certain conventional figures of speech as "literal," we fail to see that our "literal" truths are illusory fabrications. Stated another way, insofar as we accept and use the *topoi*, or "commonplaces," of the dominant discourse, we erroneously believe that we are able to discern truths that are in fact commonplace. Insofar as we accept certain privileged protocols of argument as "valid," we erroneously believe that the conclusions of our arguments provide an objective or external criterion for assessing the validity of those very arguments. We thus grant *logos* the power to judge as well as regulate what we are able to see and say, willingly assenting to its restrictions and confinements. And while we permit *logos* to determine our external reality, we also permit it to shape our internal character. We believe that to be a moral individual, to have "character," is to adhere to *principles*, to be unbending in our attachment to the moral dictates of reason. We thereby fail to see that what we consider our deepest, most moral self is in fact a product of the persuasive tropes of *logos*, the chains of the dominant rhetoric (H15). In its surreptitious insinuations, its power to stamp our psyches as it wishes, the dominant *logos* becomes a "secret police."

But what will our lives be like if we overcome the deceptions and constraints of *logos*? Gorgias offers several models of romantic, subjectivist heroes who eschew reason and follow their passions, living intensely and authentically. For Mario Untersteiner (1954), Gorgias' hero is an "irrationalist" in his ethical choices. Untersteiner depicts Gorgias as positing a tragic gulf or abyss between the nonrational chaos of the universe and the deceptive "rational" order that is fabricated in rational discourse. This tragic gulf has profound ethical consequences, for it renders every ethical choice ultimately irrational and makes human life, wherein we must often choose between incompatible or antithetical ends, potentially tragic. Given the inescapable antithesis between the rationally ordered world of *logos* and the chaos of the universe, we encounter an unbridgeable epistemological and ethical gulf between ourselves and an indifferent universe. We cannot rely on reason to help us decide what to do in a crisis when we are faced with incompatible courses of action, for while reason may provide guidance in taking means to achieve an end, it can never provide guidance in choosing which of two (or more) incompatible ends to pursue. Untersteiner identifies a paradigmatic instance of Gorgias' irrationalist morality in his account of the warriors in the *Epitaphios,* who, in facing death, must decide between two antithetical but morally justifiable actions, that of "the duty to respect the divine sanctity of life and that of fulfilling a divine end by the preservation of the polis" (1954, 177). Since there is no universal law that reconciles these antithetical moral directives, the warrior must decide irrationally, on the basis of his own subjective will. Indeed, Untersteiner reads Gorgias as implying that the sole universal or "divine" law is itself inescapably "irrational," one that "corresponds to the irrational *kairos*" wherein any course of action is "irrationally endowed with power by a will of the individual who decides" (178–79). Just as every act of cognition requires a nonrational, subjective intuition into the tragic antithesis between the domains of the rational and the irrational, so every moral choice requires a subjective, irrational choice to the extent that "the virtues also are irrational" (181). The consequence is that in rejecting universal moral law, Gorgias renders morality "relative" to the irrational choice of the individual (182); and "in the face of all idealistic dogmatism he stands for the inner turmoil of a tragic decision which gives so profound a meaning to life" (182). Gorgias is thus more courageous than the conventional moralist, insisting that every moral choice must be made by an individual on the basis of his own will. Virtue, for the irrationalist Gorgias, is the courage to make moral choices without the guidance of reason.

Each of Gorgias' romantic heroes strives to overcome the limits of reason, motivated by an intense passion that enables them to overcome their limits. The hero must continually fight against conventional-minded people who do not understand him and who fear that his great creations will disturb their secure social and intellectual universe. By eschewing the limits of *logos,* the hero becomes godlike, a creative genius who creates his own rules and lives by them. Gorgias thus extols the Athenian warriors who repudiate the constraints of everyday morality and do what they deem fitting in each moment. Rather than heeding written laws, the warrior acts from his own personal dictates; and in doing what he considers "fitting," he reenacts the "most divine and universal" law (E11). The warrior displays hubris (E24), rising above the constraints imposed on ordinary mortals and becoming godlike in his striving. The warrior is familiar with the innate passions of Ares (*emphutos areos*), the frenzy and "fire of battle in the blood" (E31), and with the intensities of "civilized erotics" as well (E32).

In Untersteiner's terms, Gorgias' warrior is a tragic hero who strives to liberate himself from the constraints imposed by reason and who recognizes that mere rational analysis can never lead to an authentic moral choice, that such a choice requires an "irrational" act of will. The heroic warrior sees that reason alone is never the instrument of morality, for it confines him to the choices made available by conventional, logical thought. The excellence of the warrior raises him above the level of ordinary men, who envy him; and it leads him to provoke the anger or nemesis of the gods, the emotion arising from a challenge to their privilege. For the warriors display hubris and thus appear "insolent" when they consider it needed. For Gorgias this hubris is warranted, and he praises the warrior who acts with hubris when he wishes to do so (E24). The warrior abandons the secure everyday life and embraces a life of danger, one in which he is continually challenged and in which he overcomes his limitations. He strives for excellence, and his virtue is one of overcoming of conventional limits. His courage is divine, that of the god Ares, and he engages in continual warfare or striving. In this respect, the warrior exhibits the same excellence that Gorgias praises in Aeschylus' *Seven against Thebes,* a drama he says is "filled with Ares" (B24).

If he extols the warriors for being filled with Ares, the romantic Gorgias applauds Helen for embodying the passions of her patroness Aphrodite, overcoming the constraints of reason and heeding her erotic desires. Helen is motivated by erotic passion, as are her motivated suitors; for as Gorgias observes, "On many did she work the greatest passions of love, and by her one body she brought together many bodies of men" (H4). In his praise of Helen, Gorgias lauds her lust for Paris and for a more passionate life than she is permitted under the stultifying "rational" laws of Sparta and the conventional constraints of its phallocratic code. Gorgias says that *eros* is "divine," a power that moves gods as well as humans. He thus asks, "If love, a god, prevails over the divine power of the gods, how could a lesser one be able to reject and refuse it?" (H19). Exhibiting her divinity, Helen acts on the promptings of her erotic impulses and repudiates the civilization of Sparta for the exotic intensity of barbaric Troy. As William Race (1989) points out, Gorgias' exaltation of Helen embraces a life of erotic euphoria and orgasmic ecstasy. Rather than heeding the repressive mores or conventions of the community, Gorgias thus encourages people to liberate themselves by heeding their deepest desires. In this context, Gorgias draws upon the passionate expressions of the lyric poet Sappho, who also extols Helen of Troy for her choice of passionate love over rational convention. Race cites Sappho's love poem to Anactoria (Fragment 16) as a source of Gorgias' views:

> Some say cavalry and others claim
> infantry or a fleet of long oars
> is the supreme sight on the black earth.
> I say it is
> the one you love. And easily proved.
> didn't Helen, who far surpassed all
> mortals in beauty, desert the best
> of men, her king,
> and sail off to Troy and forget
> her dear daughter and her dear parents! Merely
> Aphrodite's gaze made her readily bend
> and led her far
> from her path.[2]

Sappho condones Helen's eloping with Paris and implies that she is justified for acting on her passions and rejecting conventional morality. Rather than caring for her child, respecting her parents, and remaining faithful to her husband or loyal to Greece, Helen "places primary emphasis on an individual's subjective feelings" (Race 1989, 16). Moreover, by declaring that the most beautiful thing is not the city's cavalry, infantry, or navy but whatever an *individual* loves, Sappho implies that a person does not love what is inherently beautiful, but that the subjective feeling of love renders the object beautiful.[3]

Sappho's erotic ethic foreshadows Gorgias' own encomium of Helen, for "by espousing the primacy of subjective feeling, [she] advances an argument that anticipates sophistic reasoning" (Race 1987, 16). Specifically, "by adducing the example of Helen to prove that one's perception and judgments are determined by *eros*, Sappho anticipates the sophistic defense of Helen by Gorgias" (18). Gorgias, in this construal, uses the example of Helen to support his view that we should act upon our inner erotic drive and escape the tyrannical constraints imposed upon us by a "rationally" ordered culture. Sappho's and Gorgias' subjectivist defenses of Helen contrast sharply with the conventional Greek critique of Helen, one that chastises Helen for betraying her husband, Menelaus, and Greece as a whole. This tradition, embodied in the Homeric epics, the lyrical poetry of Alkaios, and the tragedies of Aeschylus and Euripides, is "essentially ethical and political; it views life in terms of the well-being of the family, army and polis. Sappho, on the other hand, presents a radically divergent view. For her the private preference of the individual takes precedence over the concerns of family or state" (23). Race further characterizes the distinction between the "ethical and political" tradition of Homer and Aeschylus and the "romantic" or subjectivist tradition of Sappho and Gorgias as analogous to the distinction that Kierkegaard draws between the "ethical" and "aesthetic" ways of living. Citing Alasdair MacIntyre's account of this distinction, Race notes that "at the heart of the aesthetic way of life, as Kierkegaard characterizes it, is the attempt to lose the self in the *immediacy of present experience*. The paradigm of aesthetic expression is the romantic lover who is immersed in his own passion. By contrast the paradigm of the ethical is marriage, a state of commitment and obligation through time, in which the present is bound by the past and to the future. Each of the two ways of life is informed by different concepts, incompatible attitudes, rival premises" (MacIntyre 39, emphasis added). In this construal, Sappho and Gorgias implicitly praise Helen for immersing herself in the immediate present and for acting on the basis of subjective desire.

If he praises the warriors for exhibiting the excellence of Ares and applauds Helen for pursuing the passions of Aphrodite, Gorgias exalts a third romantic hero, a figure who is frequently associated with the Titan Prometheus, the creative artist Palamedes.[4] Palamedes, the creative genius whose name means 'ancient *metis*,' is akin to Prometheus, whose name, from *pro-metis*, means knowledge of the future, or foresight.[5] A passionate warrior, Palamedes combines the virtues of Ares and Aphrodite in his life of love and strife; a creative genius whose creations include the alphabet and an array of crafts, Palamedes is a titanic figure who foreshadows the European Faust in his pursuit of knowledge. He is associated with the mysterious intelligence of Asia, in particular the figure of Kadmos the Phoenician, the "Asiatic" inventor of the alphabet. The brilliant Palamedes sees through the pathetic ruse of Odysseus, who feigns madness in order to avoid participation in the Trojan War; and in so doing, Palamedes provokes the resentment of Odysseus, the Greek "everyman," who falsely accuses him of betraying the Greeks to the "barbarian" Trojans. Palamedes arouses the ire of common men like Odysseus just as the heroic warriors of the *Epitaphios* arouse the envy of common men who resent their divine excellence and just as Helen arouses a univocal and unanimous condemnation by the chorus of poets who are unable to free themselves from the constraints of convention.

Gorgias' notion that *logos* is inescapably repressive as well as deceptive has profound political implications. First, he suggests that if every use of *logos* is repressive, then every utterance is always "political" in the sense of being an attempt by a speaker to control or dominate others in a community. Just as the individual rhetors like Paris are able to dominate individuals like Helen, so persuasive rhetors are able to enslave entire groups of people through their discourse; and this discourse imposes itself upon people as it wishes (H13). Powerful individuals or groups who control *logos*, therefore, are able to control the people in the community. Indeed, Gorgias characterizes *logos* with a political metaphor, saying that it is a great dynast, or *dunastes megas* (H8). There is no aspect of life that is isolated from politics. Gorgias further suggests that the only options available to people are to control or be controlled, to be a master or a slave; and he observes that nobody would "choose slavery instead of sovereignty, the worst instead of the best" (P14). Moreover, insofar as every use of *logos* is inescapably repressive, every government is inescapably tyrannical in its enforcement of a particular "rational" order, regardless of what that order may be. This implies that every government is equally repressive, whether it is a democracy, aristocracy, monarchy, or tyranny. Every polis, in this context, is an arrangement of force. Gorgias conflates all governments, in part because he sees persuasion as being as repressive as physical force and every government as irreducibly tyrannical, whether it relies on physical force or persuasive speech to achieve its ends. Insofar as people in a democracy like Athens accept their *logos* without question and accept the deceptive illusions that it permits them to fabricate as undeniably "real," they thereby allow the despotic *logos* to control their lives as much as the people living under a tyranny. And even though people in a democracy may be persuaded that their government is acceptable, this does not change the fact that it is oppressing them as much as a tyranny would repress them. Their consent to the laws only means that they are deceived into thinking that they are not being oppressed. In every state *logos* is repressive, and its laws restrict individual freedom.

In the face of political oppression, Gorgias states that his goal is *liberation*. As he remarks to Socrates, his rhetoric is designed to liberate and empower people (*Gorgias* 452d). Unlike Protagoras, who maintains that people should be governed by rational laws, Gorgias vehemently repudiates the authority of every government. For Gorgias suggests that since every form of government is equally oppressive, we are only able to become free by rebelling against the established order and its repressive laws. The heroes that Gorgias extols are people who rebel and in doing so risk reprisals. He praises the warriors in the *Epitaphios* who reject the written laws of the polis for their own free choices, who reject the laws of propriety by displaying hubris, and who become godlike in their frenzied life of warfare. And Gorgias applauds Helen for repudiating the conventions of Sparta and for incurring the universal condemnation of others in the Greek community.

Another Gorgian hero is Daedalus, the "flying man" of *On Not-Being*, who rebels against the tyrant Minos of Crete, escapes by fashioning his own wings, and lands in Sicily, whereupon he continues to invent and to provide the Sicilians with the fruits of his creations. Gorgias' heroes and heroines are always rebels, repudiating the conventions and laws of their community and seeking a life of freedom and intensity. A human incarnation of the great man is Empedocles, Gorgias' teacher in Acragus. Like Prometheus, Palamedes, and Daedalus, he is a titanic individual, a great physician and magician, able to direct the forces of nature; but he is also a man who helps others in the community and is an ardent democrat to boot. The hero's rebelliousness, his hubristic flaunting of convention, may have dire consequences. For most people resent the soaring painted bird, the extraordinary beauty and elegance of Gorgias' oratory, and they attempt to destroy it through ridicule, abuse, or force. So Palamedes, maligned and misunderstood, is executed; Prometheus is punished by Zeus, chained to a rock with a bird pecking his liver. And Gorgias himself is assaulted and misunderstood.

In his praise of heroes and heroines who repudiate the conventions of the community, Gorgias may seem to promote anarchy. As such, he may seem to warrant the condemnation by Thucydides' Alcibiades that his Sicily is one in which people have no allegiance to any one city and the condemnation by Isocrates that he is a nomadic *alazon* without obligations to any city. For Gorgias' romantic hero seems condemned to a life of solitary self-creation and restless seeking, a nomad who withdraws from the politics and conventions of every city. As a titanic individualist, Gorgias repudiates all social constraints, the "moral" limitations imposed upon people who live ordinary lives; and he chooses instead the life of a wanderer, an *alazon*, who travels from city to city in pursuit of whatever he desires. The romantic would become a wanderer, freeing himself from obligations to any city. But if Gorgias is indeed a nomadic *alazon*, it is not because he is a dishonest charlatan; on the contrary it is because he is all too honest, absolutely true to himself, and indifferent to the everyday chatter of the madding crowd. A romantic soul unwilling to settle for the conventional, an exile whose Sicilian home has been destroyed, Gorgias wanders restlessly through Greece in pursuit of what he loves.

A portrait of Gorgias that was known to the ancients may support this romantic image. Plutarch reports that the tomb of Isocrates portrays Gorgias as gazing at an astronomical globe (A17). Perhaps in his gaze, Gorgias again anticipates Shelley, who sees himself as a wanderer who gazes on the earth. In his fragment "To the Moon," Shelley poses a rhetorical question that may be asked of Gorgias as well as of himself:

> Art thou pale for weariness
> Of climbing heaven and gazing on the earth,
> Wandering companionless
> Among the stars that have a different birth,
> And ever changing, like a joyless eye
> That finds no object worth its constancy?

But rather than anarchy, the romantic Gorgias promotes another form of community, the euphoric and rapturous *festival*. His "conspicuous" participation in the festivals, where he appears to have performed regularly, appears scandalous to his classical critics. To Plato, Gorgias' oratory itself is a "feast" of words akin to the banquets of decadent Sicilian orgies. For Gorgias, the festival is not merely a convenient venue for performance; it is integral to his politics of euphoria, his rhetoric of transgression, and his epistemology of passion. At the festival, intoxicated participants mingle with others in a Dionysian intensity, experience the frenzy of dithyrambic music, and repudiate conventional morality. During its rapturous intensity, they may forge a new temporary community, a nonhierarchical collectivity in which the individual is able to remove the socially approved "masks" he must wear in everyday life, expose his true self, and indulge in all modes of uncontrolled excess. The festival, in this sense, is socially liberating, promoting a revolutionary fusion of people in a politics of ecstasy.

Greek festival, like carnival, challenges the institutions and hierarchies of the polis, inverts their hierarchies, and displaces the polis with a temporary popular fusion. During festival, the conventional institutions of the courts, assembly, and military are suspended, as are the constraints of conventional morality. The festival is thus a transgression of the social order with its rules and hierarchies. Festival, like its medieval descendant, carnival, involves "parodies, travesties, humiliations, profanations, comic crownings and uncrownings"; and it thereby "denies, but it revives and renews at the same time" (Bakhtin 1984, 11). Rather than attending to the serious business of the polis, people experience a temporary joy, a euphoric laughter that is "communal, a laughter at the world," one that is directed at everyone, including oneself (12). Rejecting conventions, the festival celebrates a "temporary liberation from the prevailing truth and from the established order"; it marks a "suspension of all hierarchical rank, privileges, norms and prohibitions" (10). Festival, like carnival, is the "feast of time, the feast of becoming, change, and renewal," and it repudiates all that is "immortalized and completed" (10).

Ending the Romance

How convincing is the romantic account of Gorgias? I believe that while the account is internally coherent, it is contradicted by several of Gorgias' assertions. First, Gorgias never suggests that moral choices are "irrational." Although on occasion he suggests that we may find ourselves in a moral dilemma in which we must choose between conflicting courses of action, he nevertheless portrays most moral choices as quite rational. It may be the case that the Athenian warriors died in defending Athens, but he suggests that defending Athens is essential if people in the city are to survive. For fighting against aggressors is essential to survival, and submission to an enemy would most likely result in their own death. Significantly, he does not state that the warriors in any way doubt their commitment to Athens. Indeed, it is a commonplace in the genre of the *Epitaphios* that the warriors' devotion to the city lies at the source of their personal commitments.

Palamedes finds himself in a similar situation. Although fighting for the Greeks involves personal risk, he never doubts his commitment, and he suggests that his commitment to the community is as deep a commitment as his desire for personal safety. There is never a question that he deliberates between, say, remaining loyal to the Greeks and advancing his own personal fortune. On the contrary, he argues that betraying his fellow countrymen would negate any possible benefit that might derive from acquiring wealth. For Palamedes, personal happiness is anchored in his participation in the community.

Concerning Helen, it may be possible to construe her as being in a dilemma in which she must choose between two incompatible ends: being with the man she loves, and fulfilling her obligations to her husband and children. But Gorgias does not characterize Helen's moral situation in this way; instead, he depicts Helen as a devoted wife who was forced or deceived into accompanying Paris to Troy. Her moral choice never becomes an issue at all. If the gods decreed her deed, if Paris physically forced her or verbally deceived her, or even if she fell in love with Paris, she is not to blame because she was powerless to resist these forces: "For she went caught by the nets around her soul not by the wishes of her mind, and by the necessity of love, not by the devices of art" (H19). Significantly, Gorgias does not depict Helen as deliberating about her act at all. In this respect, he omits the defense given to Helen by Euripides in *Trojan Women,* namely that eloping with Paris is potentially a good, for it would unite them against the Trojans. Had he used this defense, he could have portrayed Helen as facing a tragic dilemma, forced to choose between fidelity and Greek unity. But in Gorgias' characterization, Helen undertakes no such deliberation and is simply coerced or deceived into abandoning her husband and family.

Second, Gorgias does not urge us to liberate ourselves from the putative constraints of reason and heed their irrational passions. On the contrary, he explicitly rejects the notion that we should act on the promptings of erotic drives. In his defense of Helen, for instance, Gorgias never suggests that Helen is warranted in acting on the impulse of *eros* and thereby putting her own romantic passions above her responsibilities to her husband and community. On the contrary, he never questions the assumption that her obligation is to remain faithful to Menelaus and to resist the seductions of Paris, and that fulfilling this obligation is what she really wants to do. If indeed she was moved by the passion of *eros,* she is only exculpable because she was unable to resist its power over her, a power analogous to that of divine intervention, rape, or deception. Rather than liberating her from any sort of prison-house, *eros* itself imposes chains upon her and prevents her from behaving in the way she really wants to behave. Overpowered by overwhelming forces, she is "caught by the nets around her soul" and unable to follow the "wishes of her mind"; she is driven by "the necessity of love, not by the devices of art" (H20). And Gorgias never suggests that *eros* is a manifestation of Helen's truest self, a natural force the heeding of which would enable her to become an authentic being. On the contrary, he depicts *eros* as an alien force, a mischievous god who deceives and manipulates gods and humans, or a noxious disease that subverts rational deliberation and free choice (H20). Nor does Gorgias suggest that *eros* is a universal drive. It plays little if any part in motivating Palamedes, for example, who is motivated more by intellectual curiosity and honor than romantic passion. And in the *Epitaphios,* Gorgias remarks that while the warriors are not unfamiliar with *eros,* they constrain their passions with a sense of legitimacy, pursuing what Gorgias calls "legitimate love" (*nomimon eroton*) (E19).

Finally, the subjectivist account of Gorgias' political views is belied by his own activities as orator and educator. The fact that he was chosen to serve as ambassador of his native city of Leontini suggests that Gorgias was highly respected by his fellow citizens and that he was active in the politics of his city. Even his critic Plato acknowledges that Gorgias was esteemed as an ambassador, remarking that "the eminent Gorgias, the Sophist of Leontini, came here from is home on an official mission, selected because he was the ablest statesman of his city" (*Greater Hippias* 282b). Moreover, Gorgias' reputed association with Empedocles, Korax, and Tisias, each of whom was engaged in political and legal activities, further attests to Gorgias' interest in legal and political affairs, an interest that is manifested in his "legalistic" *Palamedes* and *Helen.* Moreover, the fact that Gorgias delivered an array of political addresses at various cities such as Elis, and that he was famous for his presence at the official Panhellenic festivals at Olympia and elsewhere, suggests that he was highly respected as a political thinker.

The extant fragments of his Panhellenic texts do not indicate in any way that he encouraged orgiastic indulgence; on the contrary, they indicate that he is a serious thinker intent upon promoting harmony among the Greeks. And his activities and reputation as an educator also belie that notion that he promoted a retreat from public life. As an anecdote related by Xenophon indicates, many people considered study with Gorgias to be useful for public life. Xenophon thus observes that "Proxenus of Boetia, when he was just a lad, wanted to be a man who could do great things, and because of this desire he paid a fee to Gorgias of Leontini" (A5, Xenophon. *Anabasis* II 6, 16ff.). Rather than encouraging people to withdraw from public life in order to experience irrational kairotic moments, Gorgias promotes engagement in the various political, legal, and ceremonial practices of the culture. In this respect, Gorgias appears to be the antithesis of people like the Cynics of the fourth century, who reject social conventions and who become what Dodds calls the "beatniks" or "hippies" of antiquity (1973, 13).

Gorgian Liberalism

These inconsistencies in the subjectivist reading of Gorgias' ethical and political views may lend credence to a rival construal, one that is endorsed by several scholars in the empiricist camp. In this account, Gorgias is a "liberal" who acts out of a sense of duty rather than pursuing his subjective desires. As such, he advocates what may be called an ethical "universalism" in which moral behavior is construed as that which is in accord with universal laws accessible through the faculty of reason. Empiricists have articulated two versions of this reading, which may be labeled teleological and deontological liberalism.[6] In the teleological or "utilitarian" variant, Gorgias posits happiness as the highest good and construes what is right to be that which maximizes the good of the whole community. This view is teleological in that the good is posited as the highest goal or end of human behavior, and the right is that which maximizes the good. Grote (1869) suggests that Gorgias and other Sophists advocate a utilitarian ethics, depicting the highest good to be the happiness of the community as a whole. Repudiating the notion that Gorgias and his sophistic colleagues promote a selfish hedonism, Grote argues that he encourages ethical behavior and that if we "survey the eighty-seven years of Athenian history, between the battle of Marathon [490 BC] and the renovation of the democracy after the Thirty [403 BC], we shall see no ground for the assertion, so often made, of increased and increasing moral and political corruption. It is my belief that the people had become both morally and politically better" (178). In a similar vein, Dodds (1973) argues that Gorgias and his sophistic colleagues advocate a utilitarian ethics that anticipates the utilitarianism of Bentham and Mill; for like the "Benthamites," the Sophists made utility "their standard, and based it on radical proposals for social change" (94).

A second version of Gorgias' putative liberalism may be characterized as "deontological," from the terms *de on,* or 'duty,' wherein the objective dictates of duty (or what is right) are posited as having a higher ethical claim than the achievement of any personal "good." Using Michael Sandel's terminology, deontological ethics "opposes *teleology;* it describes a form of justification in which first principles are derived in a way that does not presuppose any final human purposes or ends, nor any determinate conception foundational the human good (1998, 3). In this construal, Gorgias is seen as positing the "right" as prior to the "good", as positing justice as the primary social virtue, and as advocating democracy as the ideal form of government wherein all people are regarded as free and equal participants in a rational, just society. Reason is not an apparatus for deceiving others and achieving selfish ends, as the egoist Callicles contends; rather, it is the faculty that enables individuals to discern the validity of arguments and to identify contradictions in any position. Moreover, reason is the moral faculty that enables individuals to discern moral laws. It is the governing faculty of the autonomous individual who discerns universal rules, wills his own obedience to them, and is thereby able to liberate himself from external contingencies and his own irrational, subjective desires. All people are equal, in this sense, for all possess reason; and all people merit freedom, which is essential for their autonomy and morality. To be a moral being, in this construal, is to be autonomous, free, equal, and rational.

As a deontological liberal, Gorgias would repudiate egoism and would characterize the truly free and autonomous individual as one who wills his own obedience to universal moral laws. In a statement that appears to affirm this view, Gorgias asserts that these laws will benefit "all mankind, not only of those now alive but [also] of those to come" (P30). In order to be moral, one must be free; for only the free individual who acts from his own autonomous choice is a free moral agent. As such, a person who is enslaved by subjective passions or external forces is one who cannot follow the universal law of duty. He thus argues that if Helen is motivated by *eros*, she is a slave, not free to act morally and hence not responsible for eloping with Paris. The autonomous moral agent must be free not only of external forces but also of his own subjective inclinations, for the autonomous individual is able to legislate his own moral laws. The ethical Athenian warrior thus adheres to the most divine and universal law, doing what is "dutiful at the time of duty" (E11). Freedom involves not only freedom from the constraints of others but freedom from one's own passions as well. Gorgias emphasizes this in *Helen*, when he depicts *eros* as a powerful force that holds Helen captive. Helen's choice is not free, for she is constrained by *eros*, which is either a god or a "human disease and an ignorance of the soul"; and through *eros* she is "caught by the nets of contingency around her soul not by the wishes of her mind, and by the necessity of love, not by the devices of art" (H19). To be free is to be free of one's own passions or inclinations; it is to be free to act rationally, according to the dictates of reason, which is the voice of the universal moral law. The free, rational, and autonomous individual is the person who, like the Athenian warrior, acts according to duty, or *de on* (E11).

In this reading, Gorgias' "deontological liberalism" has important political implications and leads him to endorse a liberal and democratic conception of society. In Sandel's succinct definition, deontological liberalism is "above all a theory about justice, and in particular about the primacy of justice among moral and political ideals. Its core thesis can be staged as follows: society, being composed of a plurality of persons, each with his own aims, interests and conceptions of the good, is best arranged when it is governed by principles that do not themselves presuppose any particular conception of the good; what justifies these regulative principles above all is not that they maximize the social welfare or otherwise promote the good, but rather that they conform to the concept of right, a moral category given prior to the good and independent of it" (1998, 1). As an egalitarian democrat,

Gorgias would promote a society in which free individuals contract with others to enact principles of justice embodied in just laws. In a democracy, autonomous individuals freely enact laws that are what Palamedes calls the "guardians of justice" (P30), and they willingly obey the laws even when they are contrary to their own personal happiness. He would see justice as the principle concern for society, for just as the right is prior to the good for individuals, so justice is prior to individual happiness at the community level. The principles of justice treat people as free, equal, and autonomous agents who through reason apprehend the moral law and who freely act in accord with it. Since all people possess reason, every person merits equal consideration as speaker and member of an audience; consequently, Gorgias promotes a democratic community in which people are "just to fellow citizens by equality" (E23, Smith). As a democrat, Gorgias would oppose tyrannies such as that of Syracuse, while promoting democratic cities such as Leontini and Athens.

In this vein, Enos argues that Gorgias is a liberal whose epistemology and theory of rhetoric are integrally related to his commitment to democracy. Noting that Gorgias' rhetoric emerged as a means of operating in democratic Leontini and that it served him in defending Leontini in Athens against its adversary Syracuse, Enos suggests that Gorgias' rhetoric is firmly grounded in his commitment to the principles of liberal democracy. Enos observes that "a period of about two generations—generations spanning the lives of Corax, Tisias and Gorgias—witnessed rhetoric's emergence as a discipline within a political climate of democracy in Syracuse and Leontini" (1992, 12). In this climate, democratic Leontini formed an alliance with democratic Athens in 432; and "when Gorgias represented Leontini at Athens he did so as a sanctioned official of a democratic city, and he used his oratorical skills to sustain Athenian support based upon their earlier treaty" (1992, 9). Furthermore, Enos argues that Gorgias' success as a rhetor in Athens was due in large part to the integral connection between his rhetoric and democratic principles, and to the fact that he "made evident the effective tool rhetoric was as a source of power within a democratic context" (1992, 12). For if "Gorgias doubtlessly impressed his Athenian audience, it is also evident that he was effective (and popular) politically and it may well be equally true that ambitious democrats of Athens recognized in Gorgias' effective rhetorical composition not only eloquence but a cogency in systematic argument that could be a clear source of political power in a democracy" (1992, 12). Stated another way, Gorgias' commitment to democratic liberalism is integrally related to his empiricist epistemology, and this commitment accounts for his emphasis on freedom, tolerance, and rationality. As an advocate of liberal democracy, Gorgias would favor a society in which its citizens are free to choose their own values and goals. Such a society would not promote a single way of life or one version of the good; rather, it would operate by principles of fairness or justice wherein individuals could freely pursue their own form of life. In this respect, he would share Protagoras's commitment to democracy and would advance what Havelock calls a "*liberal scientific* view of man and society" (1957, 169; emphasis added).

Some scholars who construe Gorgias as a deontological liberal also depict him as an egalitarian who is critical of oppression of women. In this context, they read *Helen* as a proto-feminist tract in which Gorgias advocates the equality of men and women. Andy Crockett thus interprets Gorgias as a "radical feminist" who depicts Helen, and by implication all Greek women, as powerless in Greek culture (1994, 71–90). Rather than defending Helen for acting on the basis of her own desires and rejecting the norms of society, as Race contends, Crockett reads Gorgias as excusing Helen on the basis that she is completely powerless; repressed by an array of repressive religious, physical, and linguistic practices in Greek culture. Gorgias thus depicts Helen as a mere prize to be won by warriors motivated by a "passion that loved conquest and love of honor that was unconquered" (H4). Forced to be submissive to an indifferent husband and helpless before the seductive and powerful Paris, Helen is not a free individual who defies the community, a person who chooses passion instead of prudence. She is a prisoner of sex whose "subjective" erotic drive is a force over which she has no control. Gorgias' defense of Helen, in this regard, may be seen as one in which he champions Helen's cause because she is powerless in a male-dominated culture in which women are unable to resist the arbitrary whims of the gods, the desires of violent males, the verbal seductions of seducers, or their own irrepressible erotic passions. Just as he proclaims that "a woman's reputation and not her shape ought to be known by many" (B22), thereby suggesting that women ought to be seen in the same way men are treated, Gorgias' encomium challenges the "univocal and unanimous" testimony of inspired male poets and their Greek audiences, and in so doing opposes the entire patriarchal power structure of Greek culture. Gorgias' defense of Helen, in this regard, may be seen as one in which he champions Helen's cause because she is powerless in a phallocentric culture wherein religious, physical, linguistic, and psychological forces are arranged so as to perpetuate the violation and marginalization of women.[7]

Up from Liberalism

Although this reading of Gorgias as a deontological liberal may avoid the contradictions in the subjectivist account, it is itself contradicted on several occasions by Gorgias' ethical and political assertions. The difficulty with the utilitarian reading is that Gorgias never argues that moral behavior has anything to do with increasing the happiness of the greatest number of people. When Gorgias praises the warriors in the

Epitaphios, he does not say that they are admirable for promoting the happiness of the people. It may well be the case, for example, that many Greeks would be happier living in peace under the rulership of a Persian king than in a state of continual inter-city warfare. In respect to Helen, Gorgias never suggests that she is exculpable because her behavior ultimately made the Greeks a happier people, an argument raised by Euripides' Helen.[8] Instead, he depicts her as wanting to remain faithful to her husband and family, regardless of any consideration of her own or anyone else's happiness. Gorgias does not even raise the issue of whether she would have been personally "happier" living with Paris in Troy rather than with Menelaus in Sparta. Nor does Gorgias suggest that the happiness of the community is pivotal to Palamedes' virtue. Palamedes bases his decision to fight to retrieve Helen, not on the grounds that it would increase the happiness of the community, but on the fact that he, like all the suitors of Helen, promised to fight to retrieve her if she were ever taken from Menelaus. Had he based his decision on its effect on the happiness of the most people, he most likely would have concluded that many Greeks would have been far happier if they had remained at home rather than undertaking a ten-year military campaign against Troy. And while he describes himself as a "benefactor" who provides people with various means for improving their lives, Palamedes does not argue that this is what makes him morally admirable. He only asserts that the fact that he spends his time inventing things is "an indication of the fact that I abstain from shameful and wicked deeds" (P31). Palamedes' morality, like that of Helen and the Athenian warriors, is exemplified by his commitment to conventional Greek virtues, not in his attempt to increase the happiness of community as a whole (P17).

Were he a deontological liberal, Gorgias would presumably construe reason as a faculty for apprehending universally applicable moral truths. But rather than depicting reason as a faculty for apprehending any kind of truth, Gorgias argues in *On Not-Being* that there *is* no such truth and that even if there were, we would not be able to apprehend it through the use of "reason." Every such criterion is a partisan fabrication of situated rhetors rather than a standard that exists outside of all contexts and serves to justify or validate particular assertions or modes of behavior. Furthermore, as we have seen in chapter 2, Gorgias consistently depicts every use of language to be a maneuver in a rhetorical agon, and hence unavoidably partisan and partial. The faculty of reason, in this regard, is a capacity for excelling in agons and hence of being able to "trip one's opponent " (B8). Rather than being an impartial faculty for apprehending universal truths, Gorgias depicts the faculty of reasoning to be a strategic faculty for warfare.

Concerning freedom, Gorgias rejects the deontological thesis that a free individual is one who overcomes the constraints of contingency, and he repeatedly suggests that we are never able to escape the contingencies of everyday life. An individual such as Helen or Palamedes thus has obligations, duties, and commitments; neither is a free, "unbridled" agent independent of his or her community and its constraints. Furthermore, different communities may impose different sorts of constraints, and freedom for Helen differs from freedom for Palamedes or the Athenian warrior. In this respect, freedom itself has different meanings in specific communities at specific times, and there is no situation in which we are completely autonomous.

Concerning equality, Gorgias also departs from the universalist notion that all people are inherently equal because they possess the moral faculty of reason. On the contrary, he appears to condone conventional differences between individual free men, men and women, Greeks and barbarians, and free men and slaves. Gorgias does not argue that women are equal to men, and he even appears to accept their conventional roles in Greek society. As noted above, he distinguishes quite sharply between the excellences of men and of women, contending that "in the first place if you want to know what is excellence in a man, that is easy, because excellence in a man is this, to be competent to perform public duties, and in doing them to help friends and harm enemies and to avoid suffering anything of the sort himself. And if you want to know the excellence of a woman, it is not difficult to describe, for she ought to manage her household well, keeping the contents safe and being obedient to her husband. There are distinct excellences for a child, female and male, and for an older man, of one sort if free, another if a slave" (*Meno* 71e). In respect to Helen in particular, Gorgias never questions her duty to remain faithful to her husband Menelaus. Concerning the "barbarians," Gorgias never suggests that they are "naturally equal" to the Greeks. And while he does not assert, with Aristotle, that there is a "natural" difference between Greeks and barbarians such that the latter are naturally suited to be slaves, Gorgias also does not agree with Antiphon's claim that Greeks and barbarians are the same "by nature."[9]

Nor, finally, is it evident that Gorgias is an ardent advocate of democracy. He did live in Leontini, which became a democracy in the early fifth century and formed an alliance with democratic Athens. But it is not clear what the nature of this democracy was or what role Gorgias played in it. Class differences in Sicily were pronounced, and Gorgias' family appears to have been very wealthy, his brother being a physician, Gorgias himself becoming a highly paid teacher of oratory and a festival orator, and his grandnephew being wealthy enough to dedicate a gold statue to Gorgias. It may be the case that the art of rhetoric emerged in democratic Sicily in the fifth century because of the need to settle legal disputes and elect rulers and that rhetoric played an important role in democratic Athens; but the fact that Gorgias excelled in rhetoric and taught the art does not mean that he was democrat. After all, aristocrats may be very adept debaters, and many of Gorgias' students appear to have been aristocrats.

Furthermore, while Gorgias was chosen to represent Leontini in Athens as its ambassador in 427 B.C.E., this does not conclusively show that he was an ardent democrat. Plato, for example, suggests that Gorgias was chosen because of his rhetorical skills rather than because of his democratic principles, remarking that Gorgias was considered the "best able of all the citizens of Leontini to attend to the interests of the community, and it was the general opinion that he spoke excellently in the public assembly" (*Greater Hippias* 282bc). Finally, Gorgias' choice of residences suggests that he may not have been an ardent democrat. For unlike Protagoras, Gorgias did not live and work in democratic Athens; instead, he appears to have lived extensively in aristocratic Thessaly, under the rulership of the monarch Jason of Phaerae. Gorgias' choice of Thessaly suggests that he was at least not averse to living in a nondemocratic state, and that he was quite happy to teach wealthy aristocrats like Meno, rather than to promote the kind of democracy practiced in Athens (*Meno* 70a). [10]

4

THE AGONISTIC COMMUNITY

> Just as things made by mortar-makers are mortars, so also Larisians are those made by public servants, for they are a group of Larisofiers.
>
> Gorgias
>
> They deserve to be admired by many, O men of Greece.
>
> Gorgias, praising those who create national assemblies

I have argued that the subjectivist and empiricist readings cannot account for Gorgias' ethical and political views. In this chapter I provide an alternative reading, one that is consistent with his antifoundationalism. Specifically, I argue that Gorgias is a conventionalist who sees individuals as being fashioned through participation in the institutions and customs of their community, and that he construes the community as a contingent association of individuals held together by shared activities rather than by ethnicity or adherence to fixed moral principles. Although he is a conventionalist, Gorgias is not an apologist for the status quo, for he promotes the agon as the principal institution in which a community generates and displays excellence and in which they render moral judgments. The principal moral terms used by the agonistic community are *honor* and *shame*, terms in which they voice their commendation or condemnation. In his political views, Gorgias promotes Panhellenism, a political and cultural union of people from various diverse cities who participate in an array of agons and who resist attempts by imperialist Greek cities and aggressive "barbarians" to subvert those institutions.

THE FASHIONABLE SELF

In order to understand Gorgias' conventionalist model of ethics and how it differs from the subjectivist and rationalist construals of his views, it is useful to begin with his conception of the individual. In one of his most striking and pivotal metaphors, Gorgias asserts that the *demiourgoi*, the artisans of the community and the magistrates who enact the laws, *create* the citizens of the community. In what may be one of the earliest "social constructionist" accounts of the individual, he asserts that "just as things made by mortar-makers are mortars, so also Larisians are those made by public servants, for they are a group of Larisofiers" (A19). In his metaphor, Gorgias depicts the individual as an artifact or work of art, a pot, or mortar, referred to as a "larisa" that is fabricated by the potters in the community of Larisan artisans. Significantly also, Gorgias' individual is both a political and a cultural artifact, a partisan as well as an artisan, for his punning term *demiourgoi* denotes a political magistrate as well as an artisan of the district who manufactures Larisan pots. Rather than possessing an essential nature that antedates his cultural and political engagements with others, an individual's truest and most essential nature is fabricated by engaged artisans. And insofar as he is himself a member of the community of artists, an individual Larisan actively creates himself just as he creates pots. As such, each individual does not have an "essence" prior to his contingent fabrication any more than a pot or larisa has any such essence; and he thus possesses no inherent defining quality, such as natural "animal" drives, or a faculty of "reason," or a preexistent "soul." Moreover, an individual does not create himself apart from his engagement with others in the community, through an arbitrary, unbridled act of will. A cultural creator as well as creation, each craftsman is defined by the conventions of the craft or art itself. As an artisan, he is only able to make authentic larisas after mastering the craft and becoming thereby a *demiourgos*, a professional worker in the *demos*, or "artisan in the community."[1] Gorgias thus suggests that every individual who participates in the political, cultural, or economic life of the city and thereby engages in its political and cultural conventions is actively engaged in fashioning himself and other members of the community.

In a related characterization of the way people fashion themselves in society, Gorgias describes the psyche as being informed by *tropes*. The Greek term *trope* has three interrelated denotations: linguistic, social, and psychological. As noted above, the trope is a maneuver in a discursive agon, the fundamental "unit" of language itself. But the term also has a social dimension and may be translated as a "form of life" that people in the community share, a customary or habitual manner in which they behave. As such, the tropes of a community delineate their everyday routines and constitute what they consider normal and ordinary. The term also denotes the psychological or character traits of an individual, the significant features of his personality or self. A person's psyche, in this respect, is embodied in his habitual ways of behaving and speaking. As such, Gorgias posits an integral relationship among social practices, discourse, and the individual, such that the individual is "grounded" on nothing more than the practices of people in the community of which he is a member. A person's psyche, in this respect, is woven from the tropes of the community and is identical with his habitual way of behaving and thinking. An individual's psyche is not a foundational, originating source of behavior that antedates his discursive social interactions, let alone one that exists prior to his life on earth altogether, as for Pythagoras and Plato. Rather, an individual's psyche is a weaving or "text" which he participates in fabricating by engaging with other members of his community. Each person is in this respect thoroughly embedded in the conventions of the community to the extent that his deepest beliefs and desires are integrally related to the beliefs and desires of his community; and the tropes or traits that delineate his character are drawn from the customary tropes or modes of behavior that inform the ways of life of the community. The Gorgian self is a thoroughly social self.

In another metaphor expressing his notion that the psyche is shaped or "informed" by the discursive tropes of his community, Gorgias remarks that the psyche is "stamped" or molded with persuasive discourses as a coin is stamped and thereby given a face and value (H13). The very identity and value of a person, his defining psychological characteristics, derive from his position in the community. Rather than possessing a "nature" that precedes his participation in the customs of his community, the Gorgian individual acquires his identity from interaction with others. Just as he repudiates in *On Not-Being* the foundationalist notion that entities "truly exist" independently of human awareness and description of them, so Gorgias rejects the notion of an essential feature of human beings that exists outside the social contexts in which they fashion and describe themselves. The human psyche is always situated, fabricated in temporally and culturally located situations, a product of culture and contingency. The self is forged within the confines of a community and its conventions, and one's possibilities as well as opportunities are delineated by one's place in a community. Helen, for example, obtains her identity through her lineage, her relationships with her numerous suitors, her marriage to Menelaus, and her involvement with Paris. And Palamedes, similarly, acquires his identity through his commitments to his fellow Greeks, the inventions he devises to improve and enrich the life of the community, his friendship with Menelaus, his commitment to the Trojan campaign, and his rivalry with his nemesis Odysseus. As such, it is not a hyperbole when Palamedes states that he identifies so deeply with the values of his community that his very nature is indistinguishable from the community, asserting that *"in betraying Greece I was betraying myself"* (P19; emphasis added) and that his very identity is indistinguishable from his commitments to "my parents, my friends, the dignity of my ancestors, the cults of my native land, the tombs of my family, and my great country of Greece" (P19).

Gorgias' notion of the socially fashioned individual has important consequences for his account of motivation. Repudiating the notion that individuals possess fundamental or "natural" desires or motivations, Gorgias suggests that motivations originate in social interactions and that it is usually possible to describe human motivations in various ways. In the *Epitaphios*, Gorgias suggests that the warriors are motivated, not by selfish or hedonistic drives, but instead by honor, friendship, justice, legitimate love, and reverence for their parents and gods (E35–38). In *Helen*, Gorgias delineates an array of possible explanations for Helen's putative elopement with Paris, none of which is the "true" or ultimate motivation. Presenting four scenarios as plausible accounts of her action, Gorgias indicates that her behavior may be explained in terms of divine decree, fate, or contingency; physical force or rape; verbal seduction; or erotic desire. Each of these accounts of Helen's behavior is plausible, but none is the ultimate explanation. Rather than maintaining that Helen is ultimately motivated by such factors as the will of the gods, rational deliberation, or *eros*, Gorgias suggests that we must decide, as "judges" of her actions, which account we find most plausible. In *Palamedes*, Gorgias again portrays the individual as being a product of his culture whereby commitment to others in the community is as essential to his nature as personal advancement. Rather than being motivated by innate desires, Palamedes' most fundamental motivations are those of attaining honor in the community of persons he respects. Gorgias' Palamedes asserts that his principal concern is not even with staying alive, but is with maintaining his honor (P1); and he contends that life is not livable for the person who loses the trust and respect of others. And in *Palamedes*, he has Palamedes assert that the possible forms of "gain" (*kerdos*) available to him are rendered possible because of his engagement in the community. They include political rulership (13–14), wealth and money (15), honor (16), security (17). and the helping of friends and harming of foes (18). The possible losses that he would seek to avoid include fear, labor, and danger (19). Rather than seeking selfish ends, Palamedes posits social approval as his highest goal; honor is far more crucial than wealth. Conversely, the principal loss that Palamedes fears is the loss of any source of help from others, the kind of help that depends on honor and hence on *trust* (P20–21). Any other losses pale before this, for "the man who loses his money [or] who falls from power or who is exiled from his country might get on his feet again, but he who throws away good faith would not any more acquire it" (P21). The principle gain, then, becomes honor, which is a way of characterizing the highest form of trust, or *pistis;* this is so important that Gorgias can assert that "to good men death is preferable to a shameful reputation" (P35).

But though he does not see individuals as being motivated by fundamental irrational desires, Gorgias also does not see them as being motivated by a desire to adhere to the dictates of "reason." For Gorgias, there is no such thing as a "universal law" perceived by a universal human faculty of reason that is able to transcend the discourses of contingent communities. Rather, Gorgias maintains that decisions must be made anew in each circumstance, on each novel occasion. To be rational is to use means that are effective for reaching a desired end and also to consider strategies advanced by others. Stated another way, Gorgias does not depict the psyche as divided between irreducible "irrational" and "rational" forces, but instead he suggests that what counts as rational is determined by a situated community in a particular situation. In short, to be rational is to be willing to participate in an agon wherein one advances one's own views, competes with others, and accepts the conclusion of respected members of the community who adjudicate between opposed strategies. In effect, rationality, like truth or virtue, is a term of praise or endorsement that a community awards to an account, or mode of thinking, on no other basis than that it is persuaded. Gorgias thus rejects universal laws discernible through reason (*logos*), and he opposes moral and political systems that proclaim universal validity. Instead, Gorgias sees reason as contingent upon communities and suggests that individuals are able to construct themselves only through engagement in the institutions of the community. In this respect, Gorgias differs from Plato, who depicts humans as possessing a universal faculty of reason through which they are elevated from the animal and able to discern the universal moral law.

In the four scenarios he sketches for explaining Helen's behavior, Gorgias does not suggest that she strives to constrain her irrational drives by heeding the dictates of reason. Rather, he presents both *eros* and *logos* as potential adversaries, menacing forces that threaten to destroy her, rather than as features of her deepest self. Neither *eros* nor *logos* represents Helen's "true nature"; the *logos* of Paris that she finds so seductive is a fabrication designed to deceive and manipulate her, and the ostensibly natural passion she feels for Paris is the result of a disease or a mischievous daemon. She may be as readily misled by blindly following what he takes to be rational argument as by what she has been persuaded to believe are her "natural passions." So reason (or *logos*) is not a faculty that enables her to discern the truth, and her willingness to submit to argument may be as dangerous as blindly submitting to her "animal drives."

Gorgias portrays Palamedes as similarly situated vis-à-vis rational argument or *logos*. *Logos* or reason is not a reliable guide or teacher to heed in every circumstance, and Palamedes remarks that what his reason has led him to accept as the "truth" is itself more dangerous than resourceful (P5). He encounters the accusation by Odysseus, one he must demolish in order to survive. His ethical challenge is not to constrain his own irrational drives by heeding the dictates of reason or *logos* but to use the *logos* (or discursive maneuvers) of legal apology as weapons to demolish the *logos* of Odysseus and to weave an argument that persuades the judges. And Gorgias portrays the ethical situation of the Athenian warriors in a similar manner. The warriors do not control their irrational animal drives by heeding the dictates of reason. Rather, their motivations are "chaste loves" (E20), an *eros* that is constrained by the conventions of their community but also by the drive to protect their parents, friends, and fellow citizens. And rather than constraining themselves with reason, they use *logos* as a weapon, knowing when to speak and when to keep silent (E12) in order to defeat their adversaries.

Gorgias' notion of the socially constructed self also has important consequences for his conception of self-knowledge, for he suggests that self-knowledge is obtainable only through engagement with others in a variety of conventional practices. Rather than depicting such knowledge as obtainable through a private and privileged "introspection" undertaken independently of the conventional discourses of the community, Gorgias suggests that a person is able to acquire and articulate knowledge of himself only through participation in these discourses. A person who believes he is able to retreat from the tropes of his community and its discourses and discover his "true inner self" through reflection and recollection is as self-deceived as the poet who believes he is able to grasp the true nature of things through "divine inspiration." Stated another way, Gorgias repudiates the notion of a privileged standpoint from which one may observe or gain knowledge of one's "self"; for one's standpoint is itself always made possible only within the vocabulary and commonplaces of the available agons of the community.

Gorgias' notion that the individual is fabricated in the agons of a community is consistent with his notion that discourse is composed of maneuvers in socially sanctioned or customary agons, that all inquiry occurs within such agons, and that the "truth" about any subject is what a particular community considers the most persuasive account of that subject. In this respect, knowledge is not the apprehension of the way things really are, achieved by overcoming one's biases or prejudices; rather, it is a way of seeing that concurs with the way the community views a subject. All knowledge, including knowledge of one's self, is thus in this respect inseparable from the conventions, tropes, and beliefs of the community. In this regard, Palamedes asserts that "you are my companions (*suneste*) and thus you know (*suniste*) these things" (P15). Gorgias' key term, *suneimi* means 'to bring together' and 'to know'; and his term *sunistemi* means 'to stand together,' 'to stand in solidarity.' Stated another way, standing with others in the same place and thereby living with others, sharing their way of life, is the way in which people are able to know ourselves and each another. Self-knowledge cannot be obtained through inner reflection or introspection undertaken independently of discourse; rather, it is obtained through engagement with others in an array of customary or conventional discourses.

The Ungrounded Community

Gorgias thus depicts individuals as fashioning themselves and one another through participation in the customs and institutions of their community. But if Gorgias' individual is not grounded on anything more than the conventions of the community, his community in turn is not grounded on anything other than the contingent, shared activities of its members. In this respect, Gorgias differs from foundationalists such as Aristotle, who depicts the community as arising "naturally" from households and villages. For Aristotle, the household is a natural unit based on the natural superiority of men over women; the village is a natural unit that arises from a collection of households; and the ultimate community, that of the polis, emerges from a natural association of villages (*Politics* 1252b).

Gorgias also differs from Isocrates, who sees his city as morally superior and "racially pure," because it is grounded on the "earth." Isocrates, parroting an Athenian stereotype, asserts that the Athenians are autochthonous and have their birth from the earth itself. He claims that "our city is the oldest and the greatest in the world and in the eyes of all men the most renowned. But noble as is the foundation of our claims, the following grounds give us even a clearer title to distinction: for we did not become dwellers in this land by driving others out of it, nor by finding it uninhabited, nor by coming together here a motley horde composed of many races; but we are of a lineage so noble and so pure throughout our history we have continued in possession of the very land which gave us birth, since we are sprung from its very soil" (*Panegyricus* 4.23–24).[2]

Unlike Isocrates, who prides himself on his "natural" ethnic purity and superiority and who scorns the "motley hordes" outside Athens, Gorgias holds that people fashion themselves in various regions, none of which is privileged, through their day-to-day creative activities. His Larisan citizens, for instance, are humble craftsmen rather than leisured imperial Athenians; and his community is not grounded on any natural traits but is a contingent arrangement of people who share forms of life. Gorgias' community of artisans also differs from that of Plato, who anchors his ideal "republic" on what he considers an objective moral order that dictates where and how everyone in the hierarchy will live. For Gorgias the "order" of a community originates, not in an absolute domain of Platonic forms, but in the everyday practices of its citizens: the source of order or *kosmos*, which is also the community's "fairest ornament," is its *euandria*, its "good men and true" (H1).

Gorgias differentiates his views of the community from those of his foundationalist rivals most explicitly in the *Epitaphios*, in which he departs dramatically from the Athenian orators who depict Athens as the foundation and origin of virtue. Gorgias achieves his goal through a selection and arrangement of the conventional *topoi* of the *epitaphios*, omitting those *topoi* that depict Athens as a "foundational" city, including those *topoi* that render Athens to be a free association of good men, and arranging the *topoi* so as to emphasize the importance of what he depicts as the warriors' chief excellence, that of doing what is "fitting." In so doing, he removes the foundational role of Athens that it has in other extant Athenian funeral orations, namely those of Pericles, Aspasia in Plato's *Menexenus*, Lysias, Demosthenes, and Hyperides. To these orators, the Athenians are autochthonous, originating from the land of Athens rather than being immigrants; they possess a unique education; they originate a democratic form of government; they possess singular virtues; and they have a destiny to rule. Pericles, for example, praises the warriors' ancestors who "dwelt in the country without break" (2.36.1); he contends that Athens is self-sufficient, able to depend on "her own resources whether for war or peace" (2.36.3). He notes that Athens' democratic government is unique and original, for "our constitution does not copy the laws of neighboring states; we are rather a pattern to others than imitators ourselves" (2.37.1). He asserts that Athenians differ from all other Greek people in their military enterprises, daring, and deliberation, all of which are "singular" (2.40.3; 2.40.4). Athens differs in its democratic government, its education, its military policies, and its "merit to rule" (2.41.3). The warriors do not die for one another; rather, they die for the city of Athens itself (2.41.5). Hence the glory of the warriors is present insofar as they die for the city (2.42.4). Athens is itself the source of the warriors' glory or honor. Pericles thus admonishes his audience: "You must yourselves realize the power of Athens, and feed your eyes upon her from day to day, till love of her fills your hearts, and then when all her greatness shall break upon you, you must reflect that it was by courage, sense of duty, and a keen feeling of honor in action that men were enabled to win all this" (2.42.2). Pericles also characterizes his remarks as a "hymn" to the city (2.42.4), a term with religious connotations.

In his *Epitaphios,* Gorgias omits those *topoi* that render Athens foundational and unique. Unlike Pericles, Lysias, and Hyperides, he does not even mention the city of Athens; and he never suggests that Athens differs in any way from other Greek cities. As Loraux points out, all the extant *epitaphioi* save that of Gorgias award Athens and the term *polis* a predominant role (1986, 273). Gorgias omits any reference to the glorious ancestors who died at Marathon and in other battles or to the putative "destiny" of Athens as a unique city among other Greek cities. He does not mention autochthonous birth, wherein Athenians possess a "natural" origin in the land rather than being immigrants. Unlike Pericles, Plato, Lysias, and Hyperides, Gorgias omits any reference to the uninterrupted presence of the Athenians in Athens. He also omits any reference to the Athenian practice of providing for the men's burial and for their children. And though most of official orators characterize the warriors as deriving their virtue or excellence from the fact that they died for Athens, Gorgias suggests that they derive their excellence from the way they live, implying that there is no one identifiable absolute standard, that of death, to "prove" that the men are honorable. Indeed, in referring to the warriors, Gorgias uses the term *andres,* men who are "fully men." As Loraux notes, this epithet suggests that the slain warriors are "not to be reduced entirely to the classical type of Athenian citizen-soldier"; for it implies that their "divine gift, valor," is a valor they exhibit in living rather than in dying. In this way, Gorgias exalts "the choice of way of life" rather than extolling any "decision to die" (1986, 107). In Gorgias' characterization, the warriors are exemplary because they live in a fitting manner and not because they sacrifice themselves for the glorious city of Athens.

Although he omits *topoi* that affirm Athens' status as a foundational, singular city that should be looked upon every day as the source of life, Gorgias includes those conventional *topoi* that make the Athenians similar to other Greeks. He says that their principle virtue is the capacity to see what is fitting at the fitting time and to act upon it (E11), a capacity that characterizes his own sophistic art and the art he teaches his students. Rather than heeding the exactness of law, they opt for appropriate speech (E9), gentle fairness over strict justice (E10). He then illustrates this virtue of adaptability by delineating conventional Greek virtues. For Gorgias, these virtues all exemplify the ability to adapt to the moment, to do what is "fitting" in the "fitting time." He mentions many of the virtues the other authors attribute to the Athenians, but he does so as illustrations of the virtue of doing what "fits." Like Pericles, Gorgias praises the virtues of strength and planning (E15), thinking and doing (E16–17). But unlike most other funeral orators, Gorgias does not mention the presence of Athens as an originating source or validating entity for the men's virtues. The polis, in effect, is nothing other than the actions of the people who dwell in it. Rather than saying that the warriors derive their virtue from Athens, Gorgias states that their virtue is one that *all* Greeks possess, namely the power to do what is fitting in the fitting time. He asserts that the warriors treasure "unwritten" rather than written law; they prefer adapting to new situations with words rather than "strict justice." In respect to education, the warriors do not derive their education from the city but instead "school themselves" in the qualities needed to discern what is fitting and act upon it, namely intelligence and strength, skills needed to deliberate and to perform well. Thus, while he redescribes the warriors in a way that displaces the foundational role of Athens, Gorgias does not subvert Greek civic morality.

By characterizing Athens as a contingent association of individuals, Gorgias challenges its privileged foundational role; and in so doing, he suggests that it, like every community, is dependent for its existence upon the forms of life of its members and not upon divine decree or adherence to dogmatic principles. Significantly, Gorgias does not even mention the term *polis* in the *Epitaphios,* and instead uses the term *astous* to refer to Athens' citizens (E37). In Gorgias' characterization, the polis is not a privileged entity, the highest form of human community. Rather, it is no different from an *astu*, or urban conglomeration. Typically, the term *astu* refers to an urban center, without the sense of being a self-contained "polity" or possessing a particular form of government. Citizens of an *astu* do not claim to possess an autochthonous birth or singular virtues. Unlike the "divinely sanctioned" imperial city of Athens, the *astu* is not unique; it is not distinctive or original in its form of government; it has no particular military destiny; it is not inherently self-sufficient; and it has no pretense to any sacred foundation, being dependent for its integrity on the contingent associations of its citizens. Indeed, since the root of term *astu* is also the root of *asteia,* or 'urbanity,' Gorgias suggests that what is most crucial to civic unity may be the urbane, elegant discourse that its rhetors deploy in a variety of established agons.

Gorgias thus depicts individuals as artisans and artifacts, as fashioning themselves and one another through their cooperative and competitive ventures. But what, we may ask, holds the community together? What is it that leads people to accept others in the community and hence to see themselves as members of a community? Gorgias provides one possible answer in his discussion of *trust*. He frequently speaks of the importance of mutual trust in his account of community. In the *Epitaphios,* Gorgias describes the warriors as men of trust who display "respect to friends through trust" (E38); and in *Palamedes,* he identifies trust as definitive of a person and of the community of which he is a part. In seeking to expose Odysseus' deepest nature, Palamedes thus asks, "What in the world do you trust?" (P22). Palamedes emphasizes the pivotal role of trust in his conception of morality, asserting that he is someone who is "trustworthy" (P34), and pointedly asking, "How could I be [trusted], if they knew that I had done something most untrustworthy, had betrayed my friends to my enemies" (P21). Life is so dependent upon trust in other people that Palamedes asserts that it would be impossible for him to live among either the Greeks or the barbarians once he had committed treason, because he could not gain their trust. In a striking assertion that distinguishes his ethical views from that of Plato's Socrates, for whom the unexamined life is not worth living, Gorgias asserts that "life is not livable for a man who has lost the trust of others" (P21).

Unlike foundationalists, who claim that their community is privileged because it is grounded on divine decree, universal moral principles, or ethnic purity, the Gorgian community has no such ground whatsoever. Held together by mutual trust, the community is secured by nothing more than a contingent faith its members have in each other, a confidence in, and reliance upon, one other. Trust, in this sense, is displayed or demonstrated in the shared practices, behavior, or forms of life of the community. Significantly, Gorgias' term for trust, *pistis,* also denotes 'belief'; and in this sense, Gorgias suggests that the community is held together because its members are persuaded to believe in each other.

The Virtues of Agonism

Given his notion that individuals fabricate themselves by engaging in the conventions or practices of their communities and his notion that a community is "grounded" on nothing more than the customary activities of its members, we may characterizes Gorgias' ethical views as "conventionalist." For Gorgias suggests that behaving morally means adhering to the conventions of a community and thus doing what is "fitting" or "appropriate." Gorgias frequently uses the term *nomos,* or 'convention' in his discussions of morality.[3] In the *Epitaphios,* he describes the warriors' capacity to speak and act in a fitting manner in the fitting moment as "the most godlike and most common *nomos*" (E11); and he praises the warriors for being

> reverent to the gods by means of justice,
> respectful to parents by means of care,
> just to fellow citizens by equality,
> loyal to friends by faithfulness
> (E35–38)

He also describes the warriors as displaying *nomimon eroton* ("legitimate love" or "civilized erotics") (E32), an ostensibly oxymoronic combination of passion and propriety. In *Helen,* Gorgias again emphasizes the importance of *nomos,* characterizing Helen as wanting to abide by the *nomoi* or conventions of the Greeks and condemning Paris for transgressing those *nomoi* (H7). When he describes the power of sight to lead human beings astray, Gorgias uses the term *nomos* to denote that which is proper, conventional, and moral. He observes, "So strong is the disregard of the *nomos* which is implanted in them because of the fear caused by the sight; when it befalls, it makes them disregard both the honor which is awarded for obeying the *nomos* and the benefit which accrues from doing right" (H16).

In *Palamedes,* Gorgias repeatedly emphasizes the centrality of *nomos* or convention in his defense. Palamedes asserts that Odysseus would be the worst of men if he would subvert the *nomoi* of the Greeks; and he condemns the traitor as a person who contravenes *nomos* and thereby undermines the community. He contends that "the traitor is the enemy of all: the laws (*nomos*), justice, the gods, the bulk of mankind. For he contravenes the law, negates justice, destroys the masses, and dishonors what is holy" (P17). And when Palamedes praises himself, he mentions one of his chief contributions as the creation of "written laws (*nomous graptous*), the guardians of justice" (P30). Gorgias also has Palamedes state that he exhibits proper respect for others and for the traditions of the Hellenic community. He thus asserts, "I am inoffensive to the older, not unhelpful to the younger nor envious of the fortunate, but merciful to the unfortunate; not heedless of poverty nor valuing wealth ahead of virtue, but virtue ahead of wealth; neither useless in council nor lazy in war, doing what is assigned to me, obeying those in command" (P32). In each instance, Gorgias extols virtues of respecting conventions and traditions, as well as the gods recognized by the community. In each of passages, Gorgias concurs with the familiar aphorism of Pindar that "custom is king" (*Gorgias* 484b).

Insofar as he depicts morality as doing what is deemed "fitting," Gorgias is a "conventionalist" in his ethical views. But he is not a conventionalist in the sense that he sees people as "freely choosing" to adhere to moral and legal conventions, consenting to restrict their actions in order to live a better and more secure life. This is how Plato's

Callicles characterizes conventionalism, in which the "weak" members of a community agree to adopt various conventions such as morality and law in order to prevent the "strong" individuals from overpowering them, as would occur in "nature" (*Gorgias* 483cd). Eric Havelock suggests that this view is common among the Sophists:

> Rather than viewing morality and law as resting on "principles which are independent of time, place and circumstance," the Sophist views human codes of behavior less as principles than as conventional patterns, embodying not eternal laws written in the heavens or printed on man's spiritual nature, but rather *common agreements elaborated by man himself as a response to collective need*. They are the rules of the game by which he finds it convenient to live, and, as such, they are subject to change and development . . . in many practical details these conventions represent historical accidents. . . . Morals and law can be viewed in this way *a posteriori* as a kind of second language, part of the historical process." (Havelock 1957, 29; emphasis added).

But if Gorgias would repudiate the notion that morality rests on universal principles, I suggest that he advocates an even moral radical form of "conventionalism" than that described by Callicles and Havelock. For Gorgias suggests that individuals do not "freely" engage in a social contract with one another but that they are themselves the products of "conventional" behavior, pots that are manufactured by artisans or magistrates. Gorgias rejects the foundationalist assumption that individuals possess an identity prior to their engagement with others and that they are thus free to choose to limit the means they use to pursue their personally chosen or naturally given "ends." Instead, he suggests that social practices or *nomoi* precede the development of the individual, his ends and desires. It is only through participation in the institutions of the community that individuals develop their goals and beliefs. Stated another way, *praxis*, or human action, precedes *theoria*, or the reflective observation and explanation of those actions; and there is no preexisting criterion or standard that justifies the contingent human practices manifested in social customs or *nomoi*.

To say that Gorgias is a conventionalist who sees individuals and communities as arising through habitual practices and who sees morality as doing what is considered "fit" or "appropriate" may seem to suggest that he is an apologist for the status quo who counsels acceptance of traditional beliefs and practices. As Plato suggests, Gorgias merely repeats platitudes and reinforces stereotypes. Unlike the gadfly Socrates, who provokes people to examine their own lives, Gorgias merely panders to his audiences, flattering them by telling them what they want to hear (*Gorgias* 503a). In Long's terms, "Plato wanted, in all seriousness, to reform society. Gorgias, worldly and playful, reinforced conventions and stereotypes" (1984, 238). Like most Sophists, Gorgias merely engages in what Irwin calls "an uncritical articulation of common sense morality" (1997, 579). Gorgias' central notion of doing what is "fitting," or appropriate, in this sense, is merely another way of affirming the status quo. In his defense of the Athenian warriors in the *Epitaphios*, for example, he praises the warriors for behaving as they "ought" to behave and for doing what is "fitting" or expected, namely, engaging in warfare. In *Palamedes*, Gorgias promotes such conventional notions as the importance of helping friends and harming enemies, of striving for wealth and power, and of honoring one's family and country. And in *Helen*, Gorgias reinforces Greek male stereotypes of women, depicting Helen as motivated by lust and easily manipulated by the clever and articulate Paris. As Ann Bergren (1983) observes, even Gorgias' own "defense" of Helen, in this reading, is another male chauvinist attempt to "control" her with his own rhetoric; for Gorgias suggests that it is only through the persuasive discourse of a clever male like himself that a hopelessly weak woman like Helen may be rescued.[4] As a conventionalist who advocates doing what is appropriate, then, Gorgias would appear to counsel an opportunistic life of "fitting in," of never questioning authority, and of simply "going with the flow."

This charge is misguided, however, for although Gorgias sees moral behavior as that which is conventional, he does not thereby maintain that all such conventions are equally desirable. On the contrary, he strongly advocates a distinctive set of conventions and institutions, namely those of the Panhellenic community. And most particularly, he promotes the institution of the agon, an institution in which people advocate opposed viewpoints and which is therefore an institution of *change* that encourages people to challenge established beliefs. It is certainly the case that in nonagonistic communities, such as those ruled by a divine king, Gorgian conventionalism would reinforce acceptance of the status quo and offer little means of resisting the established order. But in a community informed by various types of agons, conventionality *encourages* change. Unlike communities in which people are unable to challenge the dictates of their rulers, the Hellenic community is informed by agons in which challenging established positions is definitive of its very existence. In an agonistic culture everyone will not share the same views; on the contrary, individuals differentiate themselves from others by advancing their views in a variety of agons. What people share is a commitment to the institution of the agon itself and the acceptance of the decision rendered by acknowledged judges who in effect speak for the community. Without agreement about the rules or procedures of competition and agreement to abide by the outcome of the contest, the agon is not possible. Conversely, without disagreement or rivalry, the agon cannot proceed; for the agon requires disagreement, rival points of view, in order to function. The agon thus fosters *difference*, disagreement and dispute, while at the same time fostering cooperation and agreement about the rules of competition. Gorgias thus welcomes opposition and encourages challenges to him; for as Philostratus observes, upon "coming into a theater of the Athenians he had the boldness to say 'suggest a subject,' and he was the first to proclaim himself willing to take this chance, answer all such challenges" (A1). This correlation of concord and conflict is also evidenced in Gorgias' repudiation of what he deems the "unanimity and univocity" of his poetic adversaries in *Helen* (H2); for concord or agreement does not involve agreement about specific positions or points of view.

Although he engages in and thereby promotes the agon in each of his extant texts, Gorgias does not offer a "justification" of the institution of the agon. And indeed he may well repudiate the notion that any such ground, rationale, or justification is possible. Instead, he praises or *affirms* the institution of the agon, and in this sense commits himself to it. Any attempt to justify the agon, to find a further ground or criterion to justify it, is misguided and would simply return to the foundationalist position that Gorgias repudiates. He does not attempt to ground or justify his affirmation on an external, universal criterion or standard. He does not present a "system" of ethics, one that is based on a definition of the good life or on what it really means to be moral. He does not argue, for example, that the agonistic community best expresses human nature, or that it is most rational, or even that it makes most people the happiest. Indeed, many people may be happier as slaves or servants in a command society. Rather than attempting to justify his ethics by appealing to indisputable first principles, he instead affirms or praises it, exhibiting the forms of life it makes possible. Insofar as Gorgias' account is a justification, it is what John Rawls (1980) calls a process of reaching a "reflective equilibrium" of beliefs, an ongoing hermeneutic project in which "what justifies a conception of justice is not its being true to an order antecedent and given to us, but its congruence with our deeper understanding of ourselves and our aspirations, and our realization that, given our history and the traditions embedded in our public life, it is the most reasonable doctrine for us" (519). Gorgias' justification of his radical agonism is one in which he discusses the type of community and people in such communities throughout his extant works and in so doing urges us that it is a community of which we would choose to be a part. And though he does not justify the agonistic community in reference to an external criterion, he suggests that we will embrace it because it accords with the life we choose to live.

In Gorgias' characterization, the agonistic community is desirable in part because it promotes what Gorgias characterizes as the "freedom and power" of the individual in a way that also promotes the good of the community as a whole (*Gorgias* 452a). First, the agon promotes individual freedom in a manner that also affirms social order. On the one hand, the agon fosters and indeed depends upon freedom of speech and action. Without the freedom to articulate opposed points of view, the participants in the agon could not compete. In this construal, freedom does not involve enslaving others; nor does it mean escaping the practices of the community or the discourses it sanctions. That is, freedom does not mean that one must recognize a truth that obviates the need for further disputation and argument. Rather, freedom demands the persistent engagement in argumentation in order to persuade others, and a willingness to be persuaded by their views. Indeed, Gorgias suggests that willingness to submit to others' persuasiveness is a means of learning, as one submits to the persuasive deception of the tragedian (B26). Freedom, in this context, is not the overcoming of institutional constraints, but rather the opportunity to engage in competition with others. In his embrace of the institution of the agon, Gorgias thus opposes egoists such as Callicles or Alcibiades, who are willing to *subvert* or overthrow the institutions of the community in order to liberate their own putative natural or "true" self. He also opposes those who would replace agonistic institutions with a command society of the sort Plato recommends, wherein privileged rulers dictate orders to others. Freedom is not the ability of an unconstrained individual to do whatever he wants; for to Gorgias there are no such "unconstrained" individuals. Rather, because each person is created in a culture, he is already constrained, his desires and goals being shaped by the discourses of the culture. Educated individuals such as Palamedes or the Athenian warriors, persons of *sophia,* will embody the goals and values of their community and culture. A person who repudiates these values will be a traitor or criminal. Freedom, in this context, means the ability to advance oneself within the sanctioned agons of the culture. To repudiate the agonistic culture is not to become free but to reject the very institutions that permit freedom.

In a similar vein, the agon encourages cleverness, usually associated with self-advancement, in such a way that it benefits the community as a whole. As cleverness, *sophia* is akin to *metis,* or 'cunning intelligence'; and Gorgias' heroic Palamedes' very name denotes 'ancient *metis.*' The intellectual capacity of *metis*, as Detienne and Vernant point out, is an ability to adapt to novel situations, and hence is "never the same as itself" (1991, 19). The power of *metis* is one of metamorphosis; for since one encounters a mutable adversary, one must oneself become even more mutable. For "in order to seize upon the fleeting *kairos, metis* had to make itself even swifter than the latter. In order to dominate a changing situation, full of contrasts, it must become even more supple, even more shifting, more polymorphic than the flow of time: it must adapt itself constantly to events as they succeed each other and be pliable enough to accommodate the unexpected so as to implement the plan in mind more successfully" (1991, 20). The institution of the agon enables the community to appropriate individual *sophia* or *metis,* putting cleverness into the service of helping the community. For insofar as public discourse is comprised of sanctioned agons, a clever person who engages in such agons benefits the community itself, often articulating novel ways of seeing and ingenious courses of action. In this respect Gorgias, as a teacher of rhetoric, serves the community; for he trains students to compete in an array of agons, and in so doing he teaches them to cooperate as well as compete. And while he does not profess to teach his students to adhere to any strict moral principles, this does not mean that his teaching is amoral or immoral. For to Gorgias, morality is demonstrated by participation in the community's sanctioned agons, the customs or conventions of the agonistic community.

Furthermore, the agon encourages individual boldness or daring in a manner that promotes the social good. Gorgias remarks that courage or daring (*tolmes*) is the chief moral virtue needed for participants in every agon, for it enables a person to withstand the blows of a rival. An agon, he contends, "requires two kinds of excellence, daring and skill; daring is needed to withstand danger, and skill to understand how to trip [strike] the opponent" (B8). Gorgias himself displays this sort of daring in his own works, challenging the views of the Eleatic philosophers in *On Not-Being*, the official Athenian orators in the *Epitaphios*, and the entire tradition of poets in *Helen*. A courageous speaker, he invites all challenges, being willing to "speak on any subject whatsoever" (A1). Moreover, as Plato observes, Gorgias is reported to have encouraged boldness in his students, teaching them to answer "fearlessly and haughtily if someone asks something" (*Meno* 70ab). In one respect, boldness may seem to be an egoistic virtue, one that enables an individual to advance himself. But in an agonistic community, courage is not egoistic; for by boldly challenging established positions, a rhetor may articulate views that have not previously been considered but that may well benefit the community. When Gorgias argues in the *Epitaphios* that the virtue of the Athenians does not depend on autochthony, he challenges the ultimate authority of the polis and in so doing opposes the self-destructiveness that often arises from blind patriotism. But if boldness in an agonistic community may involve defending unpopular positions in the face of adversity, it does not mean that a person blindly resists all opposition. For by entering into an agon, an individual must be willing to subject his views to refutation and consequently to alter his views if he is refuted. Gorgian daring is thus a virtue of being open to change as well as a virtue of challenging the dominant paradigms of the community.

Honor and Shame

Although Gorgias does not see the agonistic community as being grounded on dogmatic moral principles or divine decrees that serve as criteria for moral behavior, this does not mean that he deprives the community of its ability to render moral judgments. On the contrary, he suggests that the members of the community themselves are the ultimate source and authority for moral judgments. The principal terms they use in rendering their judgments, in Gorgias' characterization, are *honor* and *shame*, terms that he depicts as the primary ethical notions that guide and constrain behavior.[5] The accolade of "honorable," for Gorgias, like that of "truth," is a term of praise awarded by a community to actions and people they endorse or consider worthy of approval. Gorgias emphasizes the importance of these notions throughout the *Epitaphios, Helen,* and *Palamedes,* as well as in several aphorisms. He begins the *Epitaphios* by indicating that he wants his own speech to be honorable, one that the gods do not consider shameful:

> May what I say be what I ought to say
> And what I sought to say be what I ought to say
> Free from the wrath [*nemesis*] of gods.
> (E3–5)

Nemesis is a response of shock, contempt, malice, righteous rage, and indignation to a dishonorable deed or remark; to be *aidos nemesetos,* for instance, means being sensitive to violations of one's honor among others in the community and to have a respect for the honor of others. Gorgias also refers to honor and respect as a defining characteristic of the warriors who sacrifice their lives for their city:

> As evidence of these qualities they set up a trophy over their enemies,
> an honor to Zeus, an ornament to themselves,
> not inexperienced were they in native valor or legitimate passions
> or armed strife or honorable peace.
> (E17–20)

The trophy they erect to Zeus is an "honor"; the peace they seek is always "honorable." Gorgias also posits honor as the principal ethical term in *Helen,* asserting that "man and woman and speech and deed and city and object should be honored with praise if praiseworthy and incur blame if unworthy, for it is equal error and mistake to blame the praisable and praise the blamable" (H1). He proceeds to associate Helen with that which is honorable and to identify Paris with what is shameful. He refers to Helen's suitors as motivated by passion and honor, observing that "all came because of a passion which loved to conquer and a love of *honor* which was unconquered" (H4). He excuses Helen for being persuaded by Paris, noting that "persuasion has the same power as necessity, although it may bring shame" (H12).

Gorgias also identifies honor as a key ethical term in *Palamedes.* Palamedes begins his apology by contending that his sole concern is honor and dishonor, and that his entire argument is intended to preserve his honor. He asserts, "The danger relates to dishonor and honor, whether I must die justly or whether I must die roughly with the greatest reproaches and most shameful accusation" (P1). Throughout his defense Palamedes refers to honor and shame, presenting himself as honorable, arguing that he would not betray Greece because it would diminish his honor, and contending that honor is more important to him than life itself. Treason is unthinkable, for it would entail a loss of honor. He thus asks, "Would not my life have been unlivable if I had done these things. . . . Abandoning everything important, deprived of the noblest *honor*, passing my life in *shameful* disgrace, throwing away the labors labored for virtue of my past life? And this of my own accord, although to fail through his own doing is most *shameful* for a man" (P20; emphasis added). Palamedes depicts honor as one of the standards for assessing sanity and madness, contending on the one hand that "I am honored for the most honorable reason by the most honorable men, that is by you for wisdom" (P16); and that "it is madness to undertake tasks which are impossible, inexpedient, and shameful, which will harm his friends, help his enemies, and make his own life disgraceful and perilous" (P25). In his account of his own life, honor and shame play a central role in his behavior; he asserts that he abstains from "shameful and wicked deeds" (P31). Palamedes' most succinct assertion is that dishonor is worse than death: "To good men death is preferable to a shameful reputation. For one is the end of life, and the other a disease (*nosos*) in life" (P35).

Gorgias further emphasizes the primacy of honor and shame in several of his uncollected remarks and aphorisms. In his praise of Cimon, he asserts that "Cimon acquired money to use it and used it to be honored" (B20), perhaps implying that for a politician amassing wealth is permissible if he deploys it in such a way that people consider honorable. And in a striking remark, Gorgias suggests that women as well as men are to be judged according to the same standards. He asserts that "a woman's reputation [honor] rather than her form ought to be known to many" (B22), suggesting that a woman's status in a community is more important than her physical beauty. Gorgias further suggests in this aphorism that moral judgments of honor and shame apply to a broader ranges of actions than those that involve direct social interaction. He thus asserts, "You have sown shamefully and reaped badly" (B16), suggesting that that considerations of honor and shame apply even to the agricultural activities of planting and harvesting. In this metaphor, Gorgias suggests that a person's activities as a farmer are judged, not by attending to an "objective" criterion such as the quantity of a harvest, but by what the members of his community consider honorable or shameful behavior. Finally, Gorgias is reported to have accused a bird of shameful behavior, exclaiming to a swallow that shat on him, "Shame on you, Philomela!" (A23). In his quip, Gorgias playfully alludes to the young girl Philomela, who in myth was transformed into a swallow. Aristotle remarks that Gorgias' gibe was "in the best tragic style," for "if a bird did it there was no disgrace, but it was shameful for a girl" (A23). For Gorgias, presumably, a person is subject to judgments of honor and shame even if she is transformed into a bird.

The *topos* of honor and shame is integrally related to Gorgias' antifoundationalist conception of morality. First, by privileging honor and shame, Gorgias designates the contingent community as the supreme arbiter of what is moral or immoral, virtuous or vicious. As Bernard Williams points out, shame involves being seen by others in the community that one respects, and "the operations of shame indeed relate just to the attitudes or reactions of a specified social group" (1993, 83). In Gorgias' ethics of honor and shame, members of a contingent community assess behavior, not in terms of an independent standard that grounds their action, but in respect to the judgments of others in the community.

Next, in contrast to egoism and ethical universalism, an ethics of honor and shame does not distinguish between an "inner" and "outer" self, the former being real or fundamental, the latter being mere outer appearance. The egoist holds that one's social behavior is merely a veneer or patina of politeness that conceals one's true underlying animal desires. Conversely, the moral universalist holds that one's truest self, as a moral being, can be found only by transcending one's contingent social circumstances and attending to the dictates of a universal and impartial moral law, one accessible through the faculty of reason. For Gorgias, however, who posits honor and shame as the principal ethical *topos,* there is no more "real" self that lies beneath or above one's contingent circumstances in a community. Just as there are no objects that have "real" existence apart from one's characterizations of them within one's socially contingent situation, so there are no "real selves" that lie behind or above one's rhetorically available appearances. As Gabrielle Taylor points out, "one may be tempted to say that in a shame culture one is only concerned for how one appears in public, never mind the inner man; but this formulation implies precisely that distinction between appearance and reality, between public and private, which is unacceptable within the framework of the shame-culture. If public esteem is the sole value, to which whatever else may be valued is related as means to end, then it follows that where there is no public esteem there is no value" (1985, 54–55). Or, as Gorgias has Palamedes assert, "Life under arms is carried on outdoors (for this is a camp!), in which [everybody] sees everything and everybody is seen by everybody" (P12).

For the egoist and moral universalist, being motivated by considerations of shame is an indication of moral weakness, for it amounts to a surrender of one's truest self to the dictates of others. Submitting to shame also involves deception, for it requires a person to conceal his true desires or principles. To the foundationalist, the person motivated by shame is neither autonomous nor honest. To an egoist such as Callicles, who sees people as using any necessary means to achieve their egoistic ends, the person who is constrained by a sense of shame is heteronymous, too weak or cowardly to pursue his own animal drives, fearing the reprisals by others. He is deceptive, for he conceals his true motives and pretends to assent to the desires of the group. To a moral universalist such as Socrates, shame is also a sign of cowardice and deceptiveness, but for different reasons. The truly moral person restricts his animal drives (the "beast within") by heeding a universal moral law, one that he is aware of through reason. A person who constrains his animal drives out of a sense of shame is cowardly and deceptive, for he remains egoistic, although he controls his actions to win approval from others. The truly moral person, in contrast, is honest, for he knows what is morally right and acts upon the moral law. He is morally autonomous rather than heteronymous, in that he willingly and freely follows the rule or law he wills. But he is not egoistic, since he submits to the law as *higher* than himself and indeed as universal and absolute.

Gorgias' ethics of honor and shame may be further illuminated by contrasting it with an ethics of "guilt and innocence" often advanced by ethical universalists. Indeed, as several cultural anthropologists have observed, entire cultures may be identified as "shame cultures" and "guilt cultures."[6] Stated briefly, an ethics of guilt is one in which the experience of guilt accompanies an action a person considers to be wrong; and this is typically the case upon violating a universal moral rule. Conversely, innocence characterizes the person who does not violate a universal law. In a shame culture, in contrast, people are constrained by the experience of shame, typically felt in the face of the disapproval of particular individuals in their community. In Taylor's terms, "The distinguishing mark of a [shame culture] and that which makes it different from a so-called 'guilt-culture,' is that here public esteem is the greatest good, and to be ill spoken of the greatest evil. Public esteem for the individual, or the lack of it, depends on that individual's success or failure judged on the basis of some code which embodies that society's values. Whoever fails to meet the categoric demands engendered by that code ruins his reputation and loses the esteem of the other members of that group. He loses his honor" (1985, 54–55).

There is no universal rule the violation of which inspires shame; rather it is that they are seen by a finite group of people. Conversely, virtuous actions are those that are honored by the same community; and an action is honorable only when others observe or hear about it. Morally praiseworthy behavior is that of which a community approves; and morally reprehensible behavior is that which the community rejects. There is no universal law that grounds these judgments; there is no one reason why different communities praise or blame, honor or shame an individual. The basic experience connected with shame is that of behaving inappropriately in a particular situation and being seen by people whom one respects.

THE PANHELLENIC COMMUNITY

Gorgias identifies an array of communities in his extant texts, including the community of Athenians he addresses in the *Epitaphios,* the Greek warriors whom he addresses in *Palamedes* as the "first of the first," the members of the Hellenic cultural community whom he addresses in *Helen,* and the Eleans he addresses in his speech to the people of Elis. Gorgias also identifies an array of "professional" communities, such as the philosophers he addresses in *On Not-Being,* the Hippocratic physicians he refers to in Plato's *Gorgias,* the Olympic athletes with whom he identifies in his Olympic Speech, and the Larisan potters he characterizes as *demiourgoi.* But the most encompassing community Gorgias identifies is the Panhellenic community as a whole, the community he addresses in his numerous festival orations, and that he considers to be of supreme importance. Gorgias does not provide a systematic account of his conception of the Panhellenic community, or of Panhellenism, but it is possible to identify some of its central features and to contrast his view of the community from the views advanced by some of his foundationalist rivals.

Panhellenism, for most fifth- and fourth-century Greeks, is both a political and a cultural force. As a political order, the two chief aspects of Panhellenism in Gorgias' time are "concord among the Greeks" and "hostility to the barbarians." To most Greeks during this time, Panhellenism is merely a means of advancing the interests of the polis. As S. Perelman points out, in most cases during the fifth and fourth centuries, the "Panhellenic ideal" serves as a cloak for the advancement of a particular party or the hegemonic objectives of their city. Pericles' Congress Decree in 451 B.C.E. and the Athenian establishment of the *Panathenaea,* for example, is hegemonic and imperialistic, designed to promote the religious and cultural leadership of the Athenian empire. Similarly, Athens' establishment of Panhellenic colonies such as Thurii is a means to expand into the West, a strategy for strengthening Athenian hegemony. Athenian orators in the fourth century frequently use the term *Panhellenism* as a euphemism for Athenian hegemony. Demosthenes, for example, appeals to the Panhellenic ideal to oppose the aggression of Philip of Macedon, but his real objective is to promote Athenian hegemony. Isocrates, despite his chastisement of Athenian imperialism, also typically construes Panhellenism as being dominated by a hegemonic Athens. In all of these instances, Panhellenism as a political arrangement rarely surpasses the ultimate authority of the polis or city-state. Even Aristotle, writing at the end of the fourth century B.C.E., depicts the polis as the ultimate political unit, the paradigm of the human community. In S. Perelman's terms, "In spite of the feelings of common origin, religion, language and culture, and in spite of the uniting idea of opposition to the Barbarians, there is no unity of the Greek nation, or union of the Greek *poleis* in classical times" (1976, 1–2).

The second feature of Panhellenism as a political force involves conflict with various "barbarians," notably the Persians in the East and Carthaginians in the West. Many fifth- and fourth-century Athenians posit an absolute difference between

Greeks and barbarians, viewing the barbarians as lacking the principle Greek intellectual and moral virtues.[7] Athenian comic dramatists thus typically depict barbarians as "cowardly, weak, treacherous, unreliable, stupid, mean, uncultivated, savage" (Long 1989, 132). Aristophanes, for example, has Socrates refer to Strepsiades as "Barbarian and uneducable" (*Clouds* 398). In the same vein, these authors depict the Greeks as possessing a superior language—indeed, the only real language—while the barbarians utter sounds that are often unintelligible and sound like birds (*Birds* 1572–3).

Many Athenian authors portray the Greeks as intrinsically superior to the barbarians morally, possessing the cardinal virtues of wisdom, courage, restraint, and justice; and the barbarians as naturally possessing their respective vices of ignorance, cowardice, abandonment, and lawlessness. Isocrates repeatedly affirms the right of the Greeks to destroy the barbaric Persians. And Aristotle writes that barbarians are "naturally" inferior to the Greeks and indeed are "slaves by nature." Aristotle thus advises his student, Alexander the Great, to be "a leader to the Greeks and a despot to the barbarians, to look after the former as friends and relatives, and to deal with the latter as with beasts and plants" (Fragment 685). He cites approvingly the traditional poetic saying " 'Tis meet that Greeks should rule barbarians," a saying that implies that "barbarian and slave are the same in nature" (*Politics* 1252b). And he writes that "it is manifest therefore that there are cases of people of whom some are freemen and the others slaves by nature, and for these slavery is an institution both expedient and just" (*Politics* 1255a1).

Gorgias differs sharply from these thinkers both in respect to his notion of political unity among the Greek cities and in his view of the barbarians. As noted above, he repudiates the notion of the polis as an absolute or "foundational" entity and instead implies that the polis should itself be constrained by a larger network of cities. Gorgias explicitly affirms his approval of the establishment of national assemblies that serve in this capacity. As Aristotle reports, Gorgias begins his *Olympic Speech* by extolling the men who have established Panhellenic assemblies, proclaiming that the men who create national assemblies "deserve to be admired by many, O men of Greece" (*Rhetoric* 1414b29). Although Gorgias' own remarks on the subject of national assemblies are lost, we may speculate that the type of political union he would favor would be precisely one in which such national assemblies could constrain the excesses of aggressive cities who disrupted the harmony or concord among the Greeks. As such, he would seem to promote a type of federal union that could check the aggression of imperial cities such as Athens. Such a federal union would be consistent with his notion that mutual *trust* is the sole basis of a community, for the very term *federal* denotes an association based on *fides*, or trust, rather than on any universal principle or ethnic trait. Presumably such an organization would be similar to the associations of cities responsible for running the various Panhellenic festivals. But however Gorgias conceives such an association, his conception clearly differs from those thinkers who construe the polis as the ultimate authority and who proclaim their activities to be Panhellenic as a way of justifying and concealing actions that promote the interests of their city.

Gorgias also differs from many of his contemporaries in respect to his view of the barbarians. In some of his reported remarks, Gorgias is said to have distinguished between Greeks and barbarians, advocating a vigilant struggle against barbarian aggression. In his *Olympic Speech,* he is reported to have urged Greek unity and struggle against the barbarians. According to Philostratus, "his Olympic Speech [B7, 8a] dealt with political matters of the greatest importance, for seeing Greece involved in civil dissension, he became a counselor of concord to her inhabitants, turning their attention against the Barbarians and persuading them to regard as prizes to be won by their arms, not each others' cities, but the territory of the Barbarians" (A1, 4). In his *Epitaphios,* as Philostratus observes, Gorgias "dwelt on praise of the victories over the Medes, showing them that victories over the Barbarians require hymns of celebration, victories over the Greeks require laments" (A1). Furthermore, both *Helen* and *Palamedes* may be read as promoting Panhellenism in that in each work Gorgias focuses on the topic of treason against the Greeks. In *Helen,* he condemns treason as the worst possible crime and never suggests that an individual should ignore the claims of the Hellenic community. And in *Palamedes,* he contends, "If then the accuser, Odysseus, made his accusation through good will toward Greece, either clearly knowing that I was betraying Greece to the Barbarians or imagining something that was the case, he could be best of men. For this would of course be true of one who saves his homeland, his parents, and all Greece, and in addition punishes a wrongdoer" (P3). Asserting that treason is the most serious of crimes, he contends that "the traitor is the enemy of all: the laws, justice, the gods, the bulk of mankind. For he contravenes the law, negates justice, destroys the masses, and dishonors what is holy" (P17).

But though Gorgias advocates struggle against barbarian aggression, he does not ground Panhellenism on any fundamental or absolute distinction between Greek and barbarian. On the contrary, he never suggests that the Greeks are "naturally superior" to the barbarians intellectually or morally; he never depicts the barbarians as an uncivilized "Other," an ignorant, unjust and cowardly people who exemplify the antithesis of Greek virtues. Indeed, Gorgias at times displays a sympathy for barbarians and an appreciation of their intelligence and virtue. In *Palamedes,* he portrays the barbarians as similar to the Greeks both intellectually and morally. He observes that the Greeks and barbarians speak a different language, but he does not depict the barbarian language as inferior in any respect. Instead, he states that communicating with the barbarians is quite possible through the use of an "interpreter" (P7). He praises the Athenian warriors for displaying conventional Greek virtues of wisdom, courage, restraint, and justice; but rather than asserting that these virtues are limited to the Greeks, he suggests that barbarians may well possess this same virtues. In *Helen,* he describes Paris as able to seduce Helen through his clever use of language and his physical beauty. Gorgias does not even assert that Paris necessarily acted violently or unjustly; he only argues that if Paris behaved in this manner he deserves condemnation. Stated another way, Gorgias condemns violent and illegal behavior rather than condemning persons who possess an essentially "barbaric" inherent nature. He argues that if Helen "was seized by force and illegally assaulted and unjustly insulted, it is clear that the assailant as insulter did the wrong and the assailed as insulted suffered wrongly. It is right for the Barbarian who laid barbarous hands on her by word and law and decree to meet with blame in word, disenfranchisement in law, and punishment in deed. . . . He did dread deeds, she suffered them. Her it is just to pity, him to hate" (H7). But Gorgias never describes Paris as inherently or essentially violent; it is only if he uses physical force or violence against a nonviolent person that he merits punishment.

It is not unlikely that Gorgias' antifoundationalist view of non-Greeks may have been influenced by his encounters with non-Greeks in his native Sicily, where the Greeks were colonial "invaders" and the "barbarians" were not the menacing Persians but the economically sophisticated Carthaginians, the local Sicels, Sicans, Elymians, and Etruscans. Unlike most mainland Greeks, the colonial Greeks in Sicily did not seem to perceive non-Greeks as hostile adversaries and instead lived in far greater economic, political, and cultural harmony with barbarians than did their mainland counterparts. As M. I. Finley observes, Sicilians often lived and worked closely with non-Greeks, and in instances when disputes within a city "reached the civil war stage," for example, they frequently "sought help from outside when they could, among 'Barbarians' (a term broad enough to include Carthaginians and Etruscans along with Sicels and Elymians) as well as among other Greek states" (1979, 41). Robert Osborne points out that

> whereas in mainland Greece Persians and other Barbarians were relatively rare visitors, the Greeks of Sicily lived cheek by jowl with both native Sicilians and the Phoenicians whose cities were dotted around the island. The Carthaginian empire was quite different from the Persian empire, and might reasonably be seen as offering opportunities for economic prosperity as part of a vigorous network rather than a matter of political oppression . . . .[Sicily was] a world apart where city-state politics operated according to different rules and where contact with non-Greek traditions was frequent and intimate . . . a world where Greeks were only one group among many, competing and cooperating by turns with rather scant regard for ethnic origins. (1996, 346–47).

Furthermore, there is evidence to suggest that the Greeks in fifth-century Leontini in particular had a harmonious relationship with the native Sicels. Finley notes that the Greek colonies in Sicily "differed significantly in their relations with the Sicels. Both at Naxos and Leontini there is evidence that the first Greek migrants and the Sicels lived side by side for a time. . . .[At Leontini] the Greeks first occupied the Colle S. Mauro, while the Sicels maintained their old settlement on the adjoining Colle Metapiccola" (1979, 19). In this context, Gorgias' tolerant and respectful portrayal of non-Greeks may well have been shaped by his personal experience as well as by his antifoundationalist conception of the self.

If he emphasizes the importance of the political dimension of Panhellenism, indicating that he conceives of the Panhellenic community as a federation in which cities live in harmony and resist external aggression, Gorgias also emphasizes the importance of the *cultural* dimension of Panhellenism. And in some respects, Gorgias even suggests that he may consider the Panhellenic community to be more a cultural than a political entity. Although his own remarks on this topic are lost, Gorgias' conception of cultural Panhellenism is alluded to by Isocrates, who in the *Panegyricus,* a text that appears to have been "compiled from the works of Gorgias on the same subject," asserts that "the name Hellenes suggests no longer a race but an intelligence," and that "the title Hellenes is applied rather to those who *share our culture* than to those who share a common blood" (*Panegyricus* 4.50; emphasis added).[8] That is, being a member of the Panhellenic community does not mean that a person possesses a particular ethnicity but that he participates in the Panhellenic culture. This construal is consistent with Gorgias' notion that Panhellenic culture is defined by the institution of the agon and not by any putative "physical" properties of its members. And it is consistent with his notion that individuals create themselves and each other in artistic as well as political activities; for as he suggests in his punning metaphor, the Larisan *demiourgoi* who create themselves and each other in their community are artisans as well as magistrates. Since Gorgias maintains that a person's deepest identity derives, not from any natural or supernatural foundations, but from his engagement with others in the agons of the community, and since he holds that the community is a contingent association of mutually trusting people who believe that agonistic institutions are the best available way to generate truths and values, cultural Panhellenism is the very embodiment of Gorgias' antifoundationalism.

Conceiving the Panhellenic community as a cultural entity has important consequences. First, cultural Panhellenism renders *education* to be of central importance. Indeed, the Greek term *paideia* denotes both culture and education, and attests to the importance Gorgias attaches to teaching and to presenting "epideictic" texts at Panhellenic festivals. In Gorgias' antifoundationalist model of the individual, education is of paramount importance, for the individual has no ultimate identity or ground apart from his cultural and social interactions with others, and education has the power to shape his deepest nature. For Gorgias education is learning to participate and excel in the agons. As his grandnephew writes, "No one of mortals before discovered a finer art / Than Gorgias to arm the soul for contests of excellence (A8). Insofar as Panhellenism is centered on education, it becomes radically open-ended, such that a person's community is not restricted to the time and place in which he may happen to live. A person may, through education, become a member of a community that includes Homer and Pindar, as well as the people who happen to live in his own local village. In this way, education expands his opportunities for self-creation, enabling him to participate in an array of agons from different times and places.

Conceiving of the Panhellenic community as a cultural entity also suggests that Panhellenism may thrive under a variety of political arrangements, including democracy, oligarchy, and even tyranny, depending on the specific circumstances and nature of each government. For even a tyrant may in some instances permit and even promote participation in an array of cultural agons. In this respect, there is no simple correspondence or essential relationship between the type of government and the degree to which people are allowed to engage in various intellectual and cultural agons. It may well be the case that a democratic city such as Athens may prohibit some sorts of agons and banish or even execute men who engage in them, while a community governed by a "tyrant," such as Jason of Phaerae or Gelon of Syracuse, may encourage an array of cultural agons.[9] This may explain why Gorgias may have decided to live under a tyrant like Jason rather than live in a democracy like Athens. For artistic and intellectual activities may be as important as political organizations in shaping our deepest identity. Participating in cultural agons about such matters as the guilt or innocence of Helen or Palamedes, or about such topics as the existence or nonexistence of Being and Not-Being, consequently, may be as important as engaging in daily political discussions in one's city. In this respect, poets, rhapsodes, and philosophers may be as important as lawyers and politicians in shaping the lives and identity of a people; and the fact that the community is governed by a tyrant such as Gelon or Jason may be less important than the specific ways in which the tyrant restricts participation in cultural agons.

Consequently, Gorgias would presumably not argue that engaging in political and legal agons is more important than engaging in philosophical or literary debates in assessing a person's morality and commitment to his community. In this respect, Gorgias differs sharply from Isocrates, who argues that addressing the serious matters of the city is of primary importance and that sophistic discussions such as Gorgias' *On Not-Being* are merely trivial and selfish pursuits. For Gorgias, engaging in a discussion about Being and Not-Being is as "political" as engaging in a discussion about Athenian hegemony. But Gorgias also differs from self-anointed philosophers like Plato, who maintain that public orators are unable to discover the truth because they "are always in a hurry—for the water in the water-clock urges them on—and the other party in the suit does not permit them to talk about anything they please" (*Theaetetus* 172d), while leisured philosophers are free to follow arguments all the way to the truth. (*Theaetetus* 172c-177c). For Gorgias, both philosophical and political agons provide opportunities for becoming free and responsible individuals, and neither lifestyle offers a privileged route to these ends. Unlike Plato, Gorgias does not characterize philosophers and orators as engaging in fundamentally or essentially different activities. Instead, he maintains that public orators and philosophers both engage in debates or agons, and in this respect use "rhetoric," but that the agons differ in various ways, depending on the circumstances. In some contexts, as Isocrates illustrates in *Helen,* praising a mythical character such as Helen of Troy may be an overtly political statement. Gorgias' punning metaphor about the Larisan potters is pertinent in this context, for the creative *demiourgos* who creates people in the community is both an artist and a politician.

Part Three
PERFORMANCE

5

BEYOND EPIPHANY AND TRANSPARENCY

> By revealing an essential element in his own language [Gorgias shows] how reality [is] stamped throughout with the same pattern: the irreducibility of the antithesis.
>
> Mario Untersteiner, *The Sophists*

> Gorgias' unique prose was transforming the uses to which written discourse was being put, thereby contributing to what is often called the transition from *mythos* to *logos*. . . . Gorgias' speech contains a number of literate characteristics that mark it as an example of fifth-century "rationalism."
>
> Edward Schiappa, "Gorgias' *Helen* Revisited"

I have argued that Gorgias is an antifoundationalist who depicts language as a family of tropes or maneuvers, who sees inquiry as a process of debate in socially sanctioned agons, and who construes truth as a label of endorsement awarded by communities to those accounts they deem most persuasive. I have also argued that Gorgias' ethical and political views are consistent with his antifoundationalism in that he promotes a Panhellenic community in which individuals fashion themselves and each other by engaging in a variety of agons. I now turn to a third aspect of Gorgias' work, namely the style or manner in which he articulates his views. In chapter 5 I examine the two prevailing readings of Gorgias' style, those advanced by the subjectivist and empiricist schools, and I argue that each fails to account for Gorgias' stylistic practice. The subjectivist account depicts Gorgias as using "nonrational" or "poetic" devices such as antithesis or radically novel metaphors in order to allude to truths that cannot be conveyed through "literal" discourse. I argue that this reading of Gorgias' style, while consistent with the subjectivist interpretation of his epistemology and ethics, fails to account for Gorgias' actual stylistic practice. I then discuss the empiricist or rationalist interpretation of Gorgias' style, one that characterizes him as deploying stylistic devices to convey information more clearly and effectively. I argue that this reading also fails to grasp the nature and purpose of Gorgias' style. In chapter 6 I offer an account of Gorgias' style that renders it an integral part of his antifoundationalist teachings. I suggest that in his manner of speaking and writing, Gorgias *adapts* to the conventions or protocols of existing genres, but that he playfully *differentiates* his own work from those conventions through parody, overtly artificial figuration, and theatricality. In so doing, he draws attention to the conventions of the genres in which he is writing and hence to the rhetoricity, situatedness, and artificiality of all texts.

The Integration of Style and Content

Before examining the subjectivist and empiricist readings of Gorgias' style, we may note that both schools employ a hermeneutic strategy that enables them to discern an integral connection between Gorgias' manner of writing and his substantive thought. This hermeneutic strategy is not confined to studies of Gorgias, of course, for many scholars have argued that a philosopher's style may be integral to his or her thought. Scholars have thus explored Parmenides' use of poetry, Plato's use of the dialogue, Augustine's use of the confession, Descartes' use of the meditation, Nietzsche's use of the aphorism, and Wittgenstein's use of the "remark," for example, exploring the various ways in which a philosopher's manner of writing may illuminate his ideas.[1] Scholars have found this hermeneutic approach inviting in their reading of Gorgias, for given such obstacles to understanding Gorgias' thought as the fragmentary nature of his extant texts, the dearth of information about their immediate historical context, and the biases and distortions arising from their transcriptions and paraphrases, any strategy that assists in understanding the substance of Gorgias' thought is welcome. But the strategy also seems warranted in studying Gorgias, given that he appears to attach enormous importance to his style and mode of presentation, composing each his four major extant texts, as well as his extant uncollected aphorisms, in a highly crafted and distinctive style. As the extraordinary critical attention to his style attests, Gorgias appears to have been intent on drawing attention to his own stylistic practice.

In construing Gorgias' style as integral to his ideas, both schools differ from those critics of Gorgias who make no attempt to find a connection between his style and his substantive thought. The tendency of critics to attend to either Gorgias' style or his thought, and to make little effort to discern a connection between the two, originates with Plato, who suggests that Gorgias' excessively "poetic" writing betrays a *lack* of philosophical substance. Plato reads Gorgias as attempting to please or entertain his audiences rather than to inform them or to engage them in substantive philosophical inquiry. He thus describes Gorgias' work as an "elegant feast" of words, akin to a delightful meal prepared by a cook intent upon satisfying the tastes of his diners rather than improving their health (*Gorgias* 447a). Plato also suggests that Gorgias' epideictic performances are histrionic, akin to dramatic performances, which are also designed to entertain audiences rather than instruct them (*Gorgias* 502c). Plato thus observes that "if we strip any kind of poetry of its melody, its rhythm and its meter, we get mere speeches as the residue," such that "poetry is a kind of public speaking" (*Gorgias* 502c). He further associates Gorgias with dramatic poetry by having the tragic poet Agathon, a student of Gorgias, speak in "Gorgianic" style in the *Symposium*. Plato has Socrates remark about Agathon's "fine assortment of eloquence" that "when we drew towards the close, the beauty of the words and phrases could not but take one's breath away . . .

his speech so reminded me of Gorgias that I was exactly in the plight described by Homer. I feared that Agathon in his final phrases would confront me with the eloquent gorgon's head, and by opposing his speech to mine would turn me thus dumbfounded into stone" (*Symposium* 198bc).[2]

Aristotle echoes Plato's portrayal of Gorgias as a stylist whose diction and performances are akin to those of the poets and have little or nothing to do with philosophical inquiry. In accounting for Gorgias' ostensibly "poetic" diction, Aristotle distinguishes between "fine language" and "thought," writing that "it was because poets seemed to win fame through their fine language when their thoughts were simple enough, that the language of oratorical prose at first took a poetical color, e.g., that of Gorgias. Even now most uneducated people think that poetical language makes the finest discourse. This is not true: the language of prose is distinct from that of poetry" (*Rhetoric* 3.1.4, 1404a24). It is significant in this context that Aristotle, like Plato, does not mention Gorgias' *On Not-Being;* and he does not appear to have considered either *Helen* or *Palamedes* worthy of "philosophical" consideration. When Aristotle discusses Gorgias in the *Rhetoric,* it is primarily in respect to his "poetic style," which Aristotle condemns as "frigid" and ineffective (*Rhetoric* 1406b4). Aristotle also follows Plato in characterizing Gorgias' performances as "theatrical," classifying them as "epideictic" displays or spectacles designed primarily to entertain audiences at festivals (*Rhetoric* 1366a).[3] Moreover, Aristotle appears to see Gorgias' epideictic displays as playful or nonserious; for serious encomia are delivered on such occasions as official state funerals, whereas the playful variety, in which rhetors praise baldness or mice, are often presented at festivals or theaters. As Richard Chase observes, with the influx of Gorgias and other Sophists, Athenian rhetoric divided into "the *pragmatikon,* the practical oratory of the Athenian citizen who possessed the right to speak in the court or in the assembly of the people, and *epideiktikon,* the oratory of the non-citizen who was permitted to speak only at festivals or through either the written word or, as logographers, through the Athenian citizen" (293–94).

The Platonic and Aristotelian view of Gorgias as a poetic stylist unconcerned with serious philosophical issues has been enormously influential among subsequent critics, most of whom portray Gorgias as a stylist indifferent to philosophy. Among ancient scholars, Philostratus describes Gorgias as "a man to whom as to a father we think it right to refer the art of the sophists. For if we consider how much Aeschylus contributed to tragedy by adorning it with costume and the high buskin, and types of heroes, and messengers from abroad or from the house, and with the distinction between suitable onstage and offstage action, Gorgias would correspond to this in his contribution to his fellow artists" (A1). And while he notes that Gorgias discusses philosophical issues and advocates Panhellenism, Philostratus draws no connection between Gorgias' substantive thought and the manner of his speaking and writing. Pausanias praises Gorgias for his attention to style, remarking that Gorgias "is said to have been the first to rescue care for speech, which had been generally neglected and had almost been forgotten among men" (A7); but Pausanias does not indicate what significance, if any, such "care" had in respect to Gorgias' substantive thought. The Suda, similarly, remarks that Gorgias "was the first to give to the rhetorical genre the verbal power and art of deliberate culture" (A2); but no contributor to the compilation mentions Gorgias' "philosophy," or suggests that his stylistic devices are somehow related to his ideas.

The historian Diodorus also remarks on Gorgias' style while overlooking his ideas, and in so doing implies that Gorgias is little more than a polished stylist. Gorgias, he asserts, was "the first to invent rhetorical techniques and so surpassed others in sophistry that he received a fee of one hundred minas for students. When he had arrived in Athens and been brought before the people, he addressed the Athenians on the subject of an alliance, and by the novelty of his style he amazed the Athenians, who were cultivated and fond of letters" (A4). And Cicero, finally, appears to follow the general consensus that Gorgias is a stylist without much substance, remarking that Gorgias is a leader in the use of "concinnity" in style, one exhibiting "a skillful arrangement of parts; harmony, literary elegance" (A30) and that Gorgias "immoderately abuses these 'festive decorations,' as he regards them" (A32). But nowhere in his extant writings does Cicero suggest that Gorgias' stylistic devices are in any way important for understanding his enigmatic thought.

Conversely, while most ancient scholars attend to Gorgias' style, some philosophers discuss Gorgias' putative "thought" without discussing his manner of writing. The most striking instance of this is found in discussions of *On Not-Being*, the only text by Gorgias that ancient authors appear to have considered to be of philosophical importance. Gorgias' original work appears to have been stylistically crafted as carefully as his other texts, for as Olympiodorus attests, "It is well known also that Gorgias wrote a fine [*kompsos*] treatise *On Nature* in the eighty-fourth Olympiad [444–441 B.C.E.]" (A10). Olympiodorus' term *kompsos* means 'elegant, pretty, clever, witty, and exquisite,' suggesting that Gorgias' style in the work is akin to the refined and elegant figuration of such works as *Epitaphios* and *Helen*. But in their paraphrases of Gorgias' text, neither the author of the *MXG* nor Sextus appear to have been attentive to Gorgias' style of writing. Neither shows any interest in the manner in which Gorgias presents his ideas, and neither paraphrase exhibits much "elegance" in its style. In his paraphrase, Sextus appears to use his own terminology quite freely, with little concern for Gorgias' own stylistic choices and strategies. Significantly in this regard, neither the author of the *MXG* nor Sextus appears to have considered any of Gorgias' other works, the styles of which appear to have been far more carefully preserved, as deserving attention as philosophical works. While Sextus reads Gorgias as an early skeptic, he never addresses such questions as whether such works as the *Epitaphios, Helen,* or *Palamedes* support his skeptical reading. Indeed, by omitting reference to these works, both authors suggest that they may have considered them mere rhetorical "display" pieces, quite devoid of any philosophical interest.

This bifurcated approach to Gorgias' writing has persisted in the modern era as well. On the one hand, many philologically oriented scholars attend to Gorgias' style, and in so doing depict him as a "poetic" orator, one of the first "prose stylists" or "prose rhapsodes." Nineteenth-century scholars such as Jebb and Cope suggest that there is no philosophical significance to Gorgias' style; indeed, Jebb remarks that the while he deserves credit as the "founder of artistic prose" (1876, cxxviii), nevertheless "Gorgias seems to have given little or no heed to the treatment of subject matter . . . or even to that special topic of Probability which was already engaging so much of the attention of rhetoric" (cxxiv-cxxv). Cope, similarly, suggests that his antithetical and poetic writing indicates that Gorgias "abandoned at an early period the philosophical speculations to which he had addicted himself in his youth, and . . . devoted himself exclusively to the cultivation of rhetoric," most specifically "the novel style of composition which he introduced" (1855, 65).

More recent scholars attending to Gorgias' style frequently concur: Van Hook reads Gorgias as offering "a plethora of words and a paucity of ideas" (1913, 122); Bromley Smith finds Gorgias to be "an artist in words and not a man with a message" (1921, 354); Kennedy describes Gorgias as a writer who "simply borrowed a number of the techniques of poetry and developed to an extreme the natural Greek habit of antithesis" (1963, 64); Robinson finds in Gorgias' writing "nothing of philosophical importance; only a kind of clever-silliness" (1973, 59); and Robert Connors concludes that "rhetoric for Gorgias was extremely poetical . . . abundant [in its] use of every poetic device—antithesis, isocolon, parison, homoeoteleuton—except meter. . . . His style is a result of his discovery of a *techne* by which he could most effectually tap the response of orally conditioned minds and provoke that poetic response through rhetoric" (1992, 48).

On the other hand, many of the nineteenth- and twentieth-century philosophical "rehabilitations" of the Sophists have paid little if any attention to Gorgias' style. Hegel, who reads Gorgias as a serious philosopher with a consistent ontology and epistemology, does not even mention Gorgias' style of writing. Indeed, Hegel attends only to *On Not-Being,* a work in which Gorgias' thought appears only in the paraphrases of subsequent thinkers who appear to have had little or no interest in his original style of writing. Grote, similarly, also considers only *On Not-Being* and appears quite unconcerned with Gorgias' stylistic practice. In the twentieth century, most philosophers who have examined Gorgias' thought also tend to overlook or minimize the importance of Gorgias' manner of writing. Guthrie (1971), for example, while offering an extensive analysis of *On Not-Being*, does not draw any connection between what he sees as Gorgias' "subjectivism" and his stylistic figuration. Kerferd is perhaps even more indifferent to Gorgias' manner of writing, arguing that the suggestion that Gorgias' work is a stylistic "parody" is "so obviously wrong that it is hardly necessary to devote much time to discussing it" (1955, 3). And Robinson, continuing this tradition, simply dismisses Gorgias' style as being "as repellent as it is artificial" (1973, 52).

The Poetics of *Kairos*

Subjectivist critics have articulated two correlative readings of Gorgias' style, each of which views him as using "poetic" devices to achieve goals that cannot be reached with literal prose. As noted above, scholars in the subjectivist camp read Gorgias as intensely hostile to rational discourse; for he views *logos* as a tyrant who constrains us personally and politically and as an addictive drug that deceives and enslaves us, leading us to become isolated from experience with its abstract categories and chains of reasoning. Rational discourse is a prison-house, and insofar as we believe that we are able to discern the true nature of things through clear prose, we are "liquid prisoners pent in walls of glass," our distilled rational minds isolated from passionate involvement in real life. It is only if we are able to escape the chains of reason, smashing the transparent vial of prose, that we will be able to experience life in its truest intensity and "reality," becoming one with the irrational flux of Becoming. This experience, which Gorgias characterizes with the term *kairos*, will be an opening into what is truly real, an aperture through which we may find our truest selves. Gorgias' objective is to liberate us from the logical prison in which we are confined and enable us to experience life kairotically. In order to accomplish this task, he deploys poetic, nonrational tropes that expose the ostensibly invisible prison-house, and that offer possible ways of escaping its confines.

In the first construal of Gorgias' liberating style, that advanced by Untersteiner and iterated by Gronbeck and Engnell, Gorgias is seen as using figures of *antithesis* to imitate or replicate the tragic antithesis that isolates us from experiencing reality. As noted above, Untersteiner reads Gorgias as a "tragic" thinker who sees reality as beyond human comprehension and articulation. Unlike Parmenides, for instance, who maintains that a philosophically accurate language may articulate and communicate the essence of reality, Gorgias echoes the tragic poets, positing an unbridgeable gulf between the mind and reality. Rational discourse is inescapably deceptive insofar as we believe that it accurately represents things as they are; and any attempt to articulate in "rational" or literal terms the true nature of reality is an inescapably deceptive exercise. Gorgias' achievement as an artist, according to

Untersteiner, is that he uses poetic or nonrational features of language in a manner that enables him to "communicate the incommunicable," to show his audiences poetically what cannot be stated logically without deception and thereby communicate to them the "truth" about tragic human condition. Gorgias' rhetoric is thus a "display" of the tragic antithesis between the subjective mind and the truth that is concealed by *logos*. Untersteiner asserts that Gorgias' texts are "works of art . . . in which the harmony of speculation is embodied in the forms of expression: these forms endow the harmony of speculative theories with palpitating life and consequently with absolute validity" (1954,140). Specifically, Gorgias' works are "artistic" in their use of numerous figures of speech that, "before invading Gorgias' artistic prose, [were] used by poetry, which influenced him" (200–201). Drawing on the tragic poets, Gorgias uses poetic diction to communicate his own tragic epistemology, "displaying" the nature of a reality that resists articulation in literal prose and in so doing introducing his audiences to a "philosophical concept of life and into a tragic comprehension of reality" (201).

The key to Gorgias' poetic style is his use of the antithesis; for according to Untersteiner, although Gorgias' poetic figures may appear on first reading to be quite diverse, closer inspection reveals that they each exhibit an antithetical form. Gorgias' most distinctive figures thus underscore an antithesis at the level of letters, words, and clauses; and in so doing, they gesture toward, and draw attention to, the tragic antithesis that Gorgias sees as inherent in human existence itself. Gorgias' antitheses are not merely "figures of sound," a superficial ordering of syllables, words, and clauses so as to effect a "sing-song" effect; nor are they merely a "borrowing" from the poets in order to win fame. In Untersteiner's terms, "by revealing an essential element in his own language he [shows] how reality [is] stamped throughout with the same pattern: the irreducibility of the antitheses" (194; emphasis added). Gorgias' achievement as an artist, according to Untersteiner, is that he creates a simulacrum of the antithesis inherent in the nature of things, thereby conveying through poetry what cannot be conveyed logically. To attempt to "argue" for the notion that the truth about reality cannot be proved is inherently contradictory and self-refuting; and Gorgias circumvents this dilemma with his "poetic" style, displaying, rather than merely asserting or arguing, for this truth.

It is in his style that Gorgias is able to "show" the tragic gulf between the imprisoned mind and the reality that is accessible only in kairotic moments, the tragic gulf fabricated by reason and rational discourse itself, circumventing the impossibility of rational communication of the tragic nature of things by using an antithetical style. In his poetic rhetoric, Gorgias aligns himself with the poetic tradition in which ordinary human prose differs from the inspired speech of poets and oracles, who typically speak in riddles, paradoxes, and oxymorons. As Thomas

Rosenmeyer observes, since everyday prose is unable to convey "important realities" known to the gods, the poets use "riddles and paradoxes," the ambivalence of the inspired oracles (1955, 230). The truth is available only to those poets who repudiate sobriety and rationality; poets "speak the truth in a state of intoxication induced by the eating of honey, whereas when they are sober they lie" (230). In this respect, Gorgias not only embraces the irrationalist, mythic worldview of the poets, but he iterates their antithetical speech, repudiating the notion that literal, unequivocal discourse affords an avenue to truth.

Untersteiner was not the first to attend to Gorgias' "antithetical" style. Diodorus remarks on Gorgias' "antithesis and clauses of exactly or approximately equal length and rhythm and others a such a sort" (A4). The Suda identifies several figures that effect parallelism and antithesis, notably "hyperbaton and doublings of words and repetitions and apostrophes and clauses of equal length" (A2). Cicero remarks that "Gorgias was the first to employ like joined to like with similar endings and, conversely, opposites balanced with opposites, phrases which usually come out rhythmically even if one does nothing to make them do so, but he uses them excessively" (A32). Among modern scholars, E. M. Cope characterizes Gorgias' style as one in which antithesis is found in the "sense, structure and sound" of his figuration (1855, 69). Theodore Burgess more explicitly observes that Gorgias is especially associated with six "antithetical" figures of language: antithesis itself; repetition of sound or alliteration (*parechesis*); repetition of words (*anadiplosis*); likeness of sound in final syllables of successive words or clauses (*homoioteleuton*); arrangement of words in nearly equal periods (*parisosis*, or *isokola*); and *paronomasia* or pun (1902, 102–3, n.). Douglas MacDowell, similarly, remarks that one of the most prominent features of Gorgias' style is his use of antithesis and parallelism, in that "in sentence after sentence, individual words and longer phrases are set side by side to produce symmetry in grammar and sound. Gorgias did not, of course, invent antithesis; *men/de* and *te/kai* existed long before his time.... But in Gorgias antitheses are more frequent, more compact, and more precisely balanced.... Altogether antithesis and parallelism are used far more often by Gorgias than by any other Greek author, as far as our knowledge goes; and so it seems quite likely that (as Diodorus 12.53.4 suggests) this was what struck the Athenians as novel in 427" (1982, 18). But while these scholars allude to Gorgias' use of the antithesis, Untersteiner undertakes to explain its significance, arguing that his stylistic antitheses offer a simulacrum of the tragic metaphysical and epistemological antithesis that isolates man from experiencing the chaotic flux of Becoming.

Untersteiner's notion that Gorgias uses antithesis to imitate the tragic metaphysical antithesis between the mind and truth is iterated by Gronbeck and Richard

Engnell. Gronbeck writes that Gorgias' "tragedy of knowledge" is twofold, for "man seeking true knowledge is frustrated with the gulf between the non-rationality of the gods and the attempted rationality of his own mind; further, man working to convey what partial knowledge he has must move through the medium of *logoi* and by genus psyche, which is as capable of disease as the body" (1972, 31). Because every rational account of the tragic gulf that isolates man from the chaotic universe is inherently deceptive, it is only through poetic allusion that Gorgias is able to "speak the truth." Engnell iterates the same point, contending that "for Gorgias, knowledge was tragic because when man approached the world rationally, through *logos,* he was always forced into contradiction or led to antithetical conclusions" (1973, 176). To attempt to argue for the notion that the truth about reality is itself beyond comprehension is inherently contradictory and self-refuting, and Gorgias' way to avoid such a dilemma is to use the "poetic" device of antithesis to gesture toward that truth, displaying rather than arguing for his view of the world. Since reason or *logos* is composed of abstractions and artificial patterns, it can never capture the irrational, momentary essence of experience; but Gorgias is able to circumvent the impossibility of "rationally" communicating the truly tragic nature of things by using an antithetical style, a style whose structure imitates the truth in a "nonlogical" or poetic manner.

If these critics see antitheses as central to his style, a second group of subjectivist critics who attend to Gorgias' other poetic figures of speech argue that he uses radically novel figures of speech to express his own unique kairotic experiences. Like Untersteiner, these scholars read Gorgias as positing a gulf between the rational mind and the chaos of existence, and as using poetic devices to circumvent the inescapable deceptiveness of rational or literal prose. But rather than construing Gorgias' style as persistently antithetical, they see his writing as radically novel and original, composed of an array of metaphors, paradoxes, and other nonrational figures of speech. And rather than seeing Gorgias' style as mimetic of the tragic antithesis between the mind and the chaos of the world, they read his style as a lyrical expression of subjectively generated realities. In this respect, these critics read Gorgias' style as being more akin to that of the lyric poets than of the tragic poets, wherein his writings express his own personal experience rather than imitate or replicate the tragic gulf between the mind and the world. In this vein, Laszlo Versenyi argues that "Gorgias' conception of the power of the word makes him more akin to the lyric poets who, instead of enlightening man, gratify, delight him, and provide an escape from his plight" (1963, 52; emphasis added). Because he considers "everyday life to be deluded, ignorant, unessential, and unsafe," Gorgias uses his expressive style to generate imaginative alternatives to everyday life, offering "release and salvation through an escape into a better, more essential, and sounder realm" (52). Following in the footsteps of lyric poets such as Sappho, Gorgias uses poetic figuration as a vehicle with which he is able to convey the otherwise incommunicable truth about the irrationality of the kairotic experience.

Perhaps the most extensive version of this reading of Gorgias' style is advanced by Eric White, who sees Gorgias' endlessly creative and figurative style as exemplifying a "will to spontaneity," one by which he expresses "new and illusory spheres of belief in an ever-changing moment (1987, 21). As noted above, White reads Gorgias as depicting reality as a distinct sequence of disjunctive moments in a Heraclitean flux of Becoming, an ineffable "present," different for each individual, and always beyond the reach of any language that purports to capture and label it. For words, although needed for communication, are abstractions from that which is most real, namely the immediate, irrational, unique experience of the individual subject. Literal speech is especially misleading in its accounts of what is real; for rather than attempting to capture the uniqueness of each moment, it relies on abstract categories and purports to "make sense" of experiences by assimilating one to another. Language can never accurately mirror what is real, for as soon as it is articulated in words, the unique and subjective kairotic experience is abstracted and assimilated into the abstract categories of discourse. Because he recognizes this "truth" about the world, Gorgias deploys a style that is constantly innovative, originating novel poetic figures from moment to moment. Rather than relying on one figure, the antithesis, Gorgias generates a profusion of novel figures, creating "an endlessly proliferating style deployed according to no overarching principle or rational design" (21), whereby he "restlessly experiments with the style of utterance in the hope of producing genuine novelty" (30). Unlike Untersteiner, who sees Gorgias' antithetical style as mirroring or replicating the tragic architecture of reality itself, White argues that Gorgias composes whimsical and radically original figures of speech in order to fabricate new domains wherein he "discovers in every new occasion a unique opportunity to confer meaning on the world" (14). Gorgias' style thus expresses his subjectivist epistemology, in which each novel creation is an expression of one's personal "whim," an "ultimately arbitrary imposition of form upon the teeming variety of the world" (36). Gorgias' radically novel figuration suggests that every ostensibly mimetic verbal account of an external reality is deceptive insofar as it taken as an accurate representation of how things really are.

While Untersteiner sees Gorgias as imitating the tragic gulf between the mind and the world, and White reads him as spinning new worlds of his own, several subjectivist scholars read Gorgias as using his style in a more activist, even violent manner, assaulting the chains of *logos*. They emphasize that Gorgias recognizes that *logos* is a tyrant that imposes its will on people; and they maintain that his tropes are designed to overthrow the tyrant, to raze the prison walls of the dominant *logos*, and perhaps even to "annihilate" *logos* itself. Roger Moss remarks that the Sophist "violates the sacred relationship between words and thoughts" with his violent and "paradoxical" speech. With his tropes he "wrests words out of their accustomed forms," for "paradox violates the sacred relationship between words and thoughts. Barely suppressed aggression is a real part of sophistic verbal display." He thereby effects a "euphoria," whereby we experience the "excesses, the twists and leaps of sophistic writing," and discern the "violence that is being done to language" (1982, 216).

In Poulakos' terms, Gorgias commits "symbolic violence by engaging in paradox, indulging in excesses, or turning any argument on its head" (1990, 168). The Sophist "places a high premium on novelty," and his radically novel figurative style "shatters aspects of conventional wisdom and unsettles the sensibilities of the accepted tradition" (1995, 190). In order to disrupt and rupture the deceptive order imposed by *logos,* Gorgias deploys an array of poetic tropes that destabilize ordinary prose, disrupting the smooth flow of thought with deliberately opaque figures, and consequently "freezing" the deceptive fluidity of limpid prose. In order to enable his audience to experience kairotic moments, to leap beyond the walls of the prison of rational discourse, Gorgias thus disrupts the ostensibly "natural" flow of words that effects a lucidity to the objectified mind. If his paradoxical and antithetical tropes appear to obstruct clarity, this is precisely what they are designed to do; for they thwart rational thought, or, in Keats's phrase, "tease us out of thought" in order to burst the walls of the prison in which we are pent.

Contradictions in the Subjectivist Readings

Although these accounts render Gorgias' style consistent with his putative subjectivist epistemology and ethics, I submit that they are ultimately unconvincing, for they misrepresent Gorgias' stylistic practice. Untersteiner argues that Gorgias uses antithesis to allude to the metaphysical chasm between the rational mind and the nonrational chaos of the world; however, we should note that Gorgias' style is not uniquely or excessively antithetical. Rather than being exceptional, Gorgias' use of antitheses is quite typical of Greek writing from the sixth through the fourth centuries. As John Finley has demonstrated in great detail, antithesis, though "heightened by Gorgias' use of parisosis and paromoiosis, is not in itself Gorgian but rather, characteristic of an earlier sophistic prose already widespread before 427" (1939, 75). In the genre of the philosophical *epicheireme* exemplified by *On Not-Being,* for example, authors frequently deploy antithesis in articulating their ideas. Parmenides, for instance, writes in a highly antithetical manner, as is evidenced in his assertion that there are two "routes of inquiry for thinking: the one, that it is an that it is not possible for it not be . . . the other, that it is not and that it is right for it not to be" (Fragment 2). Nor is Gorgias' antithetical style in the *Epitaphios* unique among other extant Athenian funeral orations. Gorgias' stately, formal antitheses echo those of Pericles, Lysias, Plato, Demosthenes, and Hyperides. To cite only one of myriad examples, Thucydides' Pericles asserts, "We are free and tolerant in our private lives; but in public affairs we keep to the law. . . . Our love of what is beautiful does not lead to extravagance; our love of the things of the mind does not make us soft" (2.37–40).

In the family of texts that comprise the discourse on Helen of Troy, a similarly antithetical style may be found. In *The Trojan Women,* for instance, Euripides has Helen defend herself in a style as antithetical as that which Gorgias deploys in his own defense of Helen, remarking that she "brought their houses to the sorrow of slavery instead of conquest" (935–64).[4] And in legal apologia, Gorgias "antithetical" style is quite in keeping with the style of many other forensic texts. In the *Apology,* for example, which is frequently compared to Gorgias' work, Plato frequently uses antitheses to articulate his ideas. To cite only one instance, Socrates remarks, "My accusers, then, as I maintain, have said little or nothing that is true, but from me you shall hear the whole truth—not, I can assure you, gentlemen, in flowery language like theirs, decked out with fine words and phrases" (*Apology* 17bc). Like Gorgias, Plato uses antithesis throughout the *Apology* to contrast justice and injustice, knowledge and opinion, truth and falsity. And Gorgias' use of antithesis in his witty aphorisms or *gnomai* is also quite in keeping with the style of other such aphoristic remarks. Indeed, most of the extant *gnomai,* from Homer and Theognis through fourth-century authors, are decidedly antithetical in their style. In his account of "urbanities," Aristotle observes that "antithesis" is especially useful in conveying information quickly and easily; for it enables an audience to discern a difference between two ideas or images, and thereby grasp the meaning of the aphorism more readily (*Rhetoric* 1410b).

Although it is incorrect to characterize Gorgias' style as distinctively antithetical, it is also incorrect to construe it as radically and consistently novel in its figuration. For while he does articulate several novel images, Gorgias often writes in a way that is quite conventional and imitative of other authors in the same genre. Some of Gorgias' metaphors are indeed striking and original, such as his playful quip that "those neglecting philosophy and devoting themselves to general studies were like the suitors who, though wanting Penelope, slept with her maids" (B30); that the "the sun is a red-hot stone" (B31); that the art of rhetoric differs from all other arts because "under its influence all things are willingly but not forcibly made slaves (*Philebus* 58a); that "just as things made by mortar-makers are mortars, so also Larisians are those made by public servants, or they are a group of Larisofiers" (A19); that vultures are living tombs, and Xerxes is "the Persians' Zeus" (B5a). But many of his metaphors are more conventional, and echo familiar thoughts and phrases. His deathbed remark that "sleep already begins to hand me over to his brother Death" (A15), for instance, draws on a familiar Greek myth; his remark that one of Aeschylus' dramas was "filled with Ares," namely *The Seven Against Thebes* (B29) appears to echo Aristophanes himself; and his quip that orators were like frogs because "the latter made their cry in water and the former before the water clock" (B31), is also found in Aristophanes.

I do not mean to suggest that Gorgias is always derivative in his metaphors; but it does seem to be the case that in comparison to the metaphors of such authors as Homer, Sappho, Pindar, or Sophocles, for example, Gorgias' metaphors are by no means distinctive for their originality. And if Gorgias' poetic figuration is not always original, neither is it pervasive in his writing. For he does not always use novel figures of speech, and in several texts he avoids such poetic figures as metaphor, simile, and personification altogether. In his aphorisms, as noted, he uses metaphors quite frequently. And in *Helen,* he articulates a number of playful metaphors, analogies, and similes. He repeats the familiar hyperbole that Helen has "godlike" beauty (H4); he personifies such forces as Chance, referring to it as having a "will" of its own; he personifies *logos* as a "powerful lord" (H8) and remarks that *logos* "constrained" Helen's psyche (H12). In a striking analogy, he compares *logos* to a *pharmakon* or drug (H14); he asserts that sight "engraves" upon the mind images of things which have been seen; he compares *eros* to a disease (H19). But in *Palamedes, On Not-Being,* and the *Epitaphios,* Gorgias uses far fewer metaphors. In the legalistic *Palamedes,* he observes that Nature casts a vote of death (P1) and that a shameful reputation is a "disease in life" (P35), but most of his assertions are quite literal. In the formal Eleatic language of *On Not-Being,* Gorgias uses few if any "poetic" metaphors; and in the stately *Epitaphios,* he appears to deliberately avoid playful poetic images altogether.

The Tropes of Transparency

While critics who read Gorgias as a subjectivist see his style as designed to suggest poetically what cannot be asserted literally, those who read him as an empiricist contend that Gorgias uses stylistic devices such as antithesis and metaphor to convey information and to move his audience emotionally. In this account, Gorgias does not use antitheses to allude to a putative metaphysical antithesis between an imprisoned human consciousness and an out-of-reach kairotic experience of the flux of reality, but rather to emphasize or illustrate a particular distinction he is drawing in a specific argument. He deploys antithetical figures in order to clarify ideas, thereby illustrating Aristotle's observation that antithesis is a useful way to convey information quickly and easily. Empiricist scholars also argue that Gorgias' use of analogical figures such as metaphor and simile serve the same end, namely, to convey information. For Gorgias' analogies render his ideas concrete, presenting abstract ideas in a manner that enables his audience to visualize his ideas; that is, he renders them vivid or present to the senses. In respect to his use of metaphors, Gorgias' figures render his ideas concrete, presenting abstract ideas in a manner that makes his ideas "visible"; and in this respect he may be seen as illustrating Aristotle's observation that metaphor "gives style clearness, charm, and distinction as nothing else can" and is often more effective than lengthy argumentation in conveying information to an audience (*Rhetoric* 1405a).

Several empiricist readers emphasize that Gorgias' works are *performance* pieces in which he presents his ideas orally. In an oral presentation, exaggerated antitheses are often quite appropriate, and what may seem overly antithetical in print seems far less so when heard. Bromley Smith thus observes that Gorgias frequently performed his texts and that antithesis is especially suited to conveying information in an oral setting. In Smiths' terms, a "reading aloud of the fragment [of the *Epitaphios*] will reveal that Gorgias was a consummate elocutionist, for he had constructed a speech full of rhythms and periods, cadences and melodies, so fitted to contrasting words that all the powers of his voice would be displayed" (1921, 353).

Several readers in the empiricist camp also point out that while Gorgias' prose style may appear overly poetic, it is important to situate him in the progression in Greek thought from a poetic or "mythical" way of thinking to a rational, scientific mode of analysis and to credit him for progressing beyond "mere poetry." Schiappa (1995) argues that Gorgias' principal stylistic achievement is to advance the use of rational argumentation and to promote a style in which information is conveyed through a rational rather than a "poetic" manner of writing. That is, rather than resorting to ambiguous figures of speech, Gorgias writes in a manner that relies on cogent argumentation, and he presents his ideas in a manner that is more transparent than his "poetic" predecessors and contemporaries. Thus Schiappa contends that "it is easy to fixate on Gorgias' exotic style and his 'magical' use of language and, as a result, neglect his more 'rationalistic' side. Such neglect is a mistake. There is a clear parallel in ancient Greek discourse between the transition from poetic to prose styles and the gradual proliferation of modes of reasoning. Because many texts of this era tend to combine elements of 'rationalistic' prose and 'mythic' poetry, there is a tendency to see such a 'mixed' style as a fault of the writer rather than evidence of rapid changes in modes of composition" (1995, 315). In this reading, Schiappa stresses Gorgias' contribution to what he identifies as a principal feature of Greek intellectual culture, namely the transition from *mythos* to *logos,* from a nonrational and primarily oral mode of thinking and communicating to a rational and objective mode of thinking in which writing plays a far greater role. In this vein, Schiappa contends that:

> Gorgias' unique prose was transforming the uses to which written discourse was being put, thereby contributing to what is often called the transition from *mythos* to *logos*.... Though his style is notably poetic, it is also notably rationalistic for its time.... Though Gorgias' manner of composition may strike some readers as 'irrational' or 'nonrational' compared to Aristotle's prose, for example, the more relevant comparison is between the sorts of compositions produced immediately prior to Gorgias and in his own generation.... Gorgias' speech contains a number of literate characteristics that mark it as an example of fifth-century rationalism. (1995, 315–16)

Thus in *Helen,* and presumably in his other texts as well, Gorgias writes in a manner that draws upon the poetic conventions of his own time but in a manner that advances "the art of written prose in general, and argumentative composition in particular. Though the subject mater is ostensibly mythical, the modus operandi [or style] of the discourse supplements the qualities of traditional, oral-poetic composition with such humanistic-rationalistic practices as the apagogic method of argument" (1995, 317).

Although empiricist readers see Gorgias as using antithesis and metaphor to convey information clearly and effectively in oral settings, they also point out that Gorgias uses language for its "emotive" power as well. A skilled verbal technician, Gorgias draws upon the rhythmical and acoustic properties of language to affect his audience's emotions in a manner analogous to the way a physician may affect his patient's body through the use of medicines. Indeed, Gorgias' remarks in *Helen* seem to support this reading; for he asserts that "speech, by means of the finest and most invisible body effects the divinest works; it can stop fear and banish grief and create joy and nurture pity" (H8). He also remarks that "fearful shuddering and tearful pity and grievous longing come upon its hearers, and at the actions and physical sufferings of others in good fortunes and in evil fortunes, through the agency of words, the soul is wont to experience a suffering of its own" (H9). Gorgias also asserts that the effect of speech upon the condition of the soul is comparable to the power of drugs over the nature of bodies: "For just as different drugs dispel different secretions from the body, and some bring an end to disease and others to life, so also in the case of speeches, some distress, others delight, some cause fear, others make the hearers bold, and some drug and bewitch the soul with a kind of evil persuasion" (H14). In another analogy, Gorgias uses words as a magician uses a chant, namely to manipulate and "bind" a listener.

Romilly (1975) thus argues that Gorgias, as "the master of rhetoric," draws from the poets in order to appeal to his audience and that he finds "in the poets some notion about the means by which this aim could be reached. One of the means is suggested by Gorgias' text—namely, style" (8). Although Gorgias' style may in some respects appear to be as "poetic" as that of Aeschylus or Pindar, it differs in that he uses it in a deliberate, self-conscious, and "rational" manner. Consequently, Gorgias uses his "poetical prose" not merely to win him the prestige of the poets, as Aristotle suggests, and thereby to emulate the "dignity of poetry" (8); but rather, Gorgias draws upon the poets for a decidedly practical and rational end, namely to "work upon people's emotions"; and to this end "antithesis had its place, since it enhanced the meaning and made it more powerful" (9).

Gorgias is not alone in his use of antithesis; but he uses it "more conspicuously than anybody else" (10). Through his rational *techne,* Gorgias undertakes to "bind" his listener through words (12). Through chants, he draws upon the practices of magicians and healers who use words as a therapeutic technique. As Romilly points out, the poet Orpheus was also "a master of incantations and a healer" (1975, 14); and Gorgias uses style as a mode of psychagogia, moving his listener's psyche. He emulates the power of the poet by deploying such aspects of language as "the haunting repetition of words . . . with the same view to a magical spell" (17–19). In Romilly's terms, Gorgias knew well enough that, with all the pride of a fifth-century man, he was deliberately shifting magic into something rational" (20). In this respect Gorgias is a scientific technician, moving speech from "the level of magic and incantation to the level of empirical medicine" (21).

In a similar vein, Segal (1972) remarks that Gorgias' "rationalistic" use of style anticipates the arts of Plato and Aristotle. Segal emphasizes Gorgias' use of reason to examine and explain persuasion in a way that anticipates later "scientific" studies of rhetoric. He remarks that "although Gorgias may not himself have worked out the systematic consequences, psychological and ethical, of his *techne,* nevertheless his rationalistic approach to an area of human activity that did not admit of easy systematization, namely the emotional reaction to art, suggested and stimulated a line of development which proves highly fruitful in the fourth century and culminates as a full-blown "scientific" theory in the poetics of Aristotle" (134). Drawing on the poetic use of figuration, Gorgias uses specific formal structures (specifically, the "Gorgian" figures) to manipulate the audience emotionally. In Segal's terms,

> It is Gorgias' achievement to have perceived and formulated as a *techne* that the formal structuring of the *logos* (in qualities such as *metron*) evokes emotional forces, and to have generalized this formulation (at least in terms of the emotional effects, if not of formal analysis) to include both the linguistic and the visual arts. At the same time he attempts a scientific definition of the process by seeking an analogy in the most exact empirical science which the late fifth century could offer, medicine. In so doing, he treats the psyche as a tangible reality and places its functions on a level of reasonable explicability coordinate with other physical phenomena. (133)

Segal identifies a two-stage process, a passive aesthetic state and an active state, which Gorgias effects. Gorgias "conceived of a process n which the psyche moves from the pure aesthetic state of *terpsis* to a more active condition of fear or pity, love or persuasion" (124). Presumably, Gorgias' own figuration is an embodiment of this causal theory of rhetoric, wherein his poetic figures would transport his audience to experience the "sublime."

The Limits of Lucidity

How persuasive is the empiricist construal of Gorgias' style? On the one hand, the notion that Gorgias' style is lucid when presented in an oral setting flies in the face of the assessment of nearly every ancient commentator who emphasizes that Gorgias' speech is complex, playful, inappropriate, or transgressive. Thucydides' Cleon, for example, commenting on the type of displays for which Gorgias was famous, remarks that the Sophist uses paradoxes and novelties because his audience enjoys playing the intellectual game of grasping them (Thucydides 3.8). If Gorgias' figures were too easily grasped and hence too "ordinary," he would not be a Sophist, and his speech would not entertain his sophistic audience. Plato characterizes Gorgias' style as shimmering, diverse and "gorgonesque," ornate and rich rather than "plain"; Aristotle characterizes Gorgias' obscure allusions, newly coined words, epithets, and far-fetched metaphors as too poetic for everyday practical oratory, suitable only for theatrical, epideictic performances; and Cicero remarks that Gorgias overuses playful "festivities" of style. In short, Gorgias' classical critics characterize his style as artificial, paradoxical, and complex; filled with puns, localisms, and double words; and having an excess of epithets and far-fetched metaphors. Insofar as his contemporaries and near-contemporaries tend be nearly unanimous in remarking that Gorgias' style is anything but lucid, it is unreasonable to simply assert that they were mistaken.

Furthermore, the notion that Gorgias intends his style to be lucid in oral presentations is belied by Aristotle's observation that Gorgias' epideictic works are "writerly" in that they are highly ornate, filled with elaborate artificial figures that are inappropriate for oral argument. Aristotle suggests that Gorgias' artificial style is unsuited to the debates of the courts and assembly, that nobody would be convinced by them because they are too poetic, too much like Aeschylus. Distinguishing between the written and "agonistic" style, Aristotle asserts that epideictic rhetoric is most suited to writing, emotional and ethical proof is more suited to deliberative, and forensic rhetoric is more suited to ethical and emotional proof. He adds that "a different style is suitable to each kind of rhetoric. That of written compositions is not the same as that of debate; nor, in the latter, is that of public speaking the same as that of the law courts. . . . The style of written compositions is most precise, that of debate is most suitable for delivery . . . . This is why the same orators do not excel in all these styles; where action is most effective, there the style is least finished, and this is a case in which voice, especially a loud one, is needed. The epideictic style is especially suited to written compositions, for its function is reading" (*Rhetoric* 1413b-1414a). Aristotle does not somehow "overlook" the fact that Gorgias delivered some of his speeches; on the contrary, he argues that Gorgias' "writerly" style is ineffective in oral settings because it is too artificial and playful, distracting an audience from the substance of the speech.

Nor is it very convincing to say that Gorgias' style is "emotionally moving." The notion that Gorgias uses poetic devices to transport his audiences emotionally is belied by the remarks of his contemporaries and near-contemporaries as well as by what appears moving to most readers today. Most ancient authors remark that rather than being emotionally transporting, Gorgias' style is more aptly characterized as comic and playful. Thucydides' Cleon observes that during displays by Sophists like Gorgias, people attend to the cleverness and wit of his playful figuration and are not moved "emotionally." Addressing the Athenian Assembly, he argues that "the chief wish of each one of you is to be able to make a speech himself, and, if you cannot do that, the next best thing is to compete with those who can make this sort of speech by not looking as though you were at all out of your depth while you listen to the views put forward, by applauding a good point even before it is made, and by being as quick at seeing how an argument is going to be developed as you are slow at understanding what in the end it will lead to" (3.38). In a similar vein, Plato characterizes Gorgias' style as an entertaining or delightful "feast," a banquet of rhetorical figures that pleases or delights his audience (*Gorgias* 447a). Aristotle applauds Gorgias' witty quip to a swallow, and commends his observation that the most effective response to a seriousness is jest (*Rhetoric* 1419b3). Philostratus observes that the Gorgian style is frequently comedic, remarking that Agathon, "whom Comedy regards as wise and eloquent, often Gorgianizes in his iambic verse" (A1.3), iambic being the meter of comic abuse and satire. And Athanasius complains that Gorgias' rhetoric "is concerned with something ridiculous, awakening the guffaws of the young and being basically a shameless flattery" (B5a).

Clearly, Gorgias does not appear to be attempting to move his audience's emotions when he quips that "orators are like frogs; the former perform by the water clock, the latter in water" (B30), or when he remarks that those neglecting philosophy and devoting themselves to general studies are like the suitors in the Odyssey "who, though wanting Penelope, slept with her maids" (B29). Gorgias' elegant, sophisticated style is frequently witty and occasionally bawdy, but it is rarely if ever "emotionally moving."

6

THE EPIDEICTIC PERFORMANCE

> This language, then, should be used . . . ironically, after the manner of Gorgias.
>
> Aristotle, *Rhetoric*
>
> The story is forgotten that Hippias and Gorgias appeared in purple robes.
>
> Aelian, *Miscellaneous History*

I have argued that neither the subjectivist nor empiricist reading is able to account for the style Gorgias uses in his various texts. As an alternative to these two accounts, I suggest that Gorgias uses a variety of stylistic strategies to display his antifoundationalist views, exposing the tactics used by his foundationalist rivals to conceal the rhetoricity of their own texts and showing how texts may be composed with a nonrepresentational language. Among the stylistic strategies Gorgias uses for this end are parody, artificial figuration, theatricality, and the venue of the festival.

First, Gorgias composes parodies of such established genres as the Athenian *epitaphios*, the serious encomium, the legal *apologia*, and the Eleatic *epicheireme*. In so doing, he draws upon conventions to generate his own text and to expose the ways in which his foundationalist rivals conceal their own dependence on the *topoi*, tropes, and argumentative conventions of each genre. Next, Gorgias deploys a variety of overtly artificial, "paratropic" figures, including epithets, oxymorons, localisms, coined words, puns, and metaphors that enable him to generate new perspectives and to foreground the rhetoricity of all tropes. Third, he engages in exaggerated theatricality or "acting," wearing the traditional purple robes of the rhapsodes, playing distinctive roles (the erudite metaphysician, the officially appointed Athenian funeral orator, the bold champion of a notorious woman, the mythical Palamedes), and speaking boastfully as a comedic *alazon*. In so doing, he shows how a rhetor's character shapes what he may see, draws attention to his own role as performer, and indicates that all rhetors rely on histrionic ruses to effect persuasion. Finally, Gorgias presents many of his works at festivals, venues in which participants would expect and welcome parody, novel wordplay, and theatrical display. Gorgias' parodic and figurative displays are an integral part of his educational project, displaying the rhetoricity of all discourse and inviting his audiences to become engaged in the agons of their culture.

FOUR PARODIES

In each of his four extant texts, Gorgias' governing stylistic strategy or "master trope" is *parody*, whereby he adapts his manner of writing to the conventions of existing genres while playfully exaggerating or distorting some of those conventions. The Greek term *parodia,* which combines the prefix *para* and the root *odos,* literally denotes a "singing that is adjacent to, and yet distinct from another singing."[1] The prefix *para* suggests adjacency or affinity as well as difference, transgression, and opposition; and in this respect, it may be seen as a playful instance of the rhetoric of "praise and blame" with which Gorgias is typically associated. As Margaret Rose observes, parody is often ambivalent, showing "empathy with and distance from the text imitated" (1993, 49). The "epideictic" genre in which he writes is for Gorgias an openly parodic genre that stands "alongside" various established genres in the culture; and in each of his four parodic texts, Gorgias adapts his manner of writing to the conventions of an established genre while playfully differentiating it from the conventions of that genre.[2]

Reading Gorgias' texts as parodic is not new; several ancient and modern commentators have read some or all of Gorgias' works as parodic, ironic, or satirical. Gorgias himself invites this reading, counseling his students to deploy jest as a rhetorical strategy and observing that one "should kill [one's] opponents' seriousness with jesting, and their jesting with earnestness" (*Rhetoric* 1419b). Plato suggests that Gorgias' writing is typically parodic, for when he has Agathon "Gorgianize" in the *Symposium,* he suggests that to Gorgianize is to engage in parody, since Agathon's speech is highly parodic and playful, mocking some of Gorgias' own signature figuration.[3] Aristotle, more prosaically, observes that Gorgias' manner of writing is "typically ironic" (*Rhetoric* 1408b); and Athanasius, scandalized by Gorgias' playful reference to vultures being "living tombs" in his parodic *Epitaphios,* remarks that Gorgias' rhetoric "is concerned with something ridiculous, awakening the guffaws of the young and being basically a shameless flattery" (B5a).[4]

Gorgias uses parody as both a "compositional" and an "expositional" strategy. As a strategy of composition or invention, he uses parody to situate his text vis-à-vis other texts in established genres, drawing upon the conventional *topoi,* tropes, and modes of argument of each genre to generate his own text; and in each instance, he uses the conventional rhetorical strategies of the genre to develop a persuasive argument. Thus in *On Not-Being,* he situates his work alongside the Eleatic *epicheireme;* in the *Epitaphios,* he places his text alongside the established genre of the official Athenian funeral oration; in *Helen,* he situates his playful encomium vis-à-vis the genre of the serious or *spoudaic* encomium; and in *Palamedes,* he writes a defense that draws upon the conventions of the dicanic *apologia.*

Gorgias also uses parody as an "expositional" or polemic strategy with which he exposes as deceptive the attempts by his foundationalist foes to present their work as impartial and objective accounts of the truth. As an assault on his rivals, Gorgias' parodies suggest that every speech must adhere to the conventions of the genre in which it is situated and that each is agonistic, advanced by an interested partisan or contestant. Specifically, he exposes as deceptive the attempts by Eleatic metaphysicians, officially appointed Athenian orators, self-proclaimed divinely inspired poets, and lying plaintiffs to present their views as being honest reflections of the way the world really is. By highlighting the conventions of each genre, Gorgias displays his notion that texts are not persuasive because they accurately represent the way the world really is, but are persuasive because skilled rhetors are able to deploy strategies that conceal their own rhetoricity. He thus illustrates his antifoundationalist view that arguments are generated in sanctioned agons and that "truth" is the ornament awarded to the victor by a community or audience.[5]

Gorgias' objective, as parodist, is to undeceive his audience, alerting them to various strategies of deception used by adept rhetors. Using Plato's term, we may say that Gorgias' strategy, whereby he exposes or "brings to the light the resemblances produced and disguised" by every rhetor, is "antilogical" (*Phaedrus* 261e). Using more recent jargon, we may characterize Gorgias' strategy as "deconstructive," which in Fish's construal is a strategy of demonstrating the "mediated, constructed, partial, socially constituted nature of all realities, whether they be phenomenal, linguistic, or psychological"; of showing that every persuasive text rests on "the suppression of the challengeable rhetoricity of its own standpoint, a standpoint that offers itself as if it came from nowhere in particular and simply delivered things as they really (i.e., nonperspectivally) are"; and thereby attempting to deprive the text of its "claim to be *un*rhetorical, serious, disinterested" (1989, 492–93).

Gorgias engages in this practice of undeceiving his audience in each of his texts, drawing attention to the ways in which every persuasive text conceals its rhetoricity, displaying the ways in which rhetors present themselves as "speaking the truth as it really is," and thereby unmasking the deceptive tactics that partisan rhetors use to manufacture ostensibly impartial truths. He uses parody, paratropic figuration, and histrionics in his epideictic performances to disabuse the audience of the illusion that any account of things, including his own, is an objective representation or mirror of "things as they really are." His epideictic performances enable him to show that his own assertions are themselves situated and to alert his audience to the fact that even his own arguments are deceptive insofar as they are taken to be true in a context-invariant way. Stated another way, Gorgias' performances display, or *show*, as well as *tell* his audience about the situated and fabricative dimensions of *logos*.

By showing how each text is fabricated in a specific discourse, Gorgias uses parody as an integral part of the strategy that Sextus identifies as his *epibolen* or "line of attack" on the notion of a context-invariant criterion that serves to validate claims to truth and knowledge, a strategy that differs from the line of attack used by Protagoras. Unlike Protagoras, Gorgias does not rely simply on arguments in order to demolish his foundationalist rivals; instead, he uses his epideictic style to display how his rivals use *topoi,* tropes, and modes of argument to fabricate their ostensibly impartial arguments. For Gorgias, the foundationalist conceals the fact that he is engaging in a socially sanctioned agon and that his account is shaped by the constraints of his local vocabulary. In so doing, he disguises his verbal maneuvers in the game at hand as well as his apparatus of *topoi* and tropes, and he presents his own fabrications as representative of the way the world really is. As an assault on his rivals, Gorgias exposes the attempt by foundationalist thinkers to present their account as an objectively true account of the nature of things. In James Porter's terms, "Gorgias' writings work both within and outside the discourses and genres they mimic in order to defamiliarize. . . . [They] expose not only what today we might call philosophical and ideological assumptions in literature (and rhetoric), and literary, rhetorical, and ideological assumptions in philosophy, but also the *pragmatic* assumptions of his own rhetorical situation" (1993, 292–93). Unlike rhetors who conceal their artificiality and pretend to speak the truth as it really is, Gorgias foregrounds his own rhetorical maneuvers, exaggerating the conventions used in various genres, and in so doing displaying or exposing the rhetoricity and situatedness of each text.

Each of Gorgias' four extant works is parodic in that in each text he imitates or adapts to the conventions of an established, recognizable genre; but in so doing, he draws attention to these conventions through various tactics, including the use of mocking titles, overtly playful structures and arguments, self-reflections, digressions, figurative exaggerations, and transgressions. In each work, he adapts his manner of speaking and writing to the conventions of the genre at hand, whether it is the formal and sonorous Athenian *epitaphios,* or funeral oration; the elegant and witty discourse about Helen of Troy; the lucid and logical legal or dicanic apology; or the abstract and self-effacing Eleatic *epicheireme,* or essay. Although these four genres are not fixed molds or rigid sets of rules, each exhibits a discernible family of tropes, themes, argumentative patterns, and overall structures.

In this respect, the most striking feature of Gorgias' style is not a pervasive use of antithesis, as Untersteiner contends, nor a consistently "novel" array of metaphors and other poetic figures of speech, as White argues. Nor, as the empiricist camp contends, does Gorgias attempt to convey his ideas lucidly or "transparently" to his audience by "illustrating" his abstractions with concrete figures of speech. If we attend only to one or another of Gorgias' texts and fail to situate them among other works in the genre in which he is writing, we may draw these sorts of erroneous conclusions about his style. Focusing primarily on the *Epitaphios* may lead us to conclude with Untersteiner that Gorgias' style is overtly "antithetical";

attending primarily to *Helen* and the extant aphorisms may suggest that White is correct in contending that Gorgias strives for novel metaphors; and attending primarily to *Palamedes* may seem to corroborate Schiappa's contention that Gorgias' style is lucid rather than ludic. These readings of Gorgias' style fail to take into account the contexts in which he composes each of his works and the ways in which he both complies with, and digresses from, the constraints of various genres. But if we examine all of his extant texts and situate them vis-à-vis the specific genres he parodies namely, the Athenian *epitaphios*, the serious or *spoudaic* encomium, the dicanic *apologia*, and the Eleatic *epicheireme* we will see that Gorgias playfully mimics the conventions of these various genres.

In the *Epitaphios*, Gorgias' writing is highly antithetical, such that each of his phrases is composed of carefully balanced sounds, words, and clauses. Yet when we place Gorgias' text among other extant Athenian funeral orations, we find that its antitheses emulate the expected stylistic conventions of the genre. An examination of the five other extant Athenian funeral orations those of Pericles (in Thucydides), Plato, Lysias, Demosthenes, and Hyperides all show that Gorgias' use of antithesis is quite in keeping with the conventions of the *epitaphios*, an officially sanctioned military and political oration serving to honor both the slain warriors and the great democratic city of Athens. In his extensive use of antithesis, *homoioteleuta, parisosis,* and *isokola,* Gorgias echoes the formal and antithetical figuration of the genre. In Nicole Loraux's terminology, "the Sophist, an *opportunist in form* as well as in content, has turned to the advantage of his own thought themes proper to the funeral oration . . . appropriating a fixed form to which he had first to subject himself" (1986, 227–28; emphasis added). Loraux further notes that Gorgias' work "crystallizes in itself the ambiguity of the whole genre" and that "the oration is a curious text indeed, one in which all new thought may be reduced to a received or already formulated idea, in which all formal invention follows an already established model: thus what is generally regarded as the purest statement of the Sophist's thought still sounds strangely like the declarations of some other *epitaphioi*" (53–55). Thus, Gorgias' somber sonorities, repetitions of sounds, and rigorous formality imitate the conventions of the Athenian funeral oration; and what many critics mistakenly identify as peculiarly Gorgian is better be described as paradigmatic of other works in the genre. Indeed, the paradigmatic status of Gorgias' text is underscored by examining the *Menexenus*, in which Plato parodies the genre of the funeral oration. For in his parody, Plato appears to mimic several of Gorgias' phrases, suggesting that he considers Gorgias' oration to be representative of the genre as a whole in both its content and its style.[6]

While he mimics the antithetical and formal tropes of the Athenian *epitaphios*, Gorgias playfully differentiates his parodic text from others in the genre. First, given his status as a noncitizen of Athens, Gorgias would have been unable to deliver an official funeral oration in the Athenian *kerameikos*. His very act of composing the *Epitaphios* in effect renders the text an imitation of the orations delivered by Athenian citizens selected by the city itself, much as Plato's attribution of his funeral oration to Aspasia announces its parodic objective. Gorgias thus alerts his audience, forewarning them that in his "praise" of Athens, he will adapt to the constraints of the *epitaphios* while promoting his own antifoundationalist views.

Next, throughout the *Epitaphios* Gorgias exaggerates the tropes of the genre in ways that render his text even more artificial than others in the genre. He uses antitheses, conventional *topoi,* and quasi-poetic diction employed by most of the speakers in the genre, from Pericles in the fifth century to Lysias and Hyperides in the fourth. But in so doing, he playfully exaggerates these conventions, articulating antitheses more frequently, making his alliterations, assonances, and rhymes more pronounced than those of other funeral orators. Official Athenian funeral orators such as Pericles, Lysias, and Demosthenes are quite antithetical in their phrasing. But while they are notably antithetical and sonorous in their style, their *epitaphioi* do not consist *solely* of antithetical *topoi* deployed in balanced phrases; and in this respect Gorgias' work is undeniably excessive and distinctive. Moreover, Gorgias deliberately omits several conventional themes from his oration, specifically those that glorify Athens as a "foundational" city, such as the lengthy history of the city and its distinctive practice of caring for the orphans of the warriors.

Reading the *Epitaphios* as a parody explains why some scholars see Gorgias' style as one of adaptation to the conventions of the *epitaphios,* while others see it as playful and idiosyncratic. Loraux (1986), for example, attends primarily to the conventions of the genre and sees Gorgias' text as attempting to adapt to the conventions used by Pericles, Plato, and Hyperides in their epitaphs. Richard Lanham, in contrast, ignores the conventions of the genre and instead reads Gorgias' style as pure wordplay, a string of alliterations and other figures of sound designed to entertain and divert his audience. Lanham thus asks, "How might he console us? He could not change the event. How might he change our way of looking at it? . . . How might he truly persuade us to do the only thing one can do about the dead, to forget them? He sets out a game and invites us to play. Name the tropes as they go by. Catch an antithesis by the tail. The more contrived the language, the more allegorical the style becomes—the more it serves its purpose. The meaning is not weakened by the style but reinforced. For it is style which metamorphoses the grief into pleasure, makes us forget grief in the tremendous pleasure of expressing it" (1976, 15–16).

If we read Gorgias' work as neither a complete submission to the constraints of the genre nor a completely original fabrication, but instead see it as a playful parody of the genre itself, we may discern Gorgias' purpose as one of foregrounding the ways in which a genre sanctions and facilitates the fabrication of texts. I suggest that Loraux is correct in seeing Gorgias as adapting to the constraints of the genre, but that Lanham is correct in recognizing Gorgias' overt playfulness and exaggerations. For Gorgias does not merely invent a series of antitheses and other tropes but instead adapts his style to the constraints of the genre, using the permissible *topoi* of the funeral oration and the antithetical figuration appropriate to it, while subtly exaggerating and distorting those very conventions. Gorgias does not merely entertain his audience with tropes, as Lanham contends, nor display his ability to adapt to a conventional style, as Loraux argues. Rather, he parodies an established discourse, that of the official state funeral oration, and thereby shows that it depends on an array of conventions that provide selected rhetors with the apparatus for inventing a flattering portrait of Athens as a unique, foundational city.

If Gorgias playfully distorts the overly formal style of the Athenian funeral oration in his *Epitaphios,* he parodies a very different set of conventions drawn from epic, lyric, and dramatic poetry in his *Encomium for Helen.* Indeed, his style in *Helen* differs from that of the *Epitaphios* to such an extent that several classical scholars have contended that the two texts are by different authors. Richard Jebb, for example, contends that *Helen* does not "bear any distinctive marks of the style of Gorgias" and suggests that the work may have been written by Polykrates (1876, 101). This difference in the two styles is apparent even in translation; for though Gorgias uses antithesis throughout the *Epitaphios,* he uses this technique far less frequently in *Helen,* instead deploying the more typically poetic figures of metaphor, simile, and personification. The highly restrictive conventions of the Athenian *epitaphios,* the officially sanctioned expression of the civic practice of burying Athenians slain during battle, spoken directly to the surviving family of the slain men, is designed to effect a somber mood, presumably to harmonize with what Emily Dickinson calls a "formal feeling" after great pain and loss. In contrast, the far more diverse literary discourse on Helen of Troy, developed over several centuries, in various cities, and in styles as diverse as those of Homer, Sappho, and Euripides, tends to be far more playful and encourages the use of novel and ambiguous figures of speech. Thus in *Helen,* Gorgias uses a variety of figures as personification, metaphor, and simile, describing *logos* as a "great ruler" (H8), comparing *logos* to a drug that acts on the body (H14), and asserting that *eros* is a "disease" (H18); while in the *Epitaphios* he uses none of these poetic devices and instead deploys figures of sound that effect a tone of elevated formality. Gorgias' style in *Helen* is a distinctively imaginative *literary* discourse in contrast to the official civic discourse of the funeral oration. But the predominant commonplaces and tropes in the discourse on Helen are nevertheless quite recognizable; and Gorgias' use of these devices echoes their use by such poets as Homer, Sappho, Stasinos, Stesichorus, Aeschylus, and Euripides (Lindsay 1974, 156; Suzuki 1989, 15).

But if Gorgias deploys figures found in other discussions of Helen, he presents his work as an overt parody of those works. Gorgias' title is the first clue to his parody, for in praising the reviled Helen of Troy, Gorgias in effect announces his work as a parodic or "paradoxical" encomium, one that he later describes as a *paignion,* or 'playful work' (H21). Gorgias thus presents his work as akin to those playful encomia of mice or baldness, works that stand as playful doubles of serious encomia. Moreover, Gorgias' work is parodic in that he deliberately violates the central convention of the encomium itself, namely that of praise; for although he praises Helen for her virtues, he uses the encomium as an apologia, defending her for eloping with Paris. His text is less a conventional encomium than an *apologia,* or 'defense' of Helen of Troy, a legalistic presentation in which he argues for her innocence. As Isocrates points out, Gorgias violates the conventional genre of the encomium itself: "He committed a slight inadvertence—for although he asserts that he has actually written an encomium of Helen, it turns out that he has actually spoken a defense of her conduct! But the composition in defense does not draw upon the same topics as the encomium, nor indeed does it deal with actions of the same kind, but quite the contrary; for a plea in defense is appropriate only when the defendant is charged with a crime, whereas we praise those who excel in some good quality" (*Helen* 10.14). Another tactic Gorgias uses is that of self-reference, commenting on his own process of construction. Thus, he remarks that "having now exceeded the time allotted for my introduction, I shall proceed to my intended speech (H5), and he instructs the reader to "listen as I turn from one argument to another" (H9). Moreover, at the conclusion of his speech, he refers to his own work as a *paignion,* remarking, "I wished to write a speech that would be Helen's celebration and my own recreation" (H21).

In the *Palamedes,* Gorgias adapts to and playfully distorts the conventions of yet another established genre, employing the acceptable figures of speech and thought found in typical fifth-century Athenian legal apologies. As with the case of *Helen,* classical scholars have disputed Gorgias' authorship of the work precisely because of the marked difference in style between it and his other writings.[7] In this vein, Theodor Gomperz notes that classical scholars distinguish sharply between the "ceremonial" style, which is "brilliant, exalted, stately, flowery and full of color," and a "forensic" style that is "sharp, cool, clear and sober" (1901, 477). Critics who attend primarily to Gorgias' style of the *Palamedes* may well conclude that his writing is "lucid" and "transparent," for one of the principal conventions of the dicanic *apologia* is to portray oneself as a man of reason, a sober and dispassionate individual who would have no reason to violate the laws of Athens. Writing or speaking in an overtly poetic or playful manner could only weaken one's case, betraying either ignorance of, or contempt for, the conventions of legal disputation that the Athenians treasured as central to their democracy. This does not mean that Gorgias does not use antithesis in *Palamedes,* for antithesis may be used to clarify distinctions; and it does not mean that Gorgias eschews metaphor altogether, for as Aristotle observes, a judicious and appropriate use of metaphors enhances clarity.

As in the case of the *Epitaphios,* Plato's choice of Gorgias' work to parody strengthens the argument that Gorgias' work is in some respects paradigmatic of the genre of the *apologia,* rather than idiosyncratic in its use of antithesis or radically original figuration. As James Coulter (1979) notes, Plato employs many of the same commonplaces and phrases as Gorgias, among which are reference to the defendant's modest wealth as proof of sincerity, the claim to be a benefactor of the judges, the falsity and contradictory nature of the charge, the lack of personal gain from committing such a crime, the use of logical rather than emotional appeal, the exhortation not to hurry what old age will soon bring about, the distinction between words and deeds, the future condemnation of the jury if it condemns an innocent defendant, and the preference of death to dishonor (31–67). But though his text typifies many of the conventions of the *apologia,* Gorgias renders his work parodic in several ways. First, he uses a conventional genre to defend the mythical character Palamedes. Next, as Coulter notes, Gorgias argues his case by abbreviating and even omitting some typical sections of the fifth-century legal apology while extending others, rendering his work quite "unusual in the body of conventional courtroom oratory" (40). Third, Gorgias effects parody by using so many legal *topoi* that he draws attention to the use of *topoi* themselves. Indeed, *Palamedes* is composed of so many *topoi* that some critics have read the work as a "training" or memorization text, in which some of the *topoi* may apply to some cases but not to all.

In his treatise *On Not-Being,* finally, Gorgias mimics the conventions of yet another conventional genre, that of the traditional Eleatic *epicheireme.*[8] Gorgias' original text is lost, and we have only paraphrases by Sextus and pseudo-Aristotle; hence it is impossible to draw definitive conclusions about such stylistic matters as his figures of speech.[9] But Gorgias' choice of the *topos* of existence, knowledge, and discourse; his rigorous deployment of deductive argumentation; and his overtly "abstract" voice and tone seem to imitate the "philosophical" style of Parmenides, Melissus, and others in the Eleatic tradition. In Thomas Rosenmeyer's assessment, "Gorgias' pamphlet, i.e., the original of the two versions which we now possess, is seen as an *epicheirema* in the Eleatic tradition. His technique of argumentation places him in the company of Zeno and Melissus. . . . Norden showed up the stylistic kinship between Gorgias and Heraclitus, and actually there is more than mere style to connect the thought of the two" (1955, 231). In a similar vein, Jan

Swearingen remarks that Gorgias parodies "Parmenides' use of incantatory style and terminology" (1991, 49).

In his parodic rendering, Gorgias alerts his audience to his parodic intent in several ways. His title, *On Nature; or On Not-Being*, may be seen as a ludic inversion of several treatises dealing with Nature or with "what exists," notably those of Parmenides and Melissus. As Guthrie points out, "The title of the work is itself sufficient indication of parody," for Parmenides and Melissus appear to have titled their books "On Nature or that which is," or at least to have been referred to by such a title (1971, 194). Gorgias' juxtaposition of "nature" and "what is not" in his title indicates his playful and parodic intention and provides his readers with a clue about how to read his work. Gorgias also parodies the genre in his three-part argumentative structure, which is itself a familiar rhetorical trope, that of *klimax* or amplification. Gorgias' "argument," in essence, is the proverbial legal defense used by a defendant accused of borrowing and damaging his neighbor's plow. The three-part "defense" is that he never borrowed the plow; that if he did borrow it, he didn't use it; and that if he used it he didn't break it.

Insofar as he underscores and thereby draws attention to his own rhetorical maneuvers, Gorgias does not present his own writing as free of rhetorical conventions. In this respect, he may be said to be engaging in *self-parody* as well as parody of other texts. For while parody tends to be primarily other-directed, drawing attention to the artificial conventions of existing genres, styles, and authors, self-parody draws attention to its own situatedness and artificiality. Insofar as they are self-parodic as well as parodic, Gorgias' texts thus mock themselves as well as other texts; and in this respect they are highly self-conscious, self-aware, and self-critical, underscoring their own artificiality and contingency. In Richard Poirier's terms, self-parody "makes fun of itself as it goes along: it proposes not the rewards so much as the limits of its own procedures, it shapes itself around its own dissolvents, it calls into question not any particular literary structure so much as the enterprise, the activity itself of creating any literary form, of empowering an idea with a style" (1968, 339). A self-parody is similar to parody in that it exposes the rhetoricity of the text; but while parody is frequently used "to suggest that life or history or reality has made certain literary styles outmoded, the literature of self-parody, quite unsure of the relevance of such standards, makes fun of the effort even to verify them by the act of writing" (339). Gorgias' parodies are in this sense reflexive, indicating that his own text is as artificial as the texts of his foundationalist rivals and that there is no superior or convention-free genre from within which a person is able to liberate himself from all perspectives and articulate the truth as it really is. For every such perspective is always generated from within the contingent discourses of the community.

Paratropic Figuration

As part of his overall parodic strategy, Gorgias uses a number of overtly artificial tropes that function in a quasi-parodic or what we may call a "paratropic" manner, echoing and departing from other familiar figures of speech. Several of Gorgias' tropes are paratropic in respect to sound, such as alliteration, assonance, rhyme, and repeated clauses in order to create echoes both in his own text and in other texts. Through the use of these figures, Gorgias constructs an elaborate system of sounds, syllables, words, and clauses that echo among themselves; and in so doing, he shows how he is able to create new meanings from the interplay of words themselves, whereby the figures generate a web of allusions and interactions between the words and sounds. In this manner, Gorgias creates new meanings by repetition, draws connections between words and ideas not previously noticed, and shows that readers may create new meanings with every new reading.

Like a poem in which rhymes emphasize some associations and understate others, Gorgias' resonant and echoing texts deploy modes of parallelism as an inventive technique. Gorgias' echoing and parallel sounds are derived from other discourses in the culture and hence allude to other sounds, words, phrases, arguments, texts, and genres. In this sense, each depends for its meaning on the presence of other texts, and illustrates Gorgias' antifoundationalist thesis that the meaning of words and texts does not derive from their representation of an external world but from their use in a specific context. In this respect, Gorgias uses paratropes to create meaning, fabricating new perspectives by situating his works vis-à-vis other texts in the culture. Stated another way, Gorgias shows how rhetorical invention is a "cultural" invention in which every new work has meaning in reference not to an independent "world" but to other texts.

If Gorgias creates meaning by echoing sounds in his texts, he also invents new meanings with what some scholars call "figures of sense," an array of overtly artificial figures that derive meaning by echoing and departing from other discursive tropes. Perhaps the most distinctive trope in Gorgias' repertoire is one that is specifically and overtly dependent on other words, the *paronomasia,* or pun. The pun, as *paro-nomasia,* is a word or phrase that is 'set next to' *(para)* another word or phrase; and its effect is dependent on an existing "target" term in the discourse. Like parody, puns preserve as well as mock an original text or remark; and in so doing, they underscore the situatedness of both the pun and the original use of the word or phrase being "played upon." There is no deception involved in a pun; for if there is any concealment, the audience will simply not get the point of the pun. In the pun, meaning is created by the echoing of letters, sounds, syllables, words, clauses, statements, texts, and entire genres so as to generate a new meaning or to reveal or create a connection between the two verbal entities.

Gorgias frequently uses puns, composing works by drawing on the letters, syllables, words, clauses, phrases, arguments, texts, and genres of the discourse. By yoking different fields and fusing them with a new meaning, the pun violates the conventional use of terms, and shows how meaning is fabricated by novel uses of discourse. When Gorgias states that the *demiourgos* is the creator of the citizens of Larisa, he draws on two meanings of the term, namely the artisan and the political magistrate. In another pun, Gorgias responds to the insolent Chaerephon by attending to two uses of the term *narthekas* or 'reed.' Chaerephon is said to have asked, "Why, Gorgias, do beans inflate the belly but do not fan the fire?" Gorgias, not disturbed by the question, said, "I leave this to you to consider; for my part I have long known that the earth produces reeds (*narthekas*) for such ends" (A24). The *narthekas* is a hollow reed from which are made canes, which are used to punish insolent people like Chaerephon. Being hollow, the *narthekas* may be used as a bellows to fan a fire; and in this way the reed is suitable for both "ends," namely punishment and fanning a fire. Gorgias' pun also alludes to a familiar myth, for the *narthekas* is the reed that the titan Prometheus used to carry fire to mankind, both providing them with the source of many crafts and rebelling against Zeus. Thus, in his pun Gorgias suggests that the source of crafts, and hence of invention, is intimately related to the chastisement of insolent men who taunt or ridicule the master craftsman.

Another of Gorgias' signature paratropic figures is the *paradox,* one that may be compressed into an oxymoron or expanded into a phrase or even an entire treatise such as *On Not-Being.* Gorgias thus speaks of vultures being "living tombs"; he refers to Xerxes as the "Persian Zeus" (B5a); he remarks that, under the influence of the art of rhetoric, "all things are willingly but not forcibly made slaves" (*Philebus,* 58a); and he characterizes tragedy as a genre "in which the deceiver is more honest than the nondeceiver and the deceived is wiser than the undeceived" (B23). A paradox, from *para-doxa,* or 'that which both stands alongside and transgresses or confutes *doxa,* conventional opinion, or belief,' challenges conventional ideas. Insofar as it makes sense, and indeed is persuasive, the paradox challenges the viability of conventional ideas and shows how new ideas may be formed by confuting them.

Again, Gorgias shows how a rhetor may invent new ideas by drawing upon ideas expressed in the extant discourses of the culture and playfully altering them in various ways. Invention emerges completely from the domain of discourse itself, the common tropic maneuvers of the community and hence their shared beliefs or ways of seeing and thinking. By altering conventional notions and hence fusing ostensibly divergent categories of thought, Gorgias creates striking new ideas that confound common sense and that invite his audience to reconsider their commonplace notions. By presenting his ideas in the form of paradox, Gorgias not only succinctly articulates his antifoundationalist conception of language, but he displays it as well, exhibiting the way in which we may alter our world by changing the ways we speak.

Along with pun and paradox, Gorgias uses several figures that Aristotle characterizes as "frigidities" (*Rhetoric* 1405b). For Aristotle, Gorgias' frigidities are an indication that he is inept as a writer, unable to use conventions effectively. But for Gorgias, each of these putative frigidities is part of his strategy of exposing the artifices used by every rhetor. Each draws upon conventional uses of words and departs from them in various ways.

First, Gorgias uses *dipla onoma*, or compound words, whereby he conflates two existing words to create a new word; and in this conflation he associates what his audience has conventionally treated as two distinct and independent words. Gorgias' compounds are related to his antifoundational model of language in two respects. First, the term he composes as a compound is not a completely novel word, a pure invention emerging, say, from his "inner awareness." Rather, he combines two already existing terms and thereby provides a new use for two familiar terms. In this, he suggests that familiar words may always be given new roles to play and hence new meanings in new situations. Second, in his use of compounds, Gorgias challenges the essentialist notion that individual words name distinct entities in the world. Gorgias shows that words can be fabricated by conflating two existing terms that have previously been kept separate; and he thereby suggests that there is no independent, antecedent object that a word simply "names." Fusing two terms, the compound generates a new object; and by generating the object from familiar terms, Gorgias challenges the assumption that words and things are independent items, the former representing, or mirroring, the latter. For example, in his term *ptocho-mouso-kolakas*, "begging-poet-flatterer," Gorgias humorously derides a group of people, perhaps the dogmatic Orphics, as engaging in begging, singing, and flattering.[10] Gorgias' compounds show that words do not depend on an independent, nonlinguistic domain but that they may emerge from the fusion of existing terms. In his terms *epi-orkesantas* and *eu-orkesantos* (*Rhetoric* 1406a), which may be translated roughly as "those who commit perjury and those who swear right solemnly," Gorgias creates antithetical terms with his prefixes *epi* and *eu*. Gorgias coins the term *homopsychos* (unanimous) by placing it alongside *homologos* (univocal) (H3).

As Derek Attridge observes, the compound word, which is sometimes labeled a "portmanteau" word, "challenges two myths on which most assumptions about the efficacy of language rest . . . it denies that single words must have, on any given occasion, single meanings; and . . . it denies that the manifold patterns of similarity that occur at the level of the signifier are innocent of meaning" (1988, 145). The compound or portmanteau word shows that the boundaries in language are not permanently fixed or even sharply drawn and indicates that words often dissolve into one another. As such, it shows that new meanings may be created by a new use of words, and it negates the notion that a word has meaning because it unequivocally names something in the world. Moreover, Gorgias' compound words suggest that "every word in every text is a portmanteau, a combination of sounds that echo through the entire language and through every other language, and back through the history of speech," and as such "makes us aware that we, as readers, control this explosion, allowing only those connections to effect which will give us the kinds of meanings we recognize—stories, voices, character, metaphors, images" (1988, 154).

Another of Gorgias' "frigidities" is what Aristotle calls *glotta* (tongues), words that are peripheral to ordinary use because they are strange, provincial, archaic, or obsolete and that require a glossary in order to be understood (*Poetics* 21.6). As examples of *glotta* used by Gorgias' students, Aristotle cites Lycophron's calling Xerxes a "monster man" and Alcidamus speaking of "bringing no such toys to poetry" (*Rhetoric* 1405b). In Plato's *Gorgias,* Gorgias uses terms such as *handiwork* and *effect,* which Olympiodorus identifies as localisms (*Gorgias* 450b; A27). In his use of localisms, Gorgias implies that discourse is anchored in the local biases of its users, that words are the tools of locally situated speakers, and that consequently the meaning of a word involves situating it in a particular discourse. Some words are deemed "non-local," or nonprovincial, only because we are so familiar with the folkways and conventions of the discourses in which they are used that we don't have to look them up in a glossary. Unlike a foundationalist like Aristotle, who sees language as a neutral medium with which we may represent things as they are, Gorgias suggests with his frequent *glotta* that language is located in a particular time, place, and culture. Rather than being a transparent medium for conveying ideas, discourse consists of an array of maneuvers used by partisan rhetors in specific agons, each of which is local. If we overlook the locality of all discourse, we may fail to recognize the parochiality of our own perspectives and may self-deceptively consider our own parochiality to be a universal norm.

Aristotle also characterizes Gorgias' "excessive" use of the epithet as frigid or artificial. In the *Epitaphios,* for instance, Gorgias never refers to the warriors either by name or even as Athenians; instead, he refers to them only as "these men" (*tois andrasi*) (E1–2) and as "they" (E28, E39, E40). In *Helen,* Gorgias only names Paris once, alluding to him as Alexander (H19); instead, he refers to the Trojan as "assailant" and "insulter" (H7), "barbarian" (H7), and "persuader" (H12). Indeed, Gorgias explicitly states that he will avoid mentioning Paris directly, asserting, "Who it was and why and how he sailed away, taking Helen as his love, I shall not say. To tell the knowing what they know shows it is right but brings no delight" (H5). To iterate a name, for Gorgias, is to reify, to create the illusion that the object named "exists" independently of the naming. So with each novel epithet or redescription, Gorgias in effect avoids that reification, and instead situates Hector's brother in a new way, providing him with a new family of associations, leading us to view him from yet another perspective, and reminding us that there is no viewpoint apart from the various possible perspectives made possible by our language.

Gorgias also tends to avoid naming Helen, whose very name, as he notes, has been characterized as "ill-omened" and associated with disaster (H2). Since his goal is to alter the way we view this daughter of Zeus, he uses her name a mere six times in the entire encomium and instead uses such epithets as "the accused" (H2), "the woman who is the subject of this speech" (H3), the daughter of Leda and Zeus (H3), the "assailed" who suffered dread deeds (H7), the "persuaded" (H12), and, with extraordinary understatement, "a woman" (H21). Gorgias deploys his epithetical strategy throughout *Palamedes* as well, referring only once by name to Odysseus, whose name has synonymous with the hero (P3); and he subsequently refers to the crafty Ithacan with such epithets as "the worst of men" (P3), "my accuser" (P5), "the accuser" (P22), "most daring of all men" (P24), and "a man of the sort who in a single speech says to the same man the most inconsistent things about the same subjects" (P25).

In his "excessive" use of epithets, Gorgias offers a way of referring to objects that does not rely on a representationalist or essentialist assumption that words name determinate, preexisting things. In this respect, he exemplifies Aristotle's description of the Sophist as a person who attends only to the accidental or contingent features of any person or thing and does not address what is "essential" (*Metaphysics* 6.2). For Gorgias, this deliberate epithetical strategy of repudiating the essential embodies his antifoundationalist conception of language and knowledge. By using epithets that serve as contingent characteristics, Gorgias depicts people as no more than the accidental or contingent properties we assign to them. Gorgias thus refers to people or things by assigning associations to the "thing" in its immediate context. Gorgias rejects the notion that a "thing" is an object existing independently of discourse; instead, he presents diverse "things" as identifiable through the associations people attribute to them in their discourse. These attributions and effects change through time; so rather than possessing a distinct, identifiable essence, one with a recognizable set of qualities, the person or thing in question is identifiable by the various genealogies we may construct concerning it; and these are innumerable, always open to variation, interpretation, modification, and redescription.

Gorgias thereby shows that "things" are not entities "in the world" that may simply be observed; rather, they are constructs, the product of human associations and patterns of labeling. By using epithets to label a person, Gorgias offers a mode of reference that does not rely on the stability of the name and the object. Instead, he shows that reference is made within a discourse and its categories. Aristotle complains that in his epithets the Sophist does not present us with the "meat," but only the "seasoning" (*Rhetoric* 1406a); in effect, he makes the object being described dependent upon the description, and he ruptures the putative connection between single words and single things. There is no criterion in the world to assess the validity or accuracy of epithets and to claim that any epithet is not "appropriate" to the object itself. For new epithets redescribe the object in question, and there is no essential object in itself to which the epithets can be deemed appropriate or inappropriate.

Finally, Aristotle characterizes Gorgias' metaphors as "frigid" because they are "far-fetched." Gorgias' far-fetched metaphors are paratropic or parodic in the sense that they depend on conventional metaphoric associations but exaggerate them in various ways. For Aristotle, metaphor involves the transfer of a name from its literal referent to a referent that is similar or analogous in some way. In order to be meaningful, a metaphor must be appropriate to the object being discussed; for if the newly named object is too "distant" from the original object, an audience will not easily understand the analogy. The distance may derive from a lack of ostensible similarities between the two named objects, in that "metaphors must not be far-fetched, but we must give names to things that have none by deriving the metaphor from what is akin and of the same kind, so that, as soon as it is uttered, it is clearly seen to be akin" (*Rhetoric* 1405a). Distance may also derive from improper "elevation," in that a metaphor must be neither too base or too lofty for the object it names: if it is too "base," it will be laughable; if it is too "lofty," it will be too "tragic" (*Rhetoric* 1406b). Among Gorgias' far-fetched metaphors are "you have sown shamefully and reaped badly," (*Rhetoric* 1406b) in which Gorgias applies ethical terms to agricultural activity, and "trembling and wan are the writings, grass-pale and bloodless the doings" (*Rhetoric* 1406b). Presumably, Gorgias' metaphor is too far-fetched because it associates human behavior (writing and behaving) with "natural" objects (grass, blood): just as deeds may be like pale grass in the spring, so writings may be pale. From Aristotle's perspective, these categories are too disparate, and the resulting metaphor is too far-fetched to be grasped easily. But for Gorgias, the far-fetched metaphor draws our attention to the process of metaphoric analogizing as well as to the putative entities being analogized. Rather than grounding his metaphor on a preexisting similarity inherent in the world, Gorgias shows that he is able to create similarities with his tropes.

As an example of improper metaphoric "elevation," Aristotle remarks that "Gorgias' exclamation to the swallow when she flew down and let go her droppings on him is in the best tragic manner: he said, 'Shame on you, Philomela'; for if a bird did it there was no shame, but [it would have been] shameful for a maiden. He thus rebuked the bird well by calling it what it once had been rather than what it now was" (*Rhetoric* 1406b). Aristotle considers Gorgias' remark appropriate for tragedy but, presumably, inappropriate for everyday discourse; hence, it would be considered frigid. His metaphor is inappropriate, impolite because it is too vulgar, and too "elevated" for the subject being discussed. In this remark, Gorgias cites the bird's excretions as a mark of shame, thereby associating a "base" bodily process with the dignified maiden. In this respect, his remark is simultaneously improperly elevated, and hence like tragedy, for he speaks tragically in a nontragic situation; but his remark is also improperly "base" and hence comical. Gorgias' inappropriate metaphor echoes Aristophanes' *Clouds,* in which Socrates finds himself in a similar predicament:

> He was studying the tracks of the lunar orbit
> and its revolutions, and as he skyward gaped,
> from the roof in darkness a lizard shat on him.
> (*Clouds* 172–73)

While the event is disturbing to Socrates, who "lost a great idea because of a lizard" (*Clouds* 169–70), it is one that Gorgias uses as an opportunity for wordplay.

As with parody, Gorgias uses his overtly artificial, paratropic tropes to disabuse his audience of the illusion that any views are objectively "true." In his use of localisms, oxymorons, double words, epithets, metaphors, puns, and other tropes, he offers an alternative to the foundationalist notion that language is representational, suggesting that conventional strategies of naming, coining words, and making comparisons between things are local and anchored in the discourses of the culture. With his deliberately "thick" or opaque style, he foregrounds his own situatedness; and in so doing, he invites his audience to reflect on the arbitrary assumptions and biases in their own language. Rather than presenting his own discourse as "natural" or universal, one that represents things are they really are, he repeatedly underscores its inescapable rhetoricity. Rather than presuming to speak the truth, he thereby reminds his audience that he is only offering them another picture, one that is no more "true" than that presented by the dominant *logos*. By using artificial tropes that are deliberately outlandish when judged by the conventional standards of the genre, Gorgias disabuses his audience of the notion that words are names for things in the world and that an ostensibly lucid style provides access to things as they really are. Gorgias' paratropisms thus invite his audience to become involved in the act of interpretation; and in so doing, he prevents them from adopting the role of an impartial "spectator."[11]

A Disposition for Play

In his parodies, Gorgias frequently plays with the conventional arrangement or "disposition" of conventional genres. As Mark Smeltzer points out, Gorgias is quite cognizant of the conventional quadripartite dispositional structure of many texts, that of introduction, narration, argument, and conclusion (1995, 156). But rather than simply heeding this dispositional structure, Gorgias plays freely with each section, drawing attention to the convention and showing how it serves a rhetor's overall persuasive strategy.

First, Gorgias at times completely omits the introduction. Aristotle remarks on this omission in Gorgias' Speech to the People of Elis, in which without any introductory remarks, he asserts, "Elis, happy city" (*Rhetoric* 1416a). In *Helen,* in contrast, Gorgias composes an elaborate introduction in which he asserts a general thesis, narrows his focus to Helen as an instance of this thesis, and then uses what Hayden Pellicia (1992) calls a "false start *recusatio,*" one used by Herodotus as well as Gorgias, in which the author begins with one story, and begins to develop it, but decides to abandon it for another topic. The rhetorical purpose of this device is that "something is introduced, only to be rejected in favor of something else, which is thereby highlighted by the preceding foil" (1992, 64). Gorgias further underscores the conventionality of this part of the speech, remarking that "having gone beyond the limits of my introduction I now turn to my text" (H5). Varying his introductions from brevity (or complete omission) to prolixity, he underscores the artificiality of an element of a speech that is so customary that we consider it "natural"; and he shows how a rhetor may use the convention to present his speech as "natural."

In the "narration," or statement of the facts, Gorgias also draws attention to the rhetoricity of what may appear to be an impartial delineation of information. In the *Epitaphios,* he completely omits the conventional narrative about the history of Athens, one that official orators used to extol Athens' military victories over the Amazons, the Persians, and other enemies. Gorgias' omission complements his repudiation of official orators' depiction of Athens as a unique, elite city meriting its imperial status. But his slight also foregrounds the obvious bias of the conventional narrative, one that presents a distinctly "Athenian" history of Athens. By deliberately flaunting convention, Gorgias highlights his own disruption of a "privileged" genre reserved for a select few. In *Helen,* Gorgias transgresses the convention of the narrative by explicitly announcing, "Who he was and why and how he sailed away taking Helen as his love, I shall not say; for to tell the knowing what they know is believable but not enjoyable" (H5). Gorgias' putative rationale for his omissionc that he doesn't tell his audience something they already knowc is of course disingenuous, given that poets such as Stesichorus relate quite a different variant of the tale, one in which Helen never sails to Troy but remains in Egypt. In *Palamedes,* Gorgias again omits the narrative of such putative facts as the forged letter and the money planted under Palamedes' tent, as well as the narrative of the long-standing feud between Odysseus and Palamedes, who exposed Odysseus' attempt to avoid service in the Trojan War. What Gorgias suggests is that every putative account of the "facts" involves a partisan selection and omission, and every narrative is part of the rhetor's overall strategy of persuasion.

In a similar way, Gorgias presents "arguments" as rhetorical maneuvers rather than as inherently valid modes of reasoning. As such, he suggests that arguments are not valid in and of themselves but are valid only insofar as they persuade a particular audience. For Gorgias, every argument is a *trope* or maneuver, one that does not differ in kind from any other figurative maneuver used by a rhetor to bolster his position in an agon. In this respect, there is no essential difference between, say, metaphor and paradigm, or between juxtaposition and syllogism. Unlike Aristotle, who distinguishes sharply between valid and fallacious or "paralogical" arguments, Gorgias suggests that every argument is paralogical, having its origin and justification, not in a universally valid and rational set of abstract relationships or in the inherent validity of certain procedures of thinking, but in the conventional modes of thinking of the community at hand. Stated another way, Gorgias does not delineate a privileged set of tropes as being valid or as constituting what is logical; instead, he suggests that an open-ended family of tropes may be persuasive, depending on the discourse in which they are used. In some contexts, for example, a metaphor or even a pun may be more "logical" and effective than a deduction.

What counts as valid is that which is persuasive in a given context, not that which adheres to objective rules of reasoning. In Nelson Goodman's terms, "*a rule is amended if it yields an inference we are unwilling to accept; and inference is rejected if it violates a rule we are unwilling to amend*" (1983, 64). Rational argument is not the following of objective rules of reason that begin with true first principles and lead to true conclusions, as Aristotle maintains. Rather, argumentation is a crafty process of selection and arrangement, a project of attacking a rival and defending one's own position from attack. The strategies of division and collection in a "tree" diagram and the string of arguments in a "chain" are deliberately set out to persuade, not to arrive at an objective truth.

Gorgias deploys a variety of what may be called "local" and "global" arguments in his extant texts. Among his "local" arguments are the paradigm or example, as when in the *Epitaphios* he supports his assertion that the warriors' virtue is doing what is "fitting" by presenting several examples of their fitting behavior; or when in *Helen* he supports his thesis that Helen is not responsible if she was overcome with passion by citing another example of someone controlled by emotion, namely, a soldier whose fear of an enemy leads him to contravene custom. He thus remarks that when soldiers encounter an enemy adorned in bronze and steel, they may be so alarmed that they are "panic-stricken from future danger [as though it were] present. For strong as is the habit of allegiance to the law, it is ejected by fear resulting from sights, which coming to a man causes him to be indifferent both to what is judged honorable because of the law and to the advantage to be derived from victory" (H16).

Gorgias also uses metaphors as argumentative devices, as when he asserts that *logos* is a powerful lord or a drug, metaphors that support his claim that Helen is not responsible for her behavior if she was verbally seduced by Paris (H8, H14). Moreover, Gorgias argues from "association," for instance, when he praises Helen by praising her divine genealogy, concluding that "by nature and birth the woman who is the subject of this speech was preeminent among preeminent men and women" (H3) and when he praises her because her suitors were admirable, some possessing "greatness of wealth, some the glory of ancient noblesse, some the vigor of personal prowess, some the power of acquired knowledge" (H4). Aristotle specifically reproves Gorgias for his excessive use of this fallacious or paralogical mode of reasoning, noting that when Gorgias praises someone, he typically praises them for things that are associated with him but that are not necessarily or essentially related to their specific deeds. Aristotle adds that this paralogical mode of reasoning accounts for Gorgias' ability to respond to all questions, remarking, "This is what Gorgias meant when he said that he was never at a loss for something to say; for, if he is speaking of Peleus, he praises Achilles, then Aeacus, then the god; similarly courage, which does this and that, or is of such a kind" (*Rhetoric* 1418a).

Gorgias also deploys two types of "global" arguments, overall tropes that structure the entire text. The two global arguments Gorgias most frequently uses are the "tree," a disjunctive and exhaustive set of elements; and the sequential "chain" of if-then counterfactuals, also called *klimax*. With the "tree," Gorgias delineates a finite number of possibilities, which he presents as inclusive of all possible options, and systematically addresses each option in turn. He uses this in part one of *On Not-Being* in his discussion of Being, arguing that if Being exists, it must be generated or eternal, in motion or at rest, finite or infinite, divisible or indivisible; and he argues that in each instance neither of the two alternatives is possible. In part two, he again uses a tree arrangement, arguing that knowledge of the "existent" must be attained through either mental apprehension or sensation and that neither is possible. In *Palamedes*, Gorgias uses a "tree" division to enumerate the possible motives for committing treason, his overall division being that of achieving gain or avoiding loss, since, he says, "all men do things in pursuit of these two goals, either seeking some profit or escaping some punishment" (P20). He then identifies five possible gains: ruling over Greeks or barbarians, gaining wealth, attaining honor, achieving security, and helping friends and harming enemies; and he argues that none of these motivations could be present in this case. Concerning the avoidance of pain or loss, he argues that by committing treason he would lose rather than gain, for by betraying Greece he would be "betraying myself, my parents, my friends, the dignity of my ancestors, the cults of my native land, the tombs of my family, and my great country of Greece." What he would lose is trust, and, he asserts, this would be disastrous, for "life is not livable for a man who has lost the trust of others" (P20–21).

While Gorgias uses the "tree" structure to delineate crucial elements, he also uses it to conceal alternatives that may weaken his position. Thus in *Helen,* he delineates only four possible scenarios or possible explanations for Helen' behavior, namely, that her action was determined by supernatural forces, by rape, by persuasion, or by erotic passion. In so doing, he omits scenarios that would depict Helen as being motivated by vanity, boredom, or a desire to demonstrate her "divine" superiority to ordinary men and women. In *Palamedes,* Gorgias also uses his tree arrangement to repress alternatives: he does not mention that the genius Palamedes may be motivated by sheer hubris, the desire to prove himself superior to others, to insult others, to show that he could simply get away with treason because he was more intelligent than anyone else and had not been sufficiently appreciated. Certainly Prometheus, with whom he is often identified, was not appreciated fully.

What is crucial is that in his "tree" division, the same sort that Plato extols as the way in which a dialectician collects and divides in accordance with the truth, Gorgias suggests that every such division or enumeration is selective and partisan rather than objective. In his use of the disjunctive tree, Gorgias thus differs from Plato, who sees some argumentative trees as representative of the architecture of reality itself. Plato states that the tree method of dialectic is "that of perceiving and bringing together in one idea the scattered particulars, that one may make clear by definition the particular thing which he wishes to explain," and "that of dividing things again by classes, where the natural joints are, and not trying to break any part, after the manner of a bad carver" (*Phaedrus* 265de). For Gorgias there are myriad trees we can delineate in different situations, various ways to divide and combine whatever we posit as an important element, but no one is representative of the way things really are. Instead, each ostensibly neutral tree is a trope, a maneuver to defeat a rival and to fabricate his text. Neither involves universally valid rules of reasoning; instead, they are merely tropes that can be arranged in various ways on different occasions. To a foundationalist like Aristotle or Nussbaum, Gorgias' reasoning is infuriating, for it suggests that Gorgias is disdainful of "valid" philosophical virtues of logical reasoning. But for Gorgias, the philosopher merely privileges his or her own *topoi* and tropes and thereby fails to acknowledge that she is simply one more rhetor in the game and that there are other viable means of reasoning.

Gorgias' second type of global argumentative trope is that of the sequential "chain," a mode of argument that is akin to the rhetorical figure of *klimax,* or "amplification."[12] He uses this trope in *On Not-Being:* nothing exists, if it did we could not know it, and if we knew it we could not communicate it. A sequential chain may be logical, as in *On Not-Being,* or chronological, as in the first part of *Palamedes,* where he argues that in order to commit treason he would have to complete a series of necessary steps, each of which depends on the previous step. Gorgias' sequential chain in *On Not-Being,* which Long describes as a "Chinese box" arrangement of "counterfactual conditionals," tightens a net around a rival by increasingly restricting possibilities: A is not possible; but even if A, B is not possible; even if B, C is not possible (Long, 1984, 235). Furthermore, each possibility depends on the previous event in a kind of logical or sequential chain in which each link depends logically on the previous link to be possible.

In part three of *On Not-Being,* Gorgias again uses a chain argument to show that the foundationalist model of discourse cannot account for communication. He argues that words cannot convey information about things in the world since they are merely marks or sounds, and "he who speaks does not speak a noise at all, or a color, but a word; and so it is not possible to think a color, but only to see it, nor a noise, but only to hear it." He then argues that "even if it is possible to know things, and to express whatever one knows in words, yet how can the hearer have in his mind the same thing as the speaker? For the same thing cannot be present simultaneously in several separate people; for in that case the one would be two." Third, Gorgias argues that even if "the same thing *could* be present in several persons, there is no reason why it should not appear dissimilar to them if they are not themselves entirely similar and are not in the same place; for if they were in the same place they would be one and not two" (*MXG* 980b). Fourth, he argues that even if the existent could be represented in words, and the mental image of the object were the same in both people, and the image appeared the same to both people, still communication could not occur, for "the objects which even one and the same man perceives at the same moment are not all similar, but he perceives different things by hearing and by sight, and differently now and on some former occasion; and so a man can scarcely perceive the same thing as someone else" (*MXG* 980b).

In some of his "conclusions," finally, Gorgias transgresses convention by composing "para-conclusions" that invite a response from the audience and that thereby generate further discourse, rather than attempting to "conclude" the discussion in any sense. In *On Not-Being,* Gorgias' ostensibly paradoxical conclusion is on its face self-refuting, for he argues that communication is not possible. In so doing, he challenges the audience to come to terms with his argument, either denouncing it as what Grote calls a "monstrous paradox" (1869, 173) or attempting to understand it by reexamining their own notions of existence, knowledge, and communication. In *Helen,* Gorgias again invites his audience to respond to his puzzling assertion. He concludes the work by asserting that his entire argument is a *paignion,* or playful exercise. A *paignion* is typically a playful encomium in which a rhetor praises what Pease calls "things without honor," such as baldness or mice (1926, 27). But by proclaiming that *Helen* is a *paignion,* Gorgias opens the work to further interpretation. Is a text that proclaims itself a *paignion* really a *paignion?* If so, then isn't the assertion that the text is playful itself merely playful? In both texts, Gorgias' conclusion invites a response from his audience; and this, I submit, is its real purpose. For in each conclusion, he prevents his audience from escaping the agon and challenges them to respond. Rather than concluding the discussion or indicating that discourse is unable to grasp the true nature of things altogether, Gorgias' transgression of the convention shows how clever rhetors are able to accomplish this objective through a skilled use of the contrivance itself. Gorgias' own objective, in contrast, is to use the convention as an opening rather than as a mode of closure, and in so doing, to invite his listeners and readers to enter into the agon and compose another text.

THE THEATRICALITY OF INSIGHT

A third strategy that Gorgias uses in his performances is that of acting, or *hypokrisis,* which many rhetorical theorists refer to as "delivery." The art of acting, which involves the use of vocal intonations, facial expressions, physical gestures and movements, costume, and cosmetics, enables a rhetor to create a character for himself. Gorgias, who is known to have been intimately familiar with theater both in Sicily and Athens, appears to have been quite attentive to this aspect of his performances, typically speaking in theaters, wearing the traditional purple robes of the rhapsodes, many of whom performed scenes from Homer and other poets, and speaking in an overtly "theatrical" manner (A9).[13] Several critics have commented on Gorgias' attention to acting, Plato remarking on the similarity between Gorgias' performances and those of dramatists (*Gorgias* 447a); Aristotle characterizing Gorgias' performances as drawing on the resources of the dramatic poets (*Rhetoric* 1404a); and Everett Hunt observing that in his performances "the resources of the poets, whose works were so successful in holding the attention of Greek audiences, were turned to the purposes of the orator. Gorgias was interested in style for style's sake; his foreign accent and distinguished air delighted the Athenians; and throughout his career he sought to persuade by pleasing" (1965, 78).

Deploying his accent, distinguished air, and purple robes, Gorgias uses the art of acting to create specific characters in each of his works. In *On Not-Being,* he adopts the role of an erudite metaphysician schooled in the language of Eleatic philosophy; in the *Epitaphios,* he plays the part of an official Athenian funeral orator, a prominent citizen selected by the Assembly to honor its slain warriors; in *Helen,* he takes on the character of a legal champion of a reviled woman; and in *Palamedes*, he adopts the role of Palamedes himself, the mythical hero who was unjustly executed for treason. Gorgias seems to have adopted different roles and poses even when not performing on stage: as Aristotle points out, Gorgias' remark to a swallow that had let its droppings fall on him, "Shame on you, Philomela" (A23), is comically delivered in "the best tragic style"; and even his last words, "Sleep already begins to hand me over to his brother Death" (A15), seem self-consciously histrionic.

Many of Gorgias' critics tend to dismiss his reliance upon acting as another indication that his objective is to entertain rather than inform his audiences and that he is more interested in style than in substance. For most of these critics construe acting or delivery as a supplement to the art of rhetoric, a mere finishing touch added to render a text more entertaining to an audience. To Plato, for instance, a rhetor must first develop the content or substance of his text through a process of dialectical inquiry, and only subsequently use the techniques of style and delivery to convey these truths to an audience. Similarly, for Aristotle a rhetor must ascertain the facts and invent arguments before presenting them in lucid prose. The art of delivery is a mere supplement to this project, a kind of necessary evil that a rhetor must concern himself with because most audiences are swayed more by emotion and spectacle than by rational argument (*Rhetoric* 1404a).

But these critics fail to see that for Gorgias the art of acting is not a supplementary means of dramatizing a previously composed text but an integral part of invention itself. This is the case not only in improvisational settings but in every instance of invention. For to Gorgias, every utterance is inescapably perspectival and partisan, spoken by a limited, situated individual. Every individual, for Gorgias, is fashioned or fabricated in a particular community, situated in a given time and place and culture, and every speaker, as a "character," sees the world in a distinct, biased way. The art of acting, which is the art of constructing a character, is pivotal to the task of invention, for it delineates a rhetor's initial biases, commitments, and ways of seeing and judging, each of which opens up some avenues of inquiry and closes down others. As such, the art of acting enables a rhetor to generate a text from a particular perspective, demarcating what a rhetor may say in much the same way as playing a particular role delimits what an actor may say or not say while playing a given role. Adopting the role of Palamedes, for instance, is not supplemental to Gorgias' invention of arguments in his defense; rather, it directs his inquiry and shapes what he is able to say. Similarly in the *Epitaphios*, when Gorgias speaks as an official state orator, his character, like that of Pericles, Demosthenes, or Hyperides, is that of a prominent citizen directly involved in the practical affairs of Athens. His character enables him to say some things while avoiding others; and as such it shapes the substance and style of his oration.

Gorgias uses acting as a strategy of exposition as well as composition, for it enables him to foreground the situatedness of his assertions and in so doing draw attention to the ways in which many rhetors conceal their own biases through self-effacement. By presenting his assertions as those of a distinct, recognizable character, Gorgias displays the situatedness of his works rather than presenting them as observations about the way the world really is "from its own point of view." Speaking as a character on a stage, Gorgias thus draws attention to his own situatedness, underscoring the fact that his assertions are *his own,* and are not to be mistaken for claims about the way things "really are." Reflecting on this practice, Gorgias remarks that dramatists who present their works on stage are more "honest" than deceptive, self-effacing rhetors. Theater, he asserts, involves a deception "in which the deceiver is more honest than the non-deceiver and the deceived is wiser than the undeceived" (B23). A dramatist is honest because he foregrounds the artificiality of his assertions, reminding his audiences that his remarks are his own, made in a particular time, place, and culture. Presenting his ideas on a stage, an overtly artificial setting that nobody mistakes for real life, and using such theatrical conventions as formalized discourse, masks, ritual gestures and movements, and choruses, the honest dramatist exposes his own ruses and never allows the audience to forget that they are in the presence of a play. Furthermore, Gorgias points out that the honest dramatist who does not conceal his artifice will be best able to compose a "deception" that enables his audience to become "wiser." Attending the theater, an audience may learn from the explicit "deception" of a dramatic performance if they "suspend their disbelief" and thereby allow themselves to be "persuaded." In this way, they may be able to see the world from the perspective of the dramatist and in so doing recognize that their own views are themselves limited and biased. An audience becomes wiser, moreover, because they see that every view of the world is a perspective made possible by artifice and that even the most ostensibly natural action is a performance.

The Alazon and the Eiron

Gorgias takes on various dramatic roles in his performances, but a persistent trait of the characters he creates is that of a bold self-confidence concerning his own knowledge, a person who is able to speak persuasively and authoritatively on any subject whatsoever. In *On Not-Being,* he takes on not only the venerable Parmenides but the entire array of philosophers engaged in a project of discovering the truth. In *Helen,* he brazenly challenges the "unanimous and univocal" poets from Homer to Euripides who present themselves as speaking the truth about Helen of Troy. In the *Epitaphios,* he presents himself as knowing more about the Athenian warriors than the official orators themselves; and in the guise of *Palamedes,* the heroic man of "ancient wisdom,"

Gorgias suggests that he deserves to be seen as one of the wisest of men as well as a benefactor of Greece. Gorgias appears to have presented himself as audacious in his other performances as well, proclaiming upon entering a theater that he was able to "speak on any subject whatsoever" (A1). Moreover, as Plato observes, he is reported to have encouraged his students to adopt the same pose, teaching them to answer "fearlessly and haughtily if someone asks something, as is right for those who know" (*Meno* 70ab). Philostratus remarks on Gorgias' "boldness," remarking that "the sophist of the old school assumes a knowledge of what whereof he speaks. At any rate, he introduces his speeches with such phrases as 'I know,' or 'I am aware,' or 'I have long observed,' or 'For mankind there is nothing fixed and sure.' This kind of introduction gives a tone of nobility and self-confidence to a speech and implies a clear grasp of the truth" (480).

To several of his Athenian critics, Gorgias' boastful claims to knowledge are evidence of his quackery or imposture, claims that betray his ignorance rather than his knowledge or wisdom. Indeed, his critics see this imposture as definitive of many Sophists who present themselves as wise while knowing nothing at all. Both Plato and Aristotle characterize the Sophist as a person who appears wise to his students while having no knowledge. To his critics, Gorgias is an *alazon*, a charlatan who is frequently portrayed in Greek comedy as the boastful phony who makes exaggerated claims about his knowledge or ability.[14] His antagonist is typically the wily *eiron*, who by professing ignorance is able to deflate the *alazon* and expose him as an imposter. In Cope's terms, the Sophist possesses "that combination of qualities, effrontery and imposture—summed up in the word *alazoneia*, which is the main ingredient in [his] character as portrayed by Plato" (160). Plato insists that when Gorgias presents himself as knowledgeable about an array of issues and able to speak authoritatively on them, he is a boastful charlatan or *alazon* (*Gorgias* 448a). Like other Sophists claiming to possess knowledge about everything, Gorgias in reality knows nothing and is no more than a juggler of words (*Sophist* 235a). Aristophanes also depicts Gorgias as an *alazon*, a term he uses for the Sophists who boast of their ability to speak authoritatively on any issue (*Clouds* 103, 449, 1490). And Isocrates suggests that Gorgias is one of the phony nomadic "teachers who do not scruple to vaunt their powers with utter disregard of the truth," one of "those who choose a life of careless indolence (*alazoneuesthai*) are better advised than those who devote themselves to serious study" (*Against the Sophists* 13.2).

The distinction between the boastful *alazon* and the self-effacing *eiron* illuminates a crucial difference in the views of Gorgias and Plato's Socrates. Plato draws on the comic confrontation of the *alazon* and the *eiron* in his depiction of the quarrel between Gorgias and Socrates in the *Gorgias*. He depicts Gorgias as claiming knowledge of everything, being able to answer all questions, and teaching an art whose scope is all discourse or *logos*, an art that enables him to appear wiser than any professional. But the wily *eiron* Socrates, who presents himself merely pursuing the path of reasoned argument, demolishes Gorgias' claim and reveals the Sophist to know nothing whatsoever. Through his ironic self-effacement, Socrates presents himself as an ignorant man in search of an objective truth. Through his ironic pose of ignorance, he is able to deflate Gorgias' pretensions to knowledge and to suggest that only through dialectic is it possible to approach the truth. The truth that he discovers through impartial inquiry is not his own truth but a truth that is objective, available to anyone who pursues the path of logical reasoning. In this respect he opposes those sophistic rhetors like Gorgias, Polus, and Callicles, whose objective is not to discover the truth but merely to *win the debate*. The Sophist is completely indifferent to the truth, and indeed attempts to obfuscate it, for the truth will reveal the hollowness of his own pretenses to knowledge. To Plato, Gorgias is a boastful charlatan or *alazon* who presents himself as wise while having no knowledge whatsoever; while the ironic Socrates, who proclaims his own ignorance, is able to expose the deceptiveness of Gorgias' claims.

In sharp contrast to Socrates, Gorgias adopts the boastful role of the *alazon* who proclaims that he does possess knowledge about various matters. His pose of alazonic boastfulness is integrally related to his antifoundationalism, a strategy for conveying his antifoundationalist views. In adopting the role of the *alazon*, he makes exaggerated claims to knowledge, professing expertise on all subjects. He asserts theses he seriously believes, but the flamboyant braggadocio of his claims underscores his own presence as a distinct character. In so doing, he underscores the contingency of his own assertions and accentuates the fact that his assertions are *his own*. Thus, by presenting his claims in an exaggerated manner, he underscores his own presence as a speaker in a debate or agon. Through his exaggerated presentation of himself as a boastful *alazon*, Gorgias thus underscores his own situatedness and contingency, and emphasizes that the views he presents are by no means "impartial." Gorgias' alazonic pose thus complements his use of parody and artificial tropes, for it draws attention to himself as a performer whose assertions are to be taken as his own and are not to be mistaken for claims about a putative (and nonexistent) truth. Gorgias' objective in playing an *alazon* is not to convince us that he really possesses a privileged insight into the way things are; rather, through his overt exaggeration and hyperbole, he in effect alerts us to the very contingency and situatedness of his own assertions.

For Gorgias, the Socratic strategy of self-effacement is the clever pose of the person who wishes to conceal his foundationalist commitment; and in this way it betrays deception rather than objectivity. Socrates' ironic profession of ignorance is of course a sham, for he *does* believe that he knows what is most basic to the foundationalist position, namely that there is an objective truth that antedates human inquiry. Socrates may be quite honest in saying that he does not know precisely what that truth happens to be; but there is no doubt in his mind that such a truth exists apart from the interchanges he has with his interlocutors. To Gorgias, the wily *eiron* Socrates is not more "objective" or impartial than any other situated rhetor, and his "dialectical reasoning" does not offer an impartial route to objective truth. While Socrates adopts the pose of an ignorant man engaged in an impartial search of a truth that he knows exists, Gorgias presents himself as a partisan rhetor who knows many truths but whose claims to knowledge are always open to challenge by another rhetor in the agon. The self-effacing Socrates, by professing ignorance of the truth, implies that there is a truth to be discovered and that in order to discover the truth we must overcome our biased and limited perspectives. The boastful Gorgias, by proclaiming knowledge about all subjects, provokes us to challenge his various claims.

Through his boastful pose, Gorgias is not only able to assert views that he believes but also to *show* that each of those assertions is inescapably contingent and thus does not objectively replicate the intrinsic nature of the world as it really is. By playing the role of the ironic boaster, Gorgias leads us to see his assertions as situated and fabricated rather than as objective, neutral observations about how things "really are." Gorgias' mask of the *alazon* thus works in the opposite way of Socrates' irony. Socrates, like many other foundational thinkers, *effaces* himself, and claims ignorance of the truth he pursues. The antifoundationalist Gorgias makes his presence obvious in his outrageous claims of universal knowledge. In so doing, he shows that his own assertions, like all assertions, are partisan and partial; and as such, he displays his notion that every claim to truth is inescapably situated and open to challenge.

The Venue of the Festival

Another strategy Gorgias uses in presenting his texts concerns the venue or site of his performances, the institution of the festival. As noted above, Gorgias appears to have delivered many of his works at civic and Panhellenic festivals. The institution of the festival illuminates several features of Gorgias' performances, for as several critics have argued, the nature and meaning of a text or class of texts is illuminated by attending to the institutional network in which it is produced and received. Specifically, the institutions as established practices are important, for they embody many shared practices, values, and beliefs of a community and indicate the ways in which texts are received and understood by specific audiences. In Oddone Longo's terms, "a literary genre cannot be understood as an abstract definition of formal or structural rules operating merely on the work, but rather should be understood in terms of the ensemble of *insti-*

tutions, with their many interlocking levels and connections" (1992,15).[15] I have argued that we can understand the style and substance of Gorgias' principal texts only by placing them among other works in established genres: his *Epitaphios,* for instance, can be understood only in the context of the Athenian practice of honoring slain warriors; his *Palamedes* acquires its meaning from the legal context of accusation and defense; his *On Not-Being* requires attention to the genre of the Eleatic *epicheireme;* and his encomium of Helen makes sense only in the fifth-century context in which Helen was reviled. But to understand Gorgias' works more fully, we must attend to the institution of the festival in which he performed many of these works, for his performances embody many of the features of those festivals. Indeed, it may be said that Gorgias articulates many of the beliefs, values, and practices of the participants of the Greek festival and that the festival provides the framework within which Gorgias' style and substantive beliefs are best understood.

A point of departure for understanding the Greek festival is Mikhail Bakhtin's seminal account of European *carnival,* the family of festivals held at various times and places throughout medieval Europe, for carnival shares many of the features of its festive Greek predecessor. Carnival serves an important social function, that of challenging many beliefs of the culture and celebrating or affirming what the community deems good in that culture. Carnival involves a transgression and violation of established categories, but at the same time, it celebrates those practices and beliefs that the community considers desirable. Stated another way, the carnival is an event in which people may both challenge and celebrate values and beliefs, and in so doing, purge what they consider undesirable and affirm what they find desirable. Among the techniques of transgression of carnival, according to Bakhtin, are "parodies, travesties, humiliations," for carnival "denies, but it revives and renews at the same time" (1984, 11). In its mocking celebrations, the laughter of the carnival is "communal, a laughter at the world; it is self-directed, laughing at one's self; it is also directed at those who laugh" (12). Furthermore, carnival is overtly theatrical, a grand "performance" in which people both engage in theatrical display and observe the theatrics of others. While Greek festivals differ from medieval carnival in significant ways, they share its double function of criticizing and celebrating, and they frequently achieve these goals through playful and theatrical modes of transgression.

First, Greek festivals celebrate the agon or contest. In many of the festivals—notably the Panhellenic Olympian, Pythian, Nemean, and Isthmian festivals—athletic and other forms of competition were the principal activity. Gorgias' comment about his Olympic Speech, comparing his own performance to the Olympic Games themselves, illustrates this very point. By presenting his works as overtly agonistic, upon the occasion of the Games, Gorgias is able to assume that his audience will receive his performance as partisan and not as a pronouncement that presents itself as a foundational and unassailable truth. As such, Gorgias' use of the festival venue complements his notion that every assertion is inherently agonistic, situated vis-à-vis competing viewpoints, never complete in itself, and always responding to and being responded to by people with alternative perspectives. I suggested above that the agon is one of the central institutions of Panhellenic culture that Gorgias fosters; that in an agonistic culture, the agon serves to promote excellence and diversity among the participants; and that it requires cooperation as well as competition. For while participants compete with one another, they adhere to and affirm the rules of the various agons, be they athletic, rhapsodic, theatrical, or rhetorical. In this respect, Gorgias' agonistic performances embody and reinforce the values of the Panhellenic culture he promotes, and his selection of the festival as a venue enables him to achieve his ethical and political as well as "theoretical" objectives.

A second important feature of the festival is its use of parody. The Greek festivals of the fifth and early fourth centuries tend to be joyful, exuberant gatherings in which people mocked their institutions and themselves. The prevalence of playful abuse, or *psogos,* is central to much early comedy as well as to the humor of the festival. As Parke observes, a prominent feature of many festivals is playful ridicule and abuse; in many cases singing abusive songs was "typical of these festivals" (1977, 105). Among the Athenian festivals that illustrate this are the Eleusinian festival, during which the procession of the initiates encountered men who hurled ribald insults at distinguished persons in the procession" (66); the Anthesteria festival, when the procession "riding in the carts engaged in abuse and mocking of people they met in the roadway" (109); the Thesmophoria, when women hurled abuse at one another in honor to the goddess Iambe, the attendant of Demeter from whom the term *iambizein* derives (86); the Haloa festival, when women "indulged in uninhibited obscenity of language and abuse," as in other festivals confined to women (98); and the Thargelia festival, when figures known as *pharmakoi* or scapegoats are abused in a ritual of purification (147). The venue or site of the performance is important in respect to Gorgias' use of parody, for the audience would be disposed to expect a performance to be parodic and playful. The festival audience would presumably expect the orator to challenge social and political beliefs and values during the festive, playful, and "topsy-turvy" atmosphere of the festival. Gorgias thus would be able to challenge his audience "playfully," as he remarks in *Helen* (21), offering them a *paignion,* or "festive" speech that challenged conventional views about Helen of Troy. His major texts are playful, transgressing conventional myths and logoi, exhibiting new ways to speak about traditional heroes and villains, and always emphasizing the situatedness and contingencies in human existence.

Third, the festival is overtly theatrical, a venue for performance. Gorgias' epideictic performances are what Aristotle calls spectacles, wherein audiences are not called upon to make "practical" decisions, as they may be in forensic or deliberative rhetoric, but can attend to the performance itself. The theatrical nature of Gorgias' rhetoric is indeed crucial: adorned in purple robes, Gorgias presents himself as a theatrical figure; and as such he presents his views as akin to views expressed by an actor in a drama, to be seen as his own rather than as pretending to impartiality or universality. Presenting himself as an official Athenian funeral orator, as a forensic champion of Helen of Troy, as the great warrior and inventor Palamedes himself, or, as noted above, as the boastful and hyperbolic *alazon* who claims to know everything and to be able to speak convincingly on every subject, Gorgias is able to present his work as theater; and as such he is able to presume that his audience will attend to his assertions as they do those of actors, without mistaking his pronouncements as unassailable truths.

Gorgias' festive theater differs from conventional theater, however, in that he removes the strict boundaries between himself as performer and his audience, and he invites them to become actively involved through questions and responses. By addressing topics suggested by the audience, Gorgias illustrates his view that a rhetor must often cope with unforeseen challenges, respond to an immediate charge, and find an "opening" in which to compose a response. Furthermore, by inviting questions and challenges from his audience, he encourages them to become engaged in the agon at hand. By inviting their participation, Gorgias erases the line between the theatrical and the nontheatrical, and displays his view that every utterance is a "performance," an attempt to persuade an audience that one's assertions are true and that one's attitude is unbiased. Gorgias' epideictic theater is thus a theater of exposure, one that does not reveal "the truth" itself but rather the ways in which rhetors convince us that they are telling us the truth. And in this respect, Gorgias' theater prevents us from being mere spectators and reminds us that we are engaged in the project of establishing the truth.

An Epideictic Education

Gorgias' playful epideictic performances are highly entertaining, and it is not surprising that he would be "famous" at the Panhellenic festivals. But his displays are also educational, playing a serious role in shaping or informing as well as delighting the crowd. In order to understand the educational nature of Gorgias' epideictic performances, it is useful first to examine his conception of education and to distinguish it from that of some of his foundationalist rivals.[16]

Gorgias does not construe education as a didactic process of conveying truths about the world or the self, for he sees all such truths as no more than accounts that a particular community happens to accept and endorse at a given time. Rather than teaching his students to discover any such ultimate truths, Gorgias instead teaches them how to become engaged in the agons of the culture, encouraging them to challenge accepted beliefs and to generate new "truths" and codes of behavior. In this respect, he offers an education that facilitates growth or *edification,* rather than one that conveys established truths and prescribes a method for reaffirming them. He thus asserts that his objective as educator is to promote the freedom and power of his students (*Gorgias* 452d), liberating them from the deceptive notion that received views are beyond challenge and empowering them to articulate new ways of thinking. Liberation and power are integral aspects of edification in that a person who is able to liberate himself from fixed beliefs and originate new ways of seeing is one who is able to grow. Significantly, Gorgias' term for freedom, *eleutheria,* originates in *leudh,* which means 'to grow or develop'; and his term *arche* denotes both 'power' and 'originality,' crucial features of growth or edification. The education Gorgias provides is of paramount importance, for it not only enables individuals to contribute to the generation of the knowledge and truth by which the community lives, but to fashion themselves and one another.

In order to liberate and empower his students, Gorgias provides them with the means by which they may participate effectively in the agons of the Panhellenic community. The education he offers is both practical and theoretical. The practical dimension is one of training, a "learning how" to compete in the discursive agons of the community. Gorgias' grandnephew praises Gorgias' educational method as a form of "training":

> No one of mortals before discovered a finer art
> Than Gorgias to arm [train] the soul for contests of excellence.
> (A8)

The training is analogous to the physical training one undergoes in learning to wrestle or to engage in military combat, and Gorgias' term *askeo,* or 'training,' also denotes the way warriors prepare themselves to speak effectively (E12). This training involves mastery of strategies, tactics, and tools needed to function effectively in discursive agons. As such, it involves memorization of tropes, *topoi,* and entire textsca procedure whereby an individual may increase the repertoire of devices and maneuvers available to him on any occasioncdevices that enable him to retrieve useful pieces of information in specific encounters, to challenge established assertions, and to articulate novel viewpoints. Unlike his foundationalist rivals, Gorgias does not attempt to provide his students with a systematic method, or fixed set of rules for pursuing objective truth. For in Gorgias' conception of inquiry, any such system would be misguided and counterproductive. As in wrestling, a student may learn and practice strategies and tactics, but there is no "method" to learn, no systematic procedure that one may follow; rather, the rhetor must be prepared for novel as well as familiar challenges and audiences. Gorgias' training involves becoming familiar with agons of the culture, learning the vocabularies and paradigmatic texts of various discourses and professions, and learning which procedures and maneuvers are permitted in the various agons of the culture.[17]

To some of his critics, the education Gorgias offers is intellectually unsound precisely because it is not systematic. Plato argues that the putative skill Gorgias claims to impart to his students is a mere "knack" at persuading rather than a viable *techne* or "art"; and he contrasts Gorgias' haphazard practice with a true art of rhetoric that would instruct students about the nature of the psyche, the available modes of discourse, and the truth about the world itself.[18] Aristotle elaborates on Plato's critique of Gorgias' teaching, arguing that "the educational method of those earning money by teaching controversial arguments was like the system of Gorgias. For some assigned rhetorical speeches and others question-and-answer discussions to be learned by heart. . . . As a result, the teaching was quick but unscientific for those learning from them. For they thought they were teaching, although presenting, not art, but the results of art, just as if someone claimed to present a science to prevent feet from hurting and then did not teach shoemaking, nor where it was possible to get such things, but offered many kinds of shoes of all sorts" (*Sophistical Refutations* 183b36).

But this criticism is misguided, for if fails to recognize that Gorgias rejects the notion of a method for discovering or conveying truths. Rather than providing them with a method, he trains his students to acquire a repertoire of strategies, tactics, rules of thumb, and diverse tools for dealing with a variety of unpredictable confrontations. Memorization plays an important role in this process, for it enables a student to become embedded in various "traditions" of the culture, families of texts that various authors have composed. The texts are exemplary models or paradigms that show which tools have worked in other situations and suggest ways of thinking and speaking that may enable the rhetor to address a new situation. Memorizing these texts enables a student to become familiar with the ongoing agons and issues of the culture; and it provides a repertoire of resources for inventing new arguments. Becoming embedded in a tradition does not foreclose novelty; on the contrary, it provides a context for determining what is novel. Memorization of paradigmatic texts does not mean that a rhetor must simply repeat what has been said before; indeed, Gorgias ridicules Prodicus for doing just this (A24). Instead, memorization enables the rhetor to draw freely on an array of *topoi* and tropes, deploying them in novel ways in new circumstances. It is by being embedded in a tradition that Gorgias is able to improvise freely, drawing on what is "at hand" and trusting to the moment but not being completely at the mercy of chance or contingency (A1a).

Gorgias' education is theoretical as well as practical in that his objective is to show his students that assertions are deemed true, not because they replicate an independent state of affairs, but because they win the endorsement of an audience. Parody, figuration, and theater serve his pedagogical end, *disabusing* his audience of the illusion that any account of things, including his own, is an objective representation or mirror of "things as they really are." Gorgias' parodic, figurative, and theatrical performances enable him to show that his own assertions are themselves situated and to alert his audience to the fact that even his own arguments are deceptive insofar as they are taken to be true in a context-invariant way. Gorgias' displays may thus be seen as *showing* rather than *telling* his audience about the situated and fabricative dimensions of *logos*. For his parodies, paratropical figures, and dramatic characterizations are situated vis-à-vis the genres he parodies, the conventional tropes of the culture, and the self-effacing strategies of his foundationalist adversaries. As *epideixis,* Gorgias' works thus show or expose the rhetoricity of *logos* itself; and in so doing, they unmask the deliberately deceptive attempts by most rhetors to present their accounts as objective truths.

Through his use of parody, Gorgias draws attention to the conventions of diverse discourses and depicts them as contestable partisan accounts. By distorting or exaggerating the conventions of the metaphysical *epicheireme,* the official *epitaphios,* the cultural *encomium,* and the dicanic *apologia,* he shows that every text in these genres expresses the partisan view of a situated rhetor and not the pronouncement of a foundational truth, a political absolute, a divinely inspired utterance, or an impartial accusation. Gorgias also uses his paratropic figuration to disabuse his audience of the illusion that any views are objectively "true." In his use of *glotta,* oxymorons, *dipla,* epithets, metaphors, puns, and other tropes, he offers an alternative to the foundationalist conception of representation, exposing the conventional strategies of naming, coining words, and making comparisons between things as local and arbitrary. In his deliberately "thick" or opaque style, Gorgias foregrounds his own situatedness; and in so doing, he in effect invites his students to reflect on the arbitrary assumptions and biases in their own language. Gorgias also uses theatricality to expose the deceptiveness of many speakers, educating his audiences in a manner similar to the way tragedians educate their audiences. As a pedagogic tool, Gorgias' histrionics enable him to underscore the situatedness of each of his assertions, reminding his audience that his remarks are *his own,* made in a particular time, place, and agon, and open to challenge by a rival.

While he exposes the rhetoricity of his rivals through parody, paratropic figuration, and histrionics, Gorgias does not want to circumvent or do away with rhetorical agons and to replace them with a more "direct" route to the way things really are. For Gorgias, every time a foundationalist believes that he has discovered such a privileged or direct route to the truth, whether it involves divine inspiration, recollection of a previous life of his soul, rational apprehension of essences, nonrational experience of the moment, or empirical scientific observation of the material world, he is simply failing to recognize that he is so utterly persuaded by the particular discourse that he forgets that he is engaged in an agon and fails to see that he is so captivated by his own partisan discourse that he cannot imagine an alternative to it. Gorgias' teaching is not antilogical or deconstructive in the sense that he seeks to destroy discourse and the agons in which it is used. On the contrary, he wants to *preserve* those agons and encourage people to participate in them, showing how acceptance of their constraints enables rhetors to compose new ways of seeing and thinking. In effect, he wants to keep the players in the agons honest and thereby prevent any one of them from undermining the games by claiming that all such games are futile insofar as they purport to arrive at the way things really are. By emphasizing the agonistic nature of every discourse, Gorgias prevents partisans of any one discourse from achieving a privileged status in the culture; by generating cogent arguments in diverse agons, he shows that truths can be generated in diverse vocabularies and with varied modes of argument and presentation and that none merits the accolade of primacy.

Some of Gorgias' critics also impugn his teaching as morally objectionable, maintaining that by teaching students how to excel in agons, he encourages them to be egocentric, concerned solely with winning debates and gratifying their selfish desires, and indifferent to the welfare of the community. They argue that Gorgias seduces intellectuals and artists, like his protégé Agathon, into playing trivial wordgames; while at the same time he teaches greedy and power-hungry people like Callicles how to take power in a community. Plato equates Gorgias' elegant rhetoric with cookery, a knack of concocting verbal pastries for self-indulgent banqueters, gratifying their irrational taste for unwholesome confections, just as self-indulgent entertainers and sinister demagogues gratify the people with flattering words. Gorgias' style, a debauchery of words, intemperate and ornate, is a rich banquet, a delightful feast designed to please the decadent taste of his banqueters. His playful performances lead his audience away from the pursuit of the true and the good, absorbing them in wordplay, in the delight of sounds and rhythms and related and antithetical meanings. Rather than becoming more noble, they become base, no different than animals seeking sensual gratification. Abandoning philosophy, they turn to rhetoric, the art of seducing others, deceiving, manipulating and enslaving them, and hence using them for their own gratification.

As Plato points out, Gorgias does not attempt to improve his students morally, and rather than promising to teach virtue, he "laughs at others when he hears them so promising" (*Meno* 95c). Furthermore, Gorgias' rhetoric is a menace to the community as a whole, for by encouraging the intelligentsia to become engaged in trivial pursuits and training its politicians to excel in struggles for power unconstrained by moral principles, he undermines the moral principles of the community as a whole. The disorder he promotes is one described by Thucydides' Alcibiades in his account of the unstable cities of Gorgias' Sicily, urban centers which are "peopled by motley rabbles, and easily change their institutions and adopt new ones in their stead; and consequently the inhabitants [are] without any feeling of patriotism . . . [and] every man thinks that either by fair words or by party strife he can obtain something at the public expense, and then in the event of a catastrophe settle in some other country, and makes his preparations accordingly" (*History of the Peloponnesian War* 6.17). Rather than a moral education, Gorgias offers Greece a "miseducation," corrupting individual morality and potentially subverting the social order.

But this critique fails to understand the profoundly moral dimension of Gorgias' teaching. Rather than subverting individual morality and disrupting social order, Gorgias' agonistic education enables his students to fashion their own moral views in a manner that strengthens rather than undermines the institutions of the community. By teaching them how to excel in a variety of agons, Gorgias offers a teaching that promotes both socialization and individuation. His rhetorical education promotes socialization, encouraging people to become active members of the community by learning its discourses and participating in its agons. Since the Panhellenic community is constituted and regulated by its agonistic institutions and in this respect depends on mutual trust rather than dogmatic decrees, Gorgias' agonistic education promotes what Nietzsche calls "the welfare of the whole, of the civic society" (1976, 58–59).

Correlatively, Gorgias' agonistic education promotes individuation and true moral autonomy, whereby students learn to articulate their *own* positions in a variety of socially sanctioned agons. By teaching his students how to become embedded in the agons of the culture, Gorgias emphasizes the importance of courageously challenging the beliefs and values of others, for to assert one's own views in an agon requires a person to differentiate his position from those of others in the agon. By teaching his students how to participate in the agonistic discussions of the community, Gorgias encourages them to present their own views as persuasively as possible but to remain open to the possibility of being persuaded by others. As such, he offers them the means by which they may liberate and empower themselves in a manner that strengthens rather than undermines the Panhellenic community. Gorgias does not encourage his students to retreat from the community in order to achieve an illusory "autonomy," but neither does he encourage them to reinforce the prevailing stereotypes by iterating traditional moral views. For he teaches that morality involves engagement with others in a vigorous, free, and open interchange, rather than a slavish assent to dogmatic moral principles articulated by deceptive and manipulative foundationalist thinkers.

The Place of Gorgias

> The admirers of Gorgias were noble and numerous: first, the Greeks in Thessaly, among whom "to be an orator" acquired the synonym "to Gorgianize," and secondly, all Greece.
>
> Philostratus
>
> Every advance in epistemology and moral knowledge has reinstated the Sophists.
>
> <div align="right">Nietzsche, <i>Will To Power</i></div>

In this book I have argued that Gorgias is a sophisticated thinker and an accomplished artist. To the extent that my account is an *apologia,* I have joined the ranks of those scholars who have undertaken a "rehabilitation" of Gorgias, defending him against the claims first raised by his fifth- and fourth-century Athenian rivals that he is a pretentious charlatan indifferent to truth, a shameless self-promoter subversive of morality, and an outlandish stylist unconcerned with clarity. In defending Gorgias, however, I have differentiated my account from two prevailing scholarly accounts, the subjectivist reading initiated by Hegel and the empiricist reading initiated by Grote. I have argued that although each of these interpretations of Gorgias is internally coherent, each is contradicted by a large number of Gorgias' own assertions, and each fails to account for Gorgias' distinctive manner of writing.

As an alternative to these readings, I have argued that Gorgias is an antifoundationalist who repudiates the entire foundational project of his philosophical predecessors and contemporaries. I have argued that this construal renders Gorgias' work logically consistent, thematically coherent, and stylistically purposive and that it consequently renders his work more cogent or compelling than the subjectivist and empiricist readings. But which reading of Gorgias we ultimately accept will not depend solely on the cogency it lends to Gorgias, but also on whether it is congruent with our conception of Greek and Western culture. For every interpretation involves placing an author in a cultural context, and the way we characterize his context will influence the way we place and thus read Gorgias. An adequate account of the complex and varied cultural contexts in which Gorgias composed and presented his works lies beyond the scope of this or any one text; and in this sense, deciding which reading of Gorgias is congruent with our view of Greek culture must remain tentative and speculative. But although a detailed account is not possible in any one text, it is possible to discuss the general contours of Greek culture and to situate Gorgias in it. This placement will indicate not only how we understand Gorgias but also how important we consider him to be as a thinker and writer.

In placing Gorgias in Greek culture, it is useful to attend to the two principle accounts or narratives that Gorgian scholars have articulated, namely, the *evolutionary* and the *agonal* narratives. The evolutionary narrative, adumbrated by fifth-century thinkers such as Thucydides, Plato, and Aristotle, depicts Greek culture as evolving from an archaic culture informed by *mythos* into a classical culture informed by *logos*.[1] In this narrative, the principle feature of Greek intellectual culture is identified as a development from a mythical, irrationalist, and "poetic" worldview to an enlightened, rational, and scientific orientation. According to this narrative, archaic Greek culture was dominated by mythic thought expressed and transmitted orally in poetic myths, and Greek society was governed by authoritarian rulers legitimized by those myths. During the eighth, seventh, and sixth centuries, a number of profound social and cultural transformations occurred; and a variety of thinkers, such as Parmenides, Thales, and Heraclitus, began speculating about the universe and man's role in it, challenging the authority of traditional Greek myths and using empirical observation and rational argument to support their views. Fifth-century thinkers extended the scope of empirical observation and rational argumentation to such fields as medicine, astronomy, mathematics, psychology, and rhetoric; and thinkers such as Aristotle in the fourth century further expanded the role of scientific observation and reason. The evolution from mythical to rational thinking also influenced morality and politics, for rational inquiry into morality and the social order led to a repudiation of traditional authoritarian governments and the development of democracy in Athens and its allied cities. The progress of reason also influenced the development of Greek style, whereby the poetic metaphors of epic and lyric poetry that had been transmitted orally were supplanted by the lucid, often written fourth-century prose of historians, rhetoricians, and philosophers.

Many scholars who embrace this evolutionary narrative see this evolution as progress and extol as paragons of Greek culture the enlightened rationalism of Socrates, the democratic liberalism of Periclean Athens, and the lucid prose of fourth-century oratory. Hegel thus sees this evolution in Greek culture as decidedly progressive, as the unfolding of the human spirit; and Grote applauds the development of logic and democracy. Other scholars who embrace the evolutionary narrative bemoan the disappearance of the irrational and mythical aspects of early Greek thought and depict the development of rationality and logic as a form of decadence. Rather than attending to rationalism and democracy, they instead focus on the irrational myths, the political and social upheavals in numerous Greek cities, and the nonclassical poetic styles of various poets. Often influenced by the early Nietzsche's account of the "Dionysian" forces in Greek culture, they delineate what Frederic Jameson describes as "an alternative Greece, not that of Pericles or the Parthenon, but something savage or barbaric, tribal or African, or Mediterranean sexist—a culture of masks and death, ritual ecstasies, slavery, scapegoating, phallocratic homosexuality, an utterly non- or anticlassical culture to which something of the electrifying otherness and fascination, say, of the Aztec world, has been restored" (1988, 151). Whereas the progressivist scholars depict the greatest contributions of ancient Greece to be the objectivity of science and logic, the justice of democracy, and the lucidity of scientific prose, the "regressivist" scholars tend to extol the psychological insights of myth, the violent uprisings of repressed populations such as those of Ducetius in fifth-century Sicily, and the passionate urgencies of proto-romantic poets such as Sappho.[2]

While both progressivists and regressivists embrace an evolutionary model of Greek culture, a rival group of scholars has argued for an *agonal* narrative, one that depicts Greek culture as a series of struggles between people holding rival views of rationality, knowledge, community, and art. The agonal narrative of Greek history, adumbrated by the sophistic historian Herodotus and first articulated in the modern era by Burckhardt and Nietzsche, has been developed by historians of philosophy and rhetoric such as Isjelling, Lanham, Roochnik, Fish, Jarratt, and others who argue that Greek culture may be understood, not as an evolution from unreason to reason, but as an ongoing struggle between competing models of rationality.[3] This agonal narrative is consistent with the conclusions of a wide variety of comparative mythologists, linguists, ethnologists, and anthropologists who repudiate what Jean-Pierre Vernant characterizes as "the narrow outlook of positivism" inherent in the notion that "mythical" thought is irrational, "together with its naïve belief in the inevitable progress of society from the shadows of superstition toward the light of reason" (1988, 235).

Drawing connections between myth and language, several scholars have argued that mythical thought is not "irrational" but that myths comprise a heterogeneous family of narrative and speculative texts that provide individuals with a repertoire of binary oppositions, figurative analogies, and *exempla* or "instructive cases" for making sense of their experience. In brief, these scholars show that myths are early *rhetorical texts,* composed by partisan individuals engaged in an ongoing project of interpreting their experiences and repudiating accounts offered by rivals. Vernant thus remarks that myths consist of "an institutionalized system of symbols, a codified verbal behavior that, like language, conveys various modes of . . . organizing experience" (1988, 242); and G. S. Kirk characterizes "myths" as a diverse family of traditional narratives that provide individuals with a diverse repertoire of *topoi,* tropes, and paradigms or "instructive cases" for interpreting novel experiences (1974, 290).

The agonal narrative is also consistent with the views of contemporary philosophers such as Rorty who construe "rationality" not as the capacity for following inherently valid rules of deduction or induction, but as the ability to draw upon available resources in order to cope effectively with one's situation, to welcome rival view points, and to engage in "persuasion rather than force" (1998, 187). In this context, a so-called mythical thinker is eminently rational insofar as he uses the available vocabulary of myths for terms and distinctions that enable him to articulate persuasive interpretations of a given situation.

While advocates of the evolutionary narrative tend to contrast thinkers in the "mythical" era with those in the subsequent "logical" era, many advocates of the agonal model reject this simplistic historical categorization. Instead, they discern similarities between mystical poets such as Orpheus, who proclaim their vision irrefutable and refuse to engage in competitions with others poets, and dogmatic philosophers such as Parmenides, who maintain that their vision transcends the erroneous views of the "undiscerning horde" of ordinary mortals. The principal quarrel in Greek culture, in the agonal model of history, is between pragmatic authors writing in diverse genres and eras who promote the use of the agon as a means of coping with and making sense of life, and dogmatists of various sorts who seek to flee the contingencies of everyday life to a domain of absolute truth and virtue. Rather than postulating an historic development from an era of primitive mythical thinkers to one of rational and scientific thinkers, the agonal model depicts pragmatic, clever individuals possessing *metis* in the so-called mythical era as far more similar to their fifth-century sophistic heirs than to their own foundationalist contemporaries. Indeed, in the agonal narrative, the rigorous distinction between the so-called mythical and rational thinker dissolves. For both the mythical and the rational thinker use *topoi,* tropes, examples, and narratives to articulate persuasive accounts of their situations.

In the agonal model, Greek culture emerges as a series of struggles between people who use mythical narratives and rational strategies as tools for functioning effectively or "fittingly" in novel circumstances, and people who use these narratives and arguments to discover absolute truths or moral laws. The ancient quarrel is thus between people who see *nomos* as a family of contingent traditions, practices, and conventions, and those who seek a secure foundation for human thought and value in an inward Orphic *psyche* or an outward domain of Pythagorean spheres, Eleatic Being, or Platonic forms. The ancient quarrel is not a struggle between a mythically minded herd and enlightened analytical fifth-century individuals, as Havelock (1982) maintains, but a struggle between agonists and dogmatists, between Sophists like Protagoras, who maintain that every account may be challenged by a rival account, and philosophers like Parmenides, who contend that the correct method of thinking (namely, their own) is a reliable guide to understanding the way the world really is.

I suggest that our interpretation of Gorgias is integrally related to which of these historical narratives we find most appealing. If we adopt the *evolutionary* narrative, we will be inclined to situate Gorgias in respect to this evolution and hence will tend to embrace either the subjectivist or empiricist reading. Members of the *subjectivist* school thus read Gorgias as a proponent of irrationality who depicts *logos* or reason as inherently deceptive and repressive, an advocate of liberation who seeks to overthrow the repressive regime of *logos*, and a creative artist who uses poetic devices to expose the deceptions of *logos* and to suggest new ways to recreate oneself and one's world. The subjectivist reading identifies Gorgias as a proponent of *mythos*, who sees individuals as prevented from apprehending reality and themselves by the deceptions of a rational *logos*, who urges individuals to liberate themselves from this repressive *logos*, and who uses radically new figures of speech to subvert rationality itself. In this reading, Gorgias is aligned with "irrationalist" poets such as Aeschylus, who depict the human condition as inescapably tragic, and with lyric poets such as Sappho, who urge people to follow their passions rather than heed social norms. He is associated politically with the chaos, stasis, and violence pervasive in fifth and fourth-century Sicily, and his writing is characterized as an orally delivered poetic style in which sonorous resonance and paradoxical figuration takes precedence over clarity and effective communication.

Members of the *empiricist* school, in contrast, read Gorgias as an advocate of reason or *logos* who promotes rational inquiry as a way to dispel the deceptions of myth-bound poets, a supporter of democratic governments who affirms the equality of rational individuals and rejects the repressive social orders legitimized by traditional myths, and a proponent of lucid prose who deploys antitheses, analogies, and logical reasoning to convey his ideas clearly and effectively. They place Gorgias in the camp of *logos*, promoting enlightened rationality through logical argumentation, contributing to democracy by encouraging submission to universal moral laws accessible through reason, and promoting lucidity by transforming rhetoric from the domain of figurative poetry to one of literal prose.

If we adopt the *agonal* model of Greek culture, however, we will not characterize Gorgias as a proponent of either mythic or logical thought, but as an antifoundationalist who repudiates the foundationalist claims by both poetic advocates of *mythos* and philosophical advocates of *logos*, and who instead promotes the contingent convention of the agon as the most desirable way to establish truths and values. Gorgias thus challenges claims by mythically minded poets that their inspired words reflect a divine truth, and he rejects assertions by philosophers that their rational methods provide a secure route to an immutable Being. For he repudiates their shared foundationalist assumption that knowledge and discourse about the truth must be grounded upon, and warranted by reference to, a nonlinguistic criterion or standard, whether it is obtained through careful empirical observation of the material world or wild kairotic leaps into the flux of Becoming. Instead, he sees discourse as an array of human interactions, the paradigm of which is the cooperative and competitive agon or game. He maintains that people acquire and display knowledge, not by directly observing the world as it really is, but by participating in discursive agons sanctioned by the community, contests in which they advance rival interpretations designed to persuade specific audiences in the community. And he sees truths, not as imaginative reconstructions of kairotic experiences, nor as verifiable descriptions of a material world, but as partisan interpretations that a community endorses as most persuasive.

Gorgias' views of the individual and the community are also antifoundationalist, in that he depicts individuals as Larisan potters whose creations include themselves: a community of artists fashioning themselves through active participation in the agons of the community. He characterizes the moral individual as one who heeds the conventions of the community, not one who heeds the promptings of his innate animal drives, a supernatural being, or the decrees of reason. Gorgias promotes a Panhellenic community in which people are united through mutual trust and in which the polis is composed of citizens intent on promoting and defending their agonistic form of life. In his epideictic performances, Gorgias does not use poetic devices to allude to the chaotic flux of Becoming or to transmit his ideas lucidly. Instead, he deploys strategies such as parody, overtly artificial tropes, and an exaggerated theatricality to expose the rhetoricity of every text and to show how novel works may be composed by drawing on the discourses of the culture. Gorgias' festive performances also serve his ethical and political ends, for they invite his listeners to respond and thereby to become engaged in the agons of their community.

If we adopt the agonal narrative of Greek culture and in so doing construe Gorgias as articulating the antifoundationalist position in a long-standing quarrel with foundationalist thought, we may be led to grant him a more important place in Greek culture than he has previously been given. For if we adopt either the subjectivist or empiricist readings, we will tend to assign him a relatively minor role in the putative progression from *mythos* to *logos* and will see his work as contradictory and derivative. If we read Gorgias as a subjectivist who claims that human awareness and communication are usually confined to the deceptive domain of human *logos,* then his assertions are derivative iterations of the tragic poets. If, as Untersteiner (1954) argues, Gorgias derives his subjectivism from the tragic poets, he adds little if anything original to their views, which are more effectively illustrated in the tragic dramas of Aeschylus than in Gorgias' antithetical rhetorical tropes. In respect to ethical thought, if we read Gorgias as an egoist who urges people to use any means to satisfy their individual desires, and if we see him as drawing on Sappho's apparent justification of Helen's acting from passion, then we must see Gorgias' ethical thought as derivative and self-contradictory as well. For he praises warriors who act out of duty, condemns Odysseus for his selfishness, and depicts Palamedes as a rationalist who seldom acts on the basis of passion. Nor does Gorgias articulate the premises or consequences of egoism in any of his works, as does Plato's fictional Callicles. And if we read him as using antithetical or novel and "sublime" figures of speech to communicate his subjectivist and irrationalist views, then we must judge him as inept and unsuccessful. For if his objective is to convey his ideas to his contemporaries, he clearly fails, given that they never mention any such oblique message or effect. Even if we make a concerted effort to read him in this way, we must conclude that he is inept; for while his wordplay is often clever and witty, his writing never approaches the sublimity of Pindar or the passionate intensity of Sappho.

If, conversely, we characterize Gorgias as an empiricist and rationalist, we must also assign him a minor role in the development from mythical to logical thought, for Gorgias' contributions are sparse and derivative. His contributions to science are minimal at best, confined to a few remarks about the therapeutic effect of *logos* on the psyche and to an apparent advocacy of a "theory of pores" derived from Empedocles. Gorgias may be credited for his contributions to rational argumentation, as exemplified in his systematic use of counterfactual conditionals in *On Not-Being* and *Palamedes* and his apagogic reasoning in *Helen*. But if Gorgias is skillful in his argumentation, he cannot be credited with inventing such modes of argument, which are explored in far greater depth by such thinkers as Plato and Aristotle. Furthermore, we may object that his reasoning in *On Not-Being* seems overtly contradictory, that several of his arguments in *Palamedes* seem formulaic, and that his reasoning in *Helen* has failed to convince many readers. If we read Gorgias as articulating a universalist ethics of duty and democratic politics, then he again emerges as contradictory and derivative. While he praises the conventional Greek virtues of wisdom, courage, moderation, and justice, he never attempts to define these, and he frequently appears to advocate an ethical opportunism or situational ethics in which insult and violence are permissible. We may well be inclined to accept Plato's portrayal of Gorgias as placing his own welfare above that of the cities he visited, unconcerned with the danger posed by his potentially subversive rhetorical *techne* and unwilling to accept responsibility for the immoralism of his students. As a stylist, Gorgias also merits a minor position in the struggle between clarity and obfuscation. For even if we excuse his labored antitheses, far-fetched metaphors, pronounced provincialisms, and frequent epithets as indicative of a "transition" between poetic opacity and prosaic lucidity, we may well concur with Aristotle's assessment that Gorgias' style is more frigid than fluid, more artificial than natural.

But if we read Gorgias as an antifoundationalist struggling against foundational rivals, then we will consider him a far more seminal figure in Western culture, a precursor to a variety of contemporary thinkers. Citing only a few instances of the seminality of his thought, we may observe that Gorgias' characterization of discourse as a repertoire of maneuvers in various agons anticipates Wittgenstein's characterization of language as a family of games; that his construal of inquiry as rhetorical debate within socially sanctioned agons anticipates an array of contemporary hermeneutic theorists such as Gadamer, Rorty, and Fish, who depict inquiry as a cooperative and competitive game played by various interpretive communities; and that his notion of truth as the endorsement by a community of views they deem persuasive anticipates Thomas Kuhn's notion that the history of science is a record of scientists discarding old paradigms for new ones, rather than a progression in which "successive beliefs become more and more probable or better and better approximations to the truth" (1993, 330).

Gorgias' account of the individual and the community also anticipates ideas by an array of contemporary thinkers. His notion that people construct themselves and each other in their respective communities anticipates the ideas of many social constructionists and communitarians, and his characterization of the Panhellenic community as a contingent association of people who affirm and defend their agonistic institutions anticipates Joseph Schumpeter's notion that "to realize the relative validity of one's convictions and yet stand for them unflinchingly is what distinguishes a civilized man from a Barbarian."[4] Finally, Gorgias' stylish and theatrical performances validate Philostratus' characterization of him as the father of the Sophists' art and point to Gorgias' seminal role in the fields of literature and the arts. Gorgias' account of the poet as a rhetor engaged in competition with other rhetors and poets anticipates Harold Bloom's characterization of poets engaged in an "agon" with their predecessors;[5] his use of various stylistic strategies to expose the rhetoricity of every text anticipates Derrida's project of deconstruction; and his self-conscious theatricality anticipates Jerzy Grotowski's conception of the performer as encouraging the audience to participate in their own self-creation.[6]

In these and other ways, the antifoundationalist reading renders Gorgias our precursor, a seminal thinker and artist who provides us with a compelling way to integrate our own notions of language, inquiry, truth, selfhood, community, and art. In so doing, the reading underwrites Vitanza's assertion that Gorgias is the principal precursor of our own Third Sophistic, Fish's contention that "modern antifoundationalism is old sophism writ analytic," and, perhaps, Nietzsche's claim that "every advance in epistemology and moral knowledge has reinstated the Sophists" (1968, 428). By characterizing Gorgias as our precursor, the reading enables us appreciate the various strategies he used to challenge what has become the dominant philosophical tradition in Western thought. Conversely, the reading helps to see how foundationalist thinkers from Plato and Aristotle to Robinson and

Nussbaum have been able to characterize Gorgias in their own terms and to thereby dismiss him as philosophically trivial, morally objectionable, and stylistically inept. But even if the antifoundationalist reading of Gorgias is congruent with our view of Greek and Western culture, this is not to say that the reading is "true" in the sense that it mirrors or corresponds to an independent historical reality, for every such historical "reality" is a contingent fabrication of partisan scholars. Nor is it to say that the antifoundational account is the final word on Gorgias, given that future scholars may redescribe him in new terminologies anchored in their own partisan interests and beliefs. But it is to assert that the antifoundational narrative is true insofar as it is more persuasive than its prevailing rivals, and that it will remain so until it is persuasively refuted.

Notes

Seeking the Sophist

1. Aristophanes describes Gorgias as a member of a "rascally race" who "live by their tongues / Who reap and sow / And gather in and play the sycophant / With tongues. They are / Barbarians by birth, / Gorgiases and Philips" (A5a, *Birds* 1694ff). He also rebukes Gorgias for flattering the Athenians in his appeal for military support (*Acharnians* 633–40). Plato condemns Gorgias on intellectual, moral, and stylistic grounds; repudiating his contention that probability is more important than truth (*Phaedrus* 267a); denouncing his art of rhetoric as an amoral "knack" for manipulation through flattery (*Gorgias* 463b); and parodying his style in the *Symposium*. Aristotle also disparages Gorgias, portraying him as a derivative stylist without serious views and characterizing his style as inept and "frigid" (*Rhetoric* 1405b34).

2. Some scholars distinguish between Sophists, who discuss philosophical issues, and rhetors, who are primarily concerned with composing persuasive public speeches. Among nineteenth-century scholars, Grote argues that "if the line could be clearly drawn between rhetors and sophists, Gorgias ought rather to be ranked with the former" (1869, 187). Kierkegaard (1989) also views Gorgias as a rhetor rather than a Sophist. In the twentieth century, most scholars have depicted Gorgias as a sophist, but C. J. Classen writes that "whether Gorgias is to be regarded as a sophist is an unsolved problem even today" (1981, 21); E. R. Dodds writes that "it is doubtful whether [Gorgias] should in fact be called a 'sophist' at all" (Dodds, 1990, 6–7); and T. Irwin contends, "I do not believe there is sufficient evidence to suggest that Gorgias was a Sophist" (1997, 588, n. 2).

3. Vitanza claims that while Protagoras is the principal representative of the First Sophistic, Gorgias is a "proto-Third Sophistic thinker" (1991, 125). For further development of his view, see Vitanza 1997, 244ff.

4. Whereas only twenty years ago most anthologies and collections of essays on early Greek philosophy tended to exclude Gorgias altogether, recent texts, such as A. A. Long's 1999 *Companion to Early Greek Philosophy,* tend to include a discussion of Gorgias. Gorgias is associated with Heidegger by Miller 1987, 169–84; with Derrida by Crowley 1979, 278–85; with Gusdorf by Gronbeck 1972, 36–38; with Ayer and Stevenson by Mourelatos 1987, 156; and with Nietzsche, Derrida, Rorty, and Fish by Roochnik 1990, 50; 1991, 225–46.

5. For recent discussions of Gorgias' contribution to the discourse on Helen of Troy, see Lindsay 1974, Bergren 1983, Suzuki 1989, N. Austin 1994, Crockett 1994, and Worman 1997.

6. Concerning Gorgias' influence on the style of medical writers, Ludwig Edelstein writes that "Gorgias was Hippocrates' teacher in rhetoric; the *Epidemics* to a certain extent follow the stylistic rules of Gorgias" (1994, 138). Concerning Gorgias' contributions to the development of "logotherapy," using words to assist people in securing a flourishing life, see Nussbaum 1994, 51.

7. Among recent scholars who explore Gorgias' influence on Euripides, Gregory argues that Gorgias' influence pervades *The Trojan Women* (1991, 158); Scodel (1991) asserts that Euripides

draws directly on Gorgias; Worman finds a similarity in the references each author makes to Helen's body (1997, 181); and Croally argues that an "appropriate description of this bizarre discourse called Euripidean tragedy is aesthetic Gorgianism" (1994, 227).

8. For rival accounts of Gorgias' view of women, see Bergren (1993), Jarratt (1991), and Crockett (1994).

9. For discussions of Gorgias' contribution to Greek legal theory and reasoning, see Coulter 1979 and Long 1984.

10. For accounts of the significance of Gorgias' *Epitaphios* in Greek culture, see Untersteiner 1954, 176–84; and Loraux 1986, 221–62.

11. Arthur Pease argues that Gorgias' paradoxical encomia anticipate Erasmus' *Praise of Folly* and much modern satire (1926, 41–42); Eric White argues that Gorgias' figurative style anticipates "mannerism" (1987, 30–31); and James Porter argues that Gorgias' elevated writing is an early instance of the "sublime" (1993, 267ff).

12. For recent discussions of the educational theories and practices of Gorgias and his sophistic colleagues, see Guthrie 1971, 41–44; Kerferd 1989, 30–41; Kennedy 1963, 18–21; and Jarratt 1991, 81–120.

13. Concerning the impact of Gorgias' 427 B.C.E. delegation, B. H. Williams (1931) agrees with Diodorus that Gorgias influenced the Athenian decision to support Leontini, but Donald Kagan contends that "we may safely dismiss the suggestion by Diodorus that the Athenians were convinced by the rhetorical innovations of the great sophist Gorgias who led the embassy from Leontini" (1974, 182).

14. For ancient references to the amazement and perplexity Gorgias aroused in his first Athenian audiences, see Philostratus (A1), Diodorus Siculus (A4.3), Timaeus, and Dionysius of Halicarnassus (A4.5). Socrates concedes to Polus that "indeed I do not know whether this is the rhetoric which Gorgias practices, for from our argument just now we got no very clear view as to how he conceives it" (*Gorgias* 463a). Isocrates chastises Gorgias in *Antidosis* (sections 268–69) and *Helen* (sections 14–15). For recent discussion of Isocrates' critique of Gorgias, see Poulakos 1986.

15. For discussion of scholarly dispute over the authenticity and accuracy of Gorgias' extant texts prior to the canonization by Diels and Kranz, see Untersteiner 1954, 95–97; Segal 1972, 136–137, n. 10; Kerferd 1989, 1; and Romilly 1992, ix-x.

16. The Suda is a tenth-century Byzantine Greek historical encyclopedia of the ancient Mediterranean world derived from the *scholia* to critical editions of canonical works and from compilations by earlier authors.

17. For further discussion of the authenticity and accuracy of *Helen* and *Palamedes*, see Untersteiner 1954, 99, n. 54. For a discussion of the Cripps and Palatine manuscripts in which the works appear, see MacDowell 1961.

18. For discussion of the meaning of *logos*, see Peters 1967, 110–12; Kerferd 1981, 83; Roochnik 1990, 12–13. Kerferd writes: "There are three main areas of its application or use, all related by an underlying conceptual unity. These are first of all the area of language and linguistic formulation, hence speech, discourse, description, statements, arguments (as expressed in words) and so on; secondly the area of thought and mental processes, hence thinking, reason-

ing, accounting for, explanation (cf. *orthos logos*), etc.; thirdly, the area of the world, that *about* which we are able to speak and to think, hence structural principles, formulae, natural laws and so on, provided that in each case they are regarded as actually present in and exhibited in the world-process" (1981, 31).

19. Scholars who read Gorgias as not meaning *anything* that he says in *Helen* include Poulakos, who argues that what the Sophists left behind "is not what they really believed," since their works "represent only sketchy illustrations of what can be done with language" (1995, 25). Among those who read Gorgias as meaning *some* of what he says in the text, Versenyi writes that "there is no reason to suppose that Gorgias cared much whether Helen was vindicated or not.... There is another aspect, however, under which his defense or eulogy is by no means a playful exercise: most of Helen's Encomium deals with the nature and power of *logos,* a subject whose importance and seriousness for the rhetorician are obvious" (1963, 44). Scholars who assume that Gorgias means *everything* he says in *Helen* include Race 1989, 16–33; Crockett 1994, 71–90; and Bergren 1983, 82–86. For discussion of Gorgias' "seriousness" in *On Not-Being,* see Kerferd 1955, 3; Calogero 1971, 225–27; Versenyi 1963, 40–41; and Guthrie 1971, 193–94.

20. For ancient references to the dates of Gorgias' birth and death, which range from 500/480 to 392/372 B.C.E., see A2; A6; A10; A11; A13; A14; A18; A19. For discussion of these dates, see Untersteiner 1954, 97, n. 2; and Segal 1972, 135, n. 1.

21. For Gorgias' family life, see A2, A2a, A22; A7, A8. Concerning his putative marriage, Isocrates describes Gorgias as "neither marrying a wife nor begetting children" (A18); but Plutarch writes that "when Gorgias the orator read a speech at Olympia about concord among the Greeks, Melanthius said: 'This fellow advises us about concord, though he has to persuade himself and his wife and his maid, only three in number, to life in private concord.' For it seems that Gorgias had a passion for the little maid and his wife was jealous" (B8a).

22. Gorgias is said by Philostratus (A2), Diogenes Laertius (A3), and Quintilian (A14) to have studied under Empedocles. He demonstrates his familiarity with many of the principal philosophers of his time, including Parmenides, Zeno Melissus, Empedocles, and Plato; and he was most probably familiar with the Pythagoreans, Leucippus, and the Ionians.

23. For recent discussions of Korax and Tisias, see Verall 1980, 197–210; Hinks 1940, 61–69; Cole 1990, 23–27; and Schiappa 1999.

24. Among ancient scholars who discuss Gorgias' participation at Panhellenic festivals are Aristotle (*Rhetoric* 1414b29; 1416a1); Philostratus (A1, A35); and Pausanias (A7).

25. Concerning Gorgias' putative students, Plato identifies Polus (*Gorgias*) and Meno (*Meno*); the Suda mentions "Polus of Acragus and Pericles and Isocrates and Alcidamus of Elaea" (A2); Cicero mentions Isocrates (A12); Philostratus writes that "Aspasia of Miletus is said to have sharpened the tongue of Pericles in imitation of Gorgias, and Critias and Thucydides were not unaware of how to acquire from him glory and pride" and that "the digressions and transitions of Gorgias' speeches became the fashion in many circles and especially among the epic poets" (A35).

26. Yun Lee Too challenges the commonplace that Isocrates' was a "student" of Gorgias, claiming that the assumption is "tentative" at best, and pointing out that Isocrates repeatedly attacks Gorgias (1995, 235–39).

27. For Gorgias' association with Alcidamus and Lycophron, see Aristotle (*Rhetoric* 1406a). For a discussion of Gorgias' putative influence on Thucydides, see John Finley 1939, 35–84.

28. Plato discusses Gorgias explicitly in seven dialogues (*Apology* 19e, *Gorgias, Symposium* 198c, *Philebus* 58a, *Meno* 95c, 73c, 96d, *Hippias Major* 282b, *Phaedrus* 261b, 267a), and he discusses his views or parodies his writing in several others (*Menexenus, Sophist, Theaetetus, Parmenides, Republic*).

29. Other labels that have been given to this hermeneutic approach include "factualism" (Poulakos 1990, 220), "essentialism," "platonism" (Poulakos 1990, 219), "reactionary fundamentalism" (Poulakos 1990, 219), "positivism" (Poulakos 1990, 219), intentionalism, and "semanticism" (Poulakos 1990, 220).

30. While Plato describes the "ancient quarrel" as one between philosophy and poetry in *Republic* 607b5, he remarks in *Gorgias* 501c-502d that poetry is essentially rhetoric, suggesting that the ancient quarrel is between philosophy and rhetoric.

31. Jarratt argues that the evolutionary narrative relies on positivistic conceptions of "myth" and "rationality" (1991, 31ff.). She rejects what she calls a "commonplace of ancient history: the transformation of a 'mythic' world view through the fifth-century revolution to rationality" (xxii). She suggests that *nomos,* or 'convention,' offers a salient alternative to the *mythos/logos* antithesis (xxiii). Lanham states that in the rhetorical view, reality is irreducibly social and man is a role player; whereas for the serious or philosophical person, reality is composed of an objective natural or supernatural world "standing 'out there,' independent of man," and each man "possesses a central self, an irreducible identity" (1976, 1). Fish adds that "the history of western thought could be written as the history of this quarrel . . . . The debate continues to this very day and . . . its terms are exactly those one finds in the dialogues of Plato and the orations of the sophists" (1989, 483–85).

32. Other labels for this rhapsodic approach to interpretation include subjectivist, relativist, idiosyncratic, expressionist, "solipsist" (Schiappa 1990, 309) "existentialist," (Schiappa 1991, 207), and "neosophistic" (Schiappa 1991, 198), "postmodern" (Schiappa 1990, 308), "subjectivist" (Segal 1984, 90–93), "anti-historical" (Schiappa 1991, 310).

33. Ancient skeptics include Pyrrho and Sextus Empiricus. Dostoyevsky's underground man rejects natural laws, asserting that he alone determines whether two plus two equals four; and he rejects the anthill of modern society, asserting that his primary objective is to affirm his own personal freedom.

34. This model may also be characterized as a "game" model, a "contextualist," or "agonistic" model of interpretation. Hans-Georg Gadamer writes that "tradition" is indispensable for understanding; Kenneth Burke contends that interpretation occurs within a socially shaped "orientation"; Rorty characterizes hermeneutics as a project of familiarizing that which is unfamiliar. Hiley, Bohman, and Shusterman write that interpretation "always takes place within some context or background such as a web of belief, a complex of social relations, tradition, or the practices of a form of life" (7). I suggest that the roots of this hermeneutic approach may be found in Protagoras and Gorgias.

35. I do not mean to suggest that Schiappa, Poulakos, and Vitanza fail to contribute to our understanding of Gorgias. On the contrary, they provide an array of insights into Gorgias'

thought and art. But these insights, I submit, have nothing whatsoever to do with their professed "methodologies" of reading. Rather, it is by heeding the conventions of the interpretive community and by participating in the interpretive game currently played by its members that they are able to develop their most compelling theses.

36. For discussion of the Athenians' familiarity with *On Not-Being,* see Hays 1980, 327–37.
37. For discussion of Gorgias' statues at Olympia and Delphi, see Morgan 1994, 375–86.
38. For Gorgias' relationship to Epicharmus, see Demand 1971, 453–63.
39. Scholars who dismiss Gorgias' ideas as inane platitudes include Aristotle, *Rhetoric* 1404a20; Cope 1855, 79–80; Denniston 1952, 12; Dodds 1990, 8; and Robinson 1973, 49–60.
40. Other scholars who articulate this dichotomy include Guthrie 1971, 8–10; Mansfeld 1985, 252–53; Mourelatos 1987, 140; and Poulakos 1990, 161.

Chapter 1

1. Pease describes the paradoxical encomium as a genre "in which the legitimate methods of the encomium are applied to persons or objects in themselves obviously unworthy of praise, as being trivial, ugly, useless, ridiculous, dangerous, or vicious. What brilliant mind first devised this form of intellectual gymnastics we shall perhaps never know, but it appears as early as the time of the famous Gorgias himself" (1926, 28–29).
2. Plato describes Gorgias as "the sophist from Leontini" in *Greater Hippias* 282b.
3. For Aristotle the Sophist's goal is not to attain knowledge, but to appear wise in order to gain wealth. That is, "the sophistic art consists in apparent and not real wisdom, and the sophist is one who makes money from apparent and not real wisdom" (*Sophistical Refutations* 165a). Aristotle argues that the contentious person and the Sophist both rely on fallacious arguments; but the Sophist differs in that his only concern is with appearance, and not with victory. A charlatan who is indifferent to the truth, Gorgias tries to appear wise to the crowd in order to acquire wealth.
4. Philostratus, who considers Gorgias the father of the art of the Sophists, writes that "we must regard the ancient sophistic art as philosophic rhetoric" (*Lives of the Sophists,* 5).
5. Plato explicitly criticizes or satirizes Gorgias in the *Apology* 19e; *Gorgias; Symposium* 198c; *Philebus* 58a; *Meno* 95c, 73c, 96d; *Hippias Major* 282b; and *Phaedrus* 261b, 267a. He implicitly parodies Gorgias' *Epitaphios* in the *Menexenus;* he pursues him in the *Sophist;* he rejects his epistemology in the *Theaetetus* and *Parmenides;* and he repudiates his putative conception of justice in the *Republic.*
6. Eduard Zeller 1881, 44–52; Wilhelm Nestle concurs with Zeller in the sixth edition of the text (Leipzig 1920).
7. Shakespeare, Sonnet 5. The context of the line is as follows:

> For never-resting time leads summer on
> To hideous winter and confounds him there,
> Sap checked with frost and lusty leaves quite gone,
> Beauty o'ersnowed and bareness everywhere.
> Then, were not summer's distillation left,

> A liquid prisoner pent in walls of glass,
> Beauty's effect with beauty were bereft,
> Nor it, nor no remembrance what it was.

8. Hippias: DK86 A11; B12, 13, 21. Prodicus: DK84, B4; Antiphon: DK87, B13, 26.

9. For discussion of Empedocles' conception of sensation, see Kirk and Raven 1966, 343–44.

Chapter 2

1. For recent discussions of foundationalism and antifoundationalism, see Michael Williams, *Groundless Belief: An Essay on the Possibility of Epistemology* (New Haven: Yale University Press, 1977); Ernest Sosa, "The Raft and the Pyramid: Coherence versus Foundations in the Theory of Knowledge," *Midwest Studies in Philosophy* 5 (1980): 3–25); Evan Hunter, ed. *Anti-foundationalism and Practical Reasoning : Conversations Between Hermeneutics and Analysis* (Edmonton, Al.: Academic Printing & Publishing, 1987); Stephen Crook, *Modernist Radicalism and Its Aftermath : Foundationalism and Anti-foundationalism in Radical Social Theory* (London, New York : Routledge, 1991); John Theil, *Nonfoundationalism* (Minneapolis: Fortress Press, 1994); Bernard Donals and Richard Glejzer, eds., *Rhetoric in an Antifoundational World : Language, Culture, and Pedagogy* (New Haven: Yale, 1998).

2. For discussion of Hesiod's cosmogony, see Kirk and Raven 1966, 24–34.

3. Isocrates writes, "Our city is the oldest and the greatest in the world and in the eyes of all men the most renowned. But noble as is the foundation of our claims, the following grounds give us even a clearer title to distinction: for we did not become dwellers in this land by driving others out of it, nor by finding it uninhabited, nor by coming together here a motley horde composed of many races; but we are of a lineage so noble and so pure throughout our history we have continued in possession of the very land which gave us birth, since we are sprung from its very soil (*Panegyricus* 4.23–24). Isocrates iterates this theme of ethnic purity and superiority based on autochthony in 8.49 and 12.124–25. See also Thucydides, 1.2.5, and Aristophanes, *Wasps* 1076.

4. Concerning the imagination, Shelley writes that poets and others who are able to use their imagination are able to discern and express the "indestructible order" of the world (*Defense of Poetry*, par. 4).

5. Dodds writes that "Greek rationalism makes three affirmations: first, that reason (what the Greeks called rational discourse, *logos*) is the sole and sufficient instrument of truth . . . secondly, that reality must be such that it can be understood by reason; and this implies that the structure of reality must be itself in some sense rational. Lastly, in such a universe values as well as facts will be rational: the highest Good will be either rational thought or something closely akin to it" (1973, 78).

6. Roochnik observes that "logocentrism is based upon a metaphysics of presence. . .[and] implies that we can gain direct access to that which is present out there in the world simply and essentially as itself" (154). Derrida writes that in logocentrism "between being and mind, things and feelings, there would be a relationship of translation or natural signification. . . . Logocentrism which is also a phonocentrism: absolute proximity of voice and being, of voice and the meaning of being" (1974, 11–12)

7. For discussion of Aeschylus' conception of *apate,* see Rosenmeyer 1955, 225–60.

8. Aristotle writes that "the kind of words useful to a sophist are homonyms (by means of which he does his dirty work)" (*Rhetoric* 1404b, Kennedy). When a Sophist like Gorgias uses homonyms or equivocation, he is able to deceive, for "deception comes about in the case of arguments that depend on ambiguity of words and of phrases because we are unable to divide the ambiguous term (for some terms it is not easy to divide, e.g., 'unity,' 'being,' and 'sameness')" (*Sophistical Refutations* 169a).

9. This is the account Plato attributes to Protagoras in the *Theaetetus* 151–72c.

10. Since Nietzsche, classical scholars have frequently underscored the importance of the agon in Greek culture. Richard Garner thus remarks that competition was "embedded in the culture . . . and . . . spread to all areas of human activity" and that "Greek culture and social organization were replete with figures of competition and combat. In general, this was as true of the form of poetic figures of speech as of athletic and military struggle" (1987, 60, 58). H. C. Baldry adds that "most aspects of Greek life were strongly influenced by the ideas of competition—not for profit, but for prestige, repute, glory. The rivalry between the heroes in the *Iliad* sets a pattern which is reflected later in peacetime activities as well as war: not only athletic contests at the Games, but contests between 'rhapsodes' in the recitation of Homer, between playwrights and between actors in the theater" (1972, 19). And Gouldner writes that the Greek "contest system" is a "mechanism of social mobility or a method for distributing prestige or public status among the citizen group: it is a 'game,' if you will, in which aliens or slaves do not play. The zest for competitive struggle that pervades Greek culture finds all manner of expression, particularly on the occasion of the numerous civic and Panhellenic festivals" (1965, 46).

11. For further discussion of Nietzsche's conception of the Sophists in general and Gorgias in particular, see Consigny 1994.

12. Plato thus remarks that "wonder is the only beginning of philosophy" (*Theaetetus* 155d); and Aristotle writes that it was "on account of wonder that human beings, both now and at first, began to philosophize" (*Metaphysics* 982b12–17).

13. Orpheus appears to have refused to engage in agons. According to Pausanias, "the oldest contest and the one for which they first offered prizes was, according to tradition, the singing of a hymn to the god. . . . But they say that Orpheus, a proud man and conceited about his mysteries, and Musaeus, who copied Orpheus in everything, refused to submit to the competition in musical skill" (*Description of Greece* 10.7.2).

14. The notion of *kosmos* originates in Pythagoras, who deems it the order of the universe, the orderly arrangement found in the harmony of the spheres (DK 14, 21).

Chapter 3

1. For a lively debate on the nature of sycophancy in Athens, see Harvey and Osborne 1990.

2. In this translation, Willis Barnstone has Sappho assert that what is most beautiful, or the supreme sight on earth, is "the one you love." Other translators, notably Denys Page, translate Sappho as saying more generally that what is most beautiful is "what you love." See Page 1955, 14–15.

3. H. Frankel also reads Sappho as proto-sophistic, but considers her a relativist who antic-

ipates Protagoras (1975, 187). Page Dubois suggests that Sappho is a proto-romantic philosopher, for "some value warriors, but Sappho argues that all candidates for 'the most beautiful' can be reduced to a common denominator, all characterized as being, finally, abstractly, 'whatsoever one loves' " (1997, 114).

4. Woodford writes that Palamedes' "cultural contributions in many instances overlap those attributed Prometheus" (1994, 164, n. 9).

5. The Titan Prometheus created man and gave him fire through the fennel stalk; significantly, perhaps, Gorgias refers to this stalk, the *narthekus*, as being the reed for fanning fires and caning insolent men (A24).

6. For a recent account of teleological and deontological liberalism, see Sandel 1998, 2–7.

7. Jarratt writes that "the sophists in their own time can be taken as feminist only by implication. While their texts characterize women in potentially liberating ways (Gorgias rescues Helen, Protagoras omits Pandora), neither the texts nor the doxographical accounts provide any evidence that the male sophists sought political or social change for real women" (1991, 69).

8. In *The Trojan Women,* Euripides has Helen argue that the Greeks benefited from actions, for they are "not subject to barbarian rule, neither vanquished in the strife, nor yet by tyrants crushed" (*Trojan Women* 934).

9. Rejecting distinctions between Greeks and barbarians, Antiphon argues that "by nature we all have the same nature in all particulars, barbarians and Greeks. . . . there is no distinction of barbarian and Greek" (DK87 B91).

10. Concerning Gorgias' possible aristocratism, Kenneth Freeman writes that "one of the beauties of the old Hellenic education had been that it did not make the rich a class apart from the poor by giving a widely different form of culture. The rise of the Sophists changed all this: their fees excluded the poor. The odium of resultant class-separation fell upon the teachers. Their pupils, rich, aristocratic, and cultured, inclined towards oligarchy. Hellenic sentiment held the teacher responsible for the whole career of his pupils. So for this reason again the democracies regarded the Sophists with suspicion, as the trainers of oligarchs and tyrants" (1969, 177).

CHAPTER 4

1. Gregory Nagy writes that "the professional *aoidos*, 'singer,' belongs to the category of the *demiourgoi*, 'artisans in the district' (*demos*)" (1989, 19).

2. Isocrates iterates this theme of racial superiority based on autochthony in 8.49 and 12.124–25. See also Thucydides 1.2.5, and Aristophanes *Wasps* 1076. Gorgias also differs from Aristotle, who maintains that Greeks are the standard for what it is to be human, while barbarians are naturally inferior (*Politics* 1252b).

3. The term *nomos* originally denotes a "pasture" or "place of habitation," and subsequently means "habitual practice, usage, or custom." Originally designating something apportioned, it becomes by Gorgias' time something "believed in, practiced or held to be right" (Guthrie 1971, 55). *Nomos* thus becomes "the expression of what the people as a whole regard as a valid and binding norm" (Ostwald 1986, 55).

4. Bergren writes that "Gorgias attempts an appropriation of Helen's *logos* no less total than Zeus' swallowing of *Metis*. In fact, his procedure in the *Encomium of Helen* is the very essence of

metis, that capacity to take on the shape of the enemy, to win by disguise, to create falsehoods that imitate truth. . . . Dressed in Helen's costume, as it were, Gorgias' *metis*-like *logos* tries to divide the traditional *metis* of female speech" (1983, 82–83).

5. There are two Greek roots bearing the sense of 'shame,' *aid-,* as in *aido;* and *aischun-,* as in the noun *aischune.* In general, the latter supplanted the former historically.

6. For further discussion of the distinction between shame and guilt cultures, see Dodds 1951, Taylor 1985, and Adkins 1960.

7. For discussion of the depiction by Athenian authors of the Barbarians as the "Other," particularly in the fifth century, see Hall 1989, 18ff.

8. For an ancient assessment of Isocrates' plagiarism of Gorgias' Panhellenism in the *Panegyricus,* Philostratus remarks that Isocrates text "gave rise to the charge that it had been compiled from the works of Gorgias on the same subject" (*Lives of the Sophists,* sec. 505, pp. 54–55).

9. While Athens appears to have expelled Anaxagoras and executed Socrates, for example, the tyrant Gelon of Syracuse patronized such writers as Pindar and Aeschylus. And the tyrant Jason of Phaerae appears to have patronized Gorgias.

Chapter 5

1. Concerning Parmenides' use of poetry, see Floyd 1992, 251–61. For a discussion of critics who examine Plato's use of the dialogue, see Nehamas 1999, xvii-xix; concerning Nietzsche's styles, see Derrida 1979, and Nehamas 1990; concerning Wittgenstein's style, see Binkley 1974.

2. Plato associates Gorgianic rhetoric with poetry in respect to the venue in which it is typically presented, that of the festival. Drama was typically presented at festivals, as were the rhapsodic performances of Homeric epic. Gorgias' verbal feast is ideally suited for a festival, an occasion of eating and celebrating.

3. Aristotle does not discuss Gorgias' most ostensibly philosophical work, though he was most likely aware of it. Isocrates comments openly on Gorgias' work; and, as Hays points out, "Plato was indeed aware of [*On Not-Being*] as were most of his educated contemporaries," even though he does not mention the work (1990, 336). It is not unreasonable to conclude that Aristotle dismissed Gorgias' work as an example of playful epideictic rhetoric, even though the quite serious *MXG* is included in the Aristotelian corpus.

4. John Finley argues that Sophocles uses antithesis extensively in *Ajax* and *Antigone,* as does Euripides in *Medea* and *Hippolytus,* even though neither author indulges in the so-called Gorgian poeticisms found in Agathon. In 427 B.C.E., just prior to Gorgias' arrival, Aristophanes in the *Banqueters* and Thucydides' Cleon in the *Mytilenean Debate* speak of the rhetorical movement as widespread. And in the *Archarnians,* Aristophanes describes the style in vogue among the young as *strogguloi,* the word Plato uses to describe the style of Phaedrus. See Finley 1939, 35–84.

Chapter 6

1. For discussion of the Greek term *parodia,* see Householder 1944, 1–9.

2. The techniques of parody vary, in some instances retaining the form or style of the original work while substituting "alien subject matter or content" (Kiremidjian 1969, 232).

In other cases, parody may exaggerate or distort the style of a given text in order to satirize the stylistic mannerisms themselves.

3. Nehamas writes that Agathon "proceeds, in a masterful parody of oratory, to praise *eros*. . . . This is, delightfully, the most comic of the six speeches. . . . Here the young speaker, quite drunk already in his own honor, is unmistakably playing for laughs. He indulges in an unrestrained parody of Gorgianic style and sophistic argument, enlivened with salacious double entendres" (1999, 308).

4. Contemporary scholars who read some of Gorgias' works as parodic include Guthrie 1971, 194; Coulter 1979, 32, n. 2; Moss, 216; Swearingen 1991, 49.

5. Insofar as Gorgias' parodies are designed to expose the rhetoricity of his rivals, they differ from *pastiche*, a genre of works in which an author arbitrarily pastes together pieces of other works to compose a novel text. As Frederick Jameson observes, pastiche is "a neutral practice of . . . mimicry, without any of parody's ulterior motives, amputated of the satiric impulse, devoid of laughter and of any conviction that alongside the abnormal tongue you still have momentarily borrowed, some healthy linguistic normality still exists" (1991, 16). The term *pastiche*, which derives from *pasticcio*, a pie comprised of diverse ingredients, denotes a hodge-podge of various styles, an arbitrary mixture or miscellany. Significantly, Plato characterizes Gorgias' rhetoric as a mode of *opsopoiike*, which may be translated as 'pastry-making' (Gorgias 464d); and Robinson also describes Gorgias' text as a "clever pastiche" (Robinson 1973, 59). Vitanza also reads *On Not-Being* as a pastiche, arguing that "one of the primary conventions of pastiche is that there is no origin. . . . Pastiche is a paragenre that denegates a grand narrative (1997, 261).

6. For a discussion of Plato's *Menexenus* as a parody of Athenian funeral oratory, see Loraux 1986, 263–327. Coulter acknowledges that "since we can date neither the *Palamedes* nor the *Apology* with absolute certainty, the possibility exists" that Gorgias' work is a parody of Plato's (1979, 32, n. 2)

7. For an account of scholarly dispute over the authenticity of *Palamedes*, see Untersteiner 1954, 95.

8. For an account of scholars who have read *On Not-Being* as a parody, see Untersteiner 1954, 163–65, n. 2.

9. For a discussion of some of the stylistic features of the two extant transcriptions of *On Not-Being*, see J. H. Loenen 1959, 179–80.

10. Gorgias also appears to have coined the term *homopsychos*, "with the same mind" or "unanimous" (H2), a term parallel in form to *homophonos*, or "univocal." See MacDowell 1961, 33.

11. Even Aristotle, in one of his more sophistic moments, seems to concur with Gorgias' notion that ostensibly "natural" language is a tropical fabrication. For he remarks that "those [rhetors] who practice this artifice must conceal it and avoid the appearance of speaking artificially instead of naturally; for that which is natural persuades, but the artificial does not" (*Rhetoric* 1404b).

12. Lanham describes the trope of *klimax*, or "ladder," termed *gradatio, ascendus*, and *methalemnis* in Latin, as "mounting by degrees through words or sentences of increasing weight and in parallel construction: 'Labour getteth learning, learning getteth fame, fame getteth honor, honour getteth bliss forever' (Wilson)" (Lanham 1968, 24). Gorgias uses this figure in his remark about Cimon: "Cimon earned money to use it, and used it to be honored" (B20).

13. Gorgias appears to have been quite familiar to Epicharmus, one of whose plays deals with Gorgias (Demand 1971, 454); and Gorgias appears to have been familiar with works by Athenian dramatists. Rosenmeyer writes that "Gorgias was known to be interested in tragedy, particularly in Aeschylus. The evidence is unmistakable, and has never been disputed" (1955, 225). Gorgias remarks that Aeschylus' *Seven Against Thebes,* for instance, is "full of Ares" (B24); and he asserts that a tragedy is a deception "in which the deceiver is more honest than the non-deceiver and the deceived is wiser than the undeceived" (B23). Moreover, Gorgias appears to have influenced such playwrights as Euripides and Agathon.

14. For discussion of the *alazon* as a figure in Greek comedy, see Booth 1974, 139.

15. Concerning the Dionysian festival in Athens, Longo writes that the "Athenians' dramatic performances were not conceivable as autonomous productions, in some indifferent point in time or space, but were firmly located within the framework of a civic festival, at a time specified according to the community calendar, and in a special place expressly reserved for this function. This place, which was the scene of the *collective festival,* provided a proper home not only for the dramatic contest but also for other celebrations, which were no less strictly tied to the civic system. . . . . The dramatic spectacle was one of the rituals that deliberately aimed at maintaining social identity and reinforcing the cohesion of the group" (Longo 1992, 15–16; emphasis added).

16. For discussion of the educational practices of the Sophists, see Guthrie (1971, 41–44); Kerferd (1989, 30–41); Kennedy (1963, 18–21); and Jarratt (1991, 81–120).

17. Concerning Gorgias' figuration, Nietzsche writes that "the severe constraint which the French dramatists imposed upon themselves . . . was as important a training as counterpoint and the fugue in the development of modern music, or the Gorgian figures in Greek rhetoric. To restrict oneself so may appear absurd; nevertheless there is no way to get beyond realism other than to limit oneself at first most severely (perhaps most arbitrarily). In that way one gradually learns to step with grace, even on the small bridges that span dizzying abysses, and one takes as profit the greatest suppleness of movement" (1986, section 221).

18. Plato contrasts Gorgias' mere "knack" of persuasion with a "true" rhetoric grounded on dialectic, which he delineates in the *Phaedrus.*

THE PLACE OF GORGIAS

1. Extolling rationality or *logos* over *mythos,* Thucydides writes: "The absence of romance (*mythodes*) in my history will, I fear, detract somewhat from its interest; but if it be judged useful by those inquirers who desire an exact knowledge of the past as an aid to the interpretation of the future, which in the course of human things must resemble if it does not reflect it, I shall be content. In fine, I have written my work, not as an essay which is to win the applause of the moment, but as a possession for all time" (*History of the Peloponnesian War* 1.22.4). Similarly, Aristotle writes that although "even the lover of myth is in a sense a lover of Wisdom, for the myth is composed of wonders," (*Metaphysics* 1.2), "into the subtleties of the mythologists it is not worth our while to inquire seriously; those, however, who use the language of proof we must cross-examine" (*Metaphysics* 3.3). For recent collection of essays on this topic, see Buxton 1999.

2. The progressivist and regressivist views are first articulated in the ancient world. Hesiod

writes of a golden age in which man was united with the gods and of the subsequent ages of bronze, iron, and lead. Conversely, Plato's Protagoras and others speak of the progress of man through the development of the various arts. The agonistic account in some ways parallels the third ancient model, one that Nietzsche found compelling, that of the "eternal recurrence of the same." See Dodds 1973, 1–25.

3. For an account of Herodotus' emphasis on the agon as definitive of Greek culture, Thompson writes that "as [Herodotus] depicts the Persians' acquiescing in Darius' authoritative, traditional speech [in Book 3], he captures them in their pivotal and lost opportunity to listen to the diverse claims to appreciate debate as a productive activity. This is the main thrust; the Persian debate is a debate to inhibit all future debates, and it is the predictable end of Persian truth-telling as a possible stimulus to action" (1996, 77).

4. Schumpeter, cited in Rorty 1990, 46.

5. Concerning the struggle of a poet with his rivals, Harold Bloom writes that the relationships between poetic texts "depend on a critical act, a misreading or misprision, that one poet performs upon another, and that does not differ in kind from the necessary critical acts performed by every strong reader" (1980, 3).

6. Concerning the intimate relationship between actor and spectator, Grotowski (1968) writes that "we can thus define the theatre as 'what takes place between the spectator and actor,'" (32); that "actors may build structures among the spectators and thus include them in the architecture of action" (20); that as a place of "provocation" the theater "is capable of challenging itself and its audience by violating accepted stereotypes of vision, feelings and judgment" (22); and that "once a spectator is placed in an illuminated zone, or in other words becomes visible, he too begins to play a part in the performance" (20). For discussion of the similarity of Gorgias' epideictic performances and contemporary performance art, see Consigny 1992.

Bibliography

Adkins, Arthur. 1983. "Form and Content in Gorgias' Helen and Palamedes: Rhetoric, Philosophy, Inconsistency, and Invalid Argument in Some Greek Thinkers." In *Essays in Greek Philosophy*, edited by A. P. John Anton. Albany: State University of New York Press.

Aristophanes. 1992. *Acharnians*. Translated by Jeffrey Henderson. Cambridge, Mass.: Focus Classical Library.

———. 1992. *Clouds*. Translated by Jeffrey Henderson. Cambridge, Mass.: Focus Classical Library.

Aristotle. 1932. *Poetics*. Translated by W. H. Fyfe. London: Wm. Heinemann.

———. 1934. *Nicomachian Ethics*. Translated by H. Rackham. London: Wm. Heinemann.

———. 1944. *Politics*. Translated by H. Rackham. London: Wm. Heinemann.

———. 1967. *The "Art" of Rhetoric*. Translated by John Henry Freese. London: Wm. Heinemann.

———. 1978. *On Sophistical Refutations*. Translated by D. J. Furley. London: Wm. Heinemann.

———. 1989. *Metaphysics*. Translated by Hugh Tredennick. London: Wm. Heinemann.

Attridge, Derek. 1988. "Unpacking the Portmanteau; or Who's Afraid of *Finnegans Wake?*" In *On Puns: The Foundation of Letters*, edited by Jonathon Culler. New York: B. Blackwell.

Austin, Scott. 1986. *Parmenides: Being, Bounds and Logic*. New Haven, Conn.: Yale University Press.

Austin, Norman. 1994. *Helen of Troy and Her Shameless Phantom*. Ithaca, N.Y.: Cornell University Press.

Bakhtin, Mikhail. 1984. *Rabelais and His World*. Translated by Helen Iswolsky. Bloomington: Indiana University Press.

Baldry, H. C. 1972. *The Greek Tragic Theater*. New York: Norton.

Barnes, Jonathon, ed. 1984. *The Complete Works of Aristotle*. Princeton, N.J.: Princeton University Press.

———. 1987. *Early Greek Philosophy*. London: Penguin.

———. 1989. *The Presocratic Philosophers*. London: Routledge.

Beckett, Samuel. 1954. *Waiting for Godot*. New York: Grove.

Bergren, Ann. 1983. "Language and the Female in Early Greek Thought." *Arethusa* 16:69–95.

Bernard-Donals, Michael F., and Richard R. Glejzer. 1998. *Rhetoric in an Antifoundational World: Language, Culture, and Pedagogy*. New Haven, Conn.: Yale University Press.

Bett, Richard. 1989. "The Sophists and Relativism." *Phronesis* 34:139–69.

Betti, Emilio. 1990. "Hermeneutics as the General Methodology of the *Geistewissenschaften*." Translated by Josef Bleicher. In *The Hermeneutic Tradition: From Ast to Ricoeur*, edited by Gayle L. Ormiston and Alan D. Schrift. Albany: State University of New York.

Binkley, Timothy. 1974. *Wittgenstein's Language*. The Hague: M. Nijhoff.

Bloom, Harold. 1980. *A Map of Misreading*. New York: Oxford University Press.

Booth, Wayne. 1974. *A Rhetoric of Irony*. Chicago: University of Chicago Press.

Burckhardt, Jacob. 1998. *The Greeks and Greek Civilization*. Translated by Oswyn Murray. New York: St. Martin's Press.

Burgess, Theodore C. 1902. *Epideictic Literature*. Chicago: University of Chicago Press.

Buxton, R. G. A. 1999. *From Myth to Reason? Studies in the Development of Greek Thought*. New York: Oxford University Press.

Calogero, Guido. 1971. "Gorgias and the Socratic Principle *Nemo Sua Sponte Peccat*." In *Essays in Ancient Greek Philosophy*, edited by G. K. John Anton. Albany: State University of New York Press.

Cartledge, Paul. 1985. "The Greek Religious Festivals." In *Greek Religion and Society*, edited by P. E. Easterling and J. V. Muir. Cambridge: Cambridge University Press.

Cartledge, Paul, and Stephen Todd, eds. 1990. *Nomos: Essays in Athenian Law, Politics, and Society*. Cambridge: Cambridge University Press.

Cascardi, Anthony. 1983. "The Place of Language in Philosophy; or the Use of Rhetoric." *Philosophy and Rhetoric* 16:217–27.

Cassirer, Ernst. 1946. *Language and Myth*. Translated by Susan K. Langer. New York: Harper and Brothers.

Chase, Richard. 1961. "The Classical Conception of the Epideictic." *Quarterly Journal of Speech* 47:293–300.

Classen, Carl. 1981. "Aristotle's Picture of the Sophists." In *The Sophists and Their Legacy*, edited by G. B. Kerferd. Wiesbaden: Franz Steiner Verlag.

Cole, Thomas. 1991. *The Origins of Rhetoric in Ancient Greece*. Baltimore, Md.: Johns Hopkins University Press.

Connors, Robert J. 1986. "Greek Rhetoric and the Transition for Orality." *Philosophy and Rhetoric* 19: 38–65.

Consigny, Scott. 1992. "Sophistic Challenges: Gorgias' Epideictic Rhetoric and Postmodern Performance Art." In *Rhetoric in the Vortex of Cultural Studies*, edited by A. Walzer. St. Paul: Rhetoric Society of America.

———. 1994. "Nietzsche's Reading of the Sophists." *Rhetoric Review* 13:5–26.

Cope, Edward. 1854. "The Sophists." *Journal of Classical and Sacred Philology* 1:145–88.

———. 1855. "On the Sophistical Rhetoric." *Journal of Classical and Sacred Philology* 2: 129–69.

———. 1856. "On the Sophistical Rhetoric." *Journal of Classical and Sacred Studies* 3: 34–80.

Coulter, James. 1979. "The Relation of the *Apology of Socrates* to Gorgias' *Defense of Palamedes* and Plato's Critique of Gorgianic Rhetoric." In *Plato: True and Sophistic Rhetoric*, edited by K. Erickson. Amsterdam: Rodopi.

Croally, N. 1994. *Euripidean Polemic*. Cambridge: Cambridge University Press.

Crockett, Andy. 1994. "Gorgias' *Encomium of Helen:* Violent Rhetoric or Radical Feminism?" *Rhetoric Review* 13:71–90.

Crowley, Sharon. 1979. "Of Gorgias and Grammatology." *College Composition and Communication* 30:278–85.

Deleuze, Gilles, and Felix Guattari. 1981. "Rhizome." Translated by Paul Patton. In *Ideology and Consciousness* 8:52–62.

———. 1983. *Anti-Oedipus*. Translated by Robert Hurley, Mark Seem, and Helen R. Lame. Minneapolis: University of Minnesota Press.

Demand, Nancy. 1971. "Epicharmus and Gorgias." *American Journal of Philology* 92:453–63.
Demosthenes. 1962. *Demosthenes.* Translated by Norman W. DeWitt and Norman J. DeWitt. Cambridge, Mass.: Harvard University Press.
Denniston, J. D. 1952. *Greek Prose Style.* Oxford: Clarendon.
Derrida, Jacques. 1976. *Of Grammatology.* First American ed. Baltimore, Md.: Johns Hopkins University Press.
———. 1979. *Spurs: Nietzsche's Styles.* Translated by Barbara Harlow. Chicago: University of Chicago Press.
———. 1981. *Dissemination.* Chicago: University of Chicago Press.
Detienne, Marcel, and Jean Pierre Vernant. 1991. *Cunning Intelligence in Greek Culture and Society.* Chicago: University of Chicago Press.
Dewey, John. 1901. "Nihilism." In *Dictionary of Philosophy and Psychology,* edited by J. Baldwin. New York: Macmillan.
Dodds, E. R. 1951. *The Greeks and the Irrational.* Berkeley: University of California Press.
———. 1973. *The Ancient Concept of Progress and Other Essays on Greek Literature and Belief.* Oxford: Clarendon Press.
———, trans. 1990. *Gorgias.* by Plato. Oxford: Oxford University Press.
Dostoevsky, Fyodor. 1972. *Notes from Underground.* Translated by Jessie Coulson. New York: Penguin.
Dubois, Page. 1995. *Sappho Is Burning.* Chicago: University of Chicago Press.
Edelstein, Ludwig. 1994. *Ancient Medicine: Selected Papers of Ludwig Edelstein.* Baltimore, Md.: Johns Hopkins University Press.
Engnell, Richard. 1973. "Implications for Communication of the Rhetorical Epistemology of Gorgias of Leontini." *Western Speech* 37:175–84.
Enos, Richard. 1976. "The Epistemology of Gorgias' Rhetoric: A Re-examination." *Southern Speech Communication Journal* 42:35–51.
———. 1992. "Why Gorgias of Leontini Traveled to Athens: A Study of Recent Epigraphical Evidence." *Rhetoric Review* 11:1–15.
———. 1993. *Greek Rhetoric before Aristotle.* Prospect Heights, Ill.: Waveland Press.
Finley, John. 1939. "The Origins of Thucydides' Style." *Harvard Studies in Classical Philology* 50:35–84.
Finley, M. I. 1979. *Ancient Sicily.* Totowa, N.J.: Rowman and Littlefield.
Fish, Stanley Eugene. 1980. *Is There a Text in This Class? The Authority of Interpretive Communities.* Cambridge, Mass.: Harvard University Press.
———. 1989. *Doing What Comes Naturally: Change, Rhetoric, and the Practice of Theory in Literary and Legal Studies.* Durham, N.C.: Duke University Press.
Floyd, Edwin. 1992. "Why Parmenides Wrote in Verse." *Ancient Philosophy* 12:251–65.
Frankel, H. 1975. *Early Greek Poetry and Philosophy.* Oxford: Oxford University Press.
Freeman, Kenneth. 1969. *Schools of Hellas.* New York: Teachers College Press.
Gadamer, Hans-Georg. 1975. *Truth and Method.* Translated by Garrett Barden and John Cumming. New York: Seabury.
Garner, Richard. 1987. *Law and Society in Classical Athens.* London: Croom Helm.
Gomperz, Theodore. 1901. *Greek Thinkers.* New York: Scribners.

Goodman, Nelson. 1983. *Fact, Fiction and Forecast.* Cambridge, Mass.: Harvard University Press.

Gorgias. 1982. *Encomium of Helen.* Translated by Douglas MacDowell. Glasgow: Bristol Classical Press.

Gouldner, Alvin Ward. 1965. *Enter Plato: Classical Greece and the Origins of Social Theory.* New York: Basic Books.

Gregory, Justina. 1991. *Euripides and the Instruction of the Athenians.* Ann Arbor: University of Michigan Press.

Gronbeck, Bruce. 1972. "Gorgias on Rhetoric and Poetic: A Rehabilitation." *Southern Speech Communication Journal* 38:27–38.

Grote, George. 1869. *A History of Greece: From the Earliest Period to the Close of the Generation Contemporary with Alexander the Great.* London: J. Murray.

Grotowski, Jerzy. 1968. *Towards a Poor Theater.* New York: Simon and Schuster.

Guthrie, W. K. C. 1971. *The Sophists.* Cambridge: Cambridge University Press.

Hall, Edith. 1989. *Inventing the Barbarian.* New York: Oxford University Press.

Havelock, Eric Alfred. 1957. *The Liberal Temper in Greek Politics.* New Haven, Conn.: Yale University Press.

———. 1963. *Preface to Plato.* Cambridge, Mass.: Harvard University Press.

———. 1982. *The Literate Revolution in Greece and Its Cultural Consequences: Princeton Series of Collected Essays.* Princeton: Princeton University Press.

Harvey, David. 1990. "The Sykophant and Sykophancy: Vexatious Redefinition?" In *Nomos: Essays in Athenian Law, Politics, and Society,* edited by Paul Cartledge and Stephen Todd. Cambridge: Cambridge University Press.

Hays, Steve. 1990. "On the Skeptical Influence of Gorgias' 'On Not-Being.'" *Journal of the History of Philosophy* 28:327–37.

Hegel, Georg. 1995. *Lectures on the History of Philosophy.* Translated by E. S. Haldane. Lincoln: University of Nebraska.

Herodotus. 1987. *The History.* Translated by David Greene. Chicago: University of Chicago Press.

Hesiod. 1914. *Works and Days.* Translated by Hugh Evelyn-White. Cambridge, Mass.: Harvard University Press.

———. 1914. *Theogony.* Translated by Hugh Evelyn-White. Cambridge, Mass.: Harvard University Press.

Hiley, David, James Bohman, and Richard Shusterman, eds. 1991. *The Interpretive Turn.* Ithaca, N.Y.: Cornell University Press.

Hinks, D. A. G. 1940. "Tisias and Corax and the Invention of Rhetoric." *Classical Quarterly* 34:61–69.

Hirsch, E. D. 1967. *Validity in Interpretation.* New Haven, Conn.: Yale University Press.

Homer. 1996. *The Iliad.* Translated by Robert Fagles. New York: Penguin.

Householder, Fred. 1944. "Parodia." *Classical Philology* 39:1–9.

Hunt, Everett Lee. 1965. "On the Sophists." In *The Province of Rhetoric,* edited by J. Rycenga. New York: Ronald.

Hunter, Evan, ed. 1987. *Anti-foundationalism and Practical Reasoning: Conversations between Hermeneutics and Analysis*. Edmonton: Academic Publishing and Printing.

Ijsseling, Samuel. 1976. *Rhetoric and Philosophy in Conflict: An Historical Survey*. The Hague: M. Nijhoff.

Irwin, T. I. 1997. "Plato's Objection to the Sophists." In *The Greek World*, edited by A. Powell. London: Routledge.

Isocrates. 1986. *Isocrates*. Translated by Larue Van Hook. 3 vols. Cambridge, Mass.: Harvard University Press.

Jameson, Frederic. 1988. *The Ideologies of Theory*. Minneapolis: University of Minnesota Press.

———. 1991. *Postmodernism; or the Cultural Logic of Late Capitalism*. Durham, N.C.: Duke University Press.

Jarratt, Susan. 1991. *Rereading the Sophists: Classical Rhetoric Refigured*. Carbondale: Southern Illinois University Press.

Jebb, R. C. 1876. *The Attic Orators*. London: Macmillan.

Kagan, Donald. 1974. *The Archidamean War*. Ithaca, N.Y.: Cornell University Press.

———. 1991. *Pericles of Athens and the Birth of Democracy*. New York: Free Press.

Kahn, Charles. 1976. "The Greek Verb 'to Be' and the Concept of Language." *Foundations of Language* 2:245–65.

Kennedy, George. 1963. *The Art of Persuasion in Greece*. Princeton, N.J.: Princeton University Press.

Kerferd, G. B. 1955. "Gorgias on Nature; or That Which Is Not. *Phronesis* 1:3–25.

———. 1989. *The Sophistic Movement*. Cambridge and New York: Cambridge University Press.

Kierkegaard, Soren. 1989. *The Concept of Irony*. Translated by Howard Long and Edna Hong. Princeton: Princeton University Press.

Kiremidjian, G. D. 1969. "The Aesthetics of Parody." *Journal of Aesthetics and Art Criticism* 28:211–42.

Kirk, G. S. 1974. *The Nature of Greek Myths*. New York: Penguin.

Kirk, G. S., and J. E. Raven, eds. 1966. *The Presocratic Philosophers: A Critical History with a Selection of Texts*. Cambridge: Cambridge University Press.

Kuhn, Thomas. 1993. "Afterwords." In *World Changes: Thomas Kuhn and the Nature of Science*, edited by P. Horwich. Cambridge, Mass.: MIT Press.

Lanham, Richard A. 1968. *A Handlist of Rhetorical Terms*. Berkeley: University of California Press.

———. 1976. *The Motives of Eloquence: Literary Rhetoric in the Renaissance*. New Haven, Conn.: Yale University Press.

Lindsay, Jack. 1974. "Helen of Troy: Woman and Goddess." Totowa, N.J.: Rowman and Littlefield.

Loenen, J. 1959. *Parmenides, Melissus, Gorgias: A Reinterpretation of Eleatic Philosophy*. Assen: Royal VanGorcum.

Long, A. A. 1984. "Methods of Argument in Gorgias' *Palamedes*." In *The Sophistic Movement*, edited by F. Solmsen. Athens: Greek Philosophical Association.

———, ed. 1999. *The Cambridge Companion to Early Greek Philosophy*. Cambridge: Cambridge University Press.

Longo, Odone. 1992 "The Theater of the *Polis*." In *Nothing to Do with Dionysos?* edited by John Winkler and Froma Zeitlin. Princeton, N.J.: Princeton University Press.

Loraux, Nicole. 1986. *The Invention of Athens: The Funeral Oration in the Classical City.* Translated by Alan Sheridan. Cambridge, Mass.: Harvard University Press.

Lysias. 1960. *Lysias.* Translated by W. R. M. Lamb. Cambridge: Harvard University Press.

MacDowell, Douglas. 1961. "Gorgias, Alkidamas, and the Cripps and Palatine Manuscripts." *Classical Quarterly* 11:113–34.

———. 1982. *Gorgias: Encomium of Helen.* Bristol: Bristol Classical Press.

———. 1995. *Aristophanes and Athens: An Introduction to the Plays.* New York: Oxford University Press.

MacIntyre, Alasdair. 1981. *After Virture.* Notre Dame, Ind.: University of Notre Dame Press.

Mansfeld, Jaap. 1985. "Historical and Philosophical Aspects of Gorgias' 'On What Is Not.'" *Siculorum, Gymnasium* 38:243–71.

———. 1999. "Sources." In *The Cambridge Companion to Early Greek Philosophy,* edited by A. A. Long. Cambridge: Cambridge University Press.

Margolis, Joseph. 1992. "The Limits of Metaphysics and the Limits of Certainty." In *Antifoundationalism Old and New,* edited by Tom Rockmore and Beth Singer. Philadelphia: Temple University Press.

Miller, Bernard. 1987. "Heidegger and the Gorgian *kairos.*" In *Visions of Rhetoric,* edited by C. Kneupper. Arlington, Tex.: Rhetoric Society of America.

Morgan, Kathryn. 1994. "Socrates and Gorgias at Delphi and Olympia: *Phaedrus* 235d6–236b4." *Classical Quarterly* 44:375–86.

Moss, Roger. 1982. "The Case for Sophistry." In *Rhetoric Revalued,* edited by Brian Vickers. Binghamton, N.Y.: Center for Medieval and Early Renaissance Studies.

Mourelatos, Alexander. 1987. "Gorgias on the Function of Language." *Philosophical Topics* 15:135–70.

Nagy, Gregory. 1989. "Early Greek Views of Poetry and Poetics." In *The Cambridge History of Literary Criticism,* edited by G. Kennedy. Cambridge: Cambridge University Press.

Nehamas, Alexander. 1990. *Nietzsche: Life as Literature.* Cambridge, Mass.: Harvard University Press.

———. 1999. *Virtues of Authenticity: Essays on Plato and Socrates.* Princeton, N.J.: Princeton University Press.

Nietzsche, Friedrich. 1968. *The Will to Power.* Translated by Walter Kaufmann. New York: Vintage Books.

———. 1976. *The Portable Nietzsche.* Translated by Walter Kaufmann. New York: Viking Press.

———. 1974. "Notes for *We Philologists.*" Translated by William Arrowsmith. *Arion* 1:279–380.

———. 1986. *Human, All Too Human: A Book for Free Spirits.* Translated by R. J. Hollingdale. New York: Cambridge University Press.

———. 1989. *Friedrich Nietzsche on Rhetoric and Language.* Translated by Sander L. Gilman, Carole Blair, and David J. Parent. New York: Oxford University Press.

———. 1990. *Twilight of the Idols.* Translated by R. J. Hollingdale. London: Penguin Books.

Nussbaum, Martha. 1986. *The Fragility of Goodness: Luck and Ethics in Greek Tragedy and Philosophy.* New York: Cambridge University Press.

———. 1990. *Love's Knowledge: Essays on Philosophy and Literature.* New York: Oxford.

———. 1994. *The Therapy of Desire: Theory and Practice in Hellenistic Ethics.* Princeton, N.J.: Princeton University Press.

O'Sullivan, Neil. 1992. *Alcidamus, Aristophanes, and the Beginnings of Greek Stylistic Theory.* Stuttgart: Franz Steiner Verlag.

Ong, Walter. 1982. *Orality and Literacy: The Technologizing of the Word.* London: Methuen.

Onians, Richard. 1973. *The Origins of European Thought.* New York: Arno Press.

Osborne, Robin. 1990. "Vexatious Litigation in Classical Athens: Sykophancy and the Sykophant." In *Nomos: Essays in Athenian Law, Politics, and Society,* edited by Paul Cartledge and Stephen Todd. Cambridge: Cambridge University Press.

Osborne, Robert. 1996. *Greece in the Making, 1200–479 B.C.* London: Routledge.

Ostwald, Martin. 1986. *From Popular Sovereignty to the Sovereignty of Law: Law, Society, and Politics in Fifth-century Athens.* Berkeley: University of California Press.

Page, Denys. 1955. *Sappho and Alcaeus: An Introduction to the Study of Ancient Lesbian Poetry.* Oxford: Oxford University Press.

Parke, H. W. 1977. *Festivals of the Athenians.* Ithaca, N.Y.: Cornell University Press.

Pease, Arthur. 1926. "Things without Honor." *Classical Philology* 21:27–41.

Pellicia, Hayden. 1992. "Sappho 16, Gorgias' *Helen,* and the Preface to Herodotus' *Histories.*" *Yale Classical Studies* 29:63–84.

Perelman, Chaïm, and Lucie Olbrechts-Tyteca. 1969. *The New Rhetoric: A Treatise on Argumentation.* Translated by John Wilkinson and Purcell Weaver. Notre Dame, Ind.: University of Notre Dame Press.

Perelman, S. 1976. "Panhellenism, the Polis, and Imperialism." *Historia* 15:1–30.

Peters, F. E. 1967. *Greek Philosophical Terms: A Historical Lexicon.* New York: New York University Press.

Philostratus. 1968. *Lives of the Sophists.* Translated by Wilmer Cave Wright. London: Wm. Heinemann.

Pindar. 1937. *The Odes of Pindar.* Translated by John Sandys. London: Wm. Heinemann.

Plato. 1962. *Phaedrus.* Translated by W. R. M. Lamb. London: Wm. Heinemann.

———. 1967. *Gorgias.* Translated by W. R. M. Lamb. London: Wm. Heinemann.

———. 1967. *Symposium.* Translated by W. R. M. Lamb. London: Wm. Heinemann.

———. 1977. *Greater Hippias.* Translated by H. N. Fowler. London: Wm. Heinemann.

———. 1977. *Parmenides.* Translated by H. N. Fowler. London: Wm. Heinemann.

———. 1982. *Republic.* Translated by Paul Shorey. 2 vols. London: Wm. Heinemann.

———. 1982. *Apology.* Translated by W. R. M. Lamb. London: Wm. Heinemann.

———. 1987. *Theaetetus.* Translated by Harold North Fowler. London: Wm. Heinemann.

———. 1987. *Sophist.* Translated by Harold North Fowler. London: Wm. Heinemann.

———. 1989. *Menexenus.* Translated by R. G. Bury. London: Wm. Heinemann.

———. 1990. *Philebus.* Translated by W. R. M. Lamb. Cambridge, Mass.: Harvard University Press.

———. 1990. *Protagoras.* Translated by W. R. M. Lamb. London: Wm. Heinemann.

———. 1990. *Meno.* Translated by W. R. M. Lamb. London: Wm. Heinemann.

———. 1992. *Ion.* Translated by W. R. M. Lamb. Cambridge, Mass.: Harvard University Press.

Poirier, Richard. 1968. "The Politics of Self-Parody." *Partisan Review* 35:339–53.

Porter, James. 1993. "The Seductions of Gorgias. *Classical Antiquity* 12:267–99.

Poulakos, John. 1983. "Toward a Sophistic Definition of Rhetoric." *Philosophy and Rhetoric* 16:35–48.

———. 1983. "Gorgias' Encomium to Helen and the Defense of Rhetoric." *Rhetorica* 1:1–16.

———. 1984. "Rhetoric, the Sophists, and the Possible." *Communication Monographs* 51:215–26.

———. 1986. "Gorgias' and Isocrates' Use of the Encomium." *Southern Speech Communication Journal* 51:300–307.

———. 1987. "Sophistical Rhetoric as a Critique of Culture." In *Argument and Critical Practice,* edited by J. Wenzel. Annandale, Va.: Speech Communication Association.

———. 1990. "Interpreting Sophistic Rhetoric: A Reply to Edward Schiappa." *Philosophy and Rhetoric* 23:218–28.

———. 1995. *Sophistical Rhetoric in Classical Greece.* Columbia: University of South Carolina Press.

Race, William. 1989. "Sappho, Fr. 16 L-P and Alcaios, Fr. 42 L-P: Romantic and Classical Strains in Lesbian Lyric." *Classical Journal* 85:16–33.

Rawls, John. 1980. "Kantian Constructivism in Moral Theory." *Journal of Philosophy* 77:515–572.

Robinson, John. 1973. "On Gorgias." In *Phronesis: Supplementary Volume I,* edited by A. P. D. M. E. N. Lee and R. M. Rorty.

Rockmore, Tom, and Beth J. Singer. 1992. *Antifoundationalism Old and New.* Philadelphia: Temple University Press.

Romilly, Jacqueline de. 1975. *Magic and Rhetoric in Ancient Greece.* Cambridge, Mass.: Harvard University Press.

———. 1992. *The Great Sophists in Periclean Athens.* Oxford and New York: Clarendon Press.

Roochnik, David. 1990. *The Tragedy of Reason.* New York: Routledge.

———. 1991. "Stanley Fish and the Old Quarrel between Rhetoric and Philosophy." *Critical Review* 5:225–46.

Rorty, Richard. 1980. *Philosophy and the Mirror of Nature.* Princeton, N.J.: Princeton University Press.

———. 1990. *Contingency, Irony, and Solidarity.* New York: Cambridge University Press.

———. 1998. *Truth and Progress.* New York: Cambridge University Press.

Rorty, Richard, J. B. Schneewind, and Quentin Skinner. 1984. *Philosophy in History: Essays on the Historiography of Philosophy, Ideas in Context.* New York: Cambridge University Press.

Rose, Margaret A. 1993. *Parody: Ancient, Modern, and Post-modern.* Cambridge and New York: Cambridge University Press.

Rosenmeyer, Thomas. 1955. "Gorgias, Aeschylus, and *Apate.*" *American Journal of Philology* 76:225–60.

Sandel, Michael J. 1998. *Liberalism and the Limits of Justice.* 2d ed. New York: Cambridge University Press.

Sappho. 1999. *Poems.* Translated by Willis Barnstone. Los Angeles: Green Integer.

Schiappa, Edward. 1990a. "History and Neo-Sophistic Criticism: A Reply to Poulakos." *Philosophy and Rhetoric* 23:307–15.

———. 1990b. "Neo-Sophistic Rhetorical Criticism or the Historical Reconstruction of Sophistic Doctrines?" *Philosophy and Rhetoric* 23:192–217.

———. 1991. *Protagoras and Logos: A Study in Greek Philosophy and Rhetoric.* Columbia: University of South Carolina Press.

———. 1992. "*Rhetorike:* What's in a Name? Toward a Revised History of Early Greek Rhetorical Theory." *Quarterly Journal of Speech* 78:1–15.

———. 1995. "Gorgias' *Helen* Revisited." *Quarterly Journal of Speech* 81:310–24.

———. 1999. *The Beginnings of Rhetorical Theory in Classical Greece.* New Haven, Conn.: Yale University Press.

Scodel, Ruth. 1991. *The Trojan Trilogy of Euripides.* Gottingen: Vandenhoeck und Ruprecht.

Segal, Charles. 1972. "Gorgias and the Psychology of the Logos." *Harvard Studies in Classical Philology* 66:94–155.

Shelley, Percy. 1967. "A Defense of Poetry." In *Shelley's Critical Prose,* edited by B. McElderry. Lincoln: University of Nebraska Press.

Sidgwick, Henry, and James Ward. *Lectures on the Philosophy of Kant and Other Philosophical Lectures and Essays.* 1905. Reprint, New York: Kraus Reprint Co., 1968

Smeltzer, Mark. 1995. "Gorgias on Arrangement: A Search for Pragmatism amidst the Art and Epistemology of Gorgias of Leontini." *Communication Journal* 61 (2):156–65.

Smith, Bromley. 1921. "Gorgias: A Study of Oratorical Style." *Quarterly Journal of Speech Education* 7:335–359.

Sprague, Rosamund, ed. 1972. *The Older Sophists.* Columbia: University of South Carolina Press.

Suzuki, Mihoko. 1989. *Metamorphoses of Helen: Authenticity, Difference, and the Epic.* Ithaca: Cornell University Press.

Swearingen, C. Jan. 1991. *Rhetoric and Irony: Western Literacy and Western Lies.* New York: Oxford University Press.

Taylor, Gabriele. 1985. *Pride, Shame, and Guilt.* New York: Oxford University Press.

Thompson, Norma. 1996. *Herodotus and the Origins of the Political Community.* New Haven, Conn.: Yale University Press.

Thucydides. 1968. *History of the Peloponnesian War.* Translated by Richard Crawley. London: Wm. Heinemann.

Too, Yun Lee. 1995. *The Rhetoric of Identity in Isocrates: Text, Power, Pedagogy.* New York: Cambridge University Press.

Untersteiner, Mario. 1954. *The Sophists.* Translated by Kathleen Freeman. Oxford: Basil Blackwell.

Van Hook, Larue. 1913. "The *Encomium on Helen,* by Gorgias." *Classical Weekly* 6:122–23.

Verall, A. W. 1980. "Korax and Tisias." *Journal of Philology* 9:197–210.

Verdenius, W. J. 1981. "Gorgias' Doctrine of Deception." In *The Sophists and Their Legacy*, edited by G. Kerferd. Wiesbaden: Franz Steiner Verlag.

Vernant, Jean Pierre. 1988. *Myth and Society in Ancient Greece.* New York: Zone Books.

Versenyi, Laszlo. 1963. *Socratic Humanism.* New Haven, Conn.: Yale University Press.

Vitanza, Victor. 1991. "'Some More' Notes, toward a 'Third' Sophistic." *Argumentation* 5:117–39.

———. 1997. *Negation, Subjectivity, and the History of Rhetoric.* Albany: State University of New York Press.

Walters, Frank. 1994. "Gorgias as Philosopher of Being: Epistemic Foundationalism in Sophistic Thought." *Philosophy and Rhetoric* 27:143–55.

Wardy, Robert. 1996. *The Birth of Rhetoric: Gorgias, Plato, and Their Successors.* New York: Routledge.

White, Eric. 1987. *Kaironomia.* Ithaca, N.Y.: Cornell University Press.

Williams, B. H. 1931. "The Political Mission of Gorgias to Athens in 427 B.C." *Classical Quarterly* 25:52–56.

Williams, Bernard. 1993. *Shame and Necessity.* Berkeley: University of California Press.

Woodford, Susan. 1994. "Palamedes Seeks Revenge." *Journal of Hellenic Studies* 64:164–69.

Woodhead, Arthur Geoffrey. 1962. *The Greeks in the West.* New York: Praeger.

Worman, Nancy. 1997. "The Body as Argument: Helen in Four Greek Texts." *Classical Antiquity* 1:151–203.

Zeller, Eduard. 1881. *A History of Greek Philosophy from the Earliest Period to the Time of Socrates.* Translated by Sarah Frances Alleyne. London: Longmans Green and Co.

Index

Adkins, Arthur, 24, 96, 221n. 6
Aeschylus, 23, 63, 104, 106, 151, 161, 163, 165, 174, 207, 208, 219n. 7, 221n. 9, 223n. 13
Agathon, 7, 150, 151, 166, 168, 201, 221n. 4, 222n. 3, 223n. 13
agon: and a community undertaking, 83; conventions of, 86, 92; cooperation and competition in, 134; and discourse, 29, 60, 75, 83, 86, 116, 180, 208; and education, 144, 167, 198, 199, 201, 202; and excellence, 196; fabrication of persons in, 124, 143, 208; fabrication of subject matter in, 85; foundationalist's concealment of, 170, 201; and freedom, 133; and festivals, 195, 196; Gorgias' foregrounding of, 193, 200; Gorgias' promotion of, 119, 131, 133, 189, 197, 200, 201; and inquiry, 82, 84, 89, 95; Herodotus' emphasis on, 224n. 3; and invention, 87; justification of, 132; and *kairos*, 87, 88; and meaning, 78, 80, 81, 91; Orpheus' refusal to participate in, 84, 219n. 13; and Panhellenism, 119, 143, 202; and reason, 116; and self-knowledge, 124; use of *techne* in, 86; and truth, 30, 74, 90. *See also* game; contest
alazon, 108, 167, 192–94, 197, 223n. 14
Alcidamus, 7, 37, 180, 215n. 25, 216n. 27
Anaxagoras, 40, 53, 62, 221
ancient quarrel, 8, 13, 31, 47, 206, 216n. 30
antifoundationalism: and foundationalism, 60–65, 218n. 1; and rhetoric, 28; and Panhellenism, 143, 149, 193; and Gorgias' boastful pose, 193
antifoundationalist reading of Gorgias, 4, 28, 29, 210, 211
Antiphon: on Greeks and barbarians, 117, 220n. 9; scholarly interpretations of, 3; studies mathematics, 53
antithesis: tragic, 27, 46, 88, 103; trope of, 27, 59, 149, 153–64, 170–73, 175, 221n. 4
Apology (Plato) 2, 160, 216n. 28, 217n. 5, 222n. 6
Aristophanes, 1, 95, 96, 140, 161, 183, 192, 213n. 1, 218n. 3, 220n. 2, 221n. 4

Aristotle: on antithesis, 160, 161; on argumentation, 185, 186; on barbarians, 117, 140, 220n. 2; on being and not-being, 67; on community, 124, 139; foundationalism of, 62; on Gorgias, 1, 8, 25, 35, 36, 37, 136, 140, 151, 164–66, 185–87, 189, 190, 197, 199, 213n. 1, 217n. 39; and Greek philosophy, 40; on inquiry, 83; on language, 63, 64, 77, 222n. 11; on metaphor, 162, 175, 182, 183; on myth, 64, 204, 223n. 1; rationalism of, 48; on rhetoric, 190; scientific thought of, 28; on the Sophist, 67, 192, 217n.3; on stylistic frigidity, 179–83
Aspasia, 7, 125, 172, 215n. 25
Athanasius, 166, 168
Athens: allied with Leontini, 6, 114, 117; democracy of, 107, 114, 118, 126, 144, 204; funeral orations of, 82, 85, 171; foundational role of, 125, 126; Gorgias' account of, 3, 126, 127, 172, 173, 184; Gorgias' embassy to, 7, 114, 118, 152; imperialism of, 139, 140
Attridge, Derek, 179
Augustine, 38, 150
Austin, Norman, 213n. 5

Baldry, H. C., 219n. 10
barbarians: Antiphon's view of, 117, 220n. 9; Athenian portrayals of, 140, 221n. 7; Aristotle's view of, 140, 220n. 2; Gorgias' view of, 30, 119, 140–42
Beckett, Samuel, 73
Being and Becoming, 43; and the definitional sense of "exist"; cannot be known or discussed, 41, 47; Gorgias' account of, 67–70, 81; Gorgias' rejection of Parmenides' notion of, 28, 35, 53, 57, 68; and kairotic moments, 44; in logocentrism, 63; Parmenides' notion of, 62, 63; and the subjective mind, 88
Bergren, Ann, 131, 213n. 5, 214n. 5, 215n. 8, 220n. 4
Bett, Richard, 38
Betti, Emilio, 10
Binkley, Timothy, 221n. 1
Bloom, Alan, 11

Bloom, Harold, 210, 224n. 5
Booth, Wayne, 223n. 14
Burckhardt, Jacob, 74, 205
Burgess, Theodore, 156
Burke, Kenneth, 17, 216n. 34

Callicles, 7, 97, 98, 99, 112, 130, 133, 137, 193, 201, 209
Calogero, Guido, 215n. 19
Cascardi, Anthony, 47, 101
Cassirer, Ernst, 48
Charmantides, 6
Chase, Richard, 151
Cicero, 152, 156, 165, 215n. 25
Classen, Carl, 213n. 2
Cleon, 165, 166, 221n. 4
Cole, Thomas, 11
comedy, 192, 196, 223n. 14
commonplace, 29, 65, 77–79, 84–87, 91, 102, 109, 124, 173, 176. *See also* topos
contest, 30, 50, 74, 75, 77, 83, 84, 87, 88, 131, 144, 195, 198, 219n. 10, 219n. 13, 223n. 15. *See also* agon; game
Connors, Robert, 48, 153
conventions: of agons, 81, 86, 92, 134, 207; of a community, 29–31, 104, 107, 108, 120, 121, 124, 128, 129, 131; of a craft, 120; of discourses, 30, 75, 78; and festivals, 109; interpretive, 17–22; and the individual, 121, 124, 128, 130; and morality, 97, 98, 104, 107–9; 119, 128–30, 208; and parody, 169–76; 180, 200; theatrical, 192; transgression of, 18, 188, 196. *See also nomos;* custom
Cope, Edward, 5, 12, 22, 97, 99, 153, 156, 192, 217n. 39
Corax, 7, 111, 114
Coulter, James, 175, 214n. 9, 222n. 4, 222n. 6
Cripps and Palatine manuscripts, 4, 214n. 17
Critias, 7, 15, 56, 215n. 25
Croally, N., 214n. 7
Crockett, Andy, 115, 213n. 5, 214n. 8, 215n. 19
Crowley, Sharon, 213n. 4
culture: agons in, 31, 60, 74, 198, 219n. 10; anticlassical, 205; discourses of, 177, 178, 183; and education, 143, 167, 198, 199, 203; evolutionary and agonal narratives of, 13, 14, 203–11; and freedom, 133; guilt and shame, 137, 138, 222n. 6; individual a product of, 121, 122, 133, 190; informed by *mythos* or *logos*, 162; Panhellenic, 143, 196; phallocentric, 115; place of Gorgias in, 203–11; rationalistic, 12, 13, 105; spiritual, 40, 41
custom, 79, 97, 119–21, 124, 128–30, 134, 159, 184, 185, 220n. 3. *See also nomos;* conventions

deception (*apate*), avoided through use of poetry, 155; effected through ambiguity, 219n. 8; of foundationalist thought, 32; of Helen, 110; of *logos*, 31, 90, 101, 102, 207; overcoming of, 103; in Palamedes, 52; of the poets, 207; of the pseudo-sciences, 56; not used in puns, 177; of Socrates, 193; of the Sophists, 56; of tragedy, 133, 191, 223n. 13
Deleuze, Gilles, 14
delivery, 8, 16, 165, 189, 190
Delphi, 7, 79, 217n. 37
Demand, Nancy, 217n. 38, 223n. 13
Democritus, 53
Demosthenes, 125, 139, 160, 171, 172, 190
Denniston, J. D., 25, 217
deontological liberalism, 112, 113, 115, 116
Derrida, Jacques, 2, 38, 60, 63, 101, 210, 213n. 4, 218n. 6, 221n. 1
Dewey, John, 38
Diels-Kranz, 4, 12, 22, 23
Diodorus, 152, 156, 214n. 13, 214n. 14
Dionysius of Halicarnassus, 43
discourse: agonistic nature of, 201; antifoundationalist view of, 64; and civic unity, 128; conventions of, 30; and culture, 202; deceptiveness of, 91, 102; and education, 199; of the Eleatic *epicheireme*, 175; foundations of, 28, 62, 63, 65, 66; and freedom, 133; of the funeral oration, 173; games of, 29, 79, 73–82, 95, 124; 208, 210; generation of, 84; Gorgias' parodies of, 169, 170, 173, 177, 200; of Helen, 79, 80, 160, 170, 173, 213n. 5; of the horde, 83; and introspection, 124; of the legal apology, 170; literal, 149; local biases of, 180; of professions, 90; poetic, 56, 58, 151; psyche stamped by, 124; rational, 46, 47, 56, 154, 155, 159; rhetoricity of, 167; scientific, 35, 58, 59; theatrical, 191; things and, 39, 181; as avenue to truth, 156. *See also logos;* language

Dodds, E. R., 25, 27, 53, 56, 63, 95, 111, 112, 213n. 2, 217n. 39, 218n. 5, 221n. 6, 224n. 2
Dostoyevsky, Fyodor, 14, 216n. 33
doxa, 5, 50, 59, 73, 81, 178
Dubois, Page, 220n. 3

Edelstein, Ludwig, 213n. 6
education: of the Athenians, 125, 126; fosters freedom and power, 8, 198; prepares students for agons, 74, 144, 198; central to Gorgias' cultural Panhellenism, 143, 144; offered by Gorgias, 197–202
egoism, 7, 113, 137, 209
eiron, 192–94
Empedocles, 7, 37, 54, 58, 62, 63, 108, 111, 209
empiricism, 20, 25, 27, 53, 54, 57, 59
empiricist reading of Gorgias, 27, 29–31, 52, 57, 60, 65, 72, 95, 119, 150, 167, 203, 207, 208
Encomium for the People of Elis (Gorgias), 4
Encomium of Helen (Gorgias), 2, 4–7, 12, 22, 24, 29, 35, 36, 38, 43, 46, 47, 49, 50, 51, 57, 58, 73, 75, 79–82, 89–91, 99–101, 104–7, 110, 111, 113, 115, 121–23, 129, 131, 132, 134, 135, 139, 141, 142, 144, 145, 149, 151–53, 161, 163, 168, 171, 173, 174, 180, 181, 184–89, 191, 195–97, 208, 209, 213n. 5, 214n. 14, 214n. 17, 215n. 19, 220n. 4
Engnell, Richard, 154, 157
Enos, Richard, 27, 35, 54, 95, 114
Epicharmus, 23, 217n. 38, 223n. 13
epideictic, 9, 27, 30, 31, 36, 143, 151, 165–71, 197, 208, 221n. 3, 224n. 6
Epitaphios (Gorgias), 2, 4, 5, 29, 38, 43, 49, 50, 58, 73, 82, 83, 85, 89, 91, 99, 100, 103, 107, 109, 111, 116, 121, 125–29, 131, 134, 135, 138, 141, 152, 153, 160–62, 168, 170–73, 175, 180, 184, 185, 189, 190, 191, 195, 214n. 10, 217n. 5
epithets, 9, 16, 165, 167, 181–83, 200, 209
Euripides, 2, 23, 105, 110, 116, 160, 173, 174, 191, 213n. 7, 220n. 8, 221n. 4, 223n. 13
festival: and carnival, 109; Dionysian, 27, 95, 223n. 15; Gorgias' presence at, 7, 23, 111, 119, 151, 251n. 2; Panhellenic, 139, 141, 143; rapturous, 108, 109; and transgression, 109; venue of, 167, 194–97
Finley, John, 159, 216, 221n. 4
Finley, M. I., 142, 143
Fish, Stanley: on the ancient quarrel, 31; on antifoundationalism, 28, 60–62, 65, 210; on deconstruction, 169; on inquiry, 210; on interpretation, 3, 17–19; neopragmatism of, 60; views anticipated by Gorgias, 2, 213n. 4
Floyd, Edwin, 221n. 1
foundationalism, 60, 61, 65, 218n. 1
Frankel, H., 219n. 13
Freeman, Kenneth, 220n. 10

Gadamer, Hans-Georg, 17, 210, 216n. 34
game, 3, 19, 74, 75, 78–82, 87, 89, 130, 165, 170, 172, 187, 208, 210, 217n. 35, 219n. 10. *See also* agon; contest
Garner, Richard, 219n. 10
genre, 2, 7, 109, 152, 159, 160, 167, 168–76, 178, 183, 184, 194, 195, 217n. 1
Gompertz, Theodore, 174
Goodman, Nelson, 185
Gorgias (Plato), 2, 8, 10, 36, 47, 75, 76, 81, 86, 87, 98, 107, 129, 130, 132, 150, 166, 180, 189, 192, 198, 213n. 1, 214n. 14, 215n. 25
Gronbeck, Bruce, 35, 45, 154, 156, 157, 213n. 4
Grote, George, 1, 5, 22, 26, 27, 31, 35, 52, 57, 95, 112, 153, 188, 203, 204, 213n. 2
Grotowski, Jerzy, 210, 224n. 6
Guattari, Felix, 14
Guthrie, W. K. C., 27, 43, 47, 50, 51, 154, 176, 214n. 12, 215n. 19, 217n. 40, 220n. 3, 222n. 4, 223n. 16

Hall, Edith, 221n. 7
Harvey, David, 219n. 1
Havelock, Eric, 12, 48, 115, 130, 206
Hays, Steve, 221n. 3
hedonism, 97, 99, 112
Hegel, G. W. F., 1, 5, 22, 26, 27, 31, 35, 38–42, 53, 153, 203, 204
Heidegger, Martin, 2, 213n. 4
Heraclitus, 43, 61, 62, 175, 204
hermeneutic, 3, 4, 6, 9–12, 15, 17, 18, 20, 23, 95, 132, 150, 210, 216n. 29, 216n. 34.

Herodicus, 6
Herodotus, 79, 184, 205, 224n. 3
Hesiod, 62, 64, 218n. 2, 223n. 2
Hippias, 3, 8, 15, 53, 61, 167, 218n. 8
Hippias Major (Plato) 96, 111, 118, 216n. 28, 217n. 2, 217n. 5
Hippocrates, 7, 213n. 6
Hirsch, E. D., 10
Homer, 2, 14, 48, 62, 105, 106, 144, 151, 160, 161, 173, 174, 189, 191
honor: Cimon motivated by, 136; Helen's suitors motivated by, 91, 115, 135; importance in funeral orations, 171, 195; importance of, for Gorgias, 8, 29; Palamedes motivated by, 111, 122, 135, 136, 189; Pericles' account of, 126; and the *paignion*, 189; and shame, 134–38; warriors motivated by, 121; of women, 136
Hunt, Everett, 189
Hyperides, 125, 126, 160, 171, 172, 190

interpretive community, 3, 17–20, 217n. 35
Ion (Plato), 10, 14
Irwin, T. I., 130, 213n. 2
Isjelling, Samuel, 205
Isocrates: on autochthony, 62, 125, 218n. 3; on Gorgias, 35–38, 96, 108, 174, 192, 214n. 14; on Helen, 145; influenced by Gorgias, 7, 143, 215n. 26, 221n. 8; on Panhellenism, 139

Jameson, Frederic, 204, 222n. 5
Jarratt, Susan, 27, 28, 205, 214n. 8, 214n. 12, 216n. 31, 220n. 7, 223n. 16
Jason of Phaerae, 118, 144, 221n. 9
Jebb, Richard, 5, 12, 22, 153, 173

Kagan, Donald, 214n. 13
Kahn, Charles, 66
kairos: basis of Gorgias' ethic, esthetic, and rhetoric, 43; and critical events in one's life, 44; in the *Epitaphios*, 43; etymology of, 43; Gorgias the first to write about, 43; irrationality of, 45, 103; key to Gorgias' epistemology, 43; and *logos*, 42–48; not defined by Gorgias, 5; as opening to the real, 154; as opportunity in agons, 87, 88; in *Palamedes*, 44; poet of, 28; poetics of, 154–59; in sophistic rhetoric, 15, 16

kairotic moment, 27, 35, 43–47, 56, 59, 65, 73, 111, 155, 157–59, 161
Kennedy, George, 25, 153, 214n. 12, 219n. 8, 223n 16
Kerferd, George, 11, 26, 154, 214n. 12, 214n. 15, 214n. 18, 215n. 19, 223n. 16
Kierkegaard, Søren, 42, 106, 213n. 2
Kiremidjian, G. D. 221n. 2
Kirk, G. S., 205, 218n. 2, 218n. 9
knowledge: antifoundationalist view of, 28, 64, 65, 181; criterion for, 28; empiricist conception of, 52–59, 66, 73; foundationalist view of, 28, 29; 61–63, 65, 69, 71, 73, 169, 207; generated in agons, 74, 82, 84, 208; Gorgias' affirmations of, 50, 51, 60, 66, 191, 192; Gorgias' pretense to, 192, 193; impossibility of, 47, 50; neosophistic conceptions of, 15; objective, 27, 42; and opinion, 81, 89; of the self, 123, 124; sensualist theory of, 35; tragedy of, 157
Kuhn, Thomas, 210

Lacan, Jacques, 17
language: as action, 75, 76; antithetical figures of, 149, 156; agonistic model of, 29, 74, 75, 77, 81, 82; antifoundationalist view of, 179, 181, 183; antirepresentationalist model of, 29, 78, 79, 167; apparatus for naming things, 55; chaotic reality and, 27, 46; criterion for, 28; deceptive use of, 28, 35, 46, 47, 51, 90, 91; domain of, 77; a drug, 51; figurative, 30 63, 77; fundamental units of, 77; games of, 64, 65, 75, 80, 210; of Greeks and barbarians, 140, 141; and kairotic moments, 45; leap outside of, 88; limitations of, 158; literal, 78; magical use of, 162; as maneuvers in games, 28, 60, 86, 116, 120, 149; and myth, 205; neutrality of, 180; nonrational features of, 155; Parmenides' view of, 154; of poetry 151, 164; a powerful lord, 76; prison-house of, 27, 56; and reality, 45, 51; representational theory of, 56, 77; and silence, 77; and things, 72; tropical model of, 28; violence of, 159. *See also* discourse; *logos*
Lanham, Richard, 28, 172, 173, 205, 216n. 31, 222n. 12
Larisa, 6, 7, 178
Leontini, 1, 6, 7, 13, 23, 60, 66, 96, 111, 114, 117, 118, 143, 214n. 13, 217n. 2

Lindsay, Jack, 174, 213n. 5
Loenen, J., 27, 35, 53–56, 222n. 9
logos: annihilation of, 159; antithetical to chaotic universe, 103, 157; deceptiveness of, 31, 101, 102, 106, 155, 159; a drug, 2, 47, 80; a dunastes or lord, 5, 45, 101; effects divinest works, 101; and *eros*, 123; and *kairos*, 42–48; meanings of, 5, 214n. 18; and *mythos*, 12, 13, 20, 31, 56, 149, 162, 163, 207–09, 216n. 31, 223n. 1; prison-house of, 101; Protagoras on, 8; rhetoricity of, 60–92; stamps the psyche, 58; and truth, 5, 89; tyranny of, 95, 101, 154, 158; repressiveness of, 106, 107; situatedness exposed, 169, 200; and things, 39, 71, 72. See also discourse; language; reason
Long, A. A., 27, 89, 130, 140, 188, 213n. 4, 214n. 9
Longo, Oddone, 194, 223n. 4
Loraux, Nicole, 29, 85, 126, 171–73, 214n. 10, 222n. 6
Lycophron, 7, 37, 180, 216n. 27
Lysias, 125, 126, 160, 171, 172

MacDowell, Douglas, 27, 35, 156, 214n. 17, 222n. 10
MacIntyre, Alasdair, 106
Mansfeld, Jaap, 217n. 40
Margolis, Joseph, 61
Menexenus (Plato), 2, 125, 171, 216n. 28, 217n. 5, 222n. 6
Meno, 7, 78, 118, 215n. 25
Meno (Plato) 7, 8, 55, 78, 96, 117, 118, 134, 192, 201, 215n. 25, 216n. 28, 217n. 5
metaphor, 37, 47, 59, 75, 76, 107, 119, 121, 136, 143, 145, 161–63, 173, 175, 182, 183, 185
Metaphysics (Aristotle), 36, 67, 181, 219n. 12, 223n. 1
metis, 106, 133, 206, 221n. 4
Miller, Bernard, 27, 35, 44, 45, 213n. 4
Morgan, Kathryn, 217n. 37
Moss, Roger, 159, 222n. 4
Mourelatos, Alexander, 28, 71, 72, 213n. 4, 217n. 40
MXG (*Melissus, Xenophanes, Gorgias*), 4, 37, 38, 43, 68, 69, 71, 72, 82, 152, 188, 221n. 3
mythos, 12, 13, 20, 31, 48, 56, 149, 162, 163, 204, 207, 208, 216n. 31, 223n. 1

Nagy, Gregory, 220n. 1
Nehamas, Alexander, 61, 66, 221n. 1, 222n. 3
nemesis, 51, 104, 121, 135
Nietzsche, Friedrich, 1, 5, 22, 28, 38, 74, 77, 150, 202–05, 210, 219n. 10, 219n. 11, 221n. 1, 223n.17, 224n. 2
nihilism, 38, 39, 97
nomos, 29, 97, 128, 129, 206, 216, 220. See also conventions; custom
Nussbaum, Martha, 36, 37, 86, 96, 187, 211, 213n. 6

objectivist strategy of interpretation, 3, 10–12, 14, 18, 21, 22
Odysseus, 24, 28, 43, 49, 52, 75, 81, 89, 101, 106, 121, 123, 128, 129, 141, 181, 184, 209
Olympia, 7, 75, 111, 215n. 21, 217n. 37
Olympic Speech (Gorgias), 4, 75, 139, 140, 141, 195
Olympiodorus, 152, 180
On Not-Being (Gorgias), 1, 2, 4, 5, 7, 23, 24, 28, 29, 35, 37–39, 41, 42, 46, 48, 50, 52, 53, 57, 60, 65–69, 71–73, 77, 79, 80–83, 85, 90, 91, 97, 107, 116, 121, 134, 139, 144, 145, 151–54, 159, 161, 168, 175, 176, 178, 186, 188, 189, 191, 195, 209, 217n. 36, 221n. 3, 222n. 5, 222n. 8, 222n. 9
Ong, Walter, 12, 48
Onians, Richard, 43
Orpheus, 13, 84, 164, 206, 219n. 13
Osborne, Robert, 142, 219n. 1
O'Sullivan, Neil, 25

Page, Denys, 219n. 2
paignion, 6, 15, 16, 75, 174, 189, 196
Palamedes (Gorgias), 4, 5, 12, 22, 24, 38, 44, 46, 49, 50, 52, 55, 58, 73, 75, 76, 80–84, 89, 90, 91, 99–101, 106, 108, 110, 111, 114, 116, 117, 121–24, 128, 129, 131, 133, 135–37, 139, 141, 144, 151, 153, 161, 167, 168, 171, 174, 175, 181, 184, 186–91, 195, 197, 209, 214, 222n. 6, 222n. 7
Panhellenism: Gorgias' advocacy of, 8, 23, 30, 151; Gorgias' conception of, 30, 119, 139–44
paradox, 52, 159, 178, 179, 188
paratropic figuration, 167, 169, 177, 178, 182, 183, 200

Parke, H. W., 196
Parmenides: on Being, 28, 43, 52, 57, 62, 63, 67–69; challenged by Gorgias, 57, 191; foundationalism of, 13, 28, 61, 85; on knowledge, 63, 70; on language, 63, 83, 154; style of, 150, 159, 221; parodied by Gorgias, 176; on the undiscerning horde, 84, 206
Parmenides (Plato), 216n. 28, 217n. 5
parody: ambivalence of, 168; and festivals, 167, 196; Gorgias' use of, 167–77, 183, 193, 200, 208, 221n. 2; Plato's use of, 171, 175, 222n. 3, 222n. 6; and self-parody, 176
Pausanias, 152, 215, 219
Pease, Arthur, 35, 189, 214n. 11, 217n. 1
Pellicia, Hayden, 184
Penelope, 6, 37, 76, 160, 166
Perelman, Chaim, 84
Perelman, S., 139
Pericles, 7, 125–27, 139, 160, 171, 172, 190, 204, 215n. 25
Phaerae, 13, 144, 221n. 9
Philebus (Plato), 96, 160, 178, 216n. 28, 217n. 5
Philostratus, 23, 37, 131, 141, 151, 166, 192, 203, 210, 214n. 14, 215n. 22, 215n. 24, 215n. 25, 217n. 4, 221n. 8
Pindar, 62, 129, 144, 161, 163, 209, 221n. 9
Plato: on the ancient quarrel, 13, 47, 216n. 30; on Being and Becoming, 43, 66–69; on community, 125; foundationalism of, 28, 61–63, 68, 81, 211; on Gorgias, 1, 8, 24, 25, 35–37, 81, 96, 97, 109, 111, 118, 130, 134, 150, 151, 165, 166, 168, 169, 171, 189, 192, 193, 201, 209, 213n. 1, 216n. 28, 217n. 5, 222n. 2, 222n. 5; on interpretation, 10, 14; on introspection, 55; logic of, 38, 187, 209; on orators, 145; parodies by, 171, 175; place in Greek philosophy, 40; on the psyche, 120; on reason, 123; on reform, 130, 133; on rhetoric, 190; on the Sophist, 1, 67, 192; on the theory of pores, 54; on wonder, 82, 219n. 12. *See also Apology; Gorgias; Hippias Major; Ion; Menexenus; Meno; Parmenides; Philebus; Protagoras; Republic; Symposium; Theaetetus*
Poitier, Richard, 176
Polus, 7, 193, 214n. 14, 215n. 25

pores: theory of, 7, 35, 54, 55, 58, 59, 63, 209
Porter, James, 29, 170, 214
Poulakos, John: rhapsodic hermeneutics of, 15, 16, 20, 21; on Gorgias' symbolic violence, 159; on Isocrates, 214n. 14
Prodicus, 3, 8, 15, 16, 53, 199, 218n. 8
Protagoras: adumbrates conventionalist model of interpretation, 17, 216n. 34; argues with Socrates, 61; attacks the criterion, 60, 67; believes in progress, 224n. 2; is committed to democracy, 115; differs from Gorgias, 8; "impossible to contradict" remark of, 19; lives and works in Athens, 118; "man the measure" remark of, 3, 40; "opposed *logoi*" remark of, 8, 19, 206; opposes foundationalists, 170; pragmatism of, 3; promotes rational laws, 107; relativism of, 220, n. 3; representative of the First Sophistic, 213n. 3; scholarly interpretations of, 3; on sensation and knowledge, 69; significance of, 1; sophistic rhetoric of, 15; "make the weaker *logos* stronger" remark of, 8
Protagoras (Plato), 11
pun, 156, 177, 178, 179, 185
Pythagoras, 62, 120, 219n. 14

Quintilian, 2, 215

Race, William, 27, 95, 104, 105, 106, 115, 215n. 19
Rawls, John, 22, 132
reason: advanced by Sophists, 56; apprehending absolutes through, 55; artificiality of, 47, 157; as capacity for excelling in agons, 116; constraints of, 104, 110, 154; contemporary debates about, 61; contingency of, 123; controlling passions with, 55; correcting errors with, 55; deceptiveness of, 31, 44, 207; dictates of, 102, 122, 123; faculty of, 28, 53, 55, 62, 63, 120, 122, 123, 137; and freedom, 113, 114; grasping truth with, 81; and kairotic experience, 65; leap beyond, 45; limits of, 103; and moral laws, 112, 113, 116, 138; and myth, 48; not a reliable guide, 123; and passion, 103; progress of, 41, 204, 205; rules of, 185, 187; tyranny of, 95, 101; voice of, 30. *See also logos*

rhapsodic strategy of interpretation, 3, 10, 14–17, 21, 22, 216n. 32
Republic (Plato), 47, 216n. 28; 216n. 30, 217n. 5
rhetoric: an agonistic exercise, 75; and antifoundationalism, 28; as art of generating truths, 87; Athenian, 151; causal theory of, 165; and cookery, 201; role of delivery in, 190; and democracy, 114, 117; and enslavement, 96, 160; epideictic, 165, 221n. 3; role in festivals, 197, 221n. 2; figures of, 187, 189; forensic, 165; Gorgias' art of, 9, 16, 25, 26; and inquiry, 82–88; and *kairos*, 43, 95; as knack of manipulation and flattery, 213n. 1; as means of liberation and empowerment, 107; a menace to the community, 201; not a method, 86; of praise and blame, 168; and probability, 153; philosophical, 217n. 4; poetic nature of, 47, 153, 155, 163, 216n. 30; quarrel with philosophy, 8, 13, 31; concerned with the ridiculous, 166; scientific studies of, 164; sophistic, 8, 15, 21; theatrical nature of, 197; and transgression, 109; true art of, 199, 223n. 18; universal scope of, 86, 87
Rhetoric (Aristotle), 6, 9, 76, 140, 151, 160, 162, 166–68, 179, 180, 182–84, 186, 189, 190, 213n. 1, 215n. 24, 216n. 27, 217n. 39, 218n. 8, 219n. 8, 222n. 11
rhetoricity: concealment of, 92, 169; exposure of, 170, 172, 176, 184, 200, 208, 210, 222n. 5; of *logos*, 60–92; of every text, 30, 149
Robinson, John, 24, 25, 36, 38, 51, 153, 154, 211, 217n. 39, 222n. 5
Rockmore, Tom, 61, 63
Romilly, Jacqueline de, 11, 35, 163, 164, 214n. 15
Roochnik, David, 24, 61, 205, 213n. 4, 214n. 18, 218n. 6
Rorty, Richard, 1, 2, 13, 17, 28, 60, 64, 205, 210, 213n. 4, 216n. 34, 224n. 4
Rose, Margaret, 140, 168
Rosenmeyer, Thomas, 27, 35, 45, 156, 175, 219n. 7, 223n. 13

Sandel, Michael, 112, 113, 220n. 6
Sappho, 2, 105, 106, 158, 161, 173, 174, 205, 207–09, 219n. 2, 219n. 3

Schiappa, Edward: empiricist reading of Gorgias by, 27, 35; objectivist hermeneutics of, 11–14, 20; on *mythos* and *logos*, 12, 20, 162
Scodel, Ruth, 213n.7
Segal, Charles, 45, 53, 164, 214n. 15, 215n. 20, 216n. 32
Sextus Empiricus, 4, 37, 60, 66, 69, 71, 152, 153, 169, 175, 216n. 33
Shakespeare, 47, 217n. 7
shame, 8, 16, 29, 30, 62, 76, 98, 119, 134–38, 183, 221n. 5
Shelley, Percy, 62, 108, 218n. 4
Sicily, 6, 7, 107, 108, 117, 142, 143, 189, 202, 205, 207
Sidgwick, Henry, 1
Singer, Beth, 61
Smeltzer, Mark, 183
Smith, Bromley, 25, 38, 43, 114, 153, 162
Socrates: on Agathon's prose, 150; in the *Apology*, 160; in the *Clouds*, 183; criticizes Gorgias, 40; an *eiron*, 192–94; moral universalism of, 138; puzzled by Gorgias, 2, 214n. 14; rationalism of, 204; urges self-examination, 128, 130; opposes Sophists, 61
solipsism, 19, 73
sophistic rhetoric, 8, 15, 16, 21
Sophistical Refutations (Aristotle), 9, 199, 217n. 3, 219n. 8
Sophist(s): antifoundationalism of, 28, 61; apparent wisdom of, 36; characterization of Gorgias as, 1, 8, 21, 31, 111; concerned with contingency, 67, 181; contestive engagements of, 74; conventionalism of, 130; distinguished from rhetors, 213n. 2; educational practices of, 223n. 16; egoism of, 97; elitism of, 220n. 10; fallacious arguments of, 36, 217n. 3; feminism of, 220n. 7; impact on Athenian rhetoric, 151; imposture of, 192, 193; not concerned with reality, 67; not easy to catch and define, 1; not a serious philosopher, 35; objectivist approach to, 11–13; philosophical concerns of, 37; quarrel with philosophers, 206; rehabilitation of, 1, 5, 26, 41, 153; reinstatement of, 210; rhapsodic approach to, 14–17; scientific thinking of, 53; Socrates' opposition to, 61; stylistic novelty of, 165; stylistic opportunism of,

Sophist(s) *(continued)*
 171; subjectivism of, 35, 39–42; tropical model of language of, 28, 77; two groups of defenders of, 26; uses homonyms for dirty work, 219n. 8; utilitarianism of, 112; verbal athleticism of, 36; violent speech of, 159. *See also* Alcidamus; Antiphon; Hippias; Lycophron; Philostratus; Prodicus; Protagoras; Thrasymachus
Sophist (Plato), 1, 36, 67, 192, 216n. 28
Stesichorus, 2, 174, 184
style of Gorgias: antithetical nature of, 27, 28, 155–60; and content, 150–54; criticisms of, 9, 25, 23, 25, 26, 38; empiricist reading of, 161–66; function of, 200; novelty of, 158–59; paratropic figuration in, 177–89; parodic nature of, 167–76; Plato's parody of, 213n. 1, 222n. 3; poetic nature of, 136, 151, 163; subjectivist construal of, 154–61
subjectivism, 20, 27, 40–42, 51, 59, 154, 208
subjectivist reading of Gorgias, 35, 39, 44, 52, 112, 159, 207
Suda, 4, 152, 156, 214n. 16, 215n. 25
Suzuki, Mihoko, 174, 213n. 5
Swearingen, Jan, 176, 222n. 4
sycophant, 1, 95, 96, 213n. 1
Symposium (Plato), 7, 150, 151, 168, 213n. 1, 216n. 28, 217n. 5
Syracuse, 7, 13, 114, 144, 221n. 9

Taylor, Gabriele, 137, 138, 221n. 6
techne, 76, 86, 87, 153, 164, 199, 209
Theaetetus (Plato), 43, 145, 216n. 28, 217n. 5, 219n. 9, 219n. 12
Theil, John, 218
Thompson, Norma, 224n. 3
Thrasymachus, 3, 61
Thucydides, 7, 64, 108, 160, 165, 166, 171, 202, 204, 215n. 25, 216n. 27, 221n. 4
Tisias, 7, 111, 114, 215n. 23
Too, Yun Lee, 215n. 26
topos, 56, 84, 85, 91, 136, 137, 175. *See also* commonplace

trope, 27, 77, 120, 167, 176, 177, 185, 187, 188, 222n. 12
trust, 24, 50, 54, 81, 122, 128, 140, 187, 202, 208
truth: antifoundationalist view of, 64, 91; apprehended by poets through inspiration, 56; constructed by a community, 14, 18, 28, 29; as label of endorsement, 4, 28, 60, 61, 89–92, 123, 169; foundationalist view of, 61–63, 73, 83, 196, 197; generated in agons, 30, 73–74, 143, 87, 198, 199, 201, 207; Gorgias' putative indifference to, 36, 37, 39, 96, 217n. 3; impossibility of grasping, 39, 40, 47; independent domain of, 72, 81, 84–87; objective, 13, 28, 31, 40, 47, 92; and opinion, 79, 81; and probability, 8, 25, 55, 213n. 1; the province of philosophers, 68; subjective, 27, 30, 35, 40, 42, 44, 46, 47, 65

Untersteiner, Mario, 16, 17, 25, 27, 35, 43, 46, 95, 103, 104, 149, 154–59, 170, 208, 214n. 10, 214n. 15, 214n. 17, 215n. 20, 222n. 7, 222n. 8

Van Hook, Larue, 153
Verdenius, W. J., 27
Vernant, Jean Pierre, 133, 205
Versenyi, Laszlo, 27, 157, 215n. 19
Vitanza, Victor, 1, 16, 17, 31, 210, 213n. 3, 216n. 35, 222n. 5

Walters, Frank, 65
Wardy, Robert, 73
White, Eric, 27, 35, 43, 45, 46, 158, 170, 171, 214n. 11
Williams, 218
Williams, Bernard, 137, 214n. 13
Wittgenstein, Ludwig, 2, 60, 64, 150, 210, 221n. 1
Woodford, Susan, 220n. 4
Worman, Nancy, 213n. 5

Zeller, Eduard, 42, 217n. 6

I.S.L.?

Through June 11th Dissertation
Through June 18th Jane Austen Paper
Through July 1st Disciplinarity Article

work 4 hrs. per day.
{ Carol & My article
Native Speaker article
TESOL grad programs article
Multiculturalism effort } July & Aug.

novel also 4 hrs. per day.
{ Web sites < C.V. / Blueline } July & Aug.

Sleep 11 – 7:30
breakfast; dress – 9:00
Write novel – 9:00 – 1:00
lunch, etc. 1:00 – 2:00
Write article 2:00 – 5:30
eat 5:30 – 6:30
M/R 6:45 – 8:00 TKD
T/W/F 6:30 – 8:00 Read
8:00 – 11:00 clean, organize, read